First Principles

The Official Biography
of Keith Duckworth OBE

Front cover images: Keith Duckworth at the 1967 Dutch GP for the DFV's historic debut with (l-r) Colin Chapman, Jim Clark, Graham Hill. (Courtesy Rainer W Schlege-Imilch/Getty Images), and bottom, Keith Duckworth with the preserved DFV-engined Lotus 49 that took Graham Hill to the engine's first F1 championship. This photo appeared in the 1989 Cosworth's company accounts. (Courtesy Cosworth Engineering)
Back cover images: Andy Rouse in a WTCC Sierra Cosworth RS500 at Silverstone in 1987 (Courtesy Ford Motor Co), The first Triumph to receive design input from Keith Duckworth: the Daytona Super III. (Courtesy Roland Brown), The P&M Quik, a highly successful microlight powered by Keith Duckworth's ownership of the company. (Courtesy Steve Grimshaw/BMAA archive) and Jackie Wilson at speed in the Cosworth Hodges powerboat. (Courtesy Fast on Water)

www.veloce.co.uk

First published in April 2015, paperback edition published February 2017 by Veloce Publishing Limited, Veloce House, Parkway Farm Business Park, Middle Farm Way, Poundbury, Dorchester DT1 3AR, England. Fax 01305 268864 / e-mail info@veloce.co.uk / web www.veloce.co.uk or www.velocebooks.com.
ISBN: 978-1-787111-03-5 UPC: 6-36847-01103-1

First Principles

The Official Biography
of Keith Duckworth OBE

VELOCE PUBLISHING
THE PUBLISHER OF FINE AUTOMOTIVE BOOKS

Contents

WORKING THINGS OUT FOR YOURSELF FROM FIRST PRINCIPLES,
AND PROVIDING PROPER ENGINEERING SOLUTIONS, NEVER GOES
OUT OF FASHION.

– Keith Duckworth OBE

To Gill Duckworth

Foreword

I first became aware of Keith Duckworth through the motorsport media. His work with Mike Costin was already making the headlines in *Autosport* and *Motor Sport*, for the pair of them were the leaders of the pack, modifying mainly Ford engines for use in small GT and sports cars. From reading 'the comics,' one recognised that Duckworth and Costin were two of the great brains in motorsport technology.

When I finally got to know Keith, it was through Ken Tyrrell, who had tremendous admiration for both him and Mike. With that canny northern drawl and dry sense of humour, Keith was appealing to an awful lot of folk, myself included.

Walter Hayes was one of the great believers in the Cosworth way of doing things, of course, and without the Cosworth DFV Sir Jackie Stewart would certainly not have won three World Championships. The genius of these two men, and the people they gathered around them, was one of the great stories in motorsport history.

Keith Duckworth, however, was much more than a genius in his chosen field. Family life was hugely important to him – as was flying his helicopter: I remember many occasions on which he would arrive at a race track, sometimes in less than ideal weather, and be very cavalier about the journey.

In my early days of knowing Keith, I actually found him quite intimidating: he was never a man to suffer fools gladly, and back then, when Ken and I would go up to Cosworth to meet the people making our engines, somehow I always felt I was being judged and assessed.

Mind you, what engines they were! It was unbelievable the way Cosworth's DFV dominated Formula One – including Ferrari – for so many years.

My first season as a contracted Formula One driver, with BRM, was 1965, the year after John Surtees won the World Championship for Ferrari. I was very happy with BRM's 1.5-litre V8 engine, but in 1966 the 3-litre Formula One was introduced, and while BRM's H16 engine sounded wonderful, it weighed a ton, and carried more fuel, oil and water than most of the tankers delivering such products around the country! In the meantime Jack Brabham and his team, using a Repco V8 engine, won the World Championships for both drivers and constructors.

In 1967, glory be! Duckworth and Costin brought out the Cosworth DFV, and it was to change the world of Formula One. Why? Because the DFV was dominant. It was small, light and very driveable, and from 1968 on I never raced with any other engine in Formula One, using it to secure my three World Championships.

During this period, of course, I got to know Keith Duckworth very much better. Ken Tyrrell was a good judge of people, and he and Keith always got along very well.

My admiration for Keith Duckworth was enormous, and I believe his engineering achievements for the United Kingdom should have been more fully recognised. Almost all of my Formula One victories were scored with Cosworth DFV engines, and I count myself very lucky to have lived as a racing driver at a time when Keith and Mike, and an amazingly well chosen group of engineers, were producing them.

– Sir Jackie Stewart OBE

Preface

This book is not solely about Keith Duckworth. For as the proverb says, 'you may judge a man by the company he keeps,' and surely this was never more true than in the case of David Keith Duckworth. Despite an unspectacular academic career, the middle-class boy from Blackburn went on to design a whole series of winning race engines and to spearhead an iconic and astonishingly successful engineering company which permanently changed the face of both international motorsport and the wider motor industry.

He accomplished this not just by driving himself extremely hard, but by gathering around him a disparate group of talented and highly individualistic characters, the kind of people who in normal circumstances could be expected to move restlessly from one employer to another in search of fresh mental stimulation. It took a truly exceptional person to hold such a team together, let alone make them productive and turn their efforts into hard cash, yet this is precisely what Cosworth, under Keith Duckworth's chairmanship, achieved.

It was his endlessly enquiring mind, acerbic wit and sheer force of intellect which made the difference. Many Cosworth employees stayed at the company for decades, some for their entire career, and in the process many reinvented themselves in roles they would never even have been encouraged to consider at a less open-minded company. As the company's co-founder Mike Costin puts it: 'All Cosworth people are in some way or other a discrete personality. Most of them didn't end up doing the job they were hired for, they ended up doing something totally different.' Their stories are partly Keith's story, and I make no apology for straying from a purely Duckworth agenda in order to include portions of them in this book.

Cosworth under Keith Duckworth was indeed a one-off, but this book is not just about his company and its products, or the teamwork their creation involved. My own all-too-brief contact with him was through aviation, so when I started the biography I knew that his interests went much further than motorsport, but I'd never realised how *much* further! If it was a mechanical or electro-mechanical device, he wanted to know how it worked and how it was made, and often as not within a matter of minutes would come up with challenging ideas on how to improve it. Anyone with a liking for engineering couldn't fail to find his presence stimulating. And because he applied the same incisive analysis to life in general, many completely non-technical people relished his company every bit as much.

He was not, of course, a saint, and any biography which tried to present him as such would be doing him a disservice. If he was wrapped up in a problem he could be distant to the point of being absolutely infuriating, and although he cared deeply about people and was generous with his time and money, he was not someone who effortlessly tuned in to the worries and concerns of those around him. He would give credit where credit was due, but often not immediately, because he hated losing an argument. And at times his bluntness extended to being downright rude, his most damning remarks being reserved for the pompous and the vacuous, particularly know-alls who actually knew little.

All this made up the complex and fascinating character who is the subject of this book, a man who made an indelible mark on his chosen field, did it honestly and with good humour, and who left behind very few enemies but an enormous number of friends, plus a huge store of happy memories for those lucky enough to have known him.

Precious few people, in any walk of life, can claim as much.

– Norman Burr,
Lancaster, England

Acknowledgements

There are over 100 names in the panel here, and the length of that list tells its own story. Two and a half years elapsed between the start of this project and its completion, and during that period a huge number of people helped in myriad ways – being interviewed, writing reminiscences, finding photos, making drawings or just helping with background research.

Top of the list comes the lady without whose co-operation this biography could not have been published in its present form – Gill Duckworth. Despite the book taking far longer and ending up far larger than she (or the author!) ever envisaged, Keith's widow has kept faith with the project and for that she has both my respect and my appreciation.

Otherwise the list is alphabetical: it would be invidious to single out individual names because whoever I chose to mention, there would be sure to be someone else who had done nearly as much and had not been singled out. Common to everyone is an an astonishing level of enthusiasm and commitment, which has been truly heartening and at times almost overwhelming. Indeed it is the main reason why this book grew to its present size. My initial plan was to keep the project manageable by interviewing only key characters in the story, but that proved completely unworkable. Every time an interviewee wanted to check a point with a third party, the latter would, within days – sometimes hours – respond with a long email or phone call full of fascinating detail which it would be sin to ignore. Effectively, I'd done another interview.

I never for a moment doubted that a biography of Keith Duckworth was both justified and overdue, but if I had, the response of those close to him would have instantly quelled those doubts. Only a very special person can create such a feeling of warmth and camaraderie that the flame can be instantly relit even after several decades. The number of people who declined to become involved can be counted on the fingers and thumb of one hand; contrast that with the length of the list.

Not on the list but most definitely important are my long-suffering family and friends, who must have got thoroughly tired of my talking about a certain David Keith Duckworth. And finally, I must not forget Rod Grainger at Veloce Publishing, whose patience and support has been invaluable.

To all these people, and with apologies to anyone I have omitted, thanks for the ride. I hope you enjoy the arrival.

WITH THANKS TO ...

Gill Duckworth

Oliver Achurch
Julia Anderson
Autocar magazine
Paul Bailey
Conrad Beale
Nigel Beale
Matthias Betsch
Ian Bisco
Paul Blezard
John Blunsden (Motor Racing
    Publications)
British Microlight Aircraft
    Association
British Racing & Sports
    Car Club (*Motor Racing*
    magazine)
Dr Bill Brooks
Bill Brown
Roland Brown
Richard Bulman
John Campbell-Jones
Mike Campbell-Jones
Car magazine
Paul Carey (Triumph
    Motorcycles)
Patrick Castell
Simon Churchill (motorcycle
    research)
Roy Cooper (Fast On Water)
Chris Costin
Mike Costin
Jim Cunliffe
Stephen Curry (Veteran Car
    Club)
Peter Davenport (textile
    industry historian)
Sir Noel Davies
Pete Davies
John Dickens
Design Council
Jerry Doe (AccessNorton.com)
George Duckett
Betty Duckworth
Roger Duckworth
Trish Duckworth
Ursula Duckworth
Andrew Duerden (Vauxhall
    Motors)
Bernard Ferguson
Jack Field

Harvey Fox
Joe Freeman (Racemaker
    Archive)
Lydia French (Mercedes-Benz
    UK)
Paul Fricker
Giggleswick School
Val & John Given
Geoff Goddard
Julie Graham (National
    Motorboat Museum)
Bob Graves
Ania Grzesik
Maxine Hall
Mike Hall
Ian Hawkins
Charles Helps
Dave Hill (Ford Motor Co)
Norman Hossack
Chris Hughes (Cosworth
    Engineering)
Mario Illien
Imperial College London
Ken Jacobs
Getty Images
Graeme Jenner (Classic Car
    Portraits)
David Kemp
Ian Kew
Roger Kimbell
William Kimberley (*Race Tech*
    magazine)
Lancashire Evening Telegraph
Larry Lawrence (*Cycle News*)
Mike Lawrence (Pitpass.com)
Dave Lee
Neil Lefley
Keith Leighton
John Lievesley
Fiona Luckhurst
Alastair Lyle
Mahle Powertrain
Kees Mense
Steve Miller
John Mitchell (Ariel Owners'
    club)
John Mockett
Motor Sport magazine
Glyn Mowll
Deryck Norville

Jeff Nutt (Vintage Motorcycle
    Club)
Roger Pattrick (P&M
    Aviation)
David Phipps
Pitsford School
Colin Pritt (Blackburn Past)
Marcus Pye
RAF archives
Mick Robinson (MSR
    Photographic)
Graham Robson
Jane Rood
Nick Rossi
Royle Publications
Mark Rock (Cosworth Vega
    Owners Association)
Tom Rubython (*BusinessF1*
    magazine)
Diana Rushton (Blackburn
    with Darwen Library &
    Information Services)
Colin Russell
Cecil Schumacher
Bill Sherlock
John Skinner
    (defunctspeedway.co.uk)
David Soul
Sir Jackie Stewart
Bob Tait
Simon Taylor
Victor Thomas (Historic
    Lotus Register)
Stuart Turner
Malcolm Tyrrell
Ernie Unger
Geert Versleyen (Yesterdays
    Antique Motorcycles,
    www.yesterdays.nl)
John Watson (Historic Lotus
    Register)
Dean Weber (Ford Motor Co)
Peter Weddle (Fix Auto
    Blackburn)
Jackie Wilson
Mark Writtle (Writtle
    Productions)
www.volusiariders.com

About the author

Originally trained as an engineer at Rolls-Royce Aero Engines and Bath University, lifelong petrolhead Norman Burr has been a technical journalist practically all his working life, firstly with professional and industrial magazines, then as a freelance and subsequently through Pagefast Ltd, a small printing and publishing company which he helped found. In 2006, wanting to get off the production treadmill and give himself scope for projects like this, he left the company and reverted to freelance work. Most of his output concerns sport aviation and automotive subjects.

By the same author

Ultralight & Microlight Aircraft of the World, co-written with Alain-Yves Berger, published 1983 (also published in French as *Tous les ULM du Monde*).

Ultralight & Microlight Aircraft of the World Second Edition, co-written with Alain-Yves Berger, published 1985.

Living with Speed, a partly biographical look at the speed hillclimb scene through the eyes of Roy Lane's 1996 season, published 1997.

Mr Big Healey, official biography of racing driver John Chatham, published by Veloce, 2010.

Contributed to

32 Days to Beijing, travelogue by James Edmonds about a microlight flight from London to China, published 1994.

Gertie's Day Out, travelogue by Eve Jackson about emigrating to Tanzania by microlight, published 2006.

All images photos in this book which are not credited are from the private collections of Keith Duckworth's family, friends and colleagues. Regarding copyrighted material, the author has made every reasonable effort to contact the current copyright holder, but in some cases, particularly with older photographs, it has not been possible to locate the party concerned. The author would be obliged if those parties, or their agents, would contact him via the publisher. The same comment applies to anyone who believes a credit has been omitted or wrongly attributed.

Chapter 1

The making of the man

The girl was getting cold, very cold, as she raced the sidecar outfit along the hard, wet sands of Southport on that late winter afternoon in January 1929, but she scarcely noticed. She'd come from Blackburn with her husband, Frank, to watch the motorcycle racing, and now the meeting was drawing to a close she was having a go herself, and loving every moment. The roar of the engine, the way it responded to every twist of the wrist, the wind tearing through her hair – this was freedom! Her dress was billowing behind her in a distinctly unladylike fashion, but she didn't care; Emma was a young woman who liked doing things for herself. Flat out on the sands was a million times better than sitting in the sidecar or, worse still, side-saddle on the pillion while your husband had all the fun. Not for the first time, she understood why he was so fascinated by these machines.

The following Monday morning on the commuter train from Blackburn to Manchester, two very respectable ladies were discussing a scandalous event they had seen that weekend while taking the air on Southport sands. A woman on a motorcycle! Roaring along! With no hat! And her dress was – *well*! Words failed them, so they tut-tutted into their *Daily Mail*s until they could come up with a few more.

At this point they might have sought endorsement from the thoroughly respectable businessman sitting opposite – after all, one was travelling first class, and one only met 'the right sort' in first class. The businessman, however, seemed disinclined to talk and raised his newspaper to cover his face, for he was none other than Frank Duckworth, weekend motorcyclist and weekday cotton trader, and if they had been able to see behind the broadsheet, they would have seen a man bursting with silent laughter.

Em's weekend thrash on the Southport sands and Frank's overhearing of two affronted ladies on the train are beyond dispute; a tale told with undiminished amusement by successive generations of Duckworths. The family doesn't know the exact date of Em's race along the sands, though it must have been before she conceived her first son, Brian, which would place it before September 1930. Nor did they know whether she and Frank went there for a sporting event (there is no evidence that she actually competed) or on their own, though as they were both great motorcycle enthusiasts, the former seems more likely. But tantalisingly, a trawl through commercial archives turned up a photo, of an event at exactly the right time and place – January 1929, Southport sands (see page 17).

Frank, born in 1902, was one of the fortunate generation too young to see much of WWI and too old to be called up for WWII. The Blackburn he knew at the start of his working life was first and foremost a cotton town, and the textile industry was where he sought employment.

Frank's father had died at the age of 39 when Frank was only eight – but perhaps because of this, young Duckworth was very self-reliant. He was also intelligent, ambitious and prepared to work hard. A teetotaller, he studied at night school and by his mid-20s was a cotton trader at the Manchester Cotton Exchange, where his negotiating skills and quick-wittedness stood him in good stead.

In his spare time, Frank enjoyed woodwork and rebuilding cars. He also spent a lot of time working on motorcycles, to the point that it became a paying hobby. This ensured there were plenty of engineering influences in the household to inspire their son, Keith (actually David Keith, but no one ever called him David), who arrived on 10 August 1933, a brother to two year-old Brian, their firstborn.

Their mother, who'd married Frank in October 1927, was a formidable person in her own right. Tall, strong-limbed, strong-minded and well educated, Emma Hardman was the oldest of four children and, like her sister Margaret and brothers David and Harry, had been brought up to say exactly what she thought. She acquired a diploma in domestic science and, when the first electricity showrooms opened, became the town's first cookery demonstrator, promoting what then were newfangled electric cookers.

All her life, she was fascinated by technology. The family home at 77 Ramsgreave Drive was the first in the street to have a telephone, and during WWII, as one of the few women with a driving licence, she drove an ambulance when necessary. Even in her 80s – she lived till she was 95 and retained her mental faculties till the end – she was asking how fax machines and photocopiers worked.

Her first experience of riding a motorcycle occured when Frank took her into the hills above Blackburn, on the road leading from Wilpshire to Great Harwood. Climbing out of Blackburn, she rode pillion, then when they got up onto the quiet roads above the town, they dismounted and Frank explained the controls. Then she just got on the bike and rode it. That was it, end of tuition.

Around the time Brian was born, Frank decided that he wanted to get into textile manufacturing and entered into a partnership called Duckworth, Sagar & Ormerod. He announced his new venture to several friends on the morning train into Manchester, all of whom were steeped in the industry and none of whom was encouraging. "Eh, tha'll have to join t'masons then, won't tha!" was the response. Frank disagreed, but his fellow commuters were adamant. Frank stuck to his guns, convinced that commercial success depended on making the right products at the right price and looking after your customers, not on arcane ritual.

It was a brave decision, because in 1930s Blackburn, running a mill was certainly not a passport to riches. The proud Lancashire cotton industry, by far the largest in the world for so long, went into rapid decline soon after the end of WWI, a decline from which it never recovered. By 1931, one in three textile workers was unemployed. The reasons are many[1], but include managerial complacency, outdated technology, disruption of trade links during WWI, the Wall Street crash and the Indian boycott on imported textiles.

There was a general assumption among mill owners that all their problems were a temporary inconvenience, and that normal service would soon be resumed. Only a small minority saw the broader picture and believed that King Cotton did not occupy his throne by divine right. Was Frank one of them? His actions suggest he was, as he went on to make good money from an industry in which so many had failed. Indeed, by the time Keith came along in 1933, he was looking to leave the partnership and strike out on his own.

His chance came the following year, when Oozebooth Mill became available. Built in 1882 and with 300 looms, it was offered by the debenture holders of a defunct company, James Read Ltd, and by 1936 it was up-and-running as Oak Street Manufacturing Co Ltd[2]. Finally, the Duckworth family were mill owners.

With increasing prosperity came better housing. Ramsgreave Drive gave way to Norfield (now Norfield House), a three-bedroom semi just outside the town in Wilpshire, on the way to Clitheroe. It backed onto the course of Wilpshire Golf Club, which Frank found handy as he enjoyed a round, as did Brian later. Frank sometimes organised dance evenings at the club and, as a non-drinker, was much in demand if there was an event on elsewhere, because he could be designated as driver.

Unlike Brian, Keith was not much interested in golf. For him, the main attraction of the golf course was that it offered wide open spaces from which to fly his model aeroplanes. All he had to do was walk through the garden gate.

In fact, the brothers generally took differing approaches to life. Both admired their parents immensely, but while Brian wanted to emulate his dad, Keith preferred to go his own way. Brian had a rather more serious take on life than his younger sibling – in childhood photographs, Brian is usually the one posing carefully and correctly, while Keith has a mischievous grin.

Until Brian was nine, both boys went to Notre Dame school, about three miles from Norfield and on the same side of town. The school was, for the most part, a Catholic girls convent, with a small mixed junior section. Though the Duckworths described themselves as C of E (in reality they were not deeply religious), Notre Dame was happy to accept non-Catholics, with certain restrictions – like placing the Protestant children at the back of the class while Catholic rituals were being taught.

In due course Brian went as a boarder to Giggleswick School, near Settle in North Yorkshire, at which point Keith was moved to another local junior school rather than leave him as just one of a handful of junior boys at Notre Dame. Two years later, in 1942, he went north to join his brother.

The Blackburn Keith left behind had continued to struggle throughout those nine years, as the textile industry continued its relentless decline. How much the boys noticed it, however, is debatable, as the Duckworth family had bucked the trend. Oak Street Manufacturing had continued to generate profits and the family was now very comfortably-off. Not many families could afford a car of any kind, but the Duckworths motored in good style. Frank had a brief but underwhelming dalliance with an Alvis, but otherwise, he mostly drove Rileys and – according to Graham Robson, who interviewed Keith in the 1980s for his book on Cosworth[3] – at the outbreak of war Keith actually owned two. Gracing the drive at Norfield were a hemi-headed 2½-litre 16hp Kestrel and a 1½-litre Adelphi.

Neither would get much use in the coming years, with petrol rationing in force, but nevertheless the Riley marque seemed to sum up what the family was about – a quality product not given to ostentation, neither staid nor flashy.

Rileys were known for being very well engineered ... *thoughtfully* engineered. The engines appealed in particular to Frank, for they were among the best production units made anywhere in the prewar years, good enough to form the basis of the very successful ERA racing cars and featuring a cylinder-head design that was both innovative and effective.

"The engine is the heart of the car, and the head is the heart of the engine." It's not completely fanciful to imagine Frank saying that, on one of the rare occasions when father and son got to drive out onto the empty roads of wartime Lancashire. And maybe, just maybe, a seed was sown, for when Keith got to design his own engines, he always paid particular attention to cylinder-head design, with exceptional results.

Petrol was not, of course, the only thing in short supply in wartime Britain. The country was struggling to feed itself. Warehousing was needed so that imported food, when available, could be stockpiled and rationed. And where better than textile mills? Substantial secure structures, in easy reach of the port of Liverpool, and many of them underused. Requisitioning mills made perfect sense to the Ministry of Food. However, for some inexplicable reason, the ministry requisitioned at least one that *wasn't* underused – Oak Street Mill – and suddenly the Duckworths had no business, other than whatever income the government provided by way of compensation for having their premises filled with tinned foodstuffs from America.

Frank didn't fancy twiddling his thumbs for the duration of the war and so set about acquiring another mill, this one on Blackburn Road in Accrington. It is not clear how much fabric ever left the factory gates, however. Not only were supplies of raw cotton erratic at best during the war years, but on 13 December 1945, just a few months after the cessation of hostilities, Frank suddenly took ill and died, at the age of 43. Keith was just 12 years old, Brian 14.

It was a devastating blow for the whole family, but the boys had two things to cushion the impact. Firstly, they were now well settled at Giggleswick, so at least one part of their lives hadn't been turned upside down. Secondly, with Em being the eldest of four well-spaced children, her brothers David and Harry were young enough to relate well to the boys. They did their best to fill the gap left by Frank's death, Harry and Keith becoming particularly close. At 22, Harry was the youngest of the four, only 10 years older than Keith, and found himself filling a role somewhere between father figure and older brother.

Harry had long been used to having Keith hanging around Wellington Garage on Furthergate, where the Hardman family business was based. Like most haulage companies at the time, Hardman & Gillibrand maintained its own vehicles, and throughout his junior school days Keith had enjoyed quizzing the mechanics servicing the wagons, studying a worn component to see what was wrong with it, or helping the men bolt seats onto a flat-bed to turn it into a charabanc for a weekend trip to Blackpool. And, of course, getting thoroughly dirty.

Now, with Frank gone, Harry took on the role of mentor. Shortly before his death, Frank had fitted a window in Norfield's newly redundant air-raid shelter and equipped it as a workshop with a vertical drill, a secondhand Myford lathe and a grinder. Officially, this was to foster his young son's emerging talents. Unofficially, he was no doubt looking forward to using the equipment himself! Having a budding engineer in the family was a wonderful excuse to buy some boys' toys.

Harry couldn't hope to fill Frank's shoes as far as engineering skills were concerned, but he spent many hours with Keith in the workshop, helping where he could and watching in admiration as the boy largely trained himself by dint of sheer enthusiasm and an endlessly questioning mind. The two became great mates.

Much though he shared his father's interests in cars and motorcycles, Keith's personal passion was aircraft. His early models were schoolboy efforts from balsa wood, but he rapidly progressed to design his own, both at home in the workshop and using the facilities at Giggleswick. By the time he was in his teens he had taken a leaf out of his father's book and was using his skills to subsidise his hobby, designing and building miniature engines – steam, petrol and diesel. At a time when the national average wage was £8-9 per week, 12 shillings and sixpence for machining a crankshaft was not to be sneezed at, especially when you are only 15. Before long, if the neighbours had a mechanical or electrical problem, often as not there would come a knock at the door of Norfield, where Keith's workshop was steadily building up its collection of tools, instruments and engineering components.

Keith was not primarily an electrical engineer, but he realised the importance of the discipline and took a considerable interest in it, building his first radio-controlled equipment at the age of 16. Radio control was in its infancy at the time and, when applied to model aeroplanes, could do wondrous things. On one occasion he bet his uncle David that he could make his aircraft take off from the next field. He did, and pocketed some cash as a result.

Emboldened, he then bet uncle Harry £5 that he could turn on the electric blanket in his bed from three miles away. Harry took on the bet but, wise to his nephew's ruses, said "I'm coming with you to make sure we really are three miles away." His wife, Olive, was drafted in to ensure that the blanket in the bedroom really did switch on at the right moment. Sure enough, it worked.

When Keith went north to Giggleswick for the second term of 1942, his destination was the preparatory school, Catteral Hall, where he stayed until September 1946, when, at 13, he could move up to the main school. At the time, both were boys-only institutions and, like most public schools of that era, operated a pretty strict regime. Later, when he came to do National Service, Keith was heard to observe that the military discipline was like being in a hotel compared to what he had been used to at Giggleswick! Conscripts got better food, too.

The boy was clearly very clever, but despite this, Giggleswick didn't regard him as a towering academic; rather it was his personal and sporting qualities which were emphasised in school records. Big-framed and strong, he was an excellent swimmer and showed some ability on the rugby field, occasionally playing for the home XV. He could not, however, get on with cricket. Hand-eye coordination was never his forte – indeed, friends would later joke that he was too busy calculating the trajectory of the ball to remember to put out his hand and catch it.

The Duckworth brothers had their disagreements, Keith's mischievousness saw to that. It was, for instance, strictly forbidden to tickle trout in the school grounds, but Keith found he had a knack for it. Sometimes he got caught, but he was usually able to persuade the master in charge to look the other way, in return for a nice trout. Brian, who was genuinely proud of the fact that he would never do such a thing, was irritated by his kid brother's antics, though whether because of the transgression itself, or the fact that he often got away with it, is not clear.

Sometimes Keith's brushes with authority were more serious, for although he was not a natural rebel, if he felt something was wrong he would say so, and stand his ground.

The first indication of this trait came at 14, when everyone in his year was to be confirmed by the Church of England. Each boy had to learn by heart the Apostles, Creed, and various other texts, and then affirm that he believed in them. But Keith did not believe, and felt it would be hypocritical to say that he did. His view was broadly agnostic, and remained so for the rest of his life; interviewed later by Graham Robson he commented that the biblical story he was being asked to attest to "sounded grossly unlikely," adding "it was the first time that I actually went on my own analysis of a situation, and came to my own conclusions," (*Cosworth*, p18).

Where religion was concerned, the school did not take kindly to Keith reaching his own conclusions and he was hauled up before the padre, then the housemaster, and finally the headmaster himself, the formidable E H Partridge. He stood firm – something of an achievement when carpeted by a headmaster as forceful as Mr Partridge – and was never confirmed.

As his school days progressed, he developed an annoying (for the school) habit of asking for reasons, rather than just obeying the prevailing diktat, and occasionally this strong-mindedness led to an encounter with the Partridge cane. But by the time he left in July 1951, just before his 18th birthday, a certain mutual respect had developed, for Keith had become a praepostor (the school equivalent of prefect), head of his house (Nowell) and a corporal in the schools Combined Cadet Force. He had also managed to consume quite a lot of beer. All but the last-mentioned are summed up in his entry in the school records for that year, which says 'Duckworth D K, Nowell, came '42 (2), placed IIIB, left VI, Head of Nowell, Praepostor, Swimming colours, Librarian, Cpl CCF'. (The '2' after his entry year refers to the term of entry).

The same records detail his involvement in a rescue operation at Penyghent pothole, maintaining communication with the help of two other boys from his house, stating that "Duckworth remained at the scene of the accident on the moors throughout the night, and for most of the next day." Curiously, this incident rings no bells at all with his family; he never seems to have talked about it with anyone.

Keith's school certificate (the equivalent of today's GCSE qualification), showed distinctions in maths and chemistry, and credits in physics, Latin, French, English literature and language, and geography. Two years later he became one of the first to take the then-new A-level examinations, passing in maths, physics, chemistry and education. He also studied extra Latin, in case he wanted to go to Oxford or Cambridge, but in the event he accepted an offer from Imperial College London, one of the country's top engineering institutions.

A reference to Imperial from headmaster Partridge, dated 21 September 1951, says "Conduct good, sound character, more than average intelligence. School prefect, head of his house, played for the Int XV. I can recommend him with confidence."

The young man who left Giggleswick in 1951 had undoubtedly had a good start in life, despite the tragic loss of his father. He'd had a stable home, an excellent education at a school he had enjoyed, and had been blessed with good health and high intelligence. Thanks to his father's business acumen, he also had a bit of money to his name, £25 of which he had spent a couple of years back on an old sidevalve 250cc BSA of circa 1934 vintage, with a hand gearchange. It had needed fettling, but gave him something to do at home during the holidays.

It was now up to Keith to make the best of his good fortune. But what of the town of his birth, and the people he was about to leave behind?

By the end of 1945 Em found herself in sole charge of Oak Street Manufacturing. With neither Brian nor Keith showing any interest in taking over the business, she appointed a manager to run it, and it was eventually sold.

Both sons were undoubtedly influenced by a typically perspicacious comment Frank made not long before his death, namely that he couldn't see much future for the textile industry postwar, because of cheap imports and the like.

In fact, Brian did enter his father's industry, but not as a manufacturer. After National Service, which saw him become an officer in the Gunners, he studied textiles at Leeds University, where he also met his future wife, Betty. On graduation, Brian became a technical representative for industrial textiles, but eventually gave it up in favour of establishing the first of what was to become a series of launderettes (very much a growth sector at a time when few families had a washing machine), in the Blackburn area, a move which marked the end of the Duckworth family's involvement with the textile industry. Brian died in 2003, but his business is still trading successfully in the hands of his children.

In starting a launderette, he was following in the footsteps of his uncles Harry and David, who by now were both operating similar, but quite independent, enterprises. In 1940 they had been left the Hardman & Gillibrand haulage business in their father Walter's will, but not long after the end of WWII it was nationalised. Harry left soon after and started his first launderette, and although David stayed on to run what was now the Blackburn branch of a state-run enterprise, in due course he followed in his brother's footsteps.

Keith would live to see the town of his youth change out of all recognition, with both his father's mills demolished, the Hardman works knocked down, and his first junior school replaced by a housing estate bearing the same name, Notre Dame. Today, only the two family homes, at Ramsgreave Drive and Whalley Road, provide physical continuity.

But the ethos of the town, and more particularly of his family, had been imprinted on his psyche and would stay with him all his life. Even a well run textile business operated on small margins, and this had always informed the family's lifestyle. Work hard. Watch the pennies. Live comfortably but never extravagantly. Invest in education. Use your intelligence. Speak your mind. Tell the truth. Pay your bills on the nail. Pursue debtors determinedly. And above all, keep out of the clutches of the banks – avoid borrowing money if at all possible.

It was a set of principles that was to serve him well.

Footnotes

1 An interesting analysis of the industry in the inter-war years can be found in *Mr Gandhi Visits Lancashire: A Study in Imperial Miscommunication* by Irina Spector-Marks of Macalester College, published 2008.

2 In some documents the company is called Oak-street Manufacturing Co Ltd and in others just Oak Manufacturing Co Ltd. Some company and personal information drawn from the annual *Barretts Directory of Blackburn & District*.

3 p18 *Cosworth: the Search for Power*, by Graham Robson. First edition published by Patrick Stephens Ltd, 1990. Fifth edition published 2003. This book is referenced throughout and page numbers will be given within the main body of the text hereafter.

Motorcycle racing on the sands at Southport, on the Lancashire coast some 28 miles from Blackburn in January 1929. This event is typical of many held there in this era, and could even be the actual meeting attended by Frank and Em. *(Courtesy Getty Images)*

Daniel Duckworth, Keith's grandfather, at the wheel of a Clément Talbot (or its very similar French cousin, a Clément Bayard) in 1908. Both men are wearing buttonholes, suggesting the car was being used for a wedding. The pub was the De Tabley Arms in Ribchester near Preston, now residential accommodation. Daniel died two years after this photo was taken, leaving an eight year-old son, Frank.

Em and Frank with Frank's mother Ada and new arrival Brian, autumn 1931.

In an unsuccessful attempt to persuade Ghandi to drop his boycott of imported textiles, in 1931, Lancashire mill owners invited him to visit the county and see for himself the state of the industry. Here, he meets a group of mill workers. Incidentally, he also met a seven-year-old called Olive, who later would become Keith's aunt. *(Courtesy Blackburn & Darwen Library & Information Services)*

17

Keith as a baby.

One of the last photos of Frank with his sons, taken in 1945.

Keith (left) in the garden with Brian when he was about four.

Death of Cotton Manufacturer

A Blackburn cotton manufacturer, Mr Frank Duckworth, died suddenly at his home, Norfield, Whalley-road, Wilpshire, last night. He was 43.

Mr Duckworth was principal of Oak Manufacturing Company, which he founded in 1936 after being a partner in Duckworth, Sagar, and Ormerod, cotton manufacturers, Clayton-le-Moors.

He was a member of Wilpshire Golf Club. He leaves a widow and two sons.

COTTON MANUFACTURER'S DEATH

The cremation took place at Carleton on Tuesday of Mr. Frank Duckworth, cotton manufacturer, who died suddenly at his home, Norfield, Whalley-road, Wilpshire, the previous Thursday night. Aged 43, Mr. Duckworth, who was a native of Blackburn, was principal of Oak-street Manufacturing Co., which he founded in 1936. Previously he was a partner in the firm of Messrs. Duckworth, Sagar and Ormerod, cotton manufacturers, Clayton-le-Moors. He was a member of Wilpshire Golf Club. He leaves a widow and two sons.

Many of Mr. Duckworth's business associates met the cortege at Carleton, where a short service was held prior to cremation. Among the many beautiful floral tributes were wreaths from: Captain and Council of Wilpshire Golf Club; Employees, Oak-street Manufacturing Co.; Directors of J. Clarke, Nelson, and Messrs. J. J. Duckworth, Ltd., Nelson. Scales Funeral Service made the arrangements.

Cotton Manufacturer's Funeral

Many business associates were present at the funeral at Carleton Crematorium yesterday of Mr Frank Duckworth, cotton manufacturer, Norfield, Whalleyroad, Wilpshire.

Floral tributes included wreaths from the captain and council of Wilpshire Golf Club; employees of Oak-street Manufacturing Company; directors of J. Clarke, Nelson; and Messrs J. J. Duckworth, Ltd., Nelson. Scales Funeral Service made the arrangements.

How the *Northern Daily Telegraph* and *Blackburn Times* reported Frank's death. *(Courtesy Blackburn with Darwen Library & Information Services)*

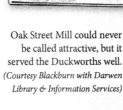

Oak Street Mill could never be called attractive, but it served the Duckworths well. *(Courtesy Blackburn with Darwen Library & Information Services)*

Early mechanical transport, and (below) the brothers when Keith was around nine.

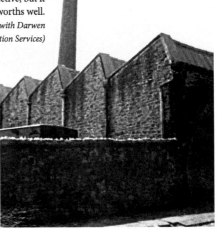

1930s picture of the area where Oak Street Mill was located. Part of Richmond Terrace is in the foreground, and St James' Church is on the skyline. *(Courtesy Blackburn with Darwen Library & Information Services)*

Keith's boyhood homes as they look today: (far left) 77 Ramsgreave Drive and Norfield (now Norfield House, 90 Whalley Road). *(Courtesy Norman Burr)*

Keith's first school, Notre Dame. *(Courtesy Lancashire Evening Telegraph)*

Envelope and contents of a letter from a Mr J A Parker, dated Monday 5 April 1948, about a model aero engine crankshaft.

Keith at Giggleswick, when about 17, third from left in front row. *(Courtesy Giggleswick School)*

Giggleswick School CCF on Speech Day 1950. Somewhere in the ranks is a young DKD.
(Courtesy Giggleswick School)

Keith in uniform with Keith Winterbottom, his best friend from Blackburn. Frostybum, as Keith always called him, was conscripted around the same time as Keith.

The Waterhouse Building, home of engineering at Imperial College, in 1957. Appropriately enough, there's an Austin Ruby parked outside – though it cannot be Keith's, because by the time this photo was taken the car was with Bill in Hartlepool. *(Courtesy Eric de Mare, from Imperial College archives)*

Neither Keith nor Noel took any photos of their bikes at university, but these pictures show a 1932 Scott Flying Squirrel (top) and 1948 Triumph Speed Twin virtually identical to Noel's 1947 example. *(Scott courtesy Yesterdays Antique Motorcycles, www. yesterdays.nl; Triumph courtesy www.volusiarider.com)*

DKD at 20. *(Courtesy Imperial College)*

Austin Seven

Austin Seven Ruby

BV

BV

© GRAEME JENNER 2014

Specifications
Engine: 4 in-line, side valve,
Bore: 56mm
Stroke: 76.2mm
Displacement: 747.5cc
Compression ratio: approx 6.5 to 1
Carburetor: horizontal Zenith
Power output: 17bhp at 3,800rpm
Maximum speed: 50.8mph
Acceleration: 0-50mph 58secs
Fuel consumption: 45mpg
Transmission: rear wheel drive syncro on top 3 gears, 4 speed manual
Clutch: single dry plate

Construction: steel body bolted to steel A-form frame chassis
Steering: worm & sector, 1¹/⁴ turns lock to lock
Brakes: cable operated drums all round

Suspension front: transverse semi-elliptic leaf
Suspension rear: quarter elliptic leaf springs Austin made friction shock absorbers
Wheels & Tyres: 17" bolt-on wire, 4.00 x 17 tyres

Dimensions
Wheelbase: 6ft 9in
Track F/R: 3ft 4in/3ft 7in
Overall length: 10ft 7in
Overall width: 4ft 3in
Height: 5ft 3in
Turning circle: 38ft
Ground clearance: 6in
Kerb weight: 12.1cwt approx.
Tank capacity: 5 gallons

Production
1935-36 price new £125
UK Austin Sevens production
Saloons & Tourers 1933-34: 43,068
Total 1922-39: 290,944

Feet: 0   1   2   3   4   5   6

Left: Ursula with Keith's Lotus Six, shortly after its completion. The Six was an important car for Lotus as it was the first of Chapman's designs to sell in any quantity – around 100 in total. Built around a spaceframe weighing only 25kg, and stiffened by rivetted-on alloy panels, it drew most of its mechanical parts from the Ford 100E and E93A, though there were several alternatives to the sidevalve engine, the Climax chosen by Keith being the top of the range. The car still exists, though at the time of writing it is not on the road.

No photos exist of Keith's Ruby, but here's what it should have looked like! The artist has added as much of the registration as we know: BV – Blackburn letters, naturally.
(Courtesy Classic Car Portraits, Graeme Jenner)

Bo in 1956, Noel at the wheel and Bill co-driving, helping with all the various levers, among which was a manual ignition advance-and-retard on the steering column which required constant adjustment to match engine speed. *(Courtesy Charles Dunn)*

Keith (left) on graduation day 1957, with fellow student Robin Barlow.

(Below) Keith at the wheel of Bo in 1956, as Bill cranks the engine, using a long handle inserted on the offside of the car. *(Courtesy L W Dowdall)*

London to Brighton run, 1955, Noel driving, Bill in the middle and Keith on the right, still recovering from glandular fever. The pair at the back are the president and secretary of the students' union.

Chapter 2

Flying low

The years following World War II saw some of the most dramatic changes Britain has ever witnessed in peacetime. During Keith's teenage years, the NHS was created, the coal, steel, railway and road transport industries were nationalised, and a massive rebuilding programme was put in place. And since the war had left the country heavily in debt to the US, industrialists everywhere were told to export or die. Materials continued to be rationed, with priority going to companies producing for export. Many products simply weren't available on the home market, even food was rationed until 1953.

One thing which didn't change, however, was that young men continued to be conscripted into the forces. With an empire still to be run, unrest in Malaya, a war in Korea, and large numbers of troops tied up in the British sector of the embryonic West German state, there was still a need for men in uniform. Moreover, unlike in wartime, being in a 'protected occupation' didn't get you off the hook. Every male had to do his two years.

There was a certain amount of flexibility, however, as to when the military duties were undertaken. For instance, those who had qualified for university could go either before or after studying for their degree, and Keith decided to go before. Conscripts were offered a choice of army, navy or air force, though there was no guarantee that you would get what you asked for. Keith asked for the RAF, the natural first choice of any aircraft-mad young man. Quite simply, he wanted to become a pilot.

So, in his final year at school, exams over, 17 year-old Keith Duckworth took the train down to Hornchurch in Essex, to take two days of aptitude tests. Hornchurch aerodrome, located near Romford in what is now the London Borough of Havering, had been a major RAF base during WWII on account of its proximity to London, but by this time (January 1951) was the RAF's Flying Training Command's Aircrew Selection Centre.

For reasons which will unfold later in this chapter, when Keith's National Service was completed and he left the RAF, it was without the coveted pilot's licence. That failure probably explains why he subsequently drew something of a veil over his time in the forces. In later interviews he would scarcely mention it, and there is only one known photo of him in Air Force uniform. He told his family and colleagues little about this period of his life, and even his closest friends remained largely in the dark. Noel – now Sir Noel – Davies, who Keith would later meet at university and who became a lifelong friend, believes that "Keith regarded his time at the RAF as a failure, and he hated to fail at anything. He didn't talk about it much at all. I don't even know where he was stationed."

As far as personal recollections of the RAF are concerned, he only opened up once on the record, and that was to Graham Robson during the preparation of the latter's book on Cosworth. As a result, quite a lot of the information in the following account of Keith's service career is drawn from that source – a fact the writer acknowledges with gratitude.

Talking about Hornchurch, he told Graham "I did a whole series of aptitude tests in those two days, and though I wanted to be a pilot, they were doubtful about this, and wanted to put me down as a navigator." Keith duly found himself drafted into the RAF in Lincolnshire, conscript number 2547108, with his service to King and country scheduled to start on 9 October 1951.

Transport between Lincolnshire and Blackburn was a challenge. He initially clubbed together with two other recruits to buy an ancient overhead-cam Singer 12 saloon, but this soon gave up the ghost. Moreover he knew from bitter experience that his recently acquired 1932 Scott Flying Squirrel could not be relied upon to produce its distinctive yowl for any length of time. Perhaps because of these complications, around this time he turned up at his Aunt Olive's house with a 1927 Norton and offered to take her for a ride on it.

Her father happened to be at her house at the time, and thought it rather risky, so he said no. Keith persisted – "We're only going round the block" – so her father relented and she climbed astride the pillion. The pair then rode to Preston and back, about eight miles each way, Keith vigorously cranking open the throttle at every opportunity. Eventually Olive shouted in his ear "Don't you think you're going a bit too fast?" and back came the reply "Yes, when the bike shakes like this, it's a lot too fast actually."

When they finally got back, her worried father asked them sternly where they'd been. With a grin, Keith replied "Well, you told me go round the block didn't you?"

Amusing though such diversions were, the fact remained that the principal task for the next two years was to do the RAF's bidding. Many school-leavers found the military discipline hard to take, but Keith took to it quite comfortably. His introduction to forces life was basic military training – square-bashing – at RAF Kirton in Lindsey, Lincolnshire.

Sixteen days into this training, on 25 October, he was formally designated as cadet navigator, and the following day was moved to another of the RAF's Lincolnshire bases, Digby near Sleaford. But he continued to agitate for transfer to a pilot's course and inside a few weeks his superiors agreed to give him a chance. Finally, he got behind the controls of an aircraft for the first time, a Tiger Moth.

This was his opportunity to go for that precious pilot's licence, and he grabbed it. His instructors were sufficiently impressed and within a few weeks, on 28 December, Keith received a belated but very welcome Christmas present – remustering as cadet pilot.

Two months later he was made up to pilot officer, ready to begin flying Chipmunks at Booker, near High Wycombe, starting in early March 1952. He logged around 60 hours on these before moving on to the advanced flying training school at Holme-on-Spalding-Moor, near Market Weighton, in June 1952. There he flew twin-engined Oxfords. Things were going well. By autumn 1952 he had about 70 hours logged on Oxfords and needed only another 10 to get his wings.

But then fate took a hand. In his leisure hours he still enjoyed flying model aircraft and one day, as he was chasing after one across a field, he tripped and sprained his ankle. The medics soon had it taped up, but what neither Keith nor anyone else knew at the time was that he was allergic to *Elastoplast*. Shortly afterwards, Keith went to sleep on duty at the controls of an aircraft on a flight back from Germany, but not until some time later did he connect this drowsiness with the allergy. With no medical explanation to offer in mitigation, he was promptly ejected from pilot training for 'dangerous and incompetent night flying' and downgraded to navigator training.

That was the end of Keith Duckworth, RAF pilot.

It was a disappointed young man who, on 18 November 1952, arrived at RAF Thorney Island near Portsmouth to train as a navigator. He had to play catch-up, as his fellow trainees had been on the course all year. Nevertheless, he found he could cope comfortably with the work, although it was not all plain sailing. The stubborn assertiveness, which had earlier seen him arraigned by his headmaster, reappeared. He had no time at all for his lecturer in astro-navigation, whom he regarded as "... a blithering idiot: we used to have lots of arguments about his theories on star shots."

Clearly, Keith was beginning to hone his view of the world, a view which in later years would be summarised by what became known as 'Duckworthisms' – pithy comments on people, engineering and life in general. Some were truisms with Keith's own slant added, others were one-offs that only made sense in the context of the moment. The remainder, more general comments, were heard so frequently that friends, family and colleagues knew much of the library by heart and regarded it as an inseparable part of his persona. From this point on – both in life and in this book – Duckworthisms appear at regular intervals.

As far as the astro-navigation lecturer is concerned, these favourite utterances fit the bill:

> *I CAN SPOT BULLSHIT AT A HUNDRED YARDS, AND I HAVE TO SAY SO ... IF SOMEONE SAYS SOMETHING TO ME WHICH HAS NO MEANING, IT JARS MY MIND. I WORRY ABOUT IT AND I LOSE THE NEXT TEN SENTENCES.*

> *WHENEVER ANYONE SAYS SOMETHING WITH WHICH I DISAGREE, I WILL TRY TO SAY 'HOW DO YOU COME TO THAT CONCLUSION?' BECAUSE OF QUESTIONING EVERYTHING, I AM MORE OR LESS SOCIALLY UNACCEPTABLE.*

Despite his assertiveness – or perhaps because of it – Keith was soon at the top of the course. However, he was never to finish it, because early in 1953 an old rugby injury flared up and he was sent to Halton hospital for a cartilage operation, followed by convalescence at Headley Court. By the time he was fit again, there simply wasn't time to complete the course before the end of his two-year military service, so he never went back. As a result, his rank on discharge remained Acting Pilot Officer / Trainee Navigator. The Keith Duckworth who rode his Scott out of the gates of RAF Thorney Island for the last time knew far more about the ways of the world than the boy who had turned up at Hornchurch two years earlier. But luck had not been on his side: apart from gaining some life skills and some piloting experience, he had little else to show for those two years.

Imperial College beckoned. Lancashire County Council had agreed to pay his tuition fees, on top of which there would be an annual grant of £159 for living expenses. So from September onwards, it was down to him. Not for the first or last time, he determined to put a setback behind him and look to the future.

Chapter 3

The Lavender Hill Mob

Walk down Lavender Gardens in Clapham today and you will see a street broadly similar to the one Keith Duckworth took in as he knocked for the first time on the door of his new lodgings, back in September 1953. Outwardly, number 15, like the rest of this Victorian terrace, has hardly changed at all, although back then it was more affordable and, perhaps, less pristine.

The other buildings that were soon to become the hub of Keith's student life are just as easy to find. Then, as now, engineering at Imperial was based at City & Guilds College (C&G), founded in 1887 and located in South Kensington, just behind the Albert Hall.

Similarly, Imperial's Students' Union is still a short walk away, on Prince Consort Road. Even the pubs which soon became his favourite watering holes remain. For a pint or three after an evening's study, The Crown on Lavender Hill was conveniently close to his digs and served a good brew. Even closer was the Cornet of Horse, just along the street at 49 Lavender Gardens, though today you will look in vain for its curious name.[1] First it was renamed the Cornet, then Bar Risa, now it's The Rise. It's all in sharp contrast to the wholesale reconstruction visited on his home town of Blackburn.

Today, most university students stay in halls for at least their first year, but in 1953, Imperial, like most universities, accommodated few of its students in university buildings – most of them took lodgings. And crucial to whether life in digs was happy or not was the landlady, whose job it was not only to accommodate and feed a houseful of (potentially) unruly students, but also to preserve some semblance of order. Many landladies were formidable characters, a few positively tyrannical.

Mrs Storey at number 15 was, by all accounts, a tolerant soul. As it turned out that was just as well, because she would find herself hosting four engineers, each with their own bits of machinery needing fettling – sometimes in the street and sometimes, when she was pretending not to notice, in the bedroom.

But on the doorstep that day was just a friendly, polite, self-confident young man from Blackburn, who in due course went along to the freshers' introductory party at the Students' Union to receive a briefing on the social and academic life he could expect for the next three years.

Immediately he headed for the motor club stand, where he found himself next to a Welsh farmer's son, Noel Davies. "Because of our common interest in motorcycles," says Noel, "we both made a beeline for the motor club, and this started our friendship." It was a friendship that would last a lifetime.

The pair soon discovered they had more in common than just bikes. "We were both enrolled for the mechanical engineering course, which qualified successful students for two degrees – BSc and ACGI[2]. Most of our student colleagues had entered university straight from school; we were part of only a small minority who had some experience of the world outside school, Keith with the RAF and me through an apprenticeship in the motor industry, at Austin. That experience set us apart from some of the others. We both felt that our route to university was better."

Noel had never had any interest in taking over the family farm near the Shropshire border. He wanted to be an engineer. It was suggested that he serve an apprenticeship at Sentinel, a well-respected maker of lorries and steam engines which was based not far away at Shrewsbury, but in the end he signed up with Austin.

It proved to be the start of a career that would take him to the very top of British engineering, and to a knighthood. Ironically, along the way he would become the notional boss of Sentinel: he went on to spend much of his career at Vickers, which in 1980 took over Rolls-Royce Motors, which itself had much earlier acquired (and eventually closed) the Shrewsbury firm.

All that, however, was in the future.

"Our friendship developed," he continues, "and we found we were joining in the same social events, lectures and project work. I regarded him as my best buddy at college; we did a lot of things together. We were both keen motorcyclists and members of the university motor club, he with his Scott Flying Squirrel and me with my Triumph Speed Twin with a sidecar. We had all sorts of adventures on those."

In later life, Keith was the first to admit that he was not the most diligent of students, but it would be wrong to say that he neglected his work. In Noel's words, "Both Keith and I maintained a responsible attitude. Keith was quickly recognised as one of the brightest students on the course, principally because of his remarkable ability to reduce a new subject to first principles. As a result, he would always produce the best design, using his philosophy of rejecting factors of safety – he described them as factors of ignorance and regarded them as a cop out – and which he would eliminate by going back to the basics. I remember one particular occasion when he did this, when we were tasked with designing a new camshaft for some engine or other. The way Keith approached it was quite different from the rest of us.

"This desire to work from first principles, coupled with his flair for detailed engineering design and manufacture, were the attributes which later became evident on the DFV.

"Keith did not depend on lecturers for his education, and often challenged staff on their approach. He didn't show disrespect for them, that wasn't Keith's nature, but he made it very clear when he thought they were wrong. I cannot recall any lecturer who could stand up to Keith on subjects he regarded as important – and they didn't seem to resent it.

"In these discussions with lecturers I was a supporter of Keith, because he was usually right! We all felt that Keith was above our level – he certainly had an edge in the laboratory, and in the classroom."

FACTORS OF SAFETY ARE ACTUALLY FACTORS OF IGNORANCE.
ACADEMICS ARE SELDOM ANY USE AT ENGINEERING. ONE MUST
HAVE A DISTRUST OF THEORISTS.

Come exam time, however, Keith's determination to build his argument from the ground up proved a liability. Noel witnessed the problem first hand. "He had a good memory, but rather than cram he would just learn the things he could understand and work out the rest during the exam. So he would run out of time. I, on the other hand, would look at the exam paper, work out all the things I could do, get writing and I'd still be writing at the end of the exam. That's how I got through." (Keith incidentally, had his own theory about Noel's examination prowess: he reckoned he has a photographic memory.)

I USED TO THINK THAT THINKING ABILITY IS THE IMPORTANT
FACTOR IN LIFE, RATHER THAN HAVING A GOOD MEMORY.
IT WASN'T UNTIL LATER THAT I REALISED THAT I HAD ALSO BEEN
GIFTED WITH WHAT APPEARS TO BE A VERY GOOD MEMORY – AND
I HADN'T REALISED THE ADVANTAGES OF THAT. HOW CAN PEOPLE
EVER LEARN FROM THEIR EXPERIENCES IF THEY'VE ALREADY
FORGOTTEN WHAT THEY WERE?

Coursework wasn't always plain sailing either. When interviewed later by Graham Robson, Keith observed that "I made quite a few mistakes. One was that we had to write reports of the work we had done on the various gas engines and oil engines. Most people just copied the previous year's reports, but not me. I actually wrote a critical analysis of whether we had learned anything, and in most cases I came to the conclusion that the measuring equipment, and the way that the experiments were done, didn't prove anything. I wrote this down at great length, and my conclusions were that it was not a worthwhile exercise.

"As this was totally new to the examiners, I got very poor marks for my coursework. But I reckon that is the foundation of why I am a good development engineer," (*Cosworth*, p32).

Life at Imperial was not all work and no play and Noel soon found himself spending a lot of time at Lavender Gardens with Keith and another of Mrs Storey's lodgers, John Coplin, who went on to be a senior designer at Rolls-Royce in Derby. Before long, the social group had expanded to four with the addition of John Chadwick. 'Chad', from Bolton, became president of the Students' Union and stayed on at Imperial for further study. Of the four, all were mechanical engineers except John Coplin, who was aeronautical. Noel always reckoned Coplin was the brightest of them all.

One night, the police caught Keith and Noel speeding on Putney Heath. Noel recalls "I was signalled to a layby while the speed cop chased after Keith before coming back to book me. It may be apocryphal, but he never caught up with the Flying Squirrel."

The motor club also provided its fair share of incidents. At that time, rallying on public roads faced virtually no restrictions (this was before even the 12-car-rally era) and the two motorcyclists were often involved in night rallies. However, as Noel recalls "The Squirrel was always breaking down and I learned to tow him, sidecar pulling solo. Very difficult, but possible, if the alternative is not getting home." Sometimes they would swap bikes, Keith making the classic mistake that all motorcyclists do when trying an outfit for the first time of running the sidecar over the kerb. "Noel was very nice about that!" Keith recalled in conversation with Graham Robson (*Cosworth*, p28).

The summer of 1954 marked the end of Keith's first year and he started the hunt for a summer job, settling on a spell at the National Oil & Gas Engine Co in Ashton-under-Lyne. The company made large stationary engines, some with bores as big as 12 inches (30cm); at one point Keith found himself helping tap out a 2½-inch Whitworth hole in the bottom of a cylinder liner.

"When I arrived," he told Graham Robson, "they'd just had a very jolly explosion, where a turbocharged gas engine had mixed gas into its crankcase, which had gone up, blown the inspection doors right off and gone out through the rear corrugated iron wall of the building."

The start of the 1954-55 academic year brought changes. When Keith arrived back from Blackburn, he found he had a new room-mate. Occupying the bed across from his was a 19 year-old from Hartlepool called Bill Brown. And in a single room elsewhere in the house, Noel was making himself at home.

Initially, Keith and Noel were not sure what to make of the newcomer, wondering if Bill would prove rather wet behind the ears. After all, he was two years younger, and had neither served an apprenticeship nor done National Service.

He had, however, worked several long school holidays on West Hartlepool Corporation Transport, first as a bus conductor, and later in the office working out timetables. This had clearly prepared him well for student life, for that very evening Bill proceeded to drink the two of them into oblivion. The following morning, Keith and Noel looked at each other, each as bleary-eyed as Bill was alert, and concluded that he definitely qualified for membership of what by then had become known as 'The Lavender Hill Mob,' after the 1951 comedy film of the same name.

Being in a different year from Keith and Noel meant attending different lectures, so out of the house Bill didn't see much of them. But inside number 15 they were good friends "... religiously crowding round a radio every Friday evening to listen to The Goons," says Bill.

Having spent many hours at Lavender Gardens the previous year, Noel had long since learned that the house rules set by Mrs Storey were non-existent. "She was a widow, and very good to us, she let us do what we wanted, including taking engines to bits in the bedroom. She expected all her lodgers to behave responsibly, and most of them did – most of the time. What must certainly have bothered her were the motorbikes at the kerbside, including my Triumph and Keith's Scott, which could not be ridden quietly under any circumstances." Noel nicknamed his Speed Twin 'Trusty,' but Bill remembers AEP289 as 'Old Rusty,' adding: "I do not remember the Scott having a pet name, but it was often referred to in strong terms."

Keith, Noel and Bill quickly became the driving force behind the college motor club, joined by Roger Brockbank (son of motoring cartoonist Russell), and John Warne, who went on to become a senior Rolls-Royce engineer. Roger, though never resident at number 15, was regarded as spiritual 'mobster.'

Weekend trips to Goodwood, Silverstone or Brands Hatch followed, sometimes three-up on Noel's outfit with Bill in the sidecar, and in 1955 Keith, Noel and Roger went to see the IoM TT. The weather was so foul that Keith spent most of the boat trip sat on the toilet, not because he felt bad but because he reckoned the gents was located at the centre of pitch of the ship, and would therefore move the least.

Eventually, Keith decided that two wheels – or even three – were no longer enough, and so he augmented the Scott with an Austin 7 Ruby. "It was horrible to look at," Noel says, "shit-coloured." The paint had originally been maroon, but some 18 years of fading, industrial grime, dirt and rust had taken their toll. "And Keith used to carry a second steering wheel, so that he could wave it through the window and pretend it had come off. This caused no end of consternation to other road users!

"But by the time he had finished breathing on it, with camshaft mods plus Keith's ideas on cylinder head and carburettor design, the thing was quick. Keith always said 'The head is the heart of the engine, you get that right and the rest will follow.'"

The Ruby's engine may have been in decent fettle by the time Keith had finished with it, but very little else was. In fact, the spare steering wheel and unappealing colour were the least of the poor thing's problems. There was a hole in the floor of the front passenger compartment. The number plate was held on by a piece of string. The passenger door was tied shut because it didn't have a handle, and the gearlever was broken. A box spanner slid over the stump provided a substitute, but not a very convenient one, as the long, spindly lever originated far under the dash and the driver was thus obliged to get his left shoulder under the dashboard to change gear – in Bill's words, "Not the best posture for driving."

Nevertheless, Keith was perversely proud of his dilapidated steed, proud enough to take a girlfriend to Claridges in it. The doorman took one look at the Ruby and said "I'm not going to park that thing," leaving Keith and the young lady no choice but to go somewhere else for the evening, there being no alternative parking nearby.

Keith's experience at Claridges was not unique, for a few years later Noel was similarly shunned. He had swapped his Triumph for an MG TA with a loose gearlever, and, to stop people stealing it and disabling the car, he developed the habit of putting the lever in his pocket along with the keys. On offering both items to the doorman, Noel was told to take his car, and, if he wished, his custom, elsewhere.

In true Austin 7 tradition the Ruby's brakes were, to put it politely, crap. Aficionados point out that, since the Austin 7's other principal characteristic was a lack of go, it didn't matter too much if its feeble cable brakes took their time about stopping. But as every vintage enthusiast knows, adjustment is everything where cable brakes are concerned. Even a useful cable setup can be turned into something grabby and unpredictable by small changes in tension, wear on a cam, or other seemingly minor mechanical defects.

Keith discovered this in dramatic fashion late one night in February 1955. He'd been to a 'hop,' a dance organised by City & Guilds College at a refectory building called Ayrton Hall (since demolished) and to which many girls from local secretarial colleges were invited, there being precisely one female engineer in C&G at the time. At the dance he'd met a girl called Ursula Cassal, who was studying French and German at the Institut Français. In Ursula's words "I went with a friend of mine who was also at the Institute, one Saturday evening for a night out. Somebody tapped me on the shoulder and there he was. He asked me to dance, and it went on from there."

Her college was quite close to C&G in South Kensington, but as her family hailed from Carshalton in Surrey and as the Institute was in any case only a gap year for her, she had continued to live at home. Keith offered her a lift to Victoria station after the dance.

"It was a very damp, dismal evening," recounts Ursula, "and in Regent Street he had to stop suddenly, because some lights went red – and in those days the road leading up to the traffic lights was paved with wooden blocks." He braked, the car started to slew on the slippery surface, he tried again and this time the Ruby did a complete one-eighty as the brakes grabbed and turned the car almost on the spot.

"Oh, that's a case for the book!" he said to Ursula, presumably referring to the fact that, had the brakes worked evenly, they probably would have locked the Ruby's skinny crossplies and sent the car slithering into the middle of the junction. The young lady from the Institut didn't share Keith's enthusiasm for this novel method of conducting an emergency stop "... but he was so calm about it that I had to be as well." Nevertheless, she was quite relieved when "... he got it pointing in the right direction and took me safely to Victoria."

That night, there was certainly no indication that the two of them would, in due course, become man and wife. In fact, they scarcely saw each other for several months. "He didn't make any definite arrangement to see me," Ursula explains, "but from time to time that year I ran into him, because I used to belong to the Imperial College choir and went there to rehearse."

The Ruby was also used for a visit home to Blackburn, during which Keith was pleased to learn that his brother Brian's patent application, for a system to ease replacement of worn-out paper-makers' endless felt belts[3], was progressing. In principle, Keith was always against the patent system – he once told Bill that if you were clever enough to invent something, you should be clever enough to stay ahead of any copiers – but he could make an exception where family was concerned, and was rather proud of what Brian had achieved.

He was also proud of his first car, despite – or perhaps because of – its condition, and couldn't resist showing it off to his favourite aunt, Olive.

"Come and have a drive," Keith said to her, pointing to his dung-coloured heap. Olive, her spirit of adventure undimmed by the memory of riding pillion with Keith some years before, duly entered from the driver's side and slid across – the passenger door was still tied shut – only to find a hole where the floor should be. "Where do I put my feet?" she asked incredulously. "Oh, put them up there, on the dashboard," came the reply, and off they went.

On their return, Uncle Harry rushed out of the house, relieved to find his wife still in one piece. "You're never to get in there again!" he berated her. That was enough to raise Harry's elder brother David's curiosity, so Keith said to him too: "Get in." Uncle David proceeded to manoeuvre himself into the curious posture necessary for any passenger to travel in the Ruby without wearing out their shoe leather, and soon, with the spanner doing sterling service as a gearlever, Keith had worked the little car up through the 'box to the dizzy heights of 90mph – or so the speedo said.

How fast was it really? A standard Ruby was good for a fraction over 50mph, and took 58 seconds to get there, courtesy of a 17bhp sidevalve four of 747cc. Noel describes Keith's example as quick, but a Ruby that managed 60mph, for example, would have been quick by Austin 7 standards. It certainly would have felt quick! Bill, who navigated for Keith in the Ruby during college motor club rallies, doesn't think

Keith did anything radical to the car, but "It certainly vibrated enough to make reading the speedo problematical – even 50mph downhill was amply exciting!"

After just a few months with the Ruby, Keith's thoughts turned towards more sporting machinery. So, by the end of the '54-55 academic year, the Ruby had a new owner, one William Brown, who thus moved across from the navigator's seat to the side of the car with a floor.

"I drove it home to Hartlepool," Bill recalls, "and somewhere in Hertfordshire I was pulled over by the police. They said they had nothing against my driving, but were not impressed by the car. They went over it, decided it was safe enough for me to proceed, but that I would be hearing from them. Shortly after I got home, a summons arrived. My father, who is also called William Brown, unfortunately opened the envelope and, being a pillar of the local community, was not amused that I had been blithely driving around Hartlepool in this menace to the populace!

"They had singled out 18 counts, one being that there was no gearlever, just a tube spanner forced over the vestigial stump. The count which most amused me (though not my father) was that 'the road could be seen from inside the car.'"

In due course Keith, who was still the legal owner at this point, found that the roadworthiness buck had stopped with him. Ursula remembers him discussing it with her:

"Apparently, the policeman walked round the car, listing one by one all the things that were wrong with it, but he burst out laughing at the same time, which rather spoiled the effect. It turned out that the constabulary in London had been trying to catch Keith for some time, but they'd always just missed out."

Back to Bill: "I then turned the Seven into a very basic aluminium-bodied two-seater special and ran it for the next five years. Even after its rebirth as my special I did nothing to the engine and I doubt if it could much exceed 60, but carrying the absolute minimum of bodywork its acceleration was definitely improved." In this form the car became well known at college motor club events during the following academic year; its driver was by then Hon Sec of the club.

In the course of that five year ownership, Bill became something of an expert on Ruby brakes, or rather the absence of them. He explains: "The reason why the brakes on the Ruby were such crap is because the actuating cables were connected directly to the levers on the front drums. When you braked, the whole solid front axle moved back on its mountings relative to the rest of the vehicle, thus loosening the cables and letting the brakes off, requiring further movement of the pedal to take up the slack. So the first application rarely had the desired effect."

Meanwhile, Keith had been busy watching motor racing and had begun to fancy himself as a budding racing driver. He noticed how Lotus Sixes could regularly beat dearer, faster machinery, by virtue of their light weight and excellent handling, and before long he was regularly spending time at the disused stables that constituted the premises of the fledgling Lotus company, behind the Railway Hotel in Hornsey. He was far from alone in this: in its early days Lotus was a magnet for anyone interested in motor racing on a budget: all sorts of people who would go on to be famous names would drop in, buy bits, chat with Chapman, work (often unpaid) on one of his customers' projects, and gradually become part of the extended, informal Lotus family.

One advantage of this system from Chapman's point of view was that it allowed him to get free first-hand experience of potential employees' usefulness, or otherwise.

If you were lucky, mucking in at Hornsey might lead to a job. If you were even luckier, you might get paid regularly.

Enthused, Keith persuaded his mother that it would be a good investment to spend a chunk of the money inherited from his father on buying a Lotus Six. Em didn't even know what a Lotus Six looked like but, knowing her son's – and her late husband's – passion for mechanical things, she didn't have the heart to put up a fight about it.

So in the spring of 1955 Keith Duckworth turned up once again at Hornsey. He'd been there many times before, but this time it was different: he was at the stores counter, chequebook open, wanting to buy a car.

On the other side of the counter stood the storeman, Jack Field. He was about Keith's age, but the two could not have had more different backgrounds if they'd tried. The very antithesis of an intellectual, Jack left school at 14, but he has never been in awe of anyone. Behind the strong Cockney accent lies a man with an honours degree from the University of Life: quick-witted, a formidable deal-maker and a first-class judge of character. In making him storeman almost from the outset of the company, Colin Chapman had decided, as would Keith later, that Jack Field was a very good person to have on your side.

"To start with I worked as a storeman at a Vauxhall-Bedford main dealer across the road from the Lotus works," Jack explains. "Chapman was living with his parents at that time, and on his way into work, if there was anything he wanted that was a bit strange, he'd pop into the dealership and explain it to me. I'd go through the GM bible, to see if I could get anything that he could make into what he wanted and, if he was lucky, on his way home he could pick it up.

"After a while he asked if I'd go and work for him: he couldn't pay me hardly any money, but he said that eventually Lotus would become one of the big six car-manufacturing companies, and it could make me a millionaire!" Jack was not that easily dazzled, but nevertheless it seemed a chance worth taking. "I was still living at home then; my living expenses were very low, so I went to work for him." This would have been around 1954, when even Mike Costin was just a part-timer.

"The company was very small at that time – Graham Hill worked in the gearbox shop, Mike Costin was often around, plus a handful of others, mostly involved in the racing side." Jack's role was to service the road-car business, dealing with kitcar customers and delivering the kits.

Jack remembers his initial meeting with Keith very clearly. "I took a bit of a dislike to him at first. This young bloke appeared at the counter, typical rich young kid, he was having the best spec, with a Climax engine, de Dion rear axle – he wanted the lot. And he asked if he could assemble the car in the garage next to our workshop, where I kept the company's stock of cars. I said, 'No you can't.' That place was my responsibility, and I reckoned that if I let a customer build a car there, if they hit any problems they'd be in and out of the workshop, borrowing tools. He said 'Mr Chapman said I could,' and I said, 'Sorry, it's my responsibility and you can't.'

"So he went away, but not long afterwards Chapman came on the phone and said 'You won't let him build in the garage?' 'No,' I repeated, 'the amount of stuff that gets nicked out of there – back-axle ratios, all sorts of things – it's bad enough as it is. And the people working in the workshop, he'll be wasting their time, we can't get enough stuff out of the door as it is.'

"But Colin insisted. 'He's going to be very useful to the company, I'd appreciate it if you'd let him use the garage.' So I said okay, though I told Colin I didn't like the idea."

As it turned out, Jack need not have worried. Shortly after this, Keith succumbed to a nasty bout of glandular fever and on 27 June the college formally notified the University of London that he was unfit to take that year's exams. He wasn't fit to build a car, either, so returned to Blackburn to recuperate, but not before Noel and Bill, themselves anxious about the forthcoming examinations, had rolled about on Keith's bed in the hope of catching the same bug. Noel remained stubbornly healthy, but roommate Bill succumbed. He didn't contract the disease severely enough or early enough to avoid the exams, but his efforts were not wasted because, when he duly failed, the college gave him the benefit of the doubt and allowed him to repeat the year.

Once in Blackburn, a combination of rest and home cooking ensured a steady recovery and, towards the end of the summer term, Keith returned to London to collect his belongings from number 15. By sheer coincidence, he bumped into Ursula again. That meeting seemed to take their relationship to another level, for when Keith returned for the next academic year, they started going out together.

Before that, however, Keith had a summer to kill. And what better convalescence project could there possibly be for a young engineer than to build a car? Keith told his mother: "I'm having a car delivered home, put it in the lounge, will you?" Em was game for most things, but she did a double-take at this. Nevertheless, that's where it landed, and where some assembly took shape. The only Lotus Six ever built in Wilpshire was registered WTD2 on 12 September 1955, and was initially left as bare aluminium, though before long it had been painted British Racing Green.

As the 1955-56 academic year at Imperial got under way, Keith found himself once again ensconced in the familiar surroundings of number 15, beginning a repeat of his second year. Bill was beginning a repeat of his first, while Noel was beginning his third and final year.

The Six became Keith's regular transport, and Ursula remembers it well. Unlike the Ruby, the nearside had the luxury of a floor, but things were still not straightforward for the passenger, as it was light alloy and a stressed component. "When we went out in it, I had to take off my shoes for fear the high heels would dent the floor."

Nonetheless, Ursula was enjoying herself. Easy-going and adaptable, she was more than happy to fit in with Keith's foibles and eccentricities, and for his part Keith, who'd had plenty of other girlfriends up to this point, loved the fact that, with Ursula, he could still be himself. There seemed to be no downside to having her around.

For Ursula, part of the attraction of life with Keith was that it was utterly different from anything she had ever known. There was always something exciting going on, such as an engine blow-up on the way to the City & Guilds fireworks party, even if it was a nuisance at the time. Living at home was very ordered: her family in Carshalton was very different to Keith's, with a much more formal and traditional approach to life. Her father was an engineer; her mother a highly respected piano teacher at Trinity College School of Music in London. Before long, Keith took Ursula to Blackburn to meet his family. She was a bit taken aback at first: they were big, they were open, they were friendly – not at all the sort of people she was used to. They welcomed her with open arms and made her feel right at home.

In winning Ursula's heart, Noel and Bill reckoned Keith had done very well for himself. Noel sums it up thus: "She was a great girl, but from a different class, she was his superior," though Ursula says she never saw herself that way. "Keith did very well to persuade her to be his girlfriend, she spoke better than any of us did. My initial impressions were of a posh young lady, you could imagine her in the foreign service or the legal profession."

By now Ursula was studying history, French and German at Kings College London in the Strand, still living at home. "It was cheaper than digs, and my parents couldn't afford to keep me in halls, but there were plenty of trains then. You could get one back at 11.30 at night, so it didn't matter much. I used to get teased about going out with somebody who wasn't from Kings: I went to Imperial's dances and he came to mine."

She also started going to race meetings with him. "My first was at Goodwood, I remember Mike Hawthorn and Colin Chapman were racing." By this point, Keith was beginning to know his way around Climax engines. "Just small jobs here and there," Ursula recalls. "That day at Goodwood, someone came to him with a Lotus Elite.

"Another day, we drove to Brands Hatch to assist one of his customers. Late and in a hurry, Keith drove along the narrow lane that led to the track, but it was an exit lane and we met a car – an old Austin I think – full on. The battery housing intruded into the passenger area and I banged my left foot on it, cracking a bone. Keith was OK, but the front of the Lotus was damaged. When it was repaired, Keith decided to have it painted red."

The other car in Keith's life at this time was also red, but otherwise it could scarcely have been more different. Then, as now, the Imperial College Motor Club owned a 1902 James & Browne (nicknamed *Boanerges*, 'son of thunder', or *Bo* for short) and at that time the students themselves used to maintain it. So it fell to Noel, as captain of the club for 1955-56, to ensure that the car was fit for its duties, such as the London-Brighton run, and to decide who should drive it. When Noel graduated in summer 1956, Keith took over as captain of the club and became responsible for *Bo*[4]. Before handing over to Keith, however, Noel was to sign off his captainship in some style.

That year, Imperial's Rag Week was in June, just before Noel was due to leave, and since traditionally *Bo* provided the Rag Week transport of the Students' Union president, he became chief taxi driver for the duration.

One of the events was a competition to see which group of students could be the first to race from the college to the Serpentine, carrying boards, rope and oil drums, make a raft, and paddle it to the other end of the lake. *Bo* was duly pressed into service to drive the president down to the lakeside to watch.

Noel takes up the story. "Reaching the lake meant crossing Rotten Row, where cars were not allowed. A policeman noticed us, caught up with us at the lakeside and, leaning his bike against the back of the makeshift raft, came round to the front of the car and proceeded to tell me 'You're not allowed to drive here, this is for horses.'

"Meanwhile the others, seeing that the policeman was busy lecturing me, took his bike and tossed it into the Serpentine. Then they all quickly disappeared, leaving me to face the music. There was nothing I could do. We did manage to retrieve the bike and the policeman allowed me to drive the president back again, but inevitably I ended up making an appearance at Great Marlborough Street accused of driving on Rotten Row, with lots of noisy supporters in the public gallery.

"The chairman of the magistrates asked 'Have you anything to say for yourself?' and I replied that the policeman had failed to mention that the car was a 50 year-old (as it was at the time) James & Browne.

"The magistrate's face lit up. 'A James & Browne? I know a lot about James & Browne.' And we had a good chat about the car, across the court."

Noel doesn't remember the details of the conversation, but there was plenty to talk about, as *Bo* is nothing if not unconventional. Its 2.5-litre transverse parallel twin has suction-operated inlet valves and is laid flat, under the driver's feet, with chain drive from either end of the crankshaft, one chain to each rear wheel. Lubrication is by total loss from reservoirs on the dashboard, with used oil dripping onto the road. The crash gearbox has a second lever to control reverse, and the throttle is hand operated, which makes for a lot of levers and means that in modern traffic conditions it is advisable to have both a driver and co-driver. On a good day, top speed is around 30mph.

All this car talk occupied judge and defendant for some time. Eventually, perhaps in response to a cough from the clerk of the court, the petrolhead magistrate remembered where he was. He abruptly stopped talking, shuffled on the bench to draw himself up to his full height and, with as much dignity as he could muster, prepared to pass sentence. Finally he said "Fined ten shillings. Don't do it again!"

A spontaneous cheer rose from the public gallery at the imposition of such a derisory fine – just 50p in modern money – a tiny sum even by 1956 standards. Up in the gallery, Keith and the other club members passed round the hat, the fine was raised in a matter of seconds, and that was that. It was a suitable high on which to end an academic year and, as it turned out, an era.

Soon afterwards Noel graduated, leaving London with very warm memories of his student days. "Imperial was the best three years of my life: tremendous fun, I wouldn't have changed it for the world. The people I met, the staff at the college, the landladies – it was all an excellent experience. Keith's late graduation spoilt a celebration of what should have been three happy years, but the friendship lasted a lifetime."

Noel's career was destined to go in a totally different direction to Keith's. Austin tried to persuade him to return, but he joined Vickers at Harwell instead. Much later he would have the chance of working with Keith, but would decide against it. Instead, his role was to be the trusted voice on the end of the phone, someone close enough to Keith to understand a problem, but far enough away to see the wood from the trees.

"Keith was very straight, but you had to be prepared to spend hours and hours on the telephone in discussions. He hated losing an argument, the only way to bring one to a close was to give in! Defeat him in logic? No! At least, I never managed it."

The departure of Noel was not the only loss at number 15, for Bill failed his first year for a second time and had to leave Imperial for good; he returned to Hartlepool to work for a chemical engineering company.

The past three years had been huge fun for the Lavender Hill Mob. Now the Mob was no more, and Lavender Gardens just wouldn't be the same. Keith wasn't sure what his final year would hold, but it was clearly going to be very different.

Footnotes

1 A cornet of horse was actually the fifth commissioned officer in a cavalry troop.

2 Affiliate of the City & Guilds Institute, one of the City & Guilds' own qualifications.

3 Patent specification 784,418, applied for 11/12/1954, filed 14/12/1955, published 09/10/1957: *Improvements in or relating to Paper-Making and like Machines.*

4 At the time of writing there is a good description of Bo and its history on www.flickr.com/photos/morven/214833881.

Chapter 4

Living with Lotus

Sad though Keith was to see his friends leave town, he consoled himself with the thought that the summer should be interesting, because Colin Chapman had offered him a vacation job – a much more exciting prospect than another spell working on huge gas engines.

Surprisingly, up to this point he had never met Mike Costin, who was already technical director of the Lotus group by this stage, having worked at Lotus since January 1953. By virtue of Keith buying the Six, Mike knew of him, but the two only got acquainted that summer, 1956. Neither could have dreamed that together they would go on to change the face of F1. Of more immediate relevance to Keith were his everyday working partners in the gearbox shop: Steve Sanville, and one Graham Hill.

Mike describes Steve Sanville as "Very tall, a bit nervous, and very gentlemanly." He was in the SAS, and every year would go off with them for a fortnight's camp. Mike thought this incredible for someone of Steve's quiet disposition, his general opinion of SAS members being that "They're marvellous, but they're like a load of terrible dogs, you should keep them locked up in a compound!" Keith had no problem working with Steve, but before long concluded that he didn't have much of an opinion of Graham Hill, as an engineer or anything else.

The grandly titled 'gearbox shop' was nothing more than a concrete garage on the way into the main factory, but to Graham's eyes it had one priceless advantage over other parts of the premises – a phone line. The outside line had been installed so that Steve could talk to customers without running in and out of the factory, but Graham, in Mike's words, "... spent all his time on the phone trying to chat up people to give him a drive, that was his main activity in life. He was totally single-minded; a pain in the arse."

It grated with Keith to see Graham taking advantage of his employer in this way. To make matters worse, Keith soon concluded that even when Graham was working, he wasn't particularly good at his job, which at that time consisted largely of assembling Austin A35-based gearboxes. Keith tackled this single-handed one day, while Graham was off racing, and decided that it was not as hard as Graham had made out. "All bull and damn-all knowledge," was Keith's withering assessment.[1]

When Keith finished his summer job and returned to Imperial for his final year, he continued – like many Lotus customers – to visit the factory regularly, and quickly became friends with the man Colin Chapman had hired to replace him, John Campbell-Jones.

John Campbell-Jones' name is not the first to come to mind when reeling off a list of 1950s and '60s F1 drivers, but in due course he would have his day in the sun – two days to be precise, at Spa with the Emeryson team in 1962, where he finished 11th after two gearbox failures, and the following year at the British Grand Prix, where he drove a Lola for Tim Parnell's team, finishing 13th after a long mid-race stop.

However in September 1956, when Keith met him, he was just an aspiring racing driver trying to pursue a 'career' in motorsport.

John explains: "One of my first jobs was at a Jaguar dealer near Hammersmith in West London. A smashed XK 120 came in and we had to get a new chassis frame out of the stores; I had to transfer all the parts to the new chassis. So I got to know Jags very well." In fact 'Shambles' – as Campbell-Jones is affectionately known to his friends, on account of the aura of barely concealed chaos which seems to forever surround his activities – still drives one to this day, a 2½-litre Daimler-engined example.

Then he left to join Cooper. "I was there during the early part of the Jack Brabham era; John Cooper was very nice, but during the winter months I was just filing chassis brackets and that sort of thing, and I fell out a bit with the workshop manager there. So I wandered into Lotus on the off-chance – I got to see Colin Chapman immediately and he said he'd got a job and introduced me to Graham Hill ... We found we had the same sense of humour, we made each other laugh, and we became firm friends. I spent a couple of years at Lotus with Graham, doing engines and gearboxes, and he became my best friend ever."

One day that autumn Keith mentioned to John that he was getting itchy feet in his digs – things just weren't the same without Noel and Bill. To his surprise John (who was still living at home at the time) replied: "Why don't you move in with us? My parents' place is in Kensington, not far away from your digs."

So he did, and early in the 1956-57 academic year his address became 44 Brunswick Gardens, Holland Park.

It wasn't an entirely successful arrangement. He liked John and got on well enough with his father, a prosperous and successful architect, but quickly discovered that his new landlady was as far removed from the easy-going Mrs Storey as could possibly be imagined. In fact, she was a harridan. Keith hated her with a passion. Even Ursula, who by nature is not disposed to speak ill of anyone, goes so far as to call Mrs C-J "A positive lady."

Nevertheless, he stayed, because fate was about to tie him to the family for a while yet. John C-J explains: "My family owned a mews and the previous tenant wanted out, so my father needed someone to run the place. It was too good an offer to turn down. We gained access to the mews in spring 1957, so I left Lotus that summer. There was a garage (called Cornwall Garage) and nine mews flats, which meant I could have an office in one and live in another.

"I was away racing a lot that year, as I had a new Series II Lotus 11, one of the first built – I built the very first one with Graham Hill. A customer bought the car and in return for my building it for him, we shared it for the first season. Half the Lotus mechanics came down to Cornwall Garage to help, so it went together very quickly. Keith's Six was kept there too."

Now that Keith had the use of Cornwall Garage, life at Brunswick Gardens seemed that bit more tolerable. He had somewhere safe and dry for the Six, and could fettle at leisure. John was just getting started racing, and sharing a house with a would-be racer encouraged Keith's own aspirations. Before long his name was appearing on the entry lists at Goodwood.

In total the Six raced three times in Keith's hands (*Cosworth*, p29), all in 1957 and all, to the best of Ursula's recollection, at the Hampshire circuit. However, Goodwood's records show only two sorties for red Lotus-Climax MkIV, WTD2 – one at the 25th Members' Meeting on 11 May and another on 31 August.[2]

Of the two, the August event produced the better result, car number 44 coming third in the five-lap Handicap Race C from a 55-second handicap. But it was the May meeting, where the Six was entered in three races wearing the number 16, which would prove the more significant, as John Campbell-Jones explains.

"It was spring 1957, one of the first races in my life. I was going to race at Goodwood in Keith's Lotus 6! He was going to do the first two races and I was going to do the third, but he shunted it at the chicane in the first event, and that was that."

The accident happened on lap three of a five-lap scratch race, for which Keith had qualified 11th, and he described it in detail in his interview with Graham Robson. "The VG95 linings picked up in the drums and the wheels didn't unlock when I took my foot off the brakes. I went straight into the chicane, which was a solid bank with a row of geranium pots on the top. I ended up against the bank with a geranium on my lap.

"Earlier on that day, I'd actually gone through Fordwater, that's the very fast kink, where there's a change of surface, and the car had leapt up and gone sideways for a way before I straightened it up. I remember thinking 'Jesus, you're not with that, not even vaguely with that, are you?'" (*Cosworth*, p29)

Keith is on record as saying that the incident at Fordwater convinced him he didn't have what it took to be a top-flight racing driver. He later observed that there seemed to be two breeds of competitive driver: those with innate ability, and those who by constant practice and sheer doggedness achieve competence. Keith concluded that he simply didn't have the hand-eye coordination to fit into the first category, and he had no desire to enter the second. He wanted to excel in his chosen field, not be a mere journeyman. So although he was a quick and competent road driver, he never again tried to prove himself on the track. Henceforth, the car would be his focus, not the race.

> *THERE SEEM TO BE TWO CATEGORIES OF RACING DRIVER: THOSE WHO CAN DRIVE BY NATURAL ABILITY, AND THOSE WHO GAIN COMPETENCE BY EXPERIENCE.*
>
> *INHERENTLY, BY NATURE, I'M ONE OF THOSE PEOPLE WHO WOULD RATHER DO A FEW THINGS VERY WELL, THAN WHAT I SEE AS THE OTHER EXTREME, WHICH IS TO MAKE A NONSENSE OF LOTS OF THINGS.*

The Six was repaired and returned to Cornwall Garage, snug and safe. But not for long: one day, John recalls, "He came zooming up the mews to the garage, having just repaired the car, and smashed it into the garage doors!"

Through all the changes at Brunswick Gardens and the mews, Keith had continued to be a student at Imperial, and that same summer, 1957, he finally graduated. Ursula doesn't believe Keith was any less committed to his studies in that final year – she remembers clearly him worrying about his finals – but mentally he was already moving on, conscious of the fact that, had he not fallen ill and had to repeat his second year, he would already be starting his career, like Noel.

At least one professor at Imperial seems to have read his mood, because many years later, when Stuart Turner (of Ford motorsport fame) by coincidence found himself seated next to the prof at an official dinner and asked what Keith had been like to teach, the lecturer replied that he "... had no idea ... he was never there, because he was always off on some madcap scheme, but he was obviously a genius so we gave him a pass degree anyway." That same lecturer suggested to Keith that he do a PhD – unheard of for a pass-degree graduate – but Keith declined.

By now Keith knew Lotus and the Lotus staff pretty well. Not only had he worked there the summer before, but the mechanics would regularly turn up at the mews. Despite this, he wasn't yet seriously considering throwing in his lot with motorsport. Instead, he did what most engineering graduates did in the 1950s, he looked for a postgraduate apprenticeship.

He had interviews at both Rolls-Royce Aero Engines and Napier, and got offers from both. At Rolls-Royce, the offer letter was accompanied by a report stating that they had "... severe doubts as to whether I was suitable to be a member of a team," (Cosworth, p34). This made him think about himself and his personality, and the more he thought, the more he concluded that they were right. The perspicacious interviewers had realised that although Keith was never an extrovert (although things did change after a few pints), and considered himself quite shy at that age, underneath was a person who wanted to plough his own furrow rather than tread in someone else's.

Impressed as he was with the calibre of R-R's personnel department, he preferred Napier and got as far as accepting its offer. He told Graham Robson "I was very tempted by Napier, because they seemed to be doing even more daft things than Rolls-Royce. I must say, there was the prospect of working with Nomads – an H24 two-stroke diesel compounded with an exhaust-driven turbine through an infinitely variable drive." (Cosworth, p34)

Then he had second thoughts. Any apprenticeship would involve going back to the basics of learning how to use hand and machine tools, and that didn't appeal. He had been honing those skills for a decade already. So he went to see Colin Chapman and was offered a job on the spot, as gearbox development engineer. Inevitably, the salary was not wonderful – £600pa – but at least he wouldn't have to spend the next six months filing test pieces, machining endless useless V-blocks, and learning for a second time how to use a four-jaw chuck. Moreover, he wouldn't have to work with Graham Hill, as the latter was about to begin his career as a full-time racing driver. Indeed, it was his imminent departure that had created the vacancy. And of course, Colin had also recently lost John Campbell-Jones due to family business commitments.

Keith felt bad about messing Napier around, but his mind was made up. That summer Lotus had won the Index of Performance at Le Mans, had come first in the 750 Class, and first and second in the 1100 Class. Colin Chapman's company was going places, and Keith wanted to be a part of it.

His family and his future in-laws both had reservations about his decision not to take a formal apprenticeship with a large company. Em didn't put up much of a fight, but Ursula's father felt more strongly about it. "My father was horrified," she relates, "because he was an engineer, he'd done an apprenticeship and thought everybody ought to do them." Mr Cassal's opinions fell on deaf ears.

Keith was the first graduate ever to be employed at Lotus, and the existing employees, no doubt mindful of the fact that an engineering degree was – and sadly still is – no guarantee of practical ability, wasted no time in winding him up. A notice appeared on his locker door saying: 'Who needs experience, I'm a college graduate' (*Cosworth*, p36). But as Mike Costin observes, "Keith had a good sense of humour, and we all had to as well, simply to survive around him."

In the coming months, he would need all of that good humour and then some, because he was about to find out what his new colleagues already suspected – namely that he had been handed a poisoned chalice, as Mike Costin explains.

"At the racing car show in 1956 we'd showed the Lotus 12, our first single-seater, with a wooden gearbox in place of the compact five-speed planned for the car. A lot of people had tried to make the box work, including the oil companies, who had got involved with trying to solve the lubrication problems." By the time the 1957 racing season was in full swing, the box actually existed in the flesh. However, it was proving extremely fragile, and the constant transmission failures were blunting the competitiveness of the Lotus 12.

Keith's brief was simple enough: to make the five-speed reliable. But the task of developing what the Lotus staff were already calling 'the Queerbox' proved anything but simple. The selector mechanism of the gearbox ran through the middle of the gears, which were all indirect. Drive came in via the lower shaft, then through the extremely short gear cluster, and thence to the crownwheel and pinion at the back, which were mated to a ZF limited-slip differential. There was a quadrant gearchange, without a positive stop. Conceptually, it was neat, clever and compact. In reality, it suffered from two major problems, which Keith quickly identified.

First, the crownwheel and pinion were inadequately lubricated, so much so that their average life was proving to be around 50 miles. Second, the compactness of the geartrain was such that it was impossible to design a decent gearchange, as the splines locating the selector linkage were so short. Drivers found it difficult to use, and all too soon the splines would strip, leaving them unable to use it at all.

Lotus aficionado Ernie Unger witnessed Keith's frustration. Though not a Lotus employee by this point, he'd continued as a mechanic and was often in and out of Hornsey. He got to know Keith quite well: "I would hear hysterical laughter coming from the gearbox shop, and when I put my head round the door, it was Keith!" In need of relief after a day's grappling with the recalcitrant device, Keith would sometimes join the lads in the pub next door, "... thump down a pint on the table and say 'right, now let's have a bloody good argument!'"

The lubrication problem proved relatively easy to solve. The crownwheel and pinion were pressure-fed with oil, but Keith decided it wasn't getting where it was needed. Using a combination of shields and jets, he redirected the feed, and, thus assembled, the first final drive "... went on forever," in Keith's words (*Cosworth*, p37). These changes needed to be built into the next batch of final drives, which meant a trip to Friedrichshafen, in what was then West Germany, to brief the ZF engineers on the new design. It was the very first time Keith had ever been outside the UK.

On his return, he turned his attention back to the gearshift problem, and concluded that what was needed was a positive-stop mechanism. Len Terry, later to have a fine career as a race car designer at Lotus, Eagle and BRM, had recently started at Lotus and drew up some of the parts, but Keith was not convinced they would work, and in the end Colin suggested he do it all himself. It proved to be a very intricate job – space was so tight – but Keith managed it.

His efforts did not go unnoticed by Mike.

"He discussed all the problems with me and I was very impressed with his thinking. Apart from getting the lubrication right and making sure the oil stayed on the crown wheel and pinion, and designing the positive stop gearchange, he got all the pieces made, did all the drawings, assembled it and demonstrated to me that it worked – very impressive for a lad straight out of college."

It proved impossible, however, to make it compact enough to fit within the existing casing, as Mike explains. "The basic problem with the unit was that it needed to be a bit longer, not because the gear teeth themselves were too small but because the dogs on the inside needed to be bigger. They had to be picked up by the dogs on the shaft that ran through the middle, and they wore too fast, with the result that they jumped out of gear or wouldn't engage, or whatever."

Keith worked out that if each gear were made just a little longer, about $\frac{1}{10}$th of an inch (2.5mm), the wear rate would be greatly reduced and the box would be viable. But that required machining new gears and casting a new casing, and Colin Chapman wouldn't sanction the expense. He insisted that Keith make do with what he had.

Had he been confronted with such obduracy later in life, Keith would have reacted strongly, and immediately. But at Lotus he was still the new boy, and moreover he hadn't worked out how to counter Chapman's formidable arguing skills, which were every bit a match for his own. Keith liked to think before he spoke, but Chapman's mind worked so fast that, out of nowhere, he could throw a red herring into a discussion and then get the other party to chase after it, losing the thrust of their argument in the process. It took Keith some time to suss out this technique, which he eventually learned to counter with words to the effect of "I understand your point Colin, but I need to sleep on it."

The box had been designed by Richard Ansdale, an engineer at Thorneycroft who would go on to do a lot of the detail design of the Lotus Twin-Cam. He wasn't a Lotus employee but often visited the works and had his own ideas about what the gearbox needed: synchromesh perhaps, or using the first-gear pair of gears as an oil pump. Keith did not agree.

Jack Field heard them arguing. "Keith had concluded that it would never work, and he told the designer his views in the yard, where everyone could hear him. Richard was really pissed off and went to Colin and said 'I don't want that young kid working on my gearbox any more.'"

Within a very short space of time, he wasn't. Realising that Chapman would never spend the money needed to make it reliable, and convinced that Richard's proposals were unworkable, Keith concluded he was on a hiding to nothing. "I'm not prepared to waste my life developing something that will never work," he told Chapman, and handed in his notice. This was March 1958: he had been a full-time employee at Lotus for just eight months.

Keith had not arrived at this decision on the spur of the moment, and it was not solely the result of his frustration over the Queerbox. In fact, before many of those eight months had passed, he had concluded that his long-term future did not lay with Lotus, because he simply didn't like the way Colin Chapman operated. He had an immense admiration for Chapman's intellect and creativity, but as far as ethics were concerned, the two men were complete opposites.

Dishonest was never a word applied to Keith, even by those – and there were a few – who disliked him. But as Keith saw it, Chapman told lies simply for intellectual stimulation. If you tell different stories to different people, sooner or later they will compare notes and confront you, demanding an explanation for the discrepancies. Far from being embarrassed at such situations, Chapman regarded them as an opportunity to test his mental agility, and revelled in the challenge of talking his way out of them. To Keith, all this was simply a waste of time: why not just tell the truth in the first place?

> *IF YOU ARE TELLING THE TRUTH, IT'S SIMPLE. IF YOU'RE LYING, YOU HAVE TO REMEMBER WHAT YESTERDAY'S LIE WAS. IT'S SAFER TO BE HONEST.*

His dislike of Chapman's behaviour was matched only by his admiration of his technical ability. The following quote sums up his view of his employer:

"I think Colin Chapman was the brightest and quickest bloke I have ever met. Technically, he was the brightest I ever met in conceptual thinking – the amount he could do in a short time was prodigious. He'd go away one day, having decided on something, and come back the following morning with a complete drawing, having done it overnight. But he wasn't that good at detail design because he didn't have enough grasp of limits, fits and running clearances," (*Cosworth*, p38).

Before handing in his notice, Keith had considered various options. Returning to a conventional career route with an established company did not appeal: he was by now convinced that Rolls-Royce had been right in its assessment of him – that he was better off doing his own thing. For some months he had been considering going into business on his own account, and he'd already taken the first step by acquiring a practical set of wheels. Predictably, the Lotus had not proved to be an ideal commuter vehicle, and he eventually sold it to racer Mike Pendleton. In autumn 1957 he had supplemented it with, of all things, a black Bradford van.

When comparing a Lotus to a Bradford, 'sublime to the ridiculous' is the phrase that comes to mind. These crude, slow, noisy flat-twin devices sold in considerable numbers in the early '50s, not because of any intrinsic merit but because they were available, and in vehicle-starved, postwar Britain, this was enough to ensure sales success. A bigger come-down from a Lotus is impossible to imagine. (As an aside, the writer's father had the use of a Bradford in the early 1950s and hated it; he was delighted when his employer replaced it with a 5cwt Ford – the Dagenham product felt positively sporty by comparison.)

Jack Field remembers the Bradford well, because he borrowed it one day.

"Apart from working for Lotus for peanuts, I was doing a little bit on the side. At that time there was retail price maintenance: if a manufacturer specified that a washing machine, for example, had to be sold for £87, that's what it cost, no matter which shop the customer went to. So if you could get stuff cheaper, say 25% off, there was always someone willing to buy it for 10% off. That little earner was working quite well, except when the goods were too big to fit in my car. On those occasions, I needed other transport.

"One day I asked Keith if I could borrow the Bradford. He said 'Yes, but the halfshaft bearing's gone. It won't take long to fix it though, about an hour.'

"So I said 'I'll stay with you and wait.' I wasn't in a hurry, I think it was a weekend. We were in the gearbox shop and we got the halfshaft in the vice and got the hydraulic press to push the halfshaft out of the hub. It wouldn't budge. We tried a bit of heat, it still wouldn't budge. He didn't know what to do. Then he tried a big club hammer and it suddenly came out – it must have gone 12 foot and stuck in the bloody breeze block wall on the other side of the shop. I thought, 'Jesus Christ, I was standing there just a minute ago, it would have gone right through me!'

"Eventually I did get the van, delivered my goods and gave it him back."

Before he left, the Queerbox had one final trick to play on Keith. In December 1957 Lotus decided to take a series II Lotus 11 to Monza for what would be the 11's third record-breaking attempt.[3] Cliff Allison was to drive, Keith was part of the support team. The car was basically a standard 11, but had been fitted with a Queerbox which, being all-indirect, had its output rotating in the opposite sense to the standard box. There was provision for the differential to be built into the gearbox casing, but this application retained the standard diff. In a fit of muddled thinking, someone – it is not clear whether at the factory or at the track – had arranged the firing order to agree with this inverse rotation.

Mike and Keith tried the starter motor. The engine coughed, at best. They tried a push-start. Ditto. They were baffled.

Eventually they twigged that while the starter motor was working in the right sense, nothing else was. So at the circuit Mike and Keith rebuilt the differential with the crown wheel on the opposite side of the pinion, to reverse the direction of rotation, and reversed the firing order to match. Hey presto! The engine fired – which was just as well, as Colin Chapman arrived soon afterwards. Mike reckons that, had the car still been dead at that point or running with five reverse gears and one forward, Colin would likely have flown into a rage and sacked them both. Much later he would also observe that, had they not fixed the 11 in time, there might never have been a company called Cosworth.

Not long after Keith returned from Italy, the Bradford died in dramatic fashion. Ursula takes up the story.

"It was just before Christmas 1957. He'd been to see me at my parents' house, we'd been out for the evening and he was driving back to Campbell-Jones' place when he fell asleep – at least that's what he reckoned happened – and went straight into a lamppost. He can't have been going all that fast – Bradford vans couldn't go all that fast! – but the steering wheel came straight up and nearly scalped him; he also lost some teeth. After that he had a great big scar on his forehead. He ended up in hospital and the van was a write-off.

"I didn't know anything about it, and I'd arranged to meet him at Campbell-Jones, place the next day. When I turned up and he wasn't there, I thought it strange – and it was also awkward, because I didn't have any money for the tube to get me home. But an Italian couple who sometimes used the garage were around, and they told me what had happened and lent me some money. I rang Keith's mother with the news and went to see him in hospital; when he got out we went up to Blackburn for Christmas."

After Christmas, Keith continued to explore his career options, for although he wanted to run his own business, he was not by nature a loner. He wanted a partner.

The first person he thought of was John Campbell-Jones, reasoning that it was in some ways the simplest option: he was already established in his premises, and they got on well. However, he decided that John's approach to motorsport would not make him a good business associate. Keith wanted to handle car preparation in general, and engine tuning in particular, methodically and professionally. He had been amazed to learn that none of the existing tuning companies used a dynamometer, an omission which he was determined to remedy. John, though, wasn't interested in that. His approach was very simple – almost simplistic: "You tune them up, then I get in them and I drive them fast around the track."

'Camworth,' Keith decided, could never become a viable operation. He didn't pursue the idea. 'Cosworth,' on the other hand, seemed to have potential. By now Keith and Mike had worked together for several months and had developed both a great personal rapport and a huge mutual respect – witness the way they had successfully worked against the clock at Monza. To speak to Mike Costin now, you would get the impression that Keith was the driver of the relationship and he the junior partner. "I was privileged to spend 40 years at the University of Duckworth," is how he describes the partnership, but Keith never saw it like that. He trusted Mike absolutely, both personally and professionally.

Mike describes his CV like this: "I wasn't a terribly well educated engineer, although I'd done a serious apprenticeship at de Havilland. At the de Havilland Aeronautical Technical School there were between 1000 and 1200 apprentices at any one time, divided into three grades: trade apprentices, engineering apprentices and premium engineering students. The latter were people who brought money in, often from abroad. I went in as a trade apprentice, but in the first two years I did pretty well academically and got upgraded to engineering apprentice. A number of aviation companies had in-house colleges at that time, but de Havilland was one of the top ones because it was in the engine business and the airframe business in an era when the two went together."

"I started with Lotus in January 1953 in my spare time ... Another ex-de Havilland apprentice suggested to Colin that I would be a useful bloke to have around because he'd just broken up with the Allen brothers with whom he had started Lotus. Colin was moaning at the 750 Motor Club that he was all on his own and had orders for MkVIs and no one to help him build them, and that's when Peter Ross suggested me. We had a very simple deal, we'd start building up these kits for sale and the ninth one would be our works car; we'd share the driving and we'd see how it went as to whether we'd go full time or not.

"In 1954 we built the MkVIII Lotus, entirely constructed by an amateur group, as the 10-15 people Lotus then employed were busy with MkVIs. By the end of 1954 we'd sold quite a few MkVIs and MkVIIIs, and a modification of the MkVIII called the MkX. That was a very hectic situation, but it wasn't until 1955 that we gave up our jobs and went full-time. And Jack Field was already there."

Unlike Keith, Mike rarely had issues with Chapman, even though he shared Keith's opinion of his ethics. Assertive but not confrontational, Mike has a canny ability to work out which battles he has a chance of winning, and to keep his own counsel when other skirmishes are looming – an approach which steered him successfully through life at Lotus and beyond. As he observes, "You won't find a lot of people with much good to say about Chapman, but funnily enough, I only ever had a couple of 'get stuffed' matches with Colin, even though – let's face it – I was his top man in engineering."

Nevertheless, Mike had sound reasons for wanting to leave. His salary may have been much higher than Keith's, but he had a wife and three children to support and the money was not enough for him to even consider buying his own house. Moreover, the stress of the job was enormous, what with test driving, spannering with the racing team, endless travelling between events and frantic all-night sessions to prepare the cars. By the end of each racing season he was exhausted. Much as he loved the sport, there must, he reasoned, be a better way to live.

"Keith and Mike discussed Cosworth up in the roof where my stores were," recalls Jack Field, "that's where the plot was hatched, or some of it at least. Maybe there was also some talk in the pub, but not all that much, as Mike didn't spend as much time there as Keith: he was living at Hatfield at the time and had a wife and kids to go home to."

The name Cosworth was suggested by Ursula's mother. Keith had been considering the obvious alternative, 'Ducktin,' but it sounded cheap and unprofessional (and in any case, would later have resulted in Sierra Cosworths being called 'Duckies,' which would never do). Cosworth, on the other hand, had a good ring to it.

Cosworth Engineering Ltd was formed to prepare cars, not just engines, as Mike explains. "At that stage the company wasn't going to do anything specific, we thought that a couple of lads like us, we considered ourselves to be reasonably knowledgeable at engineering, ought to be able to make a living in motor racing, and that was it."

IT MUST BE POSSIBLE TO MAKE AN INTERESTING LIVING, MESSING ABOUT WITH RACING CARS AND ENGINES.

Chapman's response to the news that his newly employed graduate engineer wanted out, and wanted to take his technical director with him, was understandably unenthusiastic. He could do nothing to prevent Keith going, or to prevent him and Mike setting up their own limited company, but he was keen to hang on to Mike's services for as long as possible. He insisted that Mike honour the three-year contract that he had signed only very recently. Mike reckons that, had he made a fight of it, he could have left, but in truth he simply couldn't afford to argue – he had a family to support.

Whether the timing of Mike's renewed contract was merely fortuitous for Colin, or whether someone other than Jack Field overheard Mike and Keith's conversations and forewarned the boss will remain a matter of speculation, but the result was that when Keith left Lotus, it was on his own. Not only was Mike to remain at Lotus for three years, but he was contractually prevented from moonlighting with his new business partner.

Keith left Lotus in April 1958 and the company was launched, in name at least, around the same time, but Cosworth did not actually start trading until some months later. Indeed, April 1958 was an eventful month, because on Ursula's birthday the couple got engaged, the intention being to marry the following January, when racing commitments wouldn't get in the way.

For Ursula and Keith, the summer of 1958 was an uncertain time, but an exciting one. Marriage plans were in the air, Ursula had just graduated and Cosworth had come into existence – at least on paper. Armed with a BA General in history, French and German, Ursula took a job with a publishing company, though she continued to live at home in Carshalton. Keith, by contrast, had no income.

He had to earn a living somehow, so he made the best use he could of Cornwall Garage, and tried to develop what had been the occasional evening or weekend earner into a livelihood. His reputation for tuning and repairing Climax engines ensured that a steady trickle of Climax-engined cars, particularly Elites, came his way, including that of jazzman Chris Barber.

More mundane work was also welcome, as Ursula explains. "Even one of my uncles, who was fairly interested in who his nieces married, got Keith to service his car, and was suitably impressed – so that was alright!"

Eventually, all the is were dotted and the ts crossed on the company formation, and Cosworth started trading on 30 September 1958. At Brunswick Gardens and on the floor of Cornwall Garage, nothing changed, but October that year was a watershed nevertheless; the moment when Keith went from self-employed to company director. With a share capital of £100, of which just two £1 shares were issued, one to each director, Cosworth Engineering Ltd's corporate pedigree could hardly have been more modest – especially as only one of its directors was actually able to work for it.

Neither proprietor had grand aspirations. Naturally, they wanted the business to be successful, but beyond that, Keith and Mike simply wanted to earn a decent living doing something they enjoyed. Never for a moment did they believe that their enterprise would become one of the most famous names in motorsport.

The last word from the Lotus era must go to the infamous Queerbox. Despite its limitations, the Lotus five-speed was quite widely used on racing Lotuses of the era, including the 12, 15 and 16. On Keith's departure, Steve Sanville took over its development, but the gearshift problem remained, and still frustrates historic racing enthusiasts to this day. One current owner, Nick Rossi, persuaded Cosworth engineer Neil Lefley to redesign the box into a four-speed, which of course gives ample scope to make the gears bigger. "After a few teething problems," Mike says, "they've got it working very well." So Keith's analysis seems to have been proved right, albeit 50 years too late.

Footnotes

1 p14, *Old Giggleswickians Newsletter*, November 2009, *Famous OGs*, By John Kirkpatrick, director at Jim Russell Management and himself an Old Giggleswickian.

2 These results from *A Record of Motor Racing at Goodwood* (updated 2nd Edition) by Robert Barker.

3 For more detail of the Lotus 11's record attempts at Monza, see http://lotuseleven.org/Monza/the%20MONZA%20Cars.htm.

Chapter 5

Horsepower from the stables

The first job that Cosworth Engineering Ltd ever did was for the Vanwall F1 car. That sounds impressive, but in reality it was not much of a job. Cosworth was commissioned to design and build a wooden former for the car's perspex windscreen – something for the windscreen manufacturer to shape the perspex over. Nepotism played its part in the deal, as Mike Costin's aerodynamicist brother Frank was in charge of the Vanwall's bodywork, but Keith and Mike were not complaining. The job was neither taxing nor glamorous, but the young company was glad of any work it could get.

Other than that, the first few weeks were mostly an extension of what Keith had been doing before, for by now he knew his way around Climax engines extremely well. "We used to go over to Eltham," Mike recalls, "and look after a Lotus MkXII there for Dennis Taylor, sadly killed at Monaco in 1962 driving a Formula Junior car. And we did a few jobs on a Dutchman's MkVI."

Keith was frustrated, however, by not having a dynamometer to test customers' engines on. Without that vital piece of equipment, getting the best out of a powerplant was much too hit and miss for his liking. Clearly, John Campbell-Jones had no interest in installing one at Cornwall Garage, not least because another tenant was now sharing the premises, classic car dealer and racer Dan Margulies. So almost immediately after Cosworth started trading, Keith began to hunt for premises he could call his own. It didn't take him long, and in November 1958, just one month after its launch, Cosworth was on the move.

The departure did not mark the end of Keith's relationship with Campbell-Jones, because right into the 1960s he would occasionally bump into John in the paddock. By around 1964, John had a five year-old called Mike with him, a somewhat reluctant passenger who got very fed up with being dragged from one race meeting to another. The experience put him off cars for life. Aircraft were another matter – but we are giving too much away ...

Cosworth's new home was a former coaching stable at 41a Friern Barnet Road. In Ursula's words "... between a café and the Railway Tavern pub, which was useful, and opposite a miserable little Barclays Bank, which Keith thought might be useful."

A firewood merchant had been using the stables to chop up trees, and the premises were in a bad state. The upstairs was unsafe, some stabling booths were still in place, complete with hay baskets attached to the walls, and there was a central drain in the floor to carry away the horse urine. By contrast, the only toilet for humans was in the pub next door, or at Southgate tube station nearby, and the tenants had to share the premises with the local rats, who had a habit of nipping in from the greasy café.

To Keith, the state of the building mattered less than the fact that it was affordable and sufficiently run down that no one would notice, or care, if the exhaust pipe from a dynamometer suddenly appeared through the roof. Rivals had jested at the audacity of this tiny inexperienced company claiming to offer professional race preparation, dubbing the firm 'Cosbodge & Duckfudge,' but none of them had a dyno. Installing one would demonstrate that Cosworth meant business. Keith earmarked the back booth as the home for it, and set up a tiny office under the stairs.

Initially, the mix of work was similar to that at Cornwall Garage. "There was an awful lot going on," remembers Mike, "but it was all little bits here and there. I wasn't involved because I wasn't supposed to be working at Cosworth." Customers included Graham Warner of sports car dealer Chequered Flag, Ian Walker, and Elva proprietor Frank Nichols – in particular, for John Brown's very successful racing Elva. The common link was the Climax engine, though Keith also did some suspension work on John's Elva.

The first Cosworth product appeared around this time, a fabricated manifold to mate Weber carburettors to the Climax engine. Climax gurus still rate the Cosworth manifold more highly than the older cast design from Derrington. By the end of 1958, the fledgling company was beginning to develop a reputation, and a rhythm. To help with the paperwork, Ursula would come in after her day's work at the publishing company, somehow conjuring up a meal at the same time despite the absence of anything remotely resembling a kitchen. The accounting system was simple in the extreme, based as it was on just three files: paid, unpaid and pending. They banked at the Barclays opposite, and Ursula recalls that "... at one point we had a bank statement from there with just £1.50 left in the account." In fact, Cosworth lost £744 in its first trading year, on a turnover of £3660 – but by paying on the nail and pressing customers to do likewise, Keith and Ursula could at least be confident that what little they had was actually theirs. Cosworth would grow out of all recognition in the coming years, but its straightforward and cautious approach to cash flow never varied.

I ALWAYS SEEMED TO HAVE ENOUGH NOUS TO REALISE THAT UNLESS YOUR REGULAR INCOME EXCEEDED YOUR OUTGOINGS, YOU WENT BROKE.

"Funnily enough," Ursula comments, "it never occurred to me that he wouldn't make it. I never actually worried about that, I just had a feeling that it would all be alright. And in those days it was easy enough to get jobs, so if everything did go wrong he could easily get a job instead."

The next event in Keith's life had nothing to do with Cosworth and everything to do with Ursula, for on 10 January 1959, the couple got married. The idea was that they would move straight into their first home, a newly-built maisonette not far from the works at Northwood Gardens in Friern Park, just off the main Finchley Road at Tallyho corner. "It was supposed to be ready by the time we got married," Ursula explains, "but it wasn't of course, so until the spring we took refuge with a friend of Mike Costin called Peter Mayes."

The following month, Keith finally got his dynamometer, a Heenan & Froude DPX2. He'd initially approached Barclays for a loan, but the manager didn't want to know. Fortunately, Keith had not spent all his assets on the Six, and was able to cash in some family bonds and finance the dyno himself. However, the supplier, faced with amateurish stationery and an insalubrious delivery address, was not convinced that the necessary £600 would ever be forthcoming. To reassure him, Keith offered the technical director of Lotus Cars as a reference. That seemed to do the trick!

As 1959 progressed, things in the old stable became pretty hectic, with a steady supply of Climax engines waiting to be fettled and the Formula Junior project – of which much more anon – gathering momentum. In Keith's words "I spent most of the day chasing spares, and rebuilding engines at night," (*Cosworth*, p45). Clearly, he needed an employee.

The answer came from an unexpected source: Jack Field. Having left Lotus shortly before Keith, Jack was now back working for Capital Motors. "They'd told me I could always come back, so I took them up on it. But I said I don't want a job on the front counter, I want to earn money." Coming from someone who had only worked there for 18 months, and had then gone away for three and a half years, the boss thought this rather cheeky, but Jack clearly knew exactly what he was worth, because he was offered a job.

"They told me to take a van out on the road, and not call on any existing customers. For it to be viable I had to do £1000 a month. They offered me £11 a week plus 1.5% commission. So I got my own van, I was free to do what I liked."

From time to time he would drop in at Friern Barnet, and one day a harassed Keith commented "I really need someone working with me, just part-time."

"I know just the bloke," replied Jack.

'The bloke' was an Australian called Les Spilsbury, who thus became Cosworth's first paid employee. He was a speedway rider who had come to Britain to race, for as Jack explains "A number of speedway riders from Australia and New Zealand came to Britain for experience because here they could race every week, whereas back home there might only be three events a year anywhere accessible." Les stayed at Cosworth less than a year, but Jack is sure that "If Keith was alive today, he would still say he was one of the best fitters he'd had."

His replacement stayed rather longer – until retirement in 1989, in fact. Bill Pratt had been a fitter at engine manufacturer JAP, located not far away in Tottenham, but demand for new JAP engines was declining and he was sent to the repair department at Southgate. Unhappy at the change, he left and tried selling books on his own, rather unsuccessfully, before landing on his feet at Cosworth.

Of even more significance is the next name in the story, Ben Rood. And because Ben went on to play a pivotal role in Cosworth's development, he deserves some introduction.

Born in Bethnal Green in the East End of London, where his father had a business making ice cream and confectionery (he invented a machine to make choc ices), Ben moved with his family to Loughton in Essex when he was very young. He was fascinated by mechanical devices from an early age, and his parents bought him a lathe as a boy; he put it in the attic of their big Victorian house. Although he was sent to boarding school in Margate, his education was interrupted at around 14 because WWII had started and the army wanted to use the building. So he moved back to

Loughton, to a local school, but not for long. "He found it boring, utterly boring," his widow Jane recalls, "every bit of work they gave him to do, he said 'I've already done this.' He should have gone on to university; as it was, he left and never went back."

He did his National Service in the REME (Royal Electrical & Mechanical Engineers), during which he got his first taste of motorcycle racing with a grasstracker. When he came out he helped his father maintain his confectionery-making machinery, and took a job with a local company, Browns of Loughton, at 10 shillings a week. Nowadays Browns is a Vauxhall dealer, but at that time it was involved in engineering work of many kinds.

Ben's interest in motorcycles grew and grew. He bought an Excelsior Manxman with a cracked cylinder head, and successfully machined a new head and barrel from scratch. Encouraged, he later acquired a 250cc Velocette MkVIII and converted it to twin overhead cam, doing all the design and manufacture himself. This led to a request from Gerald Smith, who owned a Norton-engined 500cc racer, for a similar conversion on his engine, and from there to a deal with Peter Hogan to manufacture complete hydroplane engines. These two-stroke powerplants were known as Hogan-Rood engines and were very successful in competition.

By the time he met Keith, while the latter was still at Lotus, what had started as a hobby had been his business for several years – Rood's Engineering, tucked away in Tower Mews, behind Hoe Street, near Walthamstow Central station in East London. Ben had by now finished riding bikes competitively and was instead interested in learning to fly and going gliding: something his continuing friendship with Gerald Smith, who had flown marine Spitfires during WWII and lived on an old airfield complete with hangar, did nothing to discourage.

Gerald was now racing an F2 car called a Smith Climax, and knew Keith because of the Climax connection. He introduced him to Ben, who initially regarded him as just another potential customer, but the pair soon realised that their approach to engineering, and to life in general, was very similar. Ursula puts it succinctly: "The two just sort of clicked, they both had the same sort of mind." For a while their contact was purely social, but that was soon to change for good, because when Keith ran into serious camshaft development problems on the Formula Junior project, it was Ben he turned to for help ...

Like many Continental race car constructors in 1959, plus Lotus and a few others in Britain, Keith was attracted by the idea of developing his own FJ car, not least because that year the formula, launched in 1958 by Count Johnny Lurani as an entry-level category where aspiring Grand Prix drivers could learn racecraft and get the feel of open-wheel cars, was given full international status. It took off rapidly, particularly on the Continent where the Fiat 1100 engine was the power unit of choice. In the UK, Formula 500 remained popular, but not for long. Within a year or two the FJ revolution would sweep it away in favour of a new breed of single-seaters based on 1000cc production car powerplants, or 1100cc if the car weighed a little more. Initially, the obvious power unit for UK constructors was the BMC A-Series, and many early British FJ cars made use of it.

The spur for Cosworth's first race car was Howard Panton, an engineer at Ford whom Keith had known from student days. He had started construction himself, intending to use a Fiat engine, but asked Keith to finish it and develop the powerplant. However, the engine was hampered by its relatively long stroke and Keith had difficulty extracting enough power from it, so he pricked up his ears when informed by Howard of the all-new Ford Anglia 105E due to be launched in time for the Motor Show that autumn. Its heavily oversquare design gave it the ability to tolerate very high revs without excessive piston speeds, and endowed the crankshaft with generous overlap, and hence great strength, so much so that Ford was able to dispense with the traditional forged crankshaft in favour of a much cheaper casting.

Racegoers got their first look at the Anglia on 4 October at Brands Hatch, when Ford – no doubt aware of the engine's potential – provided one for use as a course car at Britain's first ever FJ race. The significance of that move was not lost on the public, nor on race commentator Anthony Marsh, who remarked that the course car's engine could be developed into a real rival for the Fiat and A-Series units. What he probably didn't know was that Keith Duckworth was already doing just that.

Thanks to Howard's connections at Ford, two of the new engines had found their way to Friern Barnet, and a frantic race was on to turn the 105E motor into a race winner in time for the Boxing Day meeting at Brands Hatch. Work on Howard's car was forgotten. All Keith's efforts were concentrated on Ford's new short-stroke baby – the idea being to supply one engine to Lotus for its new FJ contender, the 18, and the other to Chequered Flag, for use in its Gemini.

By autumn 1959 Ursula had given up work at the publishing company and was with Cosworth full-time. In the run-up to Christmas, Keith would need every bit of her support, for the job of turning a 39bhp Anglia engine into an 80bhp FJ unit was far from easy. Power output would vary from day to day – one day the engine would give 80bhp on the dyno, the next only 75, and in the end Keith decided that the combustion chamber shape was wrong – it was generating so much squish that the turbulence was trying to blow out the flame and, under certain conditions of humidity, at least partially succeeding. A radical reshaping of the chamber, followed by milling the head to restore the compression ratio, solved the problem.

More serious was the issue of camshaft design. A big increase in revs from the 5000, at which the road car's maximum power was produced, to at least 7500rpm, was essential if the planned power output was to be achieved, yet despite initially using quite a conservative cam profile, the engine suffered terrible valve-spring surge around 6000rpm and would only rev through to the required speed when off load. Moreover, valve gear wear was unacceptably high.

Much later Keith concluded that the mounting of the rocker shaft was not rigid enough, but at the time it seemed the only option was to keep trying different cams.

Keith had his back to the wall. If he couldn't get the engine to rev cleanly, he couldn't satisfy his contract to deliver two engines in time for Boxing Day, and Cosworth would be broke. He approached the bank for £30 to pay the phone bill. For the second time, Barclays turned him down.

The crisis certainly focused his mind. He told Graham Robson "I do think the prospect of bankruptcy at Christmas 1959 sharpened up my thinking process. I just wasn't prepared to have to go out and get a job, with my tail between my legs, having failed to manage on my own," (*Cosworth*, p49).

Knowing that Ben Rood had had considerable success with camshaft design, Keith asked for his input. After many, many hours thinking, analysing, and experimenting, the pair decided that they should ignore everything that existing books on camshaft design recommended and go for a constant-acceleration profile. Until then, Keith had been using the then-accepted approach to valve actuation – in essence narrow timing, sharp lift and let them fall back as they will. Ben proposed a more delicate approach, markedly widening the timing and using the extra degrees to, by comparison, stroke the valves up and let them down gently, while not worrying about them being cracked open for a lot longer. With the specification decided, Ben returned to his machine shop in Walthamstow and set to work.

The new camshaft, known as the A1, wasn't perfect, but it was good enough to transform the engine. The spring surge completely disappeared and the engine revved clear through to 9000rpm. Bankruptcy had been avoided: they had an engine they could race.

"That was when I decided to stop reading books, which only tend to mislead me," Keith continued. "I decided that it was always better to work things out from first principles. One of my most important sayings, as a result, is that 'it is better to be uninformed than ill-informed.' After all, if you are uninformed your only option is to sit down and think about a solution. If you think hard enough, it is conceivable that you might get to the right answer."

IT IS BETTER TO BE UNINFORMED THAN ILL-INFORMED.

By now time was desperately short. So short, in fact, that as Christmas Eve turned into Christmas Day, the team had only managed to complete one of the two engines. So it was agreed that on Boxing Day the Gemini would run with the full Cosworth FJ unit, which would have to be fitted in the paddock on the day, while the Lotus 18 would arrive with a more standard engine, apart from twin carbs and a better exhaust manifold.

At Brands Hatch, things were chaotic. Clearly, in the run-up to Christmas, life at Hornsey had been just as hectic as at Friern Barnet, for the FJ version of the Lotus 18 had never been tested, let alone raced, when it arrived in the paddock with driver Alan Stacey. As a result, the suspension was set too soft and the car ground away its sump in practice, eventually dumping its oil all over the track and ruining the bearings.

The Gemini, with its full-race engine, was also in trouble. The team mechanics forgot to torque up the flywheel bolts, which came loose in practice, destroying the bell housing and crank. So, by the end of practice, the 105E engine's racing debut was looking like something of an embarrassment.

Desperate to see their creation used in anger, Keith, Ben and Mike removed the remains of the race engine from Graham Warner's Gemini, stripped the standard Lotus engine and, with Graham's permission, rebuilt Alan's car using as many of the Gemini's engine parts as they could, though of necessity the Lotus retained its standard crank.

Against the odds, the Lotus made the grid, but with its under-developed chassis still bottoming the sump, it was not a race-winner that day and, as the Boxing Day crowd dissipated, many would-be Formula Junior racers were more impressed by the front-engined Gemini than the more technically advanced mid-engined Lotus 18. However, the 18 had finished a respectable fourth, and even if its potential wasn't obvious to everyone, both constructor and engine supplier felt they had a package worthy of development.

As Keith and Ben drove back to North London together, they had plenty to talk about. In fact, they talked so much, and at such depth, that by the end of the journey their relationship had been taken to another level. Henceforth, Rood's Engineering would be Cosworth's preferred source of machined parts.

Encouraged by the Boxing Day result, early in 1960 Mike Costin managed to convince Colin Chapman to lay down 25 chassis for the 18, and then arranged for two cars to be fitted with potential FJ powerplants – one a Cosworth-modified 105E and the other a Speedwell-modified A-Series. With Lotus technical director Mike also being a director of Cosworth, and Lotus driver and ex-employee Graham Hill a director of Speedwell, the situation was fraught with conflicts of interest, and a straightforward performance comparison seemed the fairest route. In the event, despite the A-Series being a known quantity, whereas the Cosworth unit was still relatively unproven, Lotus opted for the Ford.

With 25 chassis being laid down, Keith decided he'd better build up a batch of engines. These used a much improved version of the camshaft, dubbed A2, but were otherwise similar to the first version, which latterly became known as the MkI.[1] Those first two engines were sold for £145 each, but issuing bills and getting cash in your account are two different things, so for the third time, Keith approached the bank.

George Duckett, a former colleague of Bill Pratt's at JAP whom Bill had recommended, started working casually for Cosworth in 1959, and early in 1960 joined the company full-time, encouraged by the prospect of having a whole batch of engines to build. Cosworth seemed to be a company that was going places, so George did not expect what happened next:

"Keith went across the road to Barclays to borrow £200 to buy a batch of five Ford short engines, and the bank turned him down. Eventually, he borrowed some money from his father-in-law. Then he bought some cylinder heads and got Benny Rood to machine them – we only had a pillar drill and a silly little lathe."

Enraged at being rebuffed three times in succession, Keith vowed never to ask any bank for one penny ever again. And he never did.

Initially, it looked as though those engines would take a long time to sell. "By March that year we'd only sold three Lotus 18s," Mike recalls, "but things changed when Jim Clark won at the first race meeting of the year on Easter Monday at Goodwood."

The victory didn't come without drama – the Lotus was using a wet sump, and it surged so badly that the bearings ran dry and new shells had to be ordered from the Ford dealer in Chichester, who sent them to the circuit by bus! Keith and Mike then fitted them in situ by tipping the car on its side in the paddock. Nevertheless, Goodwood was a turning point.

"After that we very quickly sold 25," Mike continues, "and by the end of that year we'd sold 126, and Keith had supplied all the engines. We at Lotus would buy batches of 10 and ship them to him for tuning." The price of the modified units was the same as the first pair – £145 each – and the deal allowed Cosworth to keep all the redundant standard parts. Moreover, other makers, like Gemini and Elva, were buying the powerplant, and of course all these engines needed rebuilds and spares. Suddenly, Cosworth's workload exploded. From now on, Climax engines would figures less and less in the company's activities.

George's decision to leave JAP and join Cosworth was the beginning a long relationship with the company which would embrace most of his working life. He'd started work at 14, employed by Keith & Blackman, making electric motors. "Each department was a different job, but I preferred assembly, so they left me there. By the time I was 16, I was told by the bosses to help train the new 14 year-olds, by the time I was 18 I was in charge of a section. Then I got called up – I built engines in the RAF – after which I worked at JAP."

"By this point," Mike explains, "[Keith] had Ursula, Howard Panton, Bill Pratt, George Duckett and Bill Brown working there."

Bill Brown has been absent from our story since he left Imperial, but he had not been totally absent from Keith's life.

"I had kept in vague touch with Keith [and Ursula] – I saw them occasionally in London and went to their wedding in 1959 in the scruffy, hairy uniform of an 'erk' [slang for the lowest rank in the RAF, with no stripes] where I noticed that another of the guests was an Air Vice-Marshall, someone from Ursula's side of the gathering I think!"

After leaving Imperial in 1956, he had returned to his native Hartlepool and taken a job at Steetley Magnesite, a chemical engineering business where he had already worked two college vacations. Within little more than a year, he had effectively become the works maintenance engineer. At that point his boss left and Bill took over the role officially, but although "... the MD at Steetley had several times congratulated me on good work, the full board thought I was not experienced enough and appointed a new chief engineer above me. I didn't get on well with him, so I left." Bill got the last laugh though, as on his final day he learned that a contractor charged with siting a new slurry conveyor had chosen his scheme over that of his chief engineer.

Bill's job in Hartlepool had had protected status, meaning that as long as he held it, he didn't have to do National Service. But once he left, the situation changed and he signed up for his two years, starting in mid 1958: he chose the RAF.

Bill continues "In the last quarter of my two-year stint, I was stationed at Bassingbourne in Cambridge as a radar technician." Part of the job included maintaining a rather unreliable piece of equipment, the last of the US-made CPN18 approach radars, which were about to be phased out. The radar was located only a hour's drive from Friern Barnet, for which he was provided with a car and driver – very handy if he wanted to drop in on his old drinking partner.

"I ended up as the only technician in the Air Force who knew how to make it work, or not work, as the occasion demanded. But with Cambridge being relatively close to London, in 1960 I started helping [Keith] with his business at weekends. I often stayed with him and Ursula in Friern Park."

Bill joined Cosworth full-time in mid-1960, around the same time as George. "My initial role, both during my weekends down from Bassingbourne and after I started full-time, can best be described as dogsbody. All of us turned our hands to everything and anything we could manage. Bill Pratt and George, but particularly Keith, Ursula and I, worked all the hours God sent – and then overtime! I did anything, including a bit of technical drawing of engine components, taking our blue Ford 300E 5cwt van to scour North London for any parts or equipment we needed, a bit of fitting and spannering, helping as mechanic when we went to the track, keeping records of stock and work in progress, you name it. But it gradually dawned on me that somebody was needed to keep all the balls in the air, and by default that devolved on me, nobody else being at all interested. So I gradually became office-bound."

Such was the workload that he even had to give up his beloved rugby. "When I got to Friern Barnet I skived off work on Saturday afternoons and joined the local club, Barnet, for the next season. Because of my record they put me straight into the first 15 without even a trial. The 14-hour work days were taking their toll, so the second week I was in the seconds, the third week in the thirds. I just was not up to it, which led to my giving up the unequal struggle, something I have always regretted. But work was more important to all of us."

The rugby connection did have one positive outcome, however. "I befriended another player, John Perry, at the club and talked him into having his solicitors' firm in Barnet – Boyes, Sutton and Perry – take on all the legal work for Cosworth. He was still doing it very effectively two decades later."

Once the Lotus 18 contract had put the company on the map, Keith set about developing variants of its MkII Cosworth powerplant. The MkIII had a stronger bottom end, optional dry sump lubrication and a hotter cam – the A3 – with more lift and overlap. The MkIV, introduced in 1961, was bored out to 1098cc and used larger valves. Cosworth also found itself doing a brisk trade in cams for other tuners, as by now lots of companies were modifying the 105E and no one had managed to better the Cosworth camshaft designs.

The next engine, the MkV, was a mildly modified Ford Classic engine for road-going Lotus 7s. It was of no great technical significance, but is noteworthy historically as it was the company's first non-race engine.

Predictably, by the end of 1960 some Cosworth race engines had already found their way into road cars. "I put one into a Keith's own 105E," George Duckett recalls, while Mike Costin's similarly engined Anglia was the subject of a long complimentary write-up in *The Motor*.[2] A less obviously modified engine was produced for Anne Hall's 105E, with which she won the Coupe des Dames in the 1961 Monte Carlo Rally. Externally it looked standard – no DCOEs or the like – but internally it was not, as George explains.

"The RAC scrutineer came in to measure the engine as I stripped it and I could see Keith standing behind him trying hard not to laugh – he measured the bore and stroke with a wooden rule! It was supposed to have been a standard Ford engine, but it had a special Keith-designed cam and a tuftrided crank. The scrutineer got his little stamp out to mark the crankshaft and hit it, but it only made a shiny mark. He hit it again, still no mark, but the stamp was flattened. He said 'What have you done to this crank?' We said 'Nothing, it's a standard crank.' Keith didn't tell him it had been tuftrided.

"I didn't know then what tuftriding was, I just did what I was told. I tried not to be clever with Keith, it didn't do to try to be clever with Keith. But he seemed to like the way I did up a bolt. He watched me once, torquing up a Ford engine on the dyno, he was fascinated by the way I did it, I don't know why. There were 10 bolts to tighten up, all in the right order – first to 20lbft, then 40, then 60. Every engine I built seemed to run."

Business was booming, but rapid growth always carries a risk of cash flow problems, as extra stock and salaries have to be paid for out of low financial reserves. If customers are slow to pay – and if you supplied Lotus, that was practically a given – you could simply run out of money, which is exactly what happened to Cosworth in March 1961. Lotus owed it £3000 and Keith, knowing that there was no point in even talking to Barclays, decided it was time for some straight-talking face-to-face with Fred Bushell, the Lotus financial director. He got his money, but even then it didn't turn up when Fred said it would. It was a close-run thing, but Cosworth had escaped bankruptcy for the second time.

Surviving against the odds twice, without having to beg the bank, gave Keith a very robust viewpoint on usury. A Duckworthism summarises his opinion:

*I THINK THAT BORROWING MONEY IS THE BIGGEST IMMORALITY
THAT THERE IS. THE MORE I THINK ABOUT LIFE, THE CREDIT
SOCIETY, THE MORE IRRESPONSIBLE I THINK IT IS. I DON'T THINK
THE MORAL FIBRE OF MOST PEOPLE MAKES IT POSSIBLE FOR THEM
TO BE OFFERED LOTS OF CREDIT.*

Whereas the first year's trading had been at a loss, '59-60 recorded a turnover of £21,591 and a profit of £2215, while '60-61 produced an enormous leap in turnover, to £68,507, plus a small increase in profit to £2525. The small change in profit probably reflects Keith's policy of re-investing profits in new machinery rather than taking higher salaries, despite the big increase in turnover. Some of that machinery was installed at Ben Rood's Walthamstow operation, which was now working almost exclusively for Cosworth.

By autumn 1961 it was clear that the Friern Barnet premises were hopelessly overcrowded. With the arrival of Brian Hart – a former colleague of Mike Costin's who started off buying a camshaft from Cosworth and ended up working there full-time – there could be up to 14 people in the tiny loo-less premises at any one time. So when Lotus decided to vacate its Edmonton works at 2 Kennington Road, where the Elite had been developed, Keith was more than happy to take up the lease. August 1962 was set as the moving date.

In the run-up to the move, three more significant things happened in Keith's life. First, he got his first job from Ford, a commission to design a camshaft and inlet manifold for the 1340 version of the 105E's engine, as used in the Ford Classic. In the event, the three-bearing Classic crankshaft proved too fragile to take tuning – even in standard form it was a short-life unit – and by the time of the move, Ford was planning to replace it with the far more robust five-bearing 1500 design, which duly received the upgrade originally destined for the 1340. Before long, Keith's distinctive two-ring manifold, topped with a downdraught Weber, was doing service on tens of thousands of Cortina GTs, Corsair 1500 GTs, and on the few Classic Capri GTs that were produced, though it is doubtful if many owners knew the components' pedigree. (The writer certainly didn't, when he fitted a Cortina GT camshaft in an attempt to pep up his three-bearing 1200 Cortina – helped by a bigger main jet, it revved a bit better, at the expense of the centre main bearing wearing even faster than before.)

At the time, the second event didn't register loudly – or perhaps at all – at Friern Barnet, but before long it would prove vitally important to the company. Walter Hayes was appointed head of Public Affairs & Competitions at Ford. Formally editor of *The Sunday Dispatch*, he knew nothing about motorsport and lobbied – successfully for a while – to offload the competitions part of the brief, but in 1963 Ford chairman Sir Patrick Hennessey insisted he take it back – with dramatic results that belong in subsequent chapters.

Last but not least was an event that most certainly did register – the news that Ursula was pregnant. In September, Keith would be a father!

Footnotes

1 There is a full list of Cosworth powerplants in the appendix of this book.
2 *The Motor*, 28 July 1961, p818.

Chapter 6

Three hectic years

Keith and Ursula Duckworth became parents on 20 September 1962, with the birth of their daughter, Patricia, known to all as Trish. "I was running a fortnight late," Ursula recalls, "so when we went to a Club Lotus evening we chose a route with lots of bends!"

Ursula worked until six weeks before the birth, but when Trish finally made her entrance her mother could no longer work full-time for the company. Gradually, as family commitments increased, she would reduce her hours to zero, though she always retained an active interest in the firm's affairs. She had been there for the hardest part, and her support in the difficult early years, both moral and practical, had been absolutely crucial. Without it, Cosworth might not have survived at all.

The factory might be seeing less of Ursula, but it was now seeing a great deal more of Mike, as he had at long last completed his Lotus contract and had joined full-time just the month before, around the time of the move from Friern Barnet. On his very first day as a working Cosworth director, he took great satisfaction in driving back to Lotus, this time as a supplier.

The topic of his conversation with Colin Chapman that day was the Lotus-Ford Twin-cam engine for the forthcoming Lotus Elan and Lotus Cortina. Based on the same 116E block that Keith was already familiar with, it had been designed by Climax designer Harry Mundy and drawn up by Richard Ansdale, but was in need of development to make it road reliable, and to tune it for racing. Cosworth was the obvious place to do it.

So in the last few months of 1962, Keith didn't get to see much of his baby daughter. Not only did he have the Twin-cam to think about, but Cosworth was continuing to grow at a frenetic pace – by the end of 1962 the MkIV Cosworth engine which had dominated FJ was being phased out in favour of the much improved MkXI and the company simply couldn't keep up with demand.

To relieve the pressure, Keith took on a technical assistant, John Lievesley. A young graduate, John worked at Cosworth for two years (1962-64) and developed a very good relationship with Keith, helped considerably by the discovery that they shared a similarly broad repertoire of rugby songs. He remembers those years with warmth.

"If Keith and I were working late together, as was usually the case, he would phone home to make sure that all was well with Ursula and 'Little Sprog,' as he referred to Trish, betraying his Lancashire background in a way which his mother Em apparently thought inappropriate for any son who wanted to be accepted in polite society. Ursula quite liked the term, but I suspect her mum agreed with 'Mother Duck,' because he confided in me that his mother-in-law considered him to be a dreadfully coarse northerner. Howls of mirth ensued, as we probably both fitted that description.

"I'd studied engine design at university, so when I joined I thought I knew it all. But my course had been highly theoretical and within three days I realised I knew bugger-all. Keith had great clarity of thought, the ability to get quickly to the heart of a problem and concentrate on it to the exclusion of everything else. He was wonderful to work under, a really great apprenticeship."

John had already served one apprenticeship for the Ministry of Supply in the armaments industry, and in that area of engineering traditional hand-fettled metal-to-metal joints were still the norm. So when Keith told him to design a new oil pump assembly using O-ring joints, he failed to allow for any preload on the O-ring, resulting in a cry of despair from Bill Pratt in the assembly shop and a load of scrap components – "But Keith never held my cock-up against me."

In fact, around the same time, when John fancied replacing his Austin 7 with a more girl-impressing XK 120, Keith offered to stand surety for the £400 loan – until he saw the onerous terms stipulated by the bank. "He refused to sign: instead he came into the office next day with £400 in cash and said 'pay me back when you can.' I'd only been working there four weeks!"

Despite the extra help, Keith and Mike still couldn't find time to build the FJ car they'd always promised themselves; it never got beyond the drawing board. There never seemed to be enough hours in the day, not least because the factory was still settling down after the move, which had proved a huge task, as Mike explains.

"There'd been a hell of a lot of work to do before we could move in. All the pumps for the dynos had to be put underground, and that involved excavation and planning. By the time he left Friern Barnet, Keith had two dynos, the old DPX2 and a new Heenan & Froude GB3 – the engines used to be started and run-in on one and booked onto the other for their final test."

Bill, meanwhile, travelled to Northern Ireland in November 1962 as guest of Lotus FJ driver Malcolm Templeton, for a 500 Club of Ireland annual dinner and dance. "Malcolm arranged to have me seated next to a Miss Irene Blair, also from Ballymena, and one thing led to another."

Shortly after his return, early in 1963, he went down with very bad bout of tonsillitis and Keith phoned Irene and asked her to come over "... to look after me in my scruffy flat, which cemented our relationship."

Bill's flat might have been nothing special, but neither were the new Cosworth premises – just a rather damp brick structure with a corrugated roof. There were corrugated sliding doors too, with big air gaps round them, and the only heating was a coke-burning stove in one corner which had to be relit each morning. However, at 1700ft^2 the building was larger than Friern Barnet and boasted two very welcome luxuries: a toilet, and an absence of rats.

Such was the pace of expansion that the company found itself growing out of the building almost as soon as it had moved in.

Mike describes the layout. "There was an office where Ursula and Bill worked, and a little tiny accounts office for the bookkeeper. And a little place where we had five engine builders, each with an engine stand so tight you could barely get round the back of it, and a bench for engine strip and overhaul and then a little area with a couple of machines – a mill and a lathe – plus an electric motor that could drive any test equipment we wanted, plus a welding area, plus, by the end, three dynamometers. Utterly impossible!

"Keith and I, we had an office up in the roof, we screwed a packing-case ladder vertically to the wall to go up there. I was near the door and Keith was the farthest one in. Keith was 24-hour smoking, and all the fumes from the welding area would be coming up through the door. How the hell I'm still living with secondhand smoking and all the fumes, I've no idea!"

The first product of this smoke-filled room was the production version of the Twin-cam. Discussing it with Graham Robson, Keith said "It wasn't all bad, but at the time the head joint wasn't sound, the head structure wasn't any good, and its ports didn't look like ports ought to look. So we straightened up the ports – we just arbitrarily redesigned them – then we added a bit of structure into the head too." (*Cosworth*, p60).

The thinking behind these changes was partly to render the engine fit for tuning. Keith's technical assistant at the time, John Lievesley, says "Keith had a major concern that his desired race ports, spring platforms etc, could be machined out of the standard production casting without breaking through. Thickening the sections as required was one of my first jobs on joining the firm."

Road-going Twin Cams were never produced at Cosworth – in fact the first batch was made at JAP – but from the outset Cosworth was responsible for Lotus' racing versions, the first development engine being the MkX and the subsequent racers the MkXII and MkXIII. In due course many other tuners would jump on the 'Twink' bandwagon, including Vegantune and Holbay.

From its outset, Cosworth had been closely associated with Lotus. It's not healthy for any company to rely too heavily on one customer, so when the American racing authority, the SCCA, created the Formula B category in 1965 for 1600cc production-based engines, and the MkXIII emerged as the powerplant of choice, Cosworth received not only a big boost to its income but also some much-needed diversification. It was the beginning of a US income stream which the company went on to exploit with great success over several decades.

Nineteen sixty-three brought no let-up in the pressure. In January big rule changes in single-seater racing were announced, prompted partly – and ironically – by the desire of motorsport's controlling body, the FIA, to bring more competition into the lower echelons of the sport, where Cosworth engines were utterly dominant. The 1.5-litre Formula 1 introduced in 1961 continued, but from the start of 1964 there would be two new formulae beneath it. Both would use engines of a maximum capacity of 1000cc, but whereas constructors had a free hand with the Formula 2 (F2) engine, aside from an obligation to base it on a production block, the Formula 3 (F3) engine had to use a production block and head, along with a single carburettor. Thus, F3 effectively replaced FJ.

The new rules presented a double challenge to Keith. If Cosworth was to remain dominant in sub-F1 racing after the end of 1963, by spring 1964 it had to produce two new engines – not to mention satisfy existing FJ commitments, and develop racing versions of the now in-production Twin-cam.

Something had to give, and in the event the new F3 contender, dubbed MAE (Modified Anglia Engine), was not seen on the circuits until the 1965 season, even though creating it was relatively straightforward. It took its cue from the last and most sophisticated of the twin-carb Anglia-based pushrod engines, the MkXVII, which used a radically reworked cylinder head with downdraught ports brazed in to improve gas flow. It proved expensive to make and was more of a development project than a catalogue item, but it pointed the way forward and the same principle was used shortly afterwards – albeit for one carburettor rather than two – to create the MAE. It was to prove very successful and was built in considerable quantities, many being sold as kits rather than complete engines.

Both the reworked Twin-cam and the MAE evidenced Keith's quest for the straightest possible port shape, and his F2 engine – dubbed SCA (Single Camshaft type A) – showed the same approach. The SCA appeared in March 1964, and provided Keith's biggest technical challenge to date: his first opportunity to design a head from scratch. It was a milestone in another sense too, for when Keith told Ford competition boss Walter Hayes that he'd decided to base the SCA on the 116E block (as by this point he knew it practically inside out), Walter offered £17,500 of Ford money to help with development costs, in return for Cosworth putting 'Ford' on the valve cover. It was the first time that Ford Europe had made a grant to an independent engine developer.

While the deal represented new territory for both parties, it did not come out of the blue. Unlike its great rival GM, which for many years shunned motorsport, Ford had always understood the value of competition, both as a development aid and a marketing tool. In the UK, the most obvious fruit of this policy was the Lotus Cortina, but in the US there were others, not least the AC Cobra, which arose from racer Carroll Shelby's desire to take on European marques, particularly Ferrari, in sports car racing using a US-sourced engine. Launched two years earlier, in 1962, the Ford V8-powered Cobra was a joint UK/US project by AC Cars in Surrey and Carroll Shelby in California; it did not involve Ford Europe or Cosworth, but it did illustrate the positive attitude of Ford's top management and in due course led to the development of the GT40, and victory at Le Mans.

Walter was a journalist turned marketing chief, not an engineer. In 1962, when he took the job at Ford, the only person he knew in motorsport was Colin Chapman – and then only because while editor of *The Sunday Dispatch*, he'd used him as a freelance motoring correspondent. At his own request, his brief at Ford had initially excluded competition, and by the time Ford chairman Sir Patrick Hennessey insisted he take it on, the Lotus Cortina project had already been successfully honed at Cosworth. So Walter couldn't claim credit for initiating what was to become one of the most iconic and successful '60s saloon-car racers, but as a flamboyant publicist with an incisive mind and an ability to sum up a situation quickly and accurately, he certainly knew how to exploit it to the full. To his mind, in committing Ford resources to the little firm in Edmonton, he was backing an established winner. Of course, it helps enormously if the individuals involved get along, and in the case of Duckworth and Hayes, they certainly did. Each respected the other's ability to think clearly, speak plainly and get things done – if necessary in defiance of convention.

In designing the SCA, Keith considered using a four-valve head. No one had ever succeeded in designing one that realised the theoretical advantages of the layout – the power gain over two valves was always frustratingly small – and Keith fancied the challenge. However, John Lievesley counselled caution, arguing that it might be a step too far for the company's first clean-sheet head design, and that a unit capable of bettering the performance of the Cosworth MkXI – the FJ benchmark at the time – could be designed without any such complication.

In the event, Keith decided to stick to two valves and a single overhead cam – the same basic layout he knew from Climax engines. But he opted to change from the bathtub-shaped combustion chamber he'd always worked with to a Heron head, where the combustion chamber is in the piston, the idea being to prevent the valves being masked by the edges of the combustion chamber. The camshaft cover was canted over to allow the two twin-choke downdraught Webers to feed their mixture into ports that were as straight as possible.

The SCA was a successful engine, winning the F2 championship in 1964 and '65, but Keith was not proud of it. Although the volumetric efficiency was there, the combustion efficiency was not – witness its need for a huge 49° spark advance. Despite Keith and Mike trying endless variations of piston, camshaft, port shape etc, and eventually extracting 143bhp from it in its final, 1966, fuel-injected form, they never felt it was right. Keith always said that "Development is only necessary to rectify the ignorance of designers," and with the SCA, a classic triumph of development over design, he had failed his own test.

DEVELOPMENT IS ONLY NECESSARY TO RECTIFY THE IGNORANCE OF DESIGNERS.

In Keith's eyes, the villain of the piece was the Heron head, and much later, when Harry Mundy followed Keith down what the latter regarded as a dead-end by opting for a Heron head in the Jaguar V12, Keith was aghast, and told him so. Neither man would back down though, leading Keith to observe that "... Harry Mundy was stubborn, but I wouldn't like to say I was other than that."

The 1-litre F2 formula only lasted three years and in its final year, 1966, the SCA was outclassed by Honda's four-valve twin-cam design, whose 150bhp output the Cosworth unit couldn't match. At the time there was speculation as to why Cosworth wasn't fighting back with a new design, but it simply wasn't worth the effort for a single year's competition. In any case, by that stage there were much bigger, more important, projects afoot ...

By the start of 1963 some 14 people worked at Cosworth, but to keep pace with the burgeoning workload, more were needed. And if they were to build engines, Keith insisted that they first be shown the ropes by George, as George explains.

"All the incoming men had to come through me, just for a few days. Keith would say 'I want you to work the Cosworth way, not the Aston Martin way.'"

At one point, one of the men who was a bit of an artist painted 'the master' on George's toolbox. George was a fitter, and never claimed to be anything else, but he had already attained high status simply because the boss had great faith in him. It was characteristic of Keith not to back people half-heartedly. Once he had decided a person was able and trustworthy, he would back them to the hilt and remain solidly loyal to them, unless and until their deficiencies – perceived or real – were staring him in the face. With Keith being a pretty good judge of character, that situation rarely occurred.

Keith and George understood each other very well. "If you said something to him that you thought was good, but he didn't, he'd say 'I'm going to walk behind you because you're speaking from the wrong orifice.' But he'd be smiling as he said it. He didn't frighten me at all because I felt that what I did worked. I did things my way, and Keith liked it.

"For instance, I'd check Ford blocks that Benny had modified, using an oscilloscope, and run it down the bore in four or five places to get a feeling of how thick the metal was. The bores were staggered by design and Benny would adjust the bore position

 Continued on p73

The Lotus 11 Series II record-breaker at Monza in December 1957. *(Courtesy Victor Thomas collection)*

Life at Lotus' Tottenham Lane premises around June 1957, shortly before Keith started there full-time. (Above) Bump starting an 11 along the street; DKD's Six is parked on the left. (Below) In another shot of the same series, Mike Costin trying the Le Mans 11 for size. Behind him to the right, DKD engages in conversation. *(Courtesy www.bridgetbishop.co.uk)*

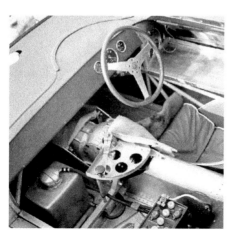

The installation of the Monza recordbreaker's Queerbox transaxle in place of the standard A35 gearbox. *(Courtesy Victor Thomas collection)*

Jowett Bradford Light Van 1946–1953

Engine: flat 2 cylinder, 4 stroke petrol, 4 side valves
Displacement: 61in³ (1,005cc)
Bore: 3¹/₈in (72.5mm)
Stroke: 4in (90mm)
Compression ratio: 5.4 to 1
Carburettors: Zenith type 30-VM
Ignition: 12 volt battery and coil
Power output: 25hp at 3,500rpm
Clutch: 7¹/₄in Borg & Beck

Construction: steel body on ladder-type chassis
Transmission: 3 forward speed and reverse, manual, column change, syncromesh on top only, rear wheel drive
Rear Axle: Spiral Bevel, ratio: 4.89 to 1
Brakes: mechanical, 10in drums all round
Steering: Bishop cam and lever
Wheels: 5 stud, 16in, pressed steel

5 x 16in crossply tyres
Suspension: semi elliptic leaf all round. Armstrong lever arm shock absorbers
Wheelbase: 90in
Track 48¹/₂in
Overall length: 144in
Width: 60in
Overall height: 69in
Track 48¹/₂in

Unladen kerb weight: 17cwt (1,904 lbs)
Ground clearance: 7¹/₂in
Turning circle: 34ft
Production: 1946–1953
38,241 built

© GRAEME JENNER 2014

www.classiccarportraits.co.uk

When it left the factory in Bradford, Keith's infamous van of the same name looked something like this. By the time DKD acquired it, the Bradford had gained a certain patina, and by the time he disposed of it, the vehicle had been terminally reshaped. (*Courtesy Classic Car Portraits, Graeme Jenner*)

The Queerbox reborn: a recent shot of Nick Rossi's re-engineered Lotus gearbox, now working nicely with only four speeds and incorporating many of the ideas proposed in 1957-8 by DKD but rejected by Colin Chapman. (*Courtesy Nick Rossi*)

Keith and Ursula on their wedding day, with Brian Duckworth on Keith's left. The wedding car is a Humber Super Snipe.

Family photo on Keith's and Ursula's wedding day. The bride and groom are flanked by Ursula's parents, Gladys and Victor Cassal (right), and Emma Duckworth, with David Hardman next to her. To the left of David are Brian and Betty Duckworth, while behind David is his brother, Harry. Aunt Olive is standing on the extreme left. Ursula's sisters are standing, both wearing flowers: eldest sister Monica is behind their mother; middle sister Anne further right.

Beginning of a legendary partnership: photos from Brands Hatch on Boxing Day 1959, of the very first Lotus 18 to receive a Cosworth engine. It is not known whether the engine photo was taken before or after the hurried rebuild. Subsequently, power output of the pushrod 105E engine was rapidly raised, as the graphs and engine shot opposite show. *(Courtesy Victor Thomas collection)*

A Lotus 18 at Goodwood in 1960. The 18 used various engines, including Climax for F1 and BMC A-Series and Ford 105E for FJ, but the latter became the definitive powerplant. *(Courtesy Ford Motor Co)*

This picture's caption on p123 of *The Motor*, 23 October 1963, read as follows: "The ultimate in engines for the now virtually extinct Formula Junior is surely this Cosworth Ford unit, which develops 124bhp and propelled Brian Hart and Mike Costin to a double victory at Brands Hatch on 6 October." *(Courtesy The Motor)*

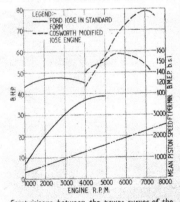

Comparisons between the power curves of the Ford 105E engine in standard form, and as developed for racing purposes by Cosworth

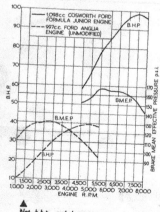

Net b.h.p. and b.m.e.p. curves for the 1,098 c.c. Cosworth Ford compared with those for the unmodified Anglia engine

Power curves of two modified 105E engines published in *The Autocar* 20 months apart. On the left (29 July 1960) is the 997cc Cosworth MkII, on the right (9 March 1962) the bored-out 1098cc MkIV. *(Courtesy The Autocar)*

George Duckett at his bench in Edmonton, assembling a Ford 105E-based engine, with his cabinet of Ford parts behind him. *(Courtesy Cosworth Engineering)*

The SCA was a milestone for Keith: the first engine to have an all-Cosworth head. *(Courtesy Cosworth Engineering)*

The ex-Lotus premises at Edmonton were far from palatial, but were a huge improvement on Friern Barnet. *(Courtesy BusinessF1 Magazine)*

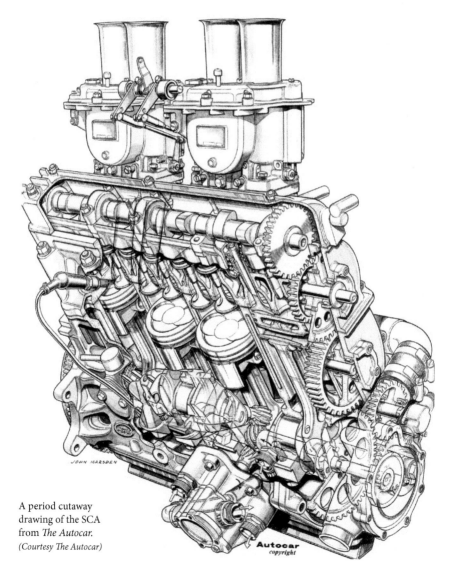

A period cutaway drawing of the SCA from *The Autocar*. *(Courtesy The Autocar)*

Jim Clark in characteristicslly exuberant style in a Lotus Cortina; its engine received a lot of development attention at Cosworth. *(Courtesy Ford Motor Co)*

(Below) A night out at Club Lotus in March 1963 – (l-r) Ben and Jane Rood, Keith and Ursula Duckworth, Stirling Moss' secretary, Val, and Bill Brown. *(Courtesy Business F1 Magazine)*

(Below) Early days at Cosworth's permanent home: how the Northampton factory – later called Factory 1 – looked around 1966, after it had been extended with a second pitched-roof workshop. The original facility was just the offices at the front with a single workshop behind, and the test cells in a separate building behind that. At the back of the second workshop were the material stores, accessed through a roller-shutter door which, in this shot, has the company Thames 15cwt van parked in front. Cosworth's buildings were the first to be constructed on the industrial estate.
(Courtesy Cosworth Engineering)

to make the most of the metal in the casting. So they could be a few thou' out of alignment, deliberately.

"Then the block had to be washed; we used bottle brushes, squirting water in with a hose. Next they would be dried in an electric oven and when they came out we'd bolt them up on to the engine stand and I'd paint them straight away, while they were still warm. Then when they cooled, I'd give them another coat. I always reckoned my engines looked better than anyone else's and when one came back for repair, I always knew whether it was one of mine."

It wasn't just engine assembly that needed more help. In particular, Cosworth needed a storeman to free up Bill to deal with engine customers – someone who could handle stock and look after the spares sales. And as Mike says "Keith and I always said that if we wanted a storeman, Jack Field would be the one." So Keith phoned him up.

"I hadn't seen Keith for months," Jack recounts, "not since he'd moved into the new premises. I'd lucked in because they were building the M1 at the time – lots of contractors were using Bedfords, and I [was] selling Bedford parts. They'd been going to a Bedford dealer, ordering their bits and waiting for them to turn up, but now they had me, this bloke with a van, if they wanted something urgent, he'd scour the whole of bloody London, he'd get it. And then, not only did I get them coming to me for the difficult stuff, I got all the easy stuff too. All I had to do was load it on the van.

"I was doing quite well, when I got the phone call from Keith. I went to see him and we stood in the yard, chatting. He said 'Come and work for me. Just do what you used to do for Chapman, it worked very well at Lotus.'

"I said 'Keith, you can't afford to employ me, I'm earning £1000 a year!' By this time I'd bought the house, got married, got a child, and I thought, I can't piss around working in motor racing earning peanuts. I didn't want another Lotus.

"Keith replied 'I don't take that much out of the company myself!'

"I went to walk out of the yard. He said 'Come back here. I'll pay you £950 a year for the first three months, then £1000 a year.' That was better in reality than Capital Motors, because it was steady, not subject to ups and downs with commission.

"I never looked back, I just grew with the company."

Behind that simple statement lies a complex relationship. Keith and Jack went on to work very successfully together over many years, and developed a great deal of mutual respect, but the pair never socialised. Keith liked company who could stretch him intellectually, and that wasn't Jack's forte. Moreover, he was not an engineer and never professed to be, which would have limited the conversation.

"I thought Keith was a bit of a snob," says Jack. "I spent a lot of time with him, I had a lot of time for his ability, he was a whizz kid. But an evening in the pub? No. With a lot of the conversation, I'd have been way out of it, especially if him and Mike had been talking engineering."

Ben Rood, despite possessing a formidable intellect in his own right, was more on Jack's wavelength. Jack went to and fro to Rood's Engineering frequently, collecting and delivering parts to what was effectively the Cosworth machine shop.

"Benny had a machine shop in Walthamstow. He was absolutely brilliant. If there was stuff I wanted next day I'd go over there, either to make sure he was working on it or to pick it up. When you arrived, the first thing you had to do was make the tea. And before that wash the cups. They were filthy, I wouldn't want to drink out of them.

"I was over there one night, about seven or eight o'clock, and Benny said 'I'm pissed off, I've had enough.'

'Why?'

'I haven't been paid!'

'I'll tell you why you haven't been paid, it's because we haven't had any invoices!'"

To Ben, who hated paperwork with a passion, operating a lathe was vastly preferable to operating a typewriter. As the workload had increased, the admin backlog had increased in tandem. The harder he worked, the less money he received.

Jack reported back to Keith. "Benny is really pissed off. He's got no money."

"Well send him some!" Keith exclaimed.

"If you want to just send him money, you do it. But the only way he's going to get money out of me is if I have an invoice, and if I sign it off to say that I've had the goods and the price is right. Then I'll bung it through, get them to write me out a cheque immediately and he'll have his money."

There was no arguing with Jack's logic, and Keith realised that something fundamental needed to be done, as Ben had clearly reached crisis point. Moreover, the workload was increasing all the time, what with the completion of the first SCAs in April 1964 and the MAE due to come on stream that December and predicted (correctly it turned out) to generate a flood of orders.

So Keith drove over to see him and they both reached the same conclusion, almost simultaneously. The obvious answer was for Cosworth to buy out Rood's Engineering, including all its machinery, and put Ben in charge of Cosworth's production.

This was done in two stages. Initially Cosworth simply bought the entire services of Rood's Engineering for a fixed sum per week, thus saving Ben the hassle of producing invoices and leaving him self-employed, but entirely working for Cosworth. This was only a stopgap though: the real answer was to find premises big enough to bring everyone under one roof, and then for Cosworth to buy out Rood's completely and integrate everything into one business.

That meeting in Walthamstow was a landmark in Cosworth's development. By the time Keith got into his car to drive home, Cosworth was, for practical purposes, operating on two sites and headed by a team of four: Keith, Mike, Bill and Ben.

In the short term, there was no alternative to Ben staying in Walthamstow, but Cosworth desperately needed a place of its own, somewhere it could consolidate and then develop. And since most of its customers were outside London, with more to the north of the metropolis than the south, the logical approach was to look for somewhere within easy reach of the newly completed M1. They got out a map, drew a line 15 miles either side of the road, and started investigating sites and grants. It was May 1963.

Wellingborough and Kettering were considered, and Bill suggested a site close to Silverstone, but the eventual choice was Northampton as it was closest to the motorway. No one knew much about the town, it just seemed to make sense. The actual site came via Harry Hook, father of Roger Hook for whom Ben had made a hydroplane engine. Harry ran the Dunmore Hotel in Shaldon, South Devon but also owned a tyre business in Northampton, and got wind of some greenfield development land in what was then known as Jimmy's End, later to become St James Mill Road. Located south-west of the town centre, it was close to the Grand Union Canal, the River Nene and the main railway line to London.

Keith regarded Harry as a straightforward reliable bloke and quickly took to him, not least because his ultra-austere office fitted with the no-nonsense approach which Keith – and the other Cosworth directors – prided themselves on.

Cosworth bought the site outright in January 1964 for £8000 cash, and local architect Rex Bryan was commissioned to draw up plans for a 6800ft² structure – four times the size of Edmonton, excluding the dynamometer cells which were to be housed in a separate building. Moreover, the site had plenty of room for further expansion, if that proved necessary. No one wanted to move a fourth time.

While the hunt for a home had been going on, a dramatic event had hit the headlines – the Great Train Robbery of August 1963. Sporting enthusiasm has never known any social boundaries, and proof of this turned up at Jack Field's spares counter that summer – Roy 'The Weasel' James.

Roy had had some success in F2 and, in Jack's words "Came over as quite a nice bloke, but he mixed with some right dodgy characters. He used to buy various tuning bits from us and he said 'one of these days I'm going to have a new MkIV engine,' – he was a quick driver even with the bits he had – and I said 'Yeah, that'll be the bleedin' day – it'll have to be in cash!' He said 'Yes, it will be.'"

Then the robbery happened. Jack recalls "One day Roy James rang up and said "Right I want it, when can I have it?"

At that time, Jack handled spares sales, but engine sales were Bill's responsibility. Next day Roy turned up at Bill's office, accompanied by two heavies and a case of money. He wanted his engine and no, he didn't want a receipt. Bill recalls "As he left he said 'When this is all over Bill, I'll see you all right.' I thought nothing of it and gave the money to Keith."

The next day someone said "Have you heard about Roy James? He was practising at Goodwood and he got a tip off that the police were on their way. He's left the circuit and done a runner. What do think that was all about? Must've been the Great Train Robbery."

Jack thought, "Bloody hell, I know where that £500 came from! And the notes are probably numbered!" Straight away he rang Keith and said urgently "I want it back. I'll write an invoice out for it, and I'll bung it in the bank."

And that's what he did. "The police did come round, but the notes didn't seem to be marked and we were allowed to keep the money."

'The Weasel' had been the getaway driver for the robbery, and later claimed he'd got involved because he'd been unable to obtain the sponsorship he needed to get into F1. He was jailed for his part in the raid and, on his release in 1975, tried to return to driving, aided by Stirling Moss' secretary Val Pirie and David Mills. But he'd lost it during his years in prison and his career soon faded. He returned to silversmithing where, thanks to one of his more upright acquaintances, a certain Bernie Ecclestone, he secured a deal making trophies for F1.

Just two months after Roy did his runner, an event occurred of far greater long-term significance to Cosworth: the FIA rewrote the rule book for F1. Having created the 1-litre F2 and F3 categories only that January, ready for 1964, in October 1963 the FIA turned its attention to the top tier of the sport and announced that from the beginning of 1966, maximum engine capacity would be doubled from 1.5-litres normally-aspirated (750cc supercharged), to 3-litres (1.5-litres supercharged). The decision left a huge power gap between F1 and F2, and is the reason the 1-litre F2 was so short-lived: from the start of 1967, F2's maximum capacity was raised to 1600cc.

The thinking behind the change to 3-litres was to bring the formula back to the top of motorsport. The 1961 reduction from 2.5-litres to 1.5-litres had been prompted by a desire to control speed and improve safety – at the time of the decision in 1958, the awful accident at the 1955 Le Mans was still very much in the public's mind and the FIA had felt obliged to act. But the subsequent arrival of big American V8s in sports racing cars had turned motorsport on its head. By the mid '60s the sports racers were setting lap times that no open-wheel car could match, and something had to be done to restore F1 to its rightful place at the top of the motorsport tree. The 3-litre formula was the answer.

The FIA's decision would have a huge effect on the whole of motorsport, and in time would completely transform Cosworth. But this was not obvious in autumn 1963: the company was not involved with F1, had no serious plans to be, and, although a new F2 unit would obviously be needed, there was plenty of time to develop it.

So as 1963 turned into 1964 and the company completed purchase of its Northampton site, the main focus was not on new formulae but on logistics: how to design the building and organise the move, without disrupting the existing Twin-cam, SCA and MAE programmes. Around 30 people worked at Edmonton by this point, but only 14 – the four directors plus 10 others – were willing to leave London. There was some recruiting to do.

However, everyone mentioned in this chapter signed up, with the exception of John Lievesley. Disappointed at Keith's decision not to take the F2 fight to Honda and redesign the SCA, he decided that his CV would be better served by a spell in engine development at Ford; his last job for Cosworth was to draw up the dyno cells for Northampton, though he never actually saw the site. Subsequently several others – notably Bill Pratt, George Duckett, Brian Hart and Jack Field – augmented their income by helping with the test cells' construction. Bricklaying and plumbing were all in a day's work.

The company was still only small, but its self-confidence was out of proportion to its size, the attitude being that it was better to have a job done properly by Cosworth people than messed up by someone else.

As 1964 wore on and Rex Bryan's building neared completion, equipment started to be moved in, and one by one the staff moved north. Keith and Ursula were among the first, as Keith wanted to handle the complexities of the dynamometer installation himself, in view of its multitude of pumps, water circuits and tanks. So that October they left their maisonette and bought their first house, 78 Larkhall Lane in the village of Harpole, on the right side of town for the factory.

Great care was taken not to disrupt production: as soon as the last engine was tested in London, the dyno in Northampton was ready for the next one.

Bill and Irene got married in August 1964 and bought a property in Creaton, north of Northampton. Ben and Jane made their home in Paulerspury, not far from Keith and Ursula, though Jane and their three sons stayed in Loughton for the first ten months, as the eldest was coming up to his O-levels. Mike and Rhoda were the last to arrive. "I carried on down in London with Jack Field and the last few blokes, overhauling engines."

Rhoda Costin, Ursula Duckworth and Jane Rood all knew very well that being a 'Cosworth wife' required tolerance and forbearance. Their husbands' hours were long and irregular, their stress levels considerable and, even when they were home, they were often preoccupied with company matters. The women put up with it because they knew their husbands loved what they were doing.

For Irene, all this was new territory, but she learned the hard way what it meant to be a Cosworth wife – on her wedding day, of all days. Bill takes up the story.

"When we married in August 1964, the wedding breakfast was attended by my three co-directors and wives, plus Howard Panton and a very pregnant Rhona Panton. As Irene and I were about to leave, we were asked where we were headed. We said 'The Mermaid at Rye for one night, then across the Channel by Silver City and drive down to Spain.'

'Oh, no, you're not! You are going to Zolder in Belgium.'

"It was Thursday, there was a race there at the weekend, and the tappets in our engines were faulty. I was given a pile of reworked tappets and told to take them to the teams involved. I was told we were booked in a hotel there. We got to Zolder, went straight to the circuit and distributed the tappets, then headed to the 'hotel,' only to be informed it was a working men's club which did have rooms, but that women were not allowed. All the hotels were full, but we got a bed that night, thanks to Richard Attwood, who was racing there and very kindly donated his room to us, and even bought champagne for a small party! Next morning we set off for L'Hospitalet near Tarragona in Spain."

After three days Bill fell asleep on the beach and got so sunburned that they drove to cooler climes in northern France. Irene, who had been looking forward to a romantic Mediterranean honeymoon, felt so short-changed that they actually came home early.

Months before the marriage, in fact, as soon as it had become clear that she and Bill were an item, the others had wanted to know, *needed* to know, if she would be able to cope with the lifestyle. As Mike says, "It was decreed, by Keith I think, that we'd better have a session and meet this lady and introduce ourselves. So Rhoda and myself and Keith and Ursula and Ben and Jane all went to a pub one Sunday lunchtime. Afterwards Keith said to me 'What do you reckon to Irene then?' and I replied 'She is going to be real trouble.'

'That's a bit unreasonable isn't it, what makes you think that?'

'It's just the way I see it.'

"Six months later he came up to me and asked 'How the bloody hell did you make up your mind so quickly?' and laughed."

Bill never knew of Mike and Keith's conversation until the writing of this book, but it does not surprise him. "I knew Rhoda did not approve of her and Mike followed suit. I thought Keith fancied her and Ben – he just liked girls!" Keith's question was almost certainly prompted by the fact that, not long after that Sunday lunch in 1963, "Jim Clark enticed her away from me and she went to stay with him at his home in Duns for a short while. That was bad enough of Clark but, much worse, he did not keep her and she came back!"

In saying this of the woman whom he would later describe as his nemesis, Bill has his tongue firmly in his cheek, for the marriage which followed the Clark affair was by no means all bad. "The first 10 years of my marriage I really loved, we produced our two wonderful children, but in retrospect I was too immersed in the business and my powerboating to realise that all was not what it seemed. After that my euphoria rapidly dissipated. Irene was a great girl to be with, but eventually proved impossible to live with."

Those troubles were all in the future, though. In December 1964, it seemed that the dust was finally settling. The company told the press that from the New Year, the phone number would no longer begin with a London code but a Northampton one, signalling the start of a new era – not only for Cosworth, but also its personnel. One merged company, in one new factory, run by four directors with four wives and seven children between them – three each to the Costins and Roods, and Trish to the Duckworths.

Soon it would be eight, for that same month, Ursula found she was pregnant again.

Chapter 7

Creating a legend

In February 1965, just two months after Cosworth had moved to Northampton, came an announcement that would change the company – and F1 – out of all recognition. Climax was pulling out of racing.

The decision came as a complete shock. Indeed, it was deemed sufficiently newsworthy to make the BBC lunchtime radio news, a very rare event for a motorsport story. Until that point, motorsport pundits had been enjoying themselves speculating about what powerplant Climax would field for the new 3-litre formula to start in 1966. Some favoured an enlarged version of the 2.5-litre V8 which had been mothballed when the outgoing 1.5-litre formula had been announced. Others, knowing that Climax had considered building a 1.5-litre flat-16 for the final year of the old formula, argued that that must be a pointer to the future.

In the event, they were all wrong – there would be no engine at all. Climax, whose principal business had always been in stationary and industrial engines, and which had slid almost by accident into racing during the 1950s, had recently been taken over by Jaguar and the new management had decided that the losses involved in providing engines for motorsport could no longer be tolerated. That was that.

The extent of the crisis this decision created among British constructors can scarcely be exaggerated. In 1964, there were six principal F1 contenders, of which three – Ferrari, BRM and Honda – made their own engines. The other three – Lotus, Cooper and Brabham – had relied on Climax power. Suddenly, just 10 months before the start of the new formula, half the field had no powerplant.

There was an uncomfortable sense of déjà vu about the situation. The last time the F1 rules had changed, in 1961, the British teams had practically gifted the championship to Ferrari because they had no competitive engine. They had opposed the downsizing to 1.5-litres, and declared they would not co-operate with the new formula, only realising much too late that the FIA was determined to go ahead anyway.[1] As a result, they were forced to contest the 1961 season with four-cylinder 1.5-litre Climax engines, which were no match for the V6 in Ferrari's beautiful 156 'Sharknose.'

The British teams recovered when BRM and Climax introduced their 1.5-litre V8s in 1962, BRM taking the title in 1962 and Lotus-Climax in 1963 and 1965. Now history was in danger of repeating itself, not because of sporting obduracy but because of commercial reality.

When the news broke, the three affected teams adopted very different strategies for tackling the crisis. Jack Brabham had a connection with the Australian engineering firm Repco, which was planning an overhead-cam engine based on GM's 3.5-litre all-alloy V8, with capacity reduced to 2.5-litres for the Australian Tasman racing series and expanded to 4.2-litres for sports car racing. Jack persuaded them to put these projects to one side in favour of a 3-litre version for installation in his new 1966 car; he knew its 300bhp would not be the class of the field, but he gambled – successfully, it turned out – that, with all the teams entering new territory and likely to hit reliabilty problems, a simple, light, robust machine might do the job.

Cooper teamed up with Maserati, whose V12 had, on paper at least, a shade more power than the Repco. But the Maserati was essentially a development of a 1950s sports car unit and was bulkier and heavier than ideal.

At Lotus, Colin Chapman had only one option, at least in the short term, and that was to buy BRM's H16 engine, which had always been intended not only for the company's own cars but also as a customer unit for other teams. Chapman believed that the way forward was to build a light monocoque car with a small frontal area and power it with a simple, light engine, with the latter acting as a stressed member and providing the pick-up points for the rear suspension. Fortunately, the H16 had been designed to be used in this way, but in every other respect the heavy, complex design was the opposite of what Chapman wanted, especially as it wasn't developing anywhere near its projected 400bhp. But it would have to do until Plan B could be put into operation, which involved using Chapman's considerable powers of persuasion to get someone else to fund a new British engine. And naturally he planned that Lotus, having taken the lead in this endeavour, would be rewarded for its initiative by getting first bite of the new British cherry.

He knew who he wanted to design it – Keith Duckworth. Chapman had already had preliminary discussions with him, and discovered that the two were thinking along very similar lines. Like Chapman, Keith was not convinced about the need for complex multi-cylinder engines.

As before, the F2 rules required the engine to be based on a production block, and initially Keith considered basing his new contender on a small straight-six, but dismissed all the potential units as having too long a crankshaft. A V6 seemed a better bet, particularly the recently introduced 2-litre V6 from Ford Germany (the first version of what came to be called the Cologne V6), but he dismissed that on learning that it was 23kg heavier than his old friend the four-cylinder Ford 116E.

He then looked carefully at Honda's SCA-beating 1-litre F2 engine, which he regarded as the best four-valve unit yet devised. It developed 150bhp thanks to twin overhead cams and a four-valve head, suggesting that a 1.5-litre engine along similar lines should be good for 200bhp. It followed that doubling up two such units to form a 3-litre V8 ought to produce a genuine 400bhp engine, an output all the other constructors were aiming at but none looked like achieving.

F1 engine or no F1 engine, Keith had every intention of building his new F2 unit, which he dubbed FVA (Four Valves series A). And in doing so, he knew he would be giving himself a head-start when it came to building an F1 design. He could take the heads and valvegear from a 1600cc FVA, confident that they worked and produced the required power, modify them slightly if necessary, to suit a 1500cc engine, and then mount two heads on a common crankcase to create a V8 F1 engine, which would then become the DFV (Double Four Valve).

So far so good. But there remained the small matter of finding someone to pay for it all. The FVA, Cosworth could fund itself, but Keith knew instinctively that the DFV was out of the question without external support. He never did any accurate calculations, but told Chapman that for designing, developing and building the five engines Lotus needed for a season "... about £100,000 will be needed to do the job properly," (*Cosworth*, p76). It was as scientific as that.

Naturally, Keith and Colin talked to Ford first, but the initial response was not encouraging. So they approached Aston Martin owner David Brown, who was interested but wanted to control the project – and effectively Cosworth – in a way Keith would not countenance. The British Sound Recording Company was tried next, then Esso Petroleum (Lotus' contracted supplier), but all the seeds fell on stony ground.

Colin's next call was on the Society of Motor Manufacturers & Traders (SMMT). British racing teams, he argued, had added great prestige to the British car industry as a whole, and now it was only fair (and good business) for the industry to provide the hard cash necessary to ensure that this continued.

He received a sympathetic ear, particularly from the then president, Ford's Sir Patrick Hennessy, but no offer of cash from the manufacturers. Hennessy, though, was intrigued enough to take the idea to Government, on the grounds that a project like this was of benefit to the whole nation. But at Whitehall he was met with utter incomprehension. The British Government either didn't understand, or didn't care, about the importance of motorsport to one of the country's largest industries. (In a telling contrast, a few years later General de Gaulle offered the equivalent of £500,000 to any company willing to develop a French F1 engine.)

Meanwhile, Colin had not given up on Ford. By this point he had developed a very good relationship with Walter Hayes, and occasionally Walter would go to dinner at the Chapmans' house in Hertfordshire. One evening, the subject of an F1 engine came up again and they discussed it at length. Either Colin was particularly persuasive that night, or perhaps Hazel's cooking did the trick, but by the time Walter drove home he was sold on the idea of a Ford F1 engine, and on Cosworth producing it.

A major attraction was that, because Keith wanted to develop the DFV from the FVA, and because the latter was based on a Cortina block, there was a direct link right through to the mainstream Ford range. No matter that the DFV, with its bespoke crankcase and Cosworth heads, would actually contain no Ford components – the lineage was there. Moreover, the choice of a V8 configuration fitted beautifully with Ford's international image. Ford didn't build the first V8 – that honour goes to Léon Levavasseur in 1902 – but the company had popularised them in the 1930s and was closely associated with the layout in the public's mind. Ford didn't offer any V8s in Britain, but there were plenty of other markets where it did, and F1 had a global following. Everything about the project fitted perfectly: what Chapman and Duckworth wanted for performance reasons, Ford needed for commercial ones. On top of all that, the value of the goodwill generated by rescuing British F1 in its hour of need was incalculable. Walter knew a PR man's dream when he saw one, and he was looking at one right now.

Moreover, a key potential ally had recently arrived from Ford headquarters in Detroit. Harley Copp, Ford UK's new vice president of engineering, was a passionate motorsport enthusiast and Walter talked at length with him about the F1 idea. Afterwards, Harley talked through all the details with Chapman, and then Keith. By the end of it, he was convinced. It was March 1965, one month after the Climax announcement. Things were moving fast, but they needed to – there were now just nine months until the new formula started. It was unrealistic to have the DFV ready for the 1966 season, especially as Keith was determined to design the FVA first, but 1967 looked feasible, and became the target.

The next challenge was for Hayes and Copp to get the project approved and the expenditure authorised. This was a two-stage process, the first being Ford of Britain's forthcoming policy committee meeting in a few weeks. If the F1 engine was approved there, it would then be put before the company's review of motorsport policy, held each September at Ford headquarters in Dearborn.

Stanley Gillen, just arrived from the US as Ford of Britain's new managing director, was chairing his first policy meeting when Hayes and Copp announced under 'any other business' that they would like to produce a Grand Prix engine. The agenda item was discussed, voted on and passed – it was as simple as that, for by mass-production motor industry standards, Walter's £100,000 pet project was small beer. Nevertheless he was putting a lot of faith in Keith: if the event was unsuccessful, his career would be on the line.

There was a gap of some three to four months between the two meetings, but back at Northampton there was no let up, for Cosworth intended to produce the FVA regardless of the answer from Detroit, and that meant more factory space. So plans were laid for a 3000ft² extension. Work started that June.

To give themselves a break, in spring 1965 the four directors went down to Harry Hook's hotel in Shaldon for a weekend of waterskiing. Jane and Ursula went too, Ursula by now visibly pregnant with her second child.

Roger Hook knew Ben because he'd used Hogan-Rood two-strokes during his hydroplane racing days, but by 1964 he'd moved on to what was called 'runabout racing,' using what were basically modified ski-boats with a co-driver. Roger always used Ford engines in these boats and this example had a 1340cc unit, tweaked with some Cosworth components.

The four pulled the boat out of the garage and decided to start it before going to the slip, but it just would not fire and, in Bill's words "The entire might of Cosworth spent the rest of the afternoon disassembling the engine, putting it back together, disassembling it further, putting it back together again etc, to no avail.

"When it was too late to get any skiing, Roger smote his forehead, went to the stern and removed the cork which was rammed up the exhaust pipe. He explained that he never tried to start the engine until he was at the water and the change in procedure had made him forget. He removed the cork and the reassembled engine started first time."

Keith had been at his wits' end trying to work out what was wrong, and had said in a low voice "That bloody thing's never going to start." Jane Rood had overheard him, and allowed herself a private smile when the engine finally ran. There was always intellectual rivalry between Keith and Ben, and it was somehow gratifying to find that Keith had missed such an obvious clue, even though the other three directors had missed it as well.

By summer 1965, the workforce had grown to about 50. One of those 50 was John Dickens, a young man who had made his first appearance at Cosworth that Easter as a work-experience trainee from Corby Technical College. A serious-minded individual, he gained Mike and Keith's confidence almost immediately and would go on to spend his entire career at Cosworth: "After Easter I continued with a Saturday-morning job during term time, cleaning out machine sumps and logging the preventative-maintenance schedule, returning each holiday for more proper experience, when I moved around each department."

In July, Keith started design work on the FVA. The month after that he became a father for the second time, when on 4 August three year-old Trish acquired a baby brother, Roger. The proud parents asked Keith's old university friend, Noel Davies, to be godfather.

September brought more good news. Walter had been unsure how an F1 engine would be received in the US, but he need not have worried. At the annual motorsport review, no less a person than Henry Ford II put his weight behind a project which, by the standards of Ford's US motorsport budget, seemed eminently affordable. Ford had decided to build its own Grand Prix engine!

A contract was promptly drawn up, but Keith was in no hurry to sign it. Rumours of the Ford-Cosworth deal had been rife in the motorsport world and in October 1965, when it was finally confirmed, the spotlight was on the Northampton company like never before. Keith was up for the challenge, but wanted to be sure of his engine's performance before he committed himself to deliver it.

Fortunately for him, Ford's corporate lawyers played right into his hands, producing page after page of convoluted legal gobbledegook that prompted Keith to say to Walter "Do you want me to read the contract, or shall I design you an engine instead? I haven't time to do both." (*Cosworth*, p80).

Keith could have hired his own lawyer to go through it, but he was always deeply suspicious of anyone who wasn't actually producing anything, regarding them as, at best, an overhead he would rather do without. When he came across someone who was self-evidently an achiever in his or her own field, like Walter Hayes, he was prepared to make an exception, but his default position, one which he expounded passionately and eloquently all his adult life, was that engineers, particularly creative engineers, were the lifeblood of society. They were the people who made the world function.

It was 23 June 1966 before the contract was finally signed, by which time the FVA was running on the testbed and the first tranche of money – £25,000 – had already been paid to Cosworth, back on 1 March! Such was the level of trust between Keith and Walter, and between the latter and senior Ford management.

The gist of the (much simplified and drafted by Keith himself!) contract was that for £100,000 Cosworth would design two Ford-badged engines for F2 and F1 respectively. At least five units of each would be produced: the F2 engines had to race in the 1967 season, the F1 engines in 1968, with the first F1 unit ready for use by May 1967. Ford would decide which F1 team received the new engine – though there were no prizes for guessing the likely recipient.

Meanwhile, the likely recipient persevered with the BRM unit. Chapman had some success – the Lotus-BRM won the 1966 US Grand Prix in the hands of Jim Clark. But in his eyes, the H16 was never more than a stop-gap.

Whole books have been written about the FVA and DFV[2], and a biography is not the place to delve into their technical minutiae, but a summary of their salient points will not go amiss. Keith always believed in designing the cylinder head first and fitting the rest of the engine around it, but until he designed the DFV he never had the chance to put this philosophy to the test without compromise, all his earlier designs having been based on production Ford iron blocks. Despite this limitation, it was the FVA's cylinder head, and in particular its combustion chamber shape, which gave this Ford 116E-based design the edge over its rivals. The general specification was state of the art at the time – gear-driven double overhead cams in an alloy head with four valves per cylinder and Lucas fuel-injection – but was by no means unique. What made the difference was the way Keith rethought the combustion process.

At the time, it was normal practice in high-performance engines to have the inlet and exhaust valves set at right angles, or nearly right angles, to each other. This made perfect sense in the days of long-stroke, narrow-bore engines, as the large valve angle allowed the valve size to be increased, and with a flat-topped piston gave a roughly hemispherical combustion chamber – an efficient shape for flame propagation. But as power requirements rose, designers resorted to fitting domed pistons to increase compression, and in doing so changed the chamber shape from a hemisphere to something with considerably less combustion efficiency, more akin to the peel from half an orange.

These same basic shapes could be found on two- and four-valve engines, but Keith reckoned that designers of four-valve engines were missing a trick. They went to great efforts to get mixture into the cylinder, with big, smooth, straight ports and maximum possible valve area, but by retaining the traditional combustion chamber shape, they were failing to make best use of the mixture once it arrived.

Keith was convinced that, if the bore was large enough, four valves could be fitted at a much shallower angle and still provide enough valve area for efficient cylinder filling. There had been a gradual trend to shallower angles, but he favoured a much more radical shift, to give a much smaller pent roof-shaped combustion chamber and obviate the need for a domed piston. Such an engine, he concluded, would have the best of both worlds – both volumetric and combustion efficiency.

Thus the FVA's valve angle was a mere 40°, with the inlets on one side of the chamber and the outlets on the other, and it is this simple-sounding arrangement which is at the heart of the engine's design.

Keith didn't arrive at this paired-valve layout immediately. Initially he planned to place the valves diametrically opposite each other, to promote the swirl whose absence, in his view, had been the SCA's weakness. He got a long way down this road, as far as detail drawings, before it dawned on him that while this layout might work with the offset plug of a two-valve head, it would actually give very little swirl relative to the single central plug of a four-valve head. Fearing that he would end up needing three plugs per cylinder to ensure efficient combustion, he scrapped the whole concept. Moreover, looking ahead to the V8, whose heads he hoped to model closely on the FVA, such a valve layout would have made for very complicated inlet and exhaust plumbing.

Keith's conclusion that the diametric layout would not work was vindicated when BMW adopted it for the company's 1967 F2 engine, designed by Ludwig Apfelbeck. The unit was not a success, and by 1970 the company had changed to a valve arrangement similar to the FVA. The FVA was designed before the BMW underperformed on the circuits, but Keith was aware of its general arrangement much earlier, as Bill confirms. "We certainly knew about its potential long before it was raced. I always thought that was a factor in Keith's rejecting its valve layout."

The rejection of diametric valves is a good example of how Keith could be completely ruthless once he had made up his mind that something had to change – even if the decision highlighted some earlier bad judgment on his part. In fact he developed a Duckworthism on the subject:

83

THE HUMAN BEING DOESN'T REALISE HE IS IN A MIRE UNTIL IT'S
ABOVE HIS HEAD – I CAN ACTUALLY RECOGNISE THAT THERE IS A
PILE OF MIRE OVER THERE, AND IF I'M NOT CAREFUL, I'M GOING
TO ARRIVE IN IT.

Correct though the decision undoubtedly was, it turned the screw on what was already a desperately tight timetable, so in November 1965, just one month after the existence of the Ford-Cosworth F1 project was announced, he left the running of the factory to Mike, Bill and Ben, and closeted himself in the dining room at 78 Larkhall Lane to concentrate absolutely on design work. Bill says "Though I say it myself, the place ran very well during that period. Things were a lot easier to do when Keith wasn't around because he would poke his nose in and he had very strong, sometimes strange, views about running a business!"

Keith knew he needed to get the FVA running by spring 1966 and have the design of the DFV complete by the following August if he was to have an F1 engine he was confident of for the 1967 season. That gave him just nine months to complete the FVA and design the DFV.

The good news was that he now had a right-hand man back at the factory, because Mike Hall had recently joined from BRM where, usefully, he had been involved with the company's successful 1.5-litre F1 V8s. Unhappy at the direction the H16 was taking, Mike asked Cosworth for a development job, was offered a design job instead and took to his new post like a duck to water, rapidly becoming a vital member of staff.

Those nine months were physically and mentally the most demanding of Keith's life. Suffering from eye strain and consuming an unhealthily large number of cigarettes, he deliberately went on a diet in an attempt to stay at least vaguely fit. Thanks to Ursula's careful ministrations, he lost 18kg (40lb) in weight. Towards the end of the period he would sometimes have young Roger for company – the lad was now finding his feet and the dining room window sill was a handy spot for a baby bouncer.

On Fridays Keith would go into the factory to discuss any problems that had arisen during the week and to progress the DFV with Mike Costin and Mike Hall, but otherwise he was at his drawing board from 9am till midnight every day, including weekends. Some components he would take right through to detail drawings, others would be started and left to Mike Hall to finish.

The link man between study and factory was George Duckett. Conveniently, George lived just round the corner from Keith "... so I became the messenger boy. On my way to work I'd call in at his house and Keith would give me a drawing. He'd say 'Take this to Mike Costin and see if we can make this.' Mike would study the drawing and then he'd ask Benny Rood 'Can we machine this?' And then I'd bring the drawing back with suggestions for changes. There was no side with Keith, he'd be on the floor, with the drawings all around him, not just on a table." Given half a chance, baby Roger would crawl all over the drawings too.

The first FVA went on the dyno in February 1966 and produced 220bhp at 9000rpm from 1600cc, a little more than its power target. Deliveries of the FVA started early in 1967, priced at £3000 each,[3] and the unit went on to dominate all four years of the the the 1600 F2 class' existence, 1967-71.

As soon as the FVA was signed off, work began on a one-off derivative to aid design of the DFV, a 1500cc version known as the FVB. This was then fitted in place of the SCB in the Brabham BT10 that Cosworth used as a test vehicle. That summer Mike began test driving, and entering the car in Formula Libre (FL) events, partly to learn and partly for fun.

Having Costin in the team was absolutely invaluable, for not only is he a very accomplished driver, but also gifted with great mechanical sensitivity. He could easily have made driving his career, had he wished. With David Phipps, Mike had written a book about race car chassis design,[4] and demonstrated that his knowledge was not merely theoretical at the 1966 *Daily Mail* International Trophy F2 race at Silverstone, when he put the Brabham on the front row next to Jim Clark, and in front of several illustrious names. Sadly, the race was rained off.

The race-shop was very much Mike's responsibility – albeit mostly an evening or weekend one. Up until recently, Brian Hart had occasionally shared the driving, but he'd left a few months before to set up his own company, coincidentally around the time John Dickens arrived. John, despite still being a very much a trainee, worked on the Brabham and remembers it well.

"At weekends I used to go testing and provide support at the races, along with George Duckett, and sometimes his wife, Pam. George was engine man; I was gearbox and chassis. We invited many top drivers to 'have a go,' to interest them in our new F2 unit, and get views on drivability – Surtees, Hulme, Brabham, Rees, Hobbs, Redman, and others. I learned a lot! Mike was keen to have a driver-primed fuelling system in the car, rather than being reliant on an electric pump, so the car was fitted with a manual Kigass plunger-pump on the dashboard. This required careful pumping, in tune with the ignition/starter motor, and few other drivers (Denny Hulme, Dickie Attwood and John Surtees come to mind) could get it right. But the system suited Mike's aviation heritage and experience.

"To the best of my recollection, though, the engine they were actually trying was the FVB, not the slightly more powerful FVA that they could actually order."

The capacity reduction was achieved by shortening the stroke. The FVA's stroke had been longer than ideal anyway; dictated as it was by limitations on bore size imposed by the wall thicknesses of the Cortina block. To keep the same compression Keith used a modified piston. This was expedient for what was, after all, a purely experimental power unit, but not ideal, so he was mightily relieved when the FVB obligingly gave precisely 200bhp on the dyno. All was set fair for the big challenge – doubling it up to produce a 400bhp DFV, Cosworth's first all-Cosworth design.

Keith's approach to design was always very thorough. Merely coming up with an arrangement that would work was not good enough: he had to satisfy himself that there wasn't a better alternative somewhere, and do that without cutting any metal, observing that:

It costs you very little to scrub out drawings on paper, and to start again. As soon as you have things in the metal, and you have to try to make a silk purse out of a sow's ear, life becomes expensive.

Because of this approach, he found the freedom to design a block from scratch simultaneously exciting and daunting. Keith often commented that "Very few straight answers are ever possible – the decisive man is a simple-minded man," and true to form he agonised long and hard about one of the first parameters, the head-stud positions. In fact, he vacillated so long that, in Mike's words, "I had to read the riot act, and point out to him that unless he made up his mind about these, we'd *never* get the DFV built," (*Cosworth*, p91).

This incident is a classic illustration of how Mike kept Keith's feet on the ground. Uniquely, he could be as blunt as he liked and Keith would just take it on the chin. He might argue the point, but criticism from Mike was never dismissed out of hand.

VERY FEW STRAIGHT ANSWERS ARE EVER POSSIBLE. THE DECISIVE

MAN IS A SIMPLE-MINDED MAN.

Keith's aim with the DFV was to achieve the target power output with maximum simplicity, neatness and lightness. He also wanted to make it practical to repair in the field and economical to produce – he would often rethink a component if it seemed to demand very tight manufacturing tolerances.

Desiring a return to a flat piston, Keith, with some trepidation, reduced the valve angle further compared to the FVB, from 40° to 32°. It was a gamble, but he hoped it would pay dividends as regards power output. Moreover, the smaller valve angle made for a slightly narrower head, no bad thing when planning a V8.

A major consideration was that the engine had to be as short as possible and have a flat front so it could bolt solidly to the bulkhead behind the driver, via the cam covers and cam carriers at the top, and the sump at the bottom. Therefore these components had to be much stronger than normal, and be able to accommodate expansion without loss of chassis stiffness. In conjunction with Lotus, Keith was also involved in designing the rear subframes, which were attached to the rear of the block, and their associated suspension.

The sump (dry of course) was a very substantial item because it also incorporated the main bearing caps, to keep weight and engine height down. The starter motor sat next to the gearbox, as the requirement for low engine height dictated a very small flywheel, whose ring gear was too far inboard to engage with a starter motor mounted conventionally, adjacent to the block.

Keith wanted to ensure that his novel sump design was up to the job, so he got George to make up a test piece which simulated the sump and main bearing assembly. "It was basically a block of alloy bored out to the diameter of the crank, cut in half and with studs and holes then added at the right places. That assembly was warmed up, measured, frozen, measured again, put under torsion, measured again, and so on. I was playing with these things for at least three months before he actually finalised the block."

Keith chose a flat-plane crank rather than the normal V8 arrangement with the crankpins at 90° to each other, largely in order to simplify the exhaust system. A flat-plane V8 crank inevitably produces an out-of-balance sideways force, and indeed the Cosworth V8 has never been the smoothest of engines, but Keith calculated – correctly it turned out – that the drivers would be able to live with it.

The DFV's block was alloy with iron liners, and Keith paid particular attention to its shape. He calculated that the crankshaft bob weights would be spinning at up to 170mph, and reasoned that the adjacent air would be dragged around at a similar speed. So he designed a barrel-shaped crankcase with smooth insides to minimise aerodynamic losses, and then got John Dickens to try the concept on a test rig. "In conjunction with Shell oils, I spent many hours on a single-cylinder test rig with specially diluted oil to replicate high-speed crankcase turbulence, with a view to trying to help DKD design a good scavenging system. I recorded lots of results, we *thought* it would work ..."

To keep width and height to a minimum, water pumps were mounted on the sides of the block at the front, with the oil pumps behind. In the middle of the vee sat an assembly which became colloquially known at Cosworth as 'the bomb', consisting of a small alternator, the fuel-injection metering unit and the distributor, though to make the latter fit it proved necessary to separate cap and base and connect them with a shaft of Cosworth's own design. A neat touch was to duct spillover fuel through a drilling in the inlet manifolds to cool the incoming fuel. The whole engine looked neat, compact and 'all of a piece', with no afterthoughts.

In August 1966, with the final drawings done, an exhausted Keith Duckworth returned to the factory full-time to supervise the construction and testing of the first engine. He had been away for nine months. Some of that time had been spent on the FVA, so he had created the DFV from scratch in around six months, an astonishing achievment in the pre-CAD era.

George Duckett built that first ever DFV. It was numbered 701 – 7 for the last digit of the season it was to be raced, and 1 because it was the first of that season's production.

"They put it on the test bed but it had valve springs from a BSA Gold Star motorcycle – they broke and a valve went through a piston. I took it apart but it was never rebuilt." George still has the piston he kept as a souvenir. So, 702 was the first engine fitted to a car.

Valve springs were not the only development problem, as John Dickens explains. "Though the results on our crankcase test rig had seemed okay, I think we proved that the test rig was worthless, because when the engines first ran, the breathing was awful! In great haste, we had to Araldite extensive external aluminium tubes into position between the crankcase and the right-hand cam carrier to equalise the pressures at the top and bottom of the engine and encourage the oil to drain. The early production engines had a neatened-up version of the same arrangement.

"The original scavenge pumps were hopeless, and one of my contributions was establishing that nylon is hydroscopic and that when running, the nylatron blades in the pump absorbed moisture from the oily atmosphere and expanded, jamming them in their grooves, rather than sliding as required in order to pump."

Several years later, a bigger roots-type pump designed by Alastair Lyle would solve the problem, but in the meantime, an improved design of blade pump was installed. A good example of the attention to detail that characterised the DFV was how Keith got George to fettle the shape of the pump's ports: "Keith got me to make up an aluminium dummy of the shape I wanted. This was mounted on a sample casting so that we could mark it up and broddle[5] the ports to the required shape. Then the production pumps were made to suit."

As soon as the breathing issues were brought under control, the engine produced 408bhp on the dyno – the magic 400bhp had been exceeded at the first attempt.

As testing proceeded, the first sign of what would become the DFV's most significant problem became apparent, when a tooth snapped off one of the timing gears. At the time, excessive backlash was suspected, but as the gear concerned had run quite a few hours by the time it broke, the problem didn't seem urgent enough to warrant delaying the schedule.

"As the FVA and DFV moved into 'production,'" John Dickens continues, "it became necessary to start keeping better records of who built what when, so I joined Bill Pratt, Alan Peck and Dick Langford in the Build Office, collating data and records and eventually working closely with Mike Costin on a failure-monitoring regime to try and predict life of components, etc. As a result I would find myself involved with Mike and Keith's discussions from time to time – usually just sitting in the corner, trying to absorb the pearls cast before me. It was a fascinating and invigorating time, building up information on the DFV and coping with FVA failures and development. Much of this work centred around our inadequate BSA Gold Star valve springs, so I became the company 'source' on such things; eventually we changed to a special design from Schmitthelm."

In December 1966, with the FVA approaching production and the DFV into its development phase, Keith briefly turned his attention away from engineering to the question of company structure. Back in 1958, just two of the 100 £1 shares had been issued, one each to Keith and Mike, and the other 98 had been in limbo ever since, despite the company changing out of all recognition in the meantime. Keith decided that the share capital should be increased from £100 to £1000 and that Mike, Bill and Ben deserved an equal share in the company. He arranged for each to be given 5% of the shares, leaving him with the remaining 85%.

"It was in our wives' names," Mike explains, "because in those days if you died as a result of doing something risky, there were tax implications for your surviving spouse. But it wasn't a long drawn-out thing, Keith just decided to do it. He said he would have preferred to give me 10% and the others 5% but decided against it because, if ever I wanted to leave, he wasn't sure the firm could find that sum of money. That was the last time he mentioned it."

At the time, the three recipients didn't pay much attention to the change, or to the percentages involved: the shares had cost them nothing and no one expected them to ever be worth much. But somehow the figure of ten per cent stuck in Keith's partners' minds.

Early in 1967, several landmarks came and went in quick succession. In January the second tranche of Ford money (£50,000) arrived, and in March the FVA took to the track in anger for the first time and performed spectacularly, Jochen Rindt winning an F2 race at Snetterton in a Brabham-Ford, with the next eight competitors all being FVA-powered. One month later, in April, Ford organised the official launch of the DFV in London, with two engines on show to the press at the company's Regent Street office. After that, it was time to install the first engine in a car: the Lotus 49.

With the FVA having performed so brilliantly, the public's expectations of the DFV were sky high. But its race performance would depend not just on the engine, but on the quality of its installation, and to optimise that you need a good test driver.

Jim Clark would have fitted the bill, but he was then living in Paris for tax reasons, and because Ford had wanted two top drivers in front of its new engine, the company persuaded Lotus to give the other seat to Graham Hill. This presented a problem, because in Mike's words "He was the last person we wanted for the first test drive. Graham Hill was a hopeless engineer. So Keith talked Colin into me driving the Lotus 49 with a DFV in it on its first testing, at the Lotus test track at Hethel." It seemed politic to choose a day when Graham was away at Indianapolis, and they got Lotus' racing manager, Dick Scammell, to share some of the driving.[6]

"Jim was a wonderful bloke. He wasn't one to sort out a car, but he would give you a very good idea of where the problems were; it was then up to us to find the solution. Quite unlike Graham, who would come in and tell you what you had to do to put it right." Was his analysis right?

"No. Never. Never ever! Graham was a wonderful bloke in so many other ways, but not with engineering."

Keith later observed that you could tell the difference between a Hill engine and a Clark engine on stripdown. Mike agrees. "The real problem of that era was that the speed limiter we had was virtually useless. So if you missed a gear, it wouldn't stop the engine over-revving. It was electronic but it worked by counting a time base for 10 explosions. By the time you'd done seven bangs too quickly, you were already way over the limit and the damage was done. And the person who was more likely to miss a gear was Graham. Much more than Jim, simply because Jim had got more time. Jim was never hurried."

The intention had been to run the F1 Lotus-Ford for the first time at Monaco, but as raceday loomed, it became clear that the package was not developed enough to compete. So the next Grand Prix, the Dutch GP at Zandvoort, became the stage on which the DFV made its debut.

Come practice in Holland, Graham had found time to do a bit of familiarisation with the new car between rushing back and forth to testing and qualification sessions at Indianapolis, but Clark had never even set eyes on it, and had to spend the first practice session getting to feel comfortable in the car and acclimatising himself to the engine's characteristics. These took some getting used to, because the power came in with a vengeance at 6500rpm, so being in the right gear at the right time was crucial.

The timing sheet at the end of Friday's first practice proved the point, for it was topped not by Clark and Hill but by Hulme in the Repco-Brabham and Rindt in the Cooper-Maserati – the Lotus' gear ratios did not suit the circuit.

This was remedied in time for second practice, which ended with Hill easily the fastest. Clark, however, was complaining about the handling and could manage no better than fourth.

Walter Hayes and Harley Copp had no intention of missing the DFV's debut, but deliberately wanted to keep a low profile, reasoning that there would be enough pressure in the Lotus pit without their presence adding to it. They travelled from England together on the Friday and stayed overnight with the managing director of Ford Holland, Ted Edwards.

On Friday evening, no problem could be found with Clark's suspension, but the cause was revealed during Saturday practice when a faulty ball joint broke, taking the hub carrier with it. New parts were fitted, but not in time for Clark to improve his Friday time, so he had to start the race from the third row. Hill was comfortably on pole, his only serious challenger being Dan Gurney in the Eagle, with its powerful but unreliable Weslake V12 engine.

Hill made an excellent start and was over a second ahead by the end of the first lap. By lap 10 he was dictating the pace, with Brabham and Rindt behind. Clark was now up to fourth and, fortunately for the Ford camp, the Eagle was out with a broken fuel metering unit.

On lap 11, however, Hill's car stopped out on the circuit with what was later diagnosed as timing gear failure. Fingers were very firmly crossed that Clark's engine, which unlike Hill's had not racked up many test miles, would hold together. It did: on lap 16 Clark took the lead and, despite almost giving everyone a heart-attack near the end, when he eased off as a precaution and spectators assumed he had a problem, Clark and the Lotus 49 crossed the line half a minute ahead of the opposition to take the chequered flag and notch up the DFV's first victory. His race average had been higher than the existing lap record.

The pits promptly exploded in scenes of enormous jubilation, not just in celebration of a historic win but also out of sheer relief. The build-up, the media attention and public expectation had been practically unbearable.

It was almost unheard of for a new Grand Prix engine to take pole and win at its first attempt, moreover by a large margin and setting a lap record along the way. Walter and Harley could scarcely believe the fairy tale that had unfolded before their eyes. To Walter, the Cosworth deal had seemed a PR man's dream: now he was actually living it, and that meant work – and lots of it. Knowing that there were press releases to write, interviews to arrange and advertisements to commission, the pair slipped quietly away long before the festivities ended and headed for Schipol airport and home, allowing themselves just a single celebratory beer en route.

Chapman, Clark, Duckworth and the rest of the team stayed and partied, long and hard – the heroes of the hour. For Keith, at that moment, it must have seemed he had the motorsport world at his feet, and that anything was possible. Accolades were heaped upon him, deservedly. He had created racing engines for FJ, F3, F2 (twice) and now F1, and every design had won on or shortly after its debut. And so far, every one had gone on to dominate its category. On the evening of 4 June 1967 at Zandvoort, no one was betting against the DFV doing exactly the same.

Footnotes

1 There is a very good description of this debacle in chapter 1 of *Such Sweet Thunder* by John Blunsden & David Phipps, published 1971 by Motor Racing Publications Ltd.

2 For those wanting more detail on the DFV's design, *Classic Racing Engines* by Karl Ludvigsen (2001, Haynes Publishing) is a good starting point. Another possibility is *The Ford Cosworth DFV*, by Andrew Noakes (2007, also by Haynes).

3 The price was calculated with every bit as much precision as the £100,000 development total for Ford; none of the directors actually knew what the engines cost to produce, so they pitched it at what they thought the market would bear, on the basis that if they couldn't produce it for £3000 they didn't deserve to be in business anyway.

4 *Racing & Sports Car Chassis Design*, by Michael Costin & David Phipps, (R Bentley, first published 1961).

5 Yorkshire dialect meaning to poke or pierce, but at Cosworth the standard term for hand-grinding ports.

6 In Ford's classic publicity film *Nine Days in Summer* (www.YouTube.com/watch?v=Ucau77iVndk), produced as a record of the 1967 season – and incidentally, featuring Keith's one and only appearance as an actor! – Graham is shown as having the first drive, but this was PR-man's licence.

Chapter 8

Two golden avenues; two dead ends

In the cold light of Northampton, after the euphoria of Zandvoort had died down, Hill's and Clark's engines were stripped and inspected. Immediately, it became apparent how a historic victory had very nearly become a DNF.

Hill's engine had failed because two teeth had broken off one of the camshaft drive gears. With a single tooth missing, drive is maintained and the engine will still run, but a gap of two teeth means no cam rotation and no power. When Clark's engine was stripped, it too had lost two teeth, but they were not adjacent – a tooth was still in place between the two. That single tooth represented the difference between success and failure – thank goodness Clark had the wisdom to back off during the closing laps!

A programme of material upgrades and design changes was promptly put in place, aimed at making the components better able to tolerate the torque being imposed on them. As race experience built up – particularly after the engine became available to other teams – a steady trickle of DFVs with broken valve trains started arriving back at Northampton. Stripped gears were not the only problem: the torsional vibration in the valve train also shattered camshafts, sometimes into as many as six pieces.

Despite the priority given to this programme, and many, many hours of midnight oil, it took several years, plus a stroke of genius at the end of the process, to conquer the problem completely.

Vacuum-remelted material for the gears, along with tighter tolerances and better heat treatment (Keith concluded that Hewlands were the only people who really understood gear manufacture), a change from cast iron to machined steel camshafts, a less aggressive cam profile that reduced the loads on the valve train, and a complete redesign of the gear pins and timing covers, so the pins were no longer cantilevered but supported at both ends – these things all reduced the problem, but did not eliminate it. Each variant would last a little longer than its predecessor, but would generate a new failure somewhere else. To an extent, the changes were merely transferring the problem from one component to another. By 1970 Keith was running out of ideas and was even considering abandoning the engine.

On the DFV, drive to the valves is taken initially by the primary gear on the end of the crankshaft, then to the first compound gear and thence to the second compound gear. The latter is a stack of three gears: a larger central gear receives the drive and is sandwiched between two smaller ones front and back, which take the drive to the left and right camshaft pairs respectively. As a last throw of the dice, Keith told one of his young development engineers, Martin Walters, to set up load cells on the second compound gear to measure the extent of the torque being transmitted through the valve train.

Martin is a man of few words but great determination, and loves engineering mathematics so much that he has been known to analyse problems purely out of curiosity – 'recreational mathematics' is what he calls it. He joined the company in 1968 and Keith quickly formed a deep respect for him, once remarking to Mike that "Martin has a better brain than me!" – a rare accolade indeed. He left Cosworth in 1972 to join the March F1 team, but in August 1978 Keith persuaded him to return as chief development engineer. He went on to become, in Mike's words, "... a vital part of Cosworth."

In 1970 in the development shop, he was being assisted by another recent recruit, Malcolm Tyrrell, who takes up the story.

"We fitted a proximity device to find out the deflection and loads on the second compound gear. I did all the testing with Martin and when he showed Keith the results, Keith said 'That's bollocks! You've done something wrong, there's no way loads in the geartrain could be that high!' The loads were greater than the torque coming out the back of the engine! So Keith decided to get involved in the calibration of the equipment. He checked all the static deflections against the readouts. Everything seemed to be in order, so we ran the test again, with very similar results."

Finally, Keith had an understanding of the magnitude of the problem, and its distribution. It was no secret that flat-crank V8s like the DFV produced torsional vibrations which tended to generate cyclic variations in the geartrain – or as Keith would have put it, "rattle the cams back and forth." But Keith had never realised the enormity of these forces, or how they would all meet at the second compound, giving rise to colossal loads which, in Malcolm's words "... just plucked teeth off the gears."

Keith went home to think: there had to be a solution somewhere. After all, one of his favourite Duckworthisms was:

IN ENGINEERING THERE IS AN ANSWER TO EVERYTHING; IT'S JUST THAT WE'RE FREQUENTLY TOO IGNORANT, OR TOO DIM, TO SEE IT.

Clearly, some form of cushioning was needed. At first he considered introducing rubber into the valvetrain, but he quickly concluded that it would never cope with the stresses involved. Instead he came up with an inspired piece of engineering which many believe to be his biggest single contribution to engine design – the second-compound quill device.

In Keith's own words "In the end I decided that [cushioning] could best be provided by mounting the second compound gears on a hub incorporating 12 tiny quill shafts, the reasoning being that with the twisting of this multiple quill we could store a certain amount of energy, and that if loads were as low as I hoped they would be, then it would survive."[1]

As Malcolm explains "That quilled drive gave the outers 1-1.5° of compliance and isolated them from the vibration. It transformed the DFV. Before it, we had huge problems, afterwards all we had were valve spring issues. Many multi-cylinder racing engines now use something similar. It worked right from the off, the only problem was an indication of some slight radial movement on the centre gear, which initially was merely an interference fit on the centre hub."

That problem was solved by drilling radial holes in the gear and using soft-iron slugs to anchor it to the shaft, rather then relying solely on the interference fit. George Duckett, who built the first quills, made this mod by hand, cutting the ends off soft-iron rivets and hitting them to expand them into their holes.

"Other than this belt-and-braces mod to stop any micro movement, it was right first time," says Malcolm. "Fantastic. It's one thing to design something with a clean sheet of paper, and quite another for Keith to come up with this when there was no room to spare. It didn't require a new front cover, it didn't need significant changes to the block casting, it just fitted. Really, really clever packaging. And not hugely expensive. This mod was fitted in 1971; the engine had four years or so without the quills, but the signs were very much there – it was strength of numbers which had helped the DFV to so many victories. If that problem hadn't been solved, eventually team owners would have gone to other engines. And where would that have left Cosworth?"

If this Duckworthism had to be applied to just one innovation, the second compound quill device was it:

THE ONLY SUBSTITUTE FOR MONEY IS GENIUS – IF YOU CAN MAKE YOUR STEPS BY THINKING ABOUT THEM, RATHER THAN BY TRIAL AND ERROR, THE END RESULT IS THE SAME, AND IN GENERAL IT COSTS LESS. A GENIUS CAN MAKE, FOR A PENNY, WHAT A GOOD ENGINEER CAN ONLY MAKE FOR 10P.

The DFV's other valve train issue was a tendency to break its double valve springs due to valve surge and, sometimes, to drop valves as a consequence. The original items, from the BSA Gold Star motorcycle, had an unacceptably short life and the company turned to German supplier Schmitthelm instead. Design engineer Geoff Goddard recalls: "When I joined Cosworth in 1971 we were having valve spring problems and I built a quick rig, put a load cell underneath it and found out that all the maths to do with what happens to a spring were wrong." He sent a copy of his rig to Schmitthelm's works at Heidelberg for the engineers there to check his findings, and between them they tried a series of designs, the object being to damp out the surge which, unchecked, would eventually break the spring.

Malcolm Tyrrell recalls "We went through lots of variations, some non-interference, some with interference rings to damp out surge – that gave scuffing, which led to surface treatments to minimise scuffing – all kinds of things were tried." The problem was never totally solved so that the springs could be relied upon to last the life of the engine, but it was brought under control, as Geoff Goddard explains.

"We got to the stage where teams could run a whole season with no valve spring failures, providing they rebuilt the heads at the specified intervals. And we were okay with springs right up to 15,000rpm."[2]

The third major development issue on the DFV was crankcase breathing. The external oil pipes hastily added to the early engines to vent crankcase to cam carrier did the job, but only after a fashion, and they looked what they were – makeshift.

There is a good description of the development of the breathing system in John Blunsden's books,[3] but basically it went through four further phases. The vent pipes were replaced by a vane-type air pump, but although this took air to the top of the engine, it carried too much oil along with it. So next its output was directed to the oil tank, so the engine effectively had two scavenge pumps and was running at a depression, with air now entering through what had been a breather. This was almost too successful: the oil tank became overwhelmed by air-oil mix and lots of oil was blown out of the tank breather as a result, sometimes enough to cause bearing failure, though the problem varied between teams as tank location and design were their responsibility.

To separate the air and oil, Keith designed a centrifugal separator for the output of the air pump, incorporating a clutch on its drive end to allow it to slip if the pump ever started to pump neat oil or if the vanes jammed. It worked on test, but the assembly showed up the air pump's limitations, so Alastair Lyle to designed a Roots-type pump to replace it. Alastair started work on this towards the end of 1969 and "... it took me well into 1970, as lots of different rotor shapes were considered and the assembly jigs and rotor cutting tools had to be designed as well."

Initially it seemed as though this new pump made things worse, as Malcolm Tyrrell explains. "We built three engines, dynoed the first one and suddenly we got oil venting, the very thing that this package was designed to eliminate.

"I can remember early 1970, an engine in each of our three test beds, Keith in cell number three on his haunches, trying to see what was going on and looking up at us – me, my development boss John Given and a couple of others – and saying 'If any of you guys have got a bright idea, [of] what we've done wrong and how we can fix it, for God's sake say something.' He was pretty down, completely baffled. However, in Keith's normal fashion, he went away, had a think about it for a while and came back saying 'Right, we're going to put some manometers on it.' In those days he was highly distrustful of mechanical or electronic pressure measurement ... with a manometer there is less to go wrong.

"We put tappings on and ran the engine. It was very obvious that the inlet of this new Roots scavenge pump was generating loads of depression, but it wasn't getting to the crankcase or the heads – there was a restriction. We found that where the scavenge pump connected in the lower crankcase, there were two channels that were limiting the amount of oil that could reach the pump. The original crankcase design had pan scrubbers to help separate oil from air, these themselves were a restriction and were removed, but adequate scavenging wasn't achieved until we opened up the feed.

"And hey presto! – the engine breathed properly. We went back and modified all that season's engines: McLaren, Lotus, Tyrrell had been sitting there with their 1971 cars waiting to go testing and they had no engines. Then we modified the drawings, to apply the mod to all subsequent blocks."

This configuration worked well and has since been echoed on a number of high-performance engines. Conceptually, it remained unchanged for the life of the DFV, though it was steadily improved to cope with increasing power outputs, blow-by and – with the advent of ground effect – cornering forces.

With three major development issues to be tackled, plus a host of work on fuel systems, electrical systems, piston design, crankshaft lubrication and more, all of which kept Keith busy for several years after the DFV's triumphant 1967 introduction, it might appear that the DFV was a troublesome engine. Certainly it was not bulletproof, but no racing engine of that era was.

Moreover, the teams who used it knew that problems would not be fudged or ignored. No other race engine supplier could match the sustained development thrust of Cosworth, or offer the same consistency of construction, thanks to Ben Rood's mastery of production techniques and equipment. Some of the very first installations of computer-controlled machine tools were made at Cosworth (the firm's first NC machine was a Cincinatti Cintamatic controlled by "... several reels of paper tape," in the words of John Dickens), production efficiency being aided by the company's policy of never preparing 'special' engines for one team (no matter how much their arm was twisted – and it was, regularly and vigorously). So all the teams had the reassurance of knowing that they were operating on a level playing field as far as powerplants were concerned. Everyone could be sure of 400bhp. Actually, 420bhp minimum by 1969, when the rev limit was raised by 500rpm to 10,000rpm.

Such was the DFV's power advantage that for the first four or five years of its life, it was the default choice for any team wanting to win. This provided an invaluable window for Cosworth, enabling the company to concentrate its development effort on improving reliability. By the time rivals' outputs had caught up and it became necessary to extract more power from the unit, Keith and his colleagues had a very solid platform to work from. This in turn helped the engine remain competitive. Add these advantages to an affordable price – £7500 initially, falling to £6500 before rising to £7150 by July 1973 – and it's easy to see why the Northampton product was such a popular choice.

The company's level of commitment paid dividends extremely quickly. The DFV achieved four victories in 1967, despite being exclusively reserved for Lotus' use that year, and the following year it won 11 of the 12 rounds, having also found its way into the back of McLarens, Ken Tyrrell's Matras, and the Lotus of privateer Rob Walker. Brabham joined the throng in 1969, when the DFV managed a clean sweep of all 11 races, taking Matra-mounted Jackie Stewart to his first world title. 1970 brought seven wins, 1971 a further eight.

By September 1972 Northampton's finest had taken its ninth win of the season in the hands of Stewart at Mosport, and Ford was taking out advertisements congratulating Keith on his engine's 50th win. Ford organised a half-century party to celebrate, and presented DKD with a memento, a splendid miniature 24cm-high drawing board, silver-plated and complete with movable set square. On the drawing surface was an engraving of the DFV, on the base a list of its 50 wins. And the victories kept on coming: when Ferrari won the World Championship in 1975 it was the first time since 1967 that an engine without Ford on the cam cover had powered the winning car.

The miniature drawing board was not Ford's first thank-you to Keith. After the victorious 1967 season, Ford commissioned a run of eight $\frac{1}{12}$-scale model Lotus 49s from fastidious model-maker Henri Baigent, each at a cost of several thousand pounds. One was given to Keith, one to Colin Chapman, and one each to drivers Clark and Hill, the other four being retained for Ford's own purposes.

That same year Keith received the Ferodo Gold Trophy, an annual award for the most outstanding contribution to motor racing, from HRH the Duke of Kent. The citation said it was for 'the design and development of the racing engines used in Formula 1

Lotus-Fords, and those which have achieved complete supremacy in Formula 2 racing.' Perhaps, as he stood there ready to receive his award, the star of the evening at a fancy London venue, the Dorchester, he reflected how times had changed in the 12 years since he was refused entry to Claridges on account of the state of his Austin Ruby.

Two years later, in 1969, he was back in central London to be honoured again, this time at the RAC headquarters in Pall Mall to receive the RAC's Dewar Challenge Trophy, which is awarded for outstanding British technical achievement in the automotive industry. Specifically, it was for the DFV, '... which has retained the supremacy of British engineering in Grand Prix racing.' Mike and Rhoda, Bill and Irene, and Ben and Jane, joined Keith and Ursula for the evening, Rhoda wearing a very nice dress-over-trousers, a fashionable ensemble at the time. But, says Bill, "... she was told that ladies in trousers were not allowed to cross the hallowed portals of the Royal Automobile Club. She promptly went back to their car, removed the trousers, and on re-presenting herself at the door was allowed in without demur!"

It's a measure of the rapidity with which the DFV transformed F1 that as early as 1969, questions were being raised as to whether such total domination was healthy for the sport. *The Autocar* of 30 October that year, for example, printed an article called *Crisis in Formula 1* with the subtitle *Does Ford domination provide a threat to the future?* Even Ford had misgivings; spectators are always turned off by predictable racing and the last thing the company wanted was fewer people taking an interest in its sporting activities. Ford engines winning lots of races was great; Ford engines winning all of them was not.

In the event, Ford would experience its share of failure in the late 1960s and early '70s, not in F1 but in endurance racing, where the DFV was markedly less successful. Although DKD once quipped that winning Le Mans must be easy, as "Someone does it every year,"[4] he knew that the vibrations inherent in a flat-crank V8 would do nothing for the DFV's long-distance reliability, and the engine's first non-F1 application, in the Len Bailey-designed P68 (also known as the Ford 3L GT or F3L), never finished a race. Sponsored by Ford Europe and built by Alan Mann Racing, it was developed for 1969 into an open car – the P69 – but this too was unsuccessful, as it relied on free-standing aerofoil wings for stability, and these were banned early in the season for safety reasons.

The first sports car application to meet with any success was the Ligier JS3, a one-off developed by Guy Ligier and driven by him and Patrick Depailler at the 1971 Le Mans. Ligier was no stranger to Cosworth products – in 1970 he had tasted sports car racing success with his FVA-engined JS1 coupé – so it was no surprise that the following year he set his sights higher and created the DFV-engined JS3, solely for one purpose: to win les vingt-quatre heurs du Mans.

The JS3 won at Montlhéry, qualified 17th for Le Mans and was lying fifth when the gearbox failed after 18 hours. A frantic gearbox rebuild ensued, but by the end the car had not covered enough distance to qualify as a finisher.

Despite never being designed for endurance racing, things did improve for the DFV, particularly at Le Mans, where it won twice, first in 1975 in the back of Jacky Ickx and Derek Bell's Mirage, and again five years later, when Jean Rondeau and Jean-Pierre Jaussaud surprised everyone by taking top spot in their Rondeau. Also noteworthy was the 1976 race, where the DFV powered four of the top ten: Mirages came home second and fifth (Jean-Louis Lafosse/François Migault and Derek Bell/Vern Schuppan

 Continued on p105

Keith Duckworth, Mike Costin and a youthful John Dickens preparing the FVB for testing in Cosworth's Brabham BT10, on the outside of Silverstone's Abbey Curve in 1966. *(Courtesy Ford Motor Co)*

Keith in the back garden of 78 Larkhall Lane around 1967, with five year-old Trish and two year-old Roger. Em can be seen in the window of the dining room, where the FVA and DFV were designed.

The Guards 100 at Snetterton in 1967: Robin Widdows in his FVA-engined Brabham Cosworth leads Jochen Rindt's similarly-powered Lotus. *(Courtesy Ford Motor Co)*

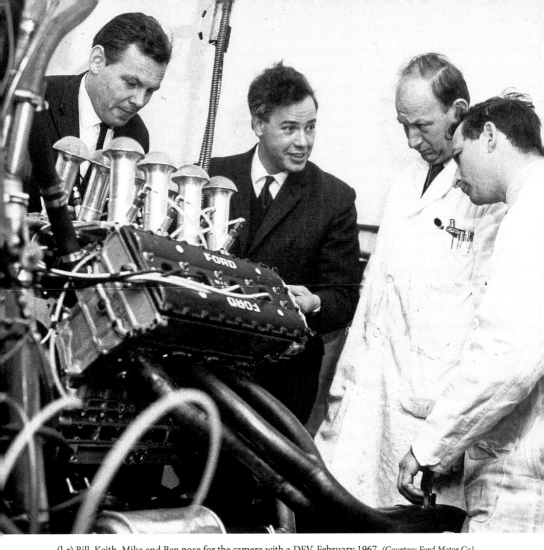

(l-r) Bill, Keith, Mike and Ben pose for the camera with a DFV, February 1967. *(Courtesy Ford Motor Co)*

Keith in the test cells with a DFV, identifiably 1967 because of Lucas Competition HT leads, unsleeved Tecalamit injection lines, front cover and inlet manifold slide cover plates in aluminium rather than magnesium, and long inlet trumpets (used on early engines to boost torque). Note non-fire-resistant plastic fuel feed! *(Courtesy Ford Motor Co)*

An original piston from 701, now serving as an ashtray in George Duckett's house. *(Courtesy Norman Burr)*

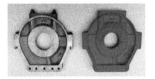

Attention to detail in the DFV: Concerned about the potential for main-bearing shells to loosen and scuff due to differential expansion, Keith suggested Vandervell use a thicker than normal steel backing that would withstand the hoop stress at room temperature, yet still provide an interference fit at operating temperatures. These test pieces were cast and machined to facilitate tests of nip and diameter at various temperatures. *(Courtesy Malcolm Tyrrell/Cosworth Enginering)*

Keith checks an early installation of the DFV in the Lotus 49. *(Courtesy Ford Motor Co)*

Mike Hall played a vital role in the design of the DFV. *(Courtesy BusinessF1 Magazine)*

Top view of 701, showing how the fuel and ignition systems fit in the vee. The photographer's foot can just be seen! *(Courtesy Ford Motor Co)*

Ford was fiercely proud of its association with
Cosworth: after the DFV's 50th win in 1972, it
organised a celebration where Henry Ford II
presented a miniature drawing board to Keith, and
(right) placed this ad in the press. *(Courtesy Ford
Motor Co)*

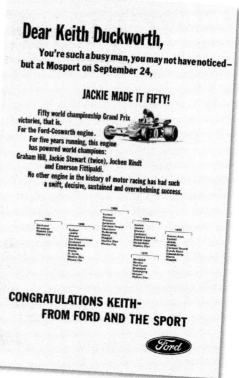

Dear Keith Duckworth,

You're such a busy man, you may not have noticed –
but at Mosport on September 24,

JACKIE MADE IT FIFTY!

Fifty world championship Grand Prix
victories, that is.
For the Ford-Cosworth engine.
For five years running, this engine
has powered world champions:
Graham Hill, Jackie Stewart (twice), Jochen Rindt
and Emerson Fittipaldi.
No other engine in the history of motor racing has had such
a swift, decisive, sustained and overwhelming success.

**CONGRATULATIONS KEITH –
FROM FORD AND THE SPORT**

Receiving the Ferodo Trophy in 1967.
(Courtesy PA Studios)

Ligier's JS3 was the first DFV-engined sports car to
meet with any success. In between pitlane duties
Cosworth's John Dickens took this snap of it at
Le Mans in 1971. *(Courtesy John Dickens)*

Ford's ill-fated DFV-engined P68, shown here in
the pits at the 1968 Nürburgring 1000km; this
example failed during the race, and the other was
totalled in practice. *(Courtesy Ford Motor Co)*

A typical broken gear from a DFV valve train, in this
case a DA0126 secondary camshaft transfer gear of
1970 vintage, using ground teeth, made of En39B
and heat-treated by Hewland. The quill drive that
cured the problem is illustrated on p276. *(Courtesy
John Dickens / Cosworth Engineering)*

Hannu Mikkola in his BDA-powered Escort
storming to victory in the 1978 Scottish Rally.
(Courtesy Ford Motor Co)

The evergreen BDA at its launch in 1969.
(Courtesy Ford Motor Co)

The DFV's finest hour in endurance racing was a 1-2-3 at Le Mans 1975. Here, the Ligier JS2 of Jean-Louis
Lafosse/Guy Chasseuil is about to take second from Jean-Pierre Jaussaud/Vern Schuppan, who went on
to hold third place in their Mirage GR8. Overall winners were Derek Bell/Jacky Ickx in another GR8.
(Courtesy Ford Motor Co)

Keith (right) with Jim Clark; Cosworth's driver of choice never got to see the car that was designed for him. *(Courtesy Ford Motor Co)*

With Robin Herd during the design stage of the 4WD car. *(Courtesy BusinessF1 Magazine)*

Two views of the Cosworth 4WD car in its original (March 1969) form, with prominent oil radiator and no wing. *(Courtesy John Dickens/ Cosworth Engineering)*

In the early '70s, after gathering dust for a while, the CA was offered to legendary hillclimber Roy Lane. Here, he tests the car at Silverstone before – wary of the complications of its bespoke transmission – rejecting it as "Too fragile." By this stage, the car had sprouted a rear wing and the oil radiator had been relocated. *(Courtesy Roy Lane collection)*

Four photos relating to the EAA and the Cosworth Vega. A 1975 example beautifully restored by Clark Kirby, and with aftermarket chin and hatch spoilers (bottom). Upper left: Ken Rock's rebuilt motor ready to be installed. Far left: Standard Cosworth Vega block during rebuild, shown with aftermarket steel sleeves fitted. Compare this with the rare heavy-duty block developed by GM, with three vertical stiffening ribs (left). *(Bottom image courtesy Clark Kirby; others courtesy Mark Rock, CVOA)*

respectively), the De Cadenet Lola T380 of Alain de Cadenet/Chris Craft was third (a remarkable result for a privateer) and the Inaltera LM of Jean-Pierre Beltoise/Henri Pescarolo finished eighth.

With so many engines out in the field, service requirements grew and grew, but as Bill Brown explains "The whole DFV operation was strictly even-handed. The engine block carried the same number from the moment its machining was finished and this number was often assigned to a customer before the engine was built; number and engine then remained the property of that customer so long as he used it. We aimed for each competing car to have three engines, one in the car, one spare, and one back at the factory being rebuilt."

As early as 1969 the volume of repairs and rebuilds coming into Northampton was becoming unmanageable at busy times. "We were really struggling to keep up with the demand," says Bill. "I was operating a strict queueing policy of 'first come, first served,' so after each GP where it was possible to drive back to Northampton, the teams' transporters were quickly loaded and they literally raced each other to the factory, sometimes arriving long before it opened on Monday morning. The engines were then rebuilt in the order they had arrived in their Transporter Grand Prix."

Mike and Keith had always intended to keep such work in-house to retain control of the job and hence of the company's reputation, but Cosworth became a victim of its own success. With considerable reluctance, they decided to encourage satellite organisations to set up as authorised service agencies – not to take all the work, but to cope with the excess. Obviously they wanted people with ability and initiative in these companies, but not too much initiative. Malcolm Tyrrell, who became responsible for technical liaison with outside service agencies, understood his management's thinking very well.

"It was almost as if they preferred people who'd never built an engine before! They didn't want people coming in who would bring their own nuances and ideas to the job, it was difficult enough controlling an engine as it was ... They wanted the engine build exactly the same, time after time after time. Otherwise, somebody could say 'I don't think we should be doing conrod bolts up that tight ...' and that could take you off down a blind alley investigating a spate of rod bolt failures, when all the time it was down to someone doing something different."

In an attempt to retain control of the rebuild process, the first satellite was actually set up as a partnership between the four Cosworth directors and John Dunn. Called Swindon Racing Engines (SRE), it now trades as Swindon Engines, and was founded in 1971. Initially it only handled FVAs, the DFV was added later.

With the workload continuing to grow, it wasn't long before SRE couldn't cope either. Other companies were authorised to join in, including Nicholson McLaren, John Judd's Engine Developments company, Hesketh, Ken Horton's Euro Racing Engines, and Langford & Peck. By 1972 the outside service network totalled six UK firms, plus Heini Mader in Switzerland. In addition, Brian Hart Racing was involved, though mainly with four-cylinder units.

The workload involved in developing the DFV meant that Keith's role in Cosworth's other major project of the late 1960s, the BDA engine, was more that of overseer than designer. The latter role went to Mike Hall, who, in 1967, was given a straightforward brief: design Ford a new 1600cc high-performance engine for road, rally and circuit use. It was to be based on the latest crossflow variant of the trusty Cortina block and would replace the twin-cam, which was now five years old.

Naturally, Mike Hall's starting point was the FVA, Cosworth's highly successful F2 engine, but although the BDA was conceived as a productionised FVA, when Mike settled down to design it he realised that in practice there could be few, if any, common parts. For a start, the blocks were different: the FVA used the 1500 casting, whereas the BDA was based on the crossflow 1600 with its less racy bore-stroke ratio. Additionally, the engine was designed for carburettors instead of fuel-injection, and the valvetrain was completely redesigned around toothed-belts – hence the name (Belt-Drive, series A). Noise was a major reason for the change to belts, which were new technology at the time, hitherto only used by Glas and Fiat, but they proved light and efficient – witness the power output of an experimental fuel-injected BDA that Cosworth constructed. It gave 238bhp on the dyno, as good as the best 1.6-litre FVA.

For test purposes, early examples of the BDA were fitted to MkII Cortina Twin-Cams, and a handful found their way into Capris (Ursula Duckworth had one), but the new unit didn't really find a niche until Keith met Ford's competition manager, Stuart Turner, at the home of journalist Graham Robson.

"I first met Keith when Graham invited me to have dinner at his house in Warwickshire, and we just got on." The three of them talked motorsport all night and by the end of the evening a plan was hatched to put the BDA into the Escort in 1970 and go rallying in it. The Escort RS1600 was born.

From that point on, Stuart's career brought him into regular contact with Keith and the pair developed a firm friendship. "I started off as competitions manager at Boreham, my first big event was the London-Mexico World Cup Rally in 1970. Then I was made head of the Advanced Vehicle Operations until that had to be closed, then I had a spell at public affairs before coming back as director of Ford Europe motorsport; I retired in 1990.

"I've always collected characters – I think life is bloody boring if you haven't got characters – and if you had to draw up a list of the hundred best characters in the world, then Mr Duckworth would be firmly in my top ten."

Not long before he met Stuart, Keith had acquired his own helicopter. "The first time he flew into Ford in it, he landed at Dunton and, being Ford, they had to have fire crews on hand with brass helmets and things. And you could see this grinning man lapping up all this nonsense, waving hello at the firemen as he walked across the apron!

"I think one reason why we got on is that I'm a total technical ignoramus – I have zero interest in technology or engineering – I couldn't explain to a five year-old how a car works. I was always prepared to play devil's advocate with Keith because he wanted people to spark it up. I could never challenge him on anything technical, but I did tell him he was talking a load of nonsense on other subjects, and I never allowed him to come on too strong – we both took the mickey out of each other."

Effectively, that evening with Graham Robson represents the beginning of the Escort's legendary rally career, a career so successful that over 40 years later the car is still the vehicle of choice for any historic rally enthusiast wanting a competitive mount that is easy to exploit, easy to maintain and offers almost unparalleled spares backup. There is no space here to chronicle the Escort's victories, but there is no doubt that the potent RS1600 got the Escort off to a flying start from which it never looked back.

Much the same could be said of the RS1600's effect on the engine itself. Just as with the twin-cam, tuners were quick to see the engine's potential, and before long many derivatives were on offer, some of which had no connection with Cosworth at all. Ford was quite relaxed about this proliferation – it was, after all, excellent free publicity.

There was never any intention that Cosworth would manufacture the BDA in quantity. The job was basically a design contract, with the first batch of engines being built for Ford by Harpers in Stevenage, who had earlier been involved with Vincent motorcycles. But as with the twin-cam, the project soon acquired a seemingly unstoppable momentum. Though volume production of the standard version was always done elsewhere, demand from many different sectors of motorsport in many countries kept Cosworth busy making seemingly endless competition variants for well over a decade, mostly as kits. The last versions were the BDP (schemed by Alastair Lyle in 1979 but not produced until 1984, methanol fuel-injected and intended for American Midget racing) and the BDR (1986, kits for Caterham to fit in the HPC version of its Seven).

The BDP is significant not just because it represented Cosworth's last throw of the BD's technical dice but also because it is the only Cosworth BD unit designed around an alloy block. It was not, however, the first alloy BD, for Brian Hart's company had taken that step much earlier, in the early 1970s. Wanting to develop the BD into a 2-litre race unit, he designed a new alloy block with siamesed bores. To maximise bore size and save weight, the engine had no cylinder liners, the alloy cylinder walls being specially hardened instead – a well-established process today, but quite new at the time.

Hart's block design was quickly adopted by Ford and other tuners, and formed the basis for the later RS1600s and the RS1800, but Keith, who had strong views about siamesed cylinder bores because of their adverse effect on block strength, was not persuaded to follow suit until over a decade later.

This reluctance to push the BD envelope typifies Keith's attitude to the BD series, which Mike Hall reckons never particularly interested him. The BD was Mike Hall's baby, just as the DFV was Keith's, and its relevance to this biography lies not in Keith's input to it, which was small, but in its significance to his company, which was huge. Cosworth made a great deal of money from the BD series for many years. Indeed, it is fair to say that the BD and DFV together were the financial bedrock of the firm throughout the 1970s.

By 1972 Cosworth's workforce was into three figures and the company was continuing to expand rapidly. Mike and Keith had never wanted it to be like this: they had gone where Keith's designs had taken them, seized opportunities as they arose, and this was the result. There was no master plan, no grand strategy, nor would there be. Neither of them ever expected their two principal series of engines to sell in such volumes and to remain competitive for decades – if they had, they would certainly have productionised the BD and DFV much sooner and more comprehensively.

Having chronicled two very successful series of engines, we must now introduce the first failure of Keith's design career – the project to build an all-Cosworth four-wheel drive (4WD) F1 car. To the public, the project never had a name, but at Northampton it was called the CA (This title arose from the drawing office lettering system adopted around this time and explained in the Appendix).

The idea of a 4WD F1 car was not new. It was pioneered by the front-engined Ferguson P99 Climax, built in 1961 by tractor magnate Harry Ferguson to showcase his transmission systems, and that car had a respectable racing career, winning a non-championship race in the hands of Stirling Moss (he rated it his favourite F1 mount) and achieving a couple of good placings in the hands of Graham Hill. It finished its career in style in the hands of Peter Westbury, who took it to victory in the British Hillclimb Championship of 1964.

That same year, BRM mated a similar Ferguson transmission to its own 1.5-litre engine to produce the mid-engined P67. It proved slow, and BRM lost interest in the idea (though the H16 was laid out with provision for a second driveshaft, just in case). The apprentice who constructed it, Mike Pilbeam, then acquired the P67 and, just as with the P99, developed it with great success as a hillclimb machine, taking the British championship in 1968 and beginning Pilbeam's long association with hillclimb single-seaters, which continues to this day.

Because the DFV was so much more powerful than earlier engines, it opened up a mismatch between power output and the ability of tyres and aerodynamics to transmit it to the tarmac (especially wet tarmac). As a result, in the late 1960s designers started revisiting the idea of 4WD, hence this Duckworthism:

THE IMPORTANT THING WITH RACING CARS IS TO MAKE MAXIMUM UTILISATION OF RUBBER.

He was not the only designer thinking this way – the Lotus 63, Matra MS84 and McLaren M9A all appeared in 1969, as did the Cosworth – but the Northampton chassis was the first to be laid down early in 1968, and the announcement of the project in 1967 probably encouraged other manufacturers to try their own 4WD designs. Such had been the impact of Cosworth's engines that, by 1967, the motorsport press afforded Keith almost godlike status, assuming that anything he touched would not only win but would probably completely change the rules of the game. Keith never encouraged this hype, though he certainly enjoyed having his efforts recognised and appreciated.

There was intense speculation in the press even before construction began, some claiming the Cosworth car was being designed at Ford's behest, others (like the well-informed Eoin Young, in his *Straight from the Grid* column in *The Autocar* of 19 October 1967) more dubious. The truth was much more ordinary. Although various people had expressed an interest in backing the project, all offers had been turned down: the car was a purely Cosworth affair, an experimental one-off. There was no suggestion of a Cosworth racing team, and Walter Hayes was merely an interested bystander.

The project was conceived in July 1967, just a few weeks after the DFV's Dutch debut, when Jim Clark, disappointed with what he saw as the fragility of Lotus designs, got talking to Keith about the problem. Out of the conversation came the idea of Cosworth building its own car, and Clark driving it for the 1969 season.

Keith, his confidence buoyed by the Zandvoort result, was not in the least fazed by the fact that he had never designed any kind of car before. After all, he told himself, he and Mike had always promised themselves they'd build a racing car. Back then, they'd planned to create an FJ contender, but there had never been time and FJ was long dead. So why not aim at the very top?

Excited as he was by the idea, with troubleshooting on the DFV still occupying much of his time, Keith realised there was no way it could become a reality if it relied totally on him. So that October, at the US GP in Watkins Glen, he and Clark jointly approached Robin Herd, chief designer at McLaren, who was rumoured to be less than happy with his current position. His M7A had won three GPs that year. Would he like to design a 4WD racing car?

The answer was yes, and Robin joined Cosworth that December, bringing McLaren colleague John Thompson with him to help with the chassis build. Cosworth engine builders Keith Leighton and Ray Buckley joined the team to look after the mechanical aspects, while Alastair Lyle and Mike Hall helped with the bespoke transmission, which remained Keith's responsibility. Unlike other 4WD designs, it used no Ferguson components, and every week Keith would come in and look at the scheme while waving his hands in circles to ensure that all four wheels would rotate in the correct direction – it was a complex transmission!

Like as not, he would then wander into the fabrication shop to see how the chassis was progressing. Occasionally, Keith Leighton recalls, the CA wasn't the only car being progressed. "One day John Thompson and I were very busy fabricating some parts for Frank Williams' first F1 car![5] Keith walks in, and there I am holding this crossbeam that the Hewland gearbox bolts to. Keith takes hold of it to have a look, so I said 'It's amazing how the TIG welder works, would you like to try it?' So I'm teaching Keith how to TIG weld – I'd only just learned myself – it was a good way of deflecting a very embarrassing situation. Frank's Brabham BT26 was fabricated at Cosworth – Piers Courage took it to second at Monaco first time out!" Did Keith cotton on but decide to turn a blind eye? It seems highly likely.

Even without the odd 'foreigner' adding to the bill, the CA represented a considerable commitment for Cosworth in personnel alone, and Bill Brown questioned the wisdom of building a car at all. "I'd always been firmly of the opinion that there are very few people who can do anything properly and, as we'd proved that we could make racing engines properly, we should stick to that and not dilute our talents."

He had a point, because the final cost of the CA was officially £30,000 – Bill reckons it was actually far more. Whatever the figure, it was certainly a lot of money for a one-off, but Keith was determined. The company was making very good money selling engines and this was something he and Mike had always wanted to do.

In public, Bill was supportive, telling journalist John Lovesey that "It just seemed a logical progression, we'd reached the top in engines, and Keith's always been interested in transmission." In the same interview Lovesey asked why Cosworth had turned down interested backers and Bill replied, with unintended prescience, that "... we'd like to be able to scrap it if we feel like it."

Drivers were not immune to the hype surrounding the Cosworth car and some started fancying themselves in the hot seat. Keith's sister-in-law Betty remembers him discussing drivers in 1967, when he flew up to Blackburn in his newly acquired helicopter for a family visit.

"He told me he'd received a letter from Graham Hill offering to drive the new car," she recalls. "It said 'I left Lotus to drive and you took my place in the factory; if you're looking for a driver, I'll drive for you.' And he sent an open cheque! Keith said 'No way, we're having Jim Clark.'"

Sadly, Keith did not get Jim Clark. Shortly afterwards, in April 1968, Clark was killed at Hockenheim in an F2 race, driving an FVA-engined Lotus. He was destined never to set eyes on the car being designed for him.

By the time of Clark's death, Keith had known him for several years, and the two had become close friends. Clark's untimely demise was deeply upsetting to Keith: with its driver dead, the 4WD project seemed in his eyes to have lost much of its urgency and some of its relevance. Robin, however, persevered and became the driving force behind the car.

He told Graham Robson "The problem was that it was always a very technically elegant piece of design, and Keith came to love it for its own sake. Once Jim had been killed, somehow it became more of a design exercise than a serious race project. After about a year, by the end of 1968, I sensed that Keith had begun to lose interest, and the building of the car went into the back shed."[6] (*Cosworth*, p133)

Nevertheless, the CA was completed, and in March 1969 Mike Costin sat behind the wheel for the first drive.

Built around a relatively conventional aluminium monocoque, the car looked good – a neat and distinctive shape with what promised to be very tidy aerodynamics. Moreover, aided by the adoption of a magnesium engine, the weight was close to the minimum permitted. Since the CA's conception in 1967, F1 cars had sprouted wings for the first time, but this 4WD was deliberately unadorned – if the transmission worked as they hoped, the new car wouldn't need them.

As Mike commenced testing, two problems manifested themselves: one proving easy to deal with, the other intractable. The engine – a DFV but with block and heads made from magnesium – was mounted with its cam drives to the rear, 180° from its normal position, and for balance reasons it was decided that its oil tank should be positioned right behind the driver. This brought a whole new meaning to the term 'heated seat,' and the tank was quickly moved back behind the engine.

Much more problematic was the transmission, which used standard Hewland gears but in Cosworth-designed housings with dry sump lubrication. Drive was taken from a forward-facing clutch to a central differential on the right-hand side of the cockpit, so the driving position was slightly offset. Shafts from the centre diff ran fore and aft to the front and rear limited-slip diffs respectively, the latter via a transfer box at the back of the engine. Torque split was 40/60 front/rear, though other ratios were considered. All brakes were inboard.

Unfortunately, the transmission didn't work well, the front driveshafts and differential proving particularly troublesome, producing, in Alastair Lyle's words "A nasty kick-back under braking." In testing Mike also found the car constantly trying to veer off in one direction: to keep it straight he'd have to apply more and more lock, but then the problem would suddenly reverse and the car would dive the other way, leaving Mike frantically unwinding the lock in an effort to catch it. Then the process would start all over again. Mike was not the only driver to experience this. Trevor Taylor and Jackie Stewart also tried the car and reported the same problem.

Things improved somewhat when the front driveshafts were redesigned and the ZF LSD up front was replaced with a free differential. However, this produced wheelspin on the exit of corners, so instead a more progressive Salisbury Powr-Lok was fitted. But the kickback problem remained and the car was still difficult to drive, and extremely demanding physically. Alastair remembers Trevor Taylor remarking that if it were to rain while he was out on circuit, he intended to stop the car, walk back to the pits and let the support crew collect it!

These problems contrived to delay the CA's launch, and it was not until 1969 that the Cosworth F1 car was entered for a race – the British GP at Silverstone, appropriately enough. But just days before, knowing that the car was hopelessly uncompetitive, Cosworth withdrew its entry. Not long afterwards, Keith abandoned the project completely. It hurt, but it had to be done.

To Keith, it must have seemed that the whole exercise had been born under a bad sign. Its driver of choice had died without even seeing it. The drivers who did try it disliked it. The heart of the car, the transmission, needed serious and sustained development, exactly the kind of programme Keith prided himself on avoiding. Most worrying of all, wing design and tyre construction were advancing by leaps and bounds, making enormous differences to traction and calling into question the CA's entire raison d'etre. Even the weather was uncooperative: in 1968, a season plagued by wet races, 4WD could perhaps have made an impact, but 1969 was much drier and two driven wheels were enough.

In fairness to Keith, three other 4WD F1 designs had debuted in the late-1960s and none were pleasant to drive or successful, with drivers complaining of heavy steering and unresponsive, unpredictable handling. Graham Hill went a step further and refused to race the Lotus 63 at the 1969 British GP, describing it as a "death trap." Johnny Servoz-Gavin reckoned the Matra MS84 was undriveable, and when Bruce McLaren tried the McLaren M9A the car was sidelined on the spot, permanently. Four-wheel drive was later banned in F1 and to date has never returned. It would take another decade, and the commitment of Ferdinand Piech and his colleagues at Audi, to make 4WD work on tarmac in a competition car.

With his project about to be canned, Robin Herd left Cosworth to found March. Not long afterwards work on the CA was officially abandoned and the Cosworth-sourced team members were reassigned. Keith tried to persuade Robin to stay – he was interested in building a small gas turbine for light aircraft and asked Robin to head up the design, even offering him shares in Cosworth as an inducement – but Robin wanted to stay in racing.

The one and only all-Cosworth Cosworth was later donated to the Donington Grand Prix Exhibition, where it can still be seen, having never turned a wheel in anger.

Fittingly perhaps, the only CA component with a long-term future at St James Mill Road was a mis-machined centre differential carrier for the car, which was mounted on a plinth and entitled the 'Cat's Arse Trophy.' Appropriately enough, it was in the shape of a cup and its mahogany base had the trophy name inscribed on one side and 'Catastrophe' on the other. It was presented to any employee who had done something stupid or totally ineffectual.

As the door was closing on the CA, another was being opened, quite out of the blue. And turning the handle was a company Cosworth had never dealt with before: General Motors. Historically, America's biggest car company had been ambivalent about motorsport, but by the late 1960s the commercial advantage being accrued by Ford from its competition programme was impossible to ignore. A chance to catch up came in 1970, following the introduction of GMs new small (by US standards) car, the Chevrolet Vega. GM asked Cosworth to 'do a BDA' with it and despatched engine designer Calvin Wade to Northampton to discuss what would become Cosworth's first non-Ford powerplant.

The idea was for the British company to create and manufacture a high-performance Vega derivative that could compete in F2 and sports car racing, while GM would develop a de-tuned road version for use in a top-of-the-range variant, to be called Cosworth Vega – the first time the company's name had appeared on a car.

Initially, everything looked very promising for the EAA, as the Vega unit was dubbed at Northampton. The BD series had always been limited by its block design – it could not be taken out to 2 litres without the complication of cylinder liners – whereas the Vega was already of 2.3-litre capacity and moreover used an alloy block, so it was much lighter. The Reynolds 390 high-silicon aluminium block was of open-deck design with the liners cast in: the pistons ran directly in the alloy bores, which were chemically treated to remove surface aluminium, leaving the harder silicon as the wearing surface. Unusually, the standard head was cast iron, but that was the first thing to be ditched.

Not surprisingly, Mike Hall's replacement head owed a lot to the BDA. An alloy casting of course, with 16 valves at a 40° included angle and belt drive to twin overhead camshafts. A dry sump completed a very promising package, which gave 275bhp on the dyno (later raised to 285hp) from 1995cc, the capacity reduction from the original 2.3-litres being achieved by a new short-stroke (and much better balanced) crankshaft. This was not far short of the 290 given by the best 2-litre BDGs, which were considerably heavier.

The bad news was that the block was simply not strong enough. In the words of Malcolm Tyrrell, who as development engineer witnessed the problems first-hand "It had a nasty habit of falling in half and caused Keith no end of problems. The big problem was that it distorted its cylinder bores. At Keith's request I made up a plate for the top and we pressurised it to simulate the normal working BMEP. Then we measured the cylinder bores – they'd gone bell-mouthed, which was why we had blow-by problems."

Sometimes the block would not just bulge in the middle, but split the bore from top to bottom. Very occasionally, the results could be even more dramatic. "We were doing an endurance run once; I was outside the test cell controlling the engine. We had about 20 minutes left to do when a colleague, John Whyatt, went inside to check if everything was okay. It seemed to be, but just as he left the cell and closed the door, the whole side of the block simply fell off, with gudgeon pins and all sorts of parts flying around."

With the block distorting so much, naturally it also had huge cylinder gasket problems. "Keith put Wills Rings in, and a sealing ring round the outside, basically to try and stop the sides of the block from flapping. We used to stick the head to the block with Dow Corning Silastic – we didn't have the technology we have now." Once that was done "... the only way you could get the head off again was to put the two outside cylinders down to BDC, feed some cord into the cylinders and slowly turn the crank over until the pistons rose, tried to compress the rope and thus broke the bond between head and block."

This was new territory for Cosworth engineers, used as they were to the sturdy sand-cast iron block of the Cortina. In the past, when faced with a block weakness or limitation, they had been able to get around it by requesting subtle changes to the cores in the casting to leave a bit more metal in the required place, but this was much more difficult with the die-cast Chevrolet block.

John Dickens, who by this time was chief quality engineer and inspection manager, saw the problems first hand. "The manufacturing process meant that there was, in effect, always a given volume of gas entrapped in the casting; gas is not a very good structural member, so when asked to carry loads like bell-housings or alternators or auxiliary pumps, they tended to fall off."

Along with Mike Costin, John found himself studying X-rays of every block, trying to assess which castings were acceptable and which required machining to accommodate replacement extruded-aluminium inserts. "This was commonplace around the bell-housing, where we became quite proficient at making good blocks, but less so in areas such as auxiliary mounting bosses which just 'grew' out of the side-walls of the block – hence the need for elaborate bracketry in these areas to spread the loads." At one point they even tried turning the engine into a closed-deck design by milling a recess into the existing deck and electron-beam welding a plate into the space created.

"The GM people came over," recalls Malcolm, "and Keith told them in his usual fashion that their product was pretty grim." This must have been hard for the American engineers to swallow, given that by this point the block was the only Chevrolet component left in the engine, but they took the criticism on the chin, changing both materials and heat treatment in an attempt to improve reliability."

The fragility of the block meant that the EAA had little development potential, so there never was an EAB, or an EAC. Nevertheless, it did achieve some competition success – not in F2, to which it never graduated, but in sports car racing, where Guy Edwards took the works Lola T290 to third overall in the 1972 European 2-litre Sports car Championship supported by Cosworth's Dick Scammell, who, as Keith's right-hand man, was on hand to monitor problems and issues. The following year he drove a Lola T292 to wins at Österreichring and Clermond-Ferrand.[7] Irish hillclimber Tommy Reid also used EAA power with considerable success.

Weary of paying for work that shouldn't have been necessary, like X-raying blocks, Keith cancelled the project in the autumn of 1972. "It was a mission going nowhere," concludes Malcolm, who heard Keith exclaim despairingly around the same time: "If anybody ever again tries to get me to make a race engine out of a production block, for Christ's sake somebody stop me!"

Despite Cosworth pulling out of the project, Chevrolet persevered, and in 1973 got McLaren USA to produce a strengthened block which went on to have a reasonably successful career in Midget racing. GM also put the standard block into production, finally getting its road-going version to the public in 1975, though the de-smogged motor developed only half the power it had in Northampton – just 140bhp – which later dropped to 122bhp as emission regulations tightened. The car had always been intended to be exclusive – just 5000 engines were built – but its introduction came shortly after the 1974 oil crisis, and performance simply wasn't in vogue. Only 3508 engines found their way into cars before the Cosworth Vega was dropped in 1976, though the model has since acquired a considerable cachet among collectors.

Footnotes

1 p47, *The Power to Win*, by John Blunsden (Motor Racing Publications Ltd, first edition 1983).

2 In talking of 15,000rpm, Geoff is referring to the company's experience with later engines; the DFV never revved that high.

3 p201, *Such Sweet Thunder*, by John Blunsden & David Phipps (Motor Racing Publications, 1971), and p59, *The Power to Win*, by John Blunsden (Motor Racing Publications Ltd, first edition 1983).

4 *Motor Sport*, October 1996.

5 At this date Frank was an entrant but not yet a constructor in his own right.

6 The back shed was an area at the rear of the factory used for the material stores and where employees – and particularly the directors – played with their personal projects; it was known throughout Cosworth as the Playpen on account of the metal mesh that enclosed it.

7 It is not certain whether Guy Edwards had the EAA fitted for every one of these races, but he definitely achieved some victories with the powerplant.

Chapter 9

Work and (a little) play

Keith Duckworth is so intimately associated with Cosworth that it's easy for a biographer to find himself simply regurgitating a history of the firm. But of course there is far more to an engineer than his company's achievements.

The previous chapter takes us roughly up to 1972, by which time the Duckworths had been settled in Northampton for some eight years. Keith was 39, had a wife three years his junior, two children aged ten and seven, and a successful company. So successful, in fact, that in the brief period since the move from London at the start of 1965, the factory had been extended almost immediately, and then supplemented by an entirely new second building, Factory 2, in 1969. By 1972, the workforce had more than doubled to around 120 ... What was Keith like to work with during that initial decade in Northampton?

The first thing to be said of Keith Duckworth is that he was not a materialistic man. Cosworth operated in a glamorous sport, and inevitably numbered many wealthy people among its clients (as well as many impecunious enthusiasts who were anything but). However, apart from his one indulgence – a helicopter – none of that big-money world rubbed off on the boss, an ethos that ran right through the firm. You might find an exotic vehicle in the company car park, but it would probably be in a visitor's spot.

For obvious reasons, many Cosworth employees opted for Ford power, and the Duckworths were no exception. When they moved from London, Keith had a green Lotus Elan and Ursula a pale blue 105E Anglia. Keith kept the Elan for many years, though, as time went by, he used it less and less.

Ursula moved on to a Cortina Estate, and then a whole series of Capris, including a red example whose matt-black bonnet hid an experimental BDA. As the children grew in stature, a Granada Estate was acquired, supplied direct from Ford. "I hated it," says Ursula, "it was an automatic and I didn't like it changing gear when I thought it shouldn't!" Ford offered Keith a personalised number plate – DFV 1 – but he declined it.

Mike, in the late 1960s, was driving a Cortina 1600GT, while Bill had a Corsair (a rare two-door example), later replaced with a Capri 3000GT. Ben's transport was even more unremarkable – he could often be seen at the wheel of his wife's Renault.

Keith was no socialist; nor did he believe that people were born equal. In fact, he had a Duckworthism about this idea:

THE PROBLEMS THAT HAVE DEVELOPED BY SUGGESTING THAT WE ARE ALL BORN EQUAL! IT JUST ISN'T SO. IT IS ABSOLUTELY PARAMOUNT TO APPRECIATE THAT OUR CHANCES IN LIFE ARE GOVERNED BY ACCIDENT OF BIRTH – 80% OF OUR POSSIBILITIES IN LIFE ARE DUE TO WHETHER WE HAVE A LOT BETWEEN THE EARS, OR VERY LITTLE BETWEEN THE EARS.

That conviction was balanced by an equally strong belief that everyone, no matter how gifted or otherwise they might be, deserved a chance. He felt it only right and proper that every person should be given the opportunity to make the best of his or her talents – just as he had been. When recruiting, Keith always backed his own judgement rather than that of examiners. Hardly surprising, as Cosworth was doing very nicely, despite its four directors having just one pass degree between them: Keith's.

When assessing talent, his basic philosophy was that, regardless of qualifications:

YOUNG FOOLS GO ON TO BECOME OLD FOOLS.

His recruitment of John Given in 1965, who was hired from diesel injection specialist CAV to mastermind the company's move from carburettors into fuel-injection, illustrates how he put this approach into practice.

"I'd been asked by the service department at CAV to engineer petrol injection on a Hillman Imp, but the project was going nowhere. So I wrote to Lotus, BRM and Cosworth; I got offered a job at Lotus and an interview at Cosworth.

"Back then I didn't understand the hierarchy at Cosworth: when I arrived I spoke to Bill Brown for half an hour or so, then I was taken into Mike Costin's office, I was with him a couple of hours, next thing I had to go and see Keith, and I didn't get away until seven at night. All he wanted to talk about was the compressibility of liquids: he knew we were injecting diesel at 175 atmospheres; he wanted to know the compressibility of the liquid we were trying to inject.

"I handled the fuel-injection work for a number of years in the test shop. In fact, I was the one who took on Malcolm Tyrrell in 1968. About a fortnight after I took [him] on, another candidate phoned from London saying 'You've got the wrong man.' I told Mike about the call and he said 'We'll interview him, if he's any good we'll find him something to do.' That was Paul Squires.[1] That was the freedom of the place, they used people's abilities as best they could."

Geoff Goddard had a similar experience in 1971. "Rolls-Royce had made lots of us redundant after the RB211 project had gone wrong and the firm had been driven into nationalisation. The job centre in Derby offered me a post as development engineer on sausage skins in Glasgow! So I leapt into the car and went to McLaren. They said 'We'd love to have you but we don't think you could afford to live here,' so on the way back up north I dropped in at Cosworth on the off-chance.

"[Keith] gave me one of his grillings, took a problem he'd been grappling with and tried all the maths on me. He decided I had a feel for engineering in his direction, and at the end of it all I had a job. He was so demanding, his questioning was designed to find out if I could keep up with him. He understood that everything moves as it works, and though the stress sums prove whether it will break or not, the design principle is to accommodate all the strain. As a company, you start with the maths, then design the insides and finally – if it's an engine – the block. That's just the wrapping."

Obviously, not every recruit was hired ad hoc, but such was the rate of expansion that in practice there was little risk of the company finding itself over-manned. The workforce was young, bright and motivated – people were happy to be flexible.

Indeed, this organic structure was an attraction in itself. At Cosworth it was first names throughout, everyone was approachable, everyone was encouraged to have their say and argue their case, and knowledge was to be shared, not manipulated or hoarded. In the 1960s and early 1970s, a workplace like this was a breath of fresh air. Most British engineering companies, particularly large, well-established ones, retained very traditional structures and seemed to new recruits to be frustratingly out of touch with the zeitgeist.

Sometimes newcomers were taken aback by the simplicity and informality of Cosworth. When Robin Herd arrived from McLaren to design the 4WD car, he was none too impressed to find his office was nothing more than a concrete cubicle inside the main factory with a flat roof for storing box files – even though Mike and Ben's offices were just the same. He was even less impressed at 5pm when he asked for the keys to the promised company car, only to find that Keith hadn't organised one. In the short term Keith loaned him his Elan – a bit of a squeeze for a man of 6ft 2 inches.

On occasion Keith could take classlessness a bit too far, as with John Given in summer 1967. "When the DFV was being developed after its first race, the gear train had a lot of problems and some of us didn't have a day off for weeks, not even a Sunday. It was round the clock for Keith, too. One Sunday he said, 'I think we've done enough, I'll take you out to lunch.' And we ended up in a Wimpy Bar! That was his idea of entertainment!"

When the chips were down, Keith asked a lot of his employees, but they responded because they knew that, when he finally sent them home at eight o'clock after grappling with some intractable problem all day, the light in his office would be burning for several more hours. It was leadership by example and inspiration, not by rulebook and hierarchy.

None of the four directors had formal job titles, and their roles often overlapped. Broadly speaking, Keith was chairman and chief designer, Mike was technical director, Ben was production director and Bill was operations director. The atmosphere both in and out of the boardroom was relaxed and jovial and, as is the way in any organisation, the whole workforce took their cue from the esprit de corps evident at the top.

Perhaps the best analogy for their respective roles was to say that, if Keith was the precociously talented and explosively energetic physics teacher, firing off ideas in all directions and inspiring his pupils, then Ben was the resourceful lab assistant whose brilliantly inventive experiments lent substance to Keith's teachings. And Mike was the tall, quietly authoritative but approachable headmaster, who heard everything and understood everything, but was content to beaver away in the background unless he sensed things were going off course.

Where does Bill fit in our analogy? Somewhere between bursar and school secretary, which may sound a lower status than the others, but is probably close to Keith's view, coloured as it was by his underlying conviction that no one who wasn't actually designing or making something could be on the same level as those who were.

However, while the analogy describes their day-to-day roles pretty well, it only goes so far, because in this case the physics teacher owned 85% of the school and had the final say over all major decisions. This was the paradox at the heart of Cosworth's management, that the boss didn't actually want to run the business, indeed had *never* wanted to. Keith loved to design, develop and manufacture. The business was simply a vehicle that enabled these passions to be pursued, and which earned him a living along the way. He was justly proud of the business, but even more proud of its engineering.

As long as the firm remained relatively small, the company could be run effectively by the existing four directors and the paradox contained. But Keith was beginning to believe that before long it would have to be resolved.

Keith, Mike and Ben lived for their work, and were happy to thrash out problems for hours in the office, then in the nearby Red Rover pub, then finally into the small hours in the pub car park. Bill preferred a more normal existence; he had shown in the early years of Cosworth that he was willing to put in very long days, but he had no desire to turn that into a lifestyle. He found endless after-hours brainstorming hard work. Truth to tell, the other three so perfectly complemented each other's skills and personalities that any contribution by Bill to their epic engineering debates was neither needed nor wanted. So for the first few years at Northampton at least, any mismatch in input was not an issue; Bill was competently fulfilling his role, and that was enough.

That role included production planning and costing. "From the beginning," Bill explains, "I'd used a simple costing system based on the time spent making a part, and it produced viable figures. Gordon Roberts, the machine shop manager, produced much of the information used for costing our machined parts, while to an extent we left Jack Field to set over-the-counter prices for bits. Not having any competitors, we were in the happy position of being able to exploit the basic law of pricing: 'get what the market will stand,' though I do not think we abused it."

Production control was similarly straightforward, "Parts were tracked – from when they entered the factory through all the manufacturing processes – using a big metal board in the general office in Factory 1, with columns of movable plastic squares which were coloured according to the state which any item had reached. So anyone could see at a glance how we were fixed for any given engine."

Cosworth turned in a profit of £36,145 for 1967, and while company policy was always to plough profits back into new machinery rather than pay big bonuses, there was clearly scope for an indulgence. Keith's days of flying fixed-wing aircraft had ended with National Service, but he was still fascinated by flying machines of all kinds, so just a month after the DFV's triumphant debut at Zandvoort, he decided the company needed a helicopter, and treated himself to a Brantly B-2B two-seater. It was for sale at British Executive Air Services at Oxford Airport and was already sporting its rather egotistical registration of G-AVIP, but Keith didn't seem to mind much – not enough to spend good money getting it changed anyway! It was just three months old when he acquired it for £10,000.

He didn't yet have a helicopter licence, but that omission was soon remedied after just 37 hours of instruction. It was a big moment for Keith: finally, 15 years after the debacle with the RAF, he had a pilot's licence ... he could fly at last! He celebrated by proudly flying the Brantly up to Blackburn with Ursula, to show the folks back home.

After frightening the life out of Ursula by hill-hopping, he eventually landed on his brother's lawn, which prompted quite a lot of curtain-twitching from the neighbours, enough to bring the police round – understandably perhaps, as it was quite a small garden. According to sister-in-law Betty, they seemed thoroughly bemused. "The police asked Keith if they should ask him something! He was the first person other than royalty to land in the area by helicopter and they didn't know what should be done, if anything." But as they couldn't work out which, if any, provisions of air law Keith had broken, they went away.

His choice helicopter is a good illustration of the pleasure Keith got from engineering for its own sake. In order to fly and remain stable, any multi-blade helicopter (ie, with more than two blades – the Brantly has three) needs its blades to be hinged in two planes: up and down (the flapping hinge), and forwards and backwards (the lead-lag hinge). The design of these hinges and their positioning along the radius of the blade is critical to the effectiveness of the helicopter. Moreover, multi-blade designs can develop potentially dangerous resonances while the helicopter is on the ground and the blades are accelerating or decelerating.

The Brantly's American designer, Newby O Brantly, devised a novel solution to the resonance problem, involving two flapping hinges per blade and a lead-lag hinge located further outboard from the hub than usual. This technically elegant arrangement made the B-2B unusually smooth for a machine of its size, but was expensive to build, which is probably why it was never widely adopted. Nevertheless, it appealed to Keith, and is one of the main reasons he chose the Brantly over rival designs.

All four directors had their boys' toys. Ben and Mike both joined the Gliding Centre at Husbands Bosworth, initially sharing a glider and later having one each. "But they couldn't talk about gliding in front of Keith ... he didn't like it," says Jane Rood. In working hours the last thing glider pilots needed, DKD discovered, was encouragement to look wistfully out of the window in search of that magical ideal soaring day.

Alone of the directors, Bill had no interest in flying. His passion, one which would increasingly dominate his life, was driving, designing and building powerboats.

Malcolm Tyrrell remembers Bill's boats very well. "When I first joined Cosworth in 1968, down in the Playpen was Bill's monohull, *Venus*, with a Cosworth twin-cam engine in it – Bill had always participated in circuit racing [...] plus Ben's sailing boat, plus Mike's Brabham."

"Factory 2 was built alongside Factory 1. The design office, manufacturing and the machine shop went into Factory 2 and the F1 car was built in the vacated space in the fabrication shop, which also involved moving Bill's boat. The back of Factory 2 dropped down to a different level and that became the new Playpen."

"It was three feet lower than the main structure," explains Mike, "so people thought it was nothing to do with the works!" Actually, the height change had been dictated by the natural slope of the site: "We said 'Sod it, might as well have a bit more headroom, no point in paying lots of money to fill it all up!'"

It didn't take long for the directors to make good use of the extra space, and soon Mike and Ben's glider and trailer and Keith's Brantly had joined the collection. Not for nothing did the new Playpen become known as the Toy Shop, but it was only for the directors. "You were very privileged if you were allowed to work in there, and you were especially privileged if Mike gave you the key to one of his cupboards," says Malcolm. However, in the main factory a blind eye was turned to employees doing their own thing after-hours, within reason. "One night, about a quarter to seven, I was still in the shop, using a Morrisflex[2] to broddle the A-Series head on my Frogeye Sprite. Keith came along and, far from telling me off, took an interest and made some suggestions. He liked people who would roll their sleeves up and get stuck into stuff."

The years between 1967 and 1972 were exciting ones for any new recruit. "At tea break in Factory 1," John Given relates, "Mary the tea lady would come with this great steaming metal teapot. She'd put it on a table under the open-plan stairs that led to Keith's office, and people would gather there – Keith, Bill Brown, Mike Hall – and of course we'd all put the world to rights. As Keith smoked a lot, he always had a fag packet on him and he often used to write stuff on the back. After BRM brought the H16 out, I remember him doing some sums on the back of a packet and exclaiming to everyone, 'It can't work!' And it didn't!

"Tea break was where most of the information got disseminated."

As the company relentlessly expanded, the chummy tea breaks faded, but expansion was imperative, given the workload. Despite his disregard for the academic world, Keith knew the best brains were likely to be found among graduates, so inside the space of a few years a whole series of talented young engineers joined the company, many of whom would go on to have distinguished careers in motorsport. John Hancock was first to arrive, followed by Geoff Goddard and Paul Morgan. They were soon joined by Martin Walters, Graham Dale-Jones, Paul Chamberlain, Kees Mense and Neil Lefley.

Nevertheless, there was still room for people with less exalted qualifications to shine – Malcolm Tyrrell for one. Another example was John Dickens, who became a specialist in quality control and would eventually retire with the status of director, but was a mere work-experience trainee when he arrived in 1965.

Not everyone was at ease with all the new arrivals. George Duckett, in particular, took a dim view of graduates.

"Sometimes you'd get one who didn't know which end of a hammer to pick up. I'd say to Mike, 'Can you take this man and put him somewhere else? He's never going to make an engine builder.' When another of my rejects went into the drawing office, his first job was to make up a build schedule for the DFV. I'd already done one, starting with the block, then the crank, and going right down to the last nut. His was totally different from mine, but his became the schedule, which annoyed me."

The last straw came in 1972 when former Lotus racing manager Dick Scammell was hired from Tom Wheatcroft's Museum Programme. As the day-to-day pressures of running the company had increased, Keith had become increasingly fond of working from home, and Dick's job was to handle routine matters in his absence. Design engineers continued to report direct to Keith, but development was a different matter.

"Initially," Malcolm Tyrrell recalls, "Dick just sat in Mike Costin's office, causing all of us to ponder who this bloke was. It would appear that Keith might have adopted his normal practice of taking someone on without informing those impacted as to what was occurring – particularly George, who'd been running the development department, a position now to be the responsibility of Dick!"

To make matters worse, one of Dick's first jobs, a supposedly improved redesign of a bracket made by George for the EAA engine, exhibited a basic error – it fitted the wrong side of the block. "I couldn't stand him and told Keith it was him or me."

This cannot have been a pleasant moment for Keith, for he had a high regard for George. Not only had he been with Cosworth since the very beginning, he was absolutely at the top of his game – on some of the DFV's less critical components, the torque figure had been decided by taking an assembly put together by George, undoing the nuts and noting how tight they'd been! That then became the build standard.

Nevertheless, Keith did not appreciate being given an ultimatum. He didn't want to lose George, but he let him leave. He went to Milson Bearings for seven years, but returned to Cosworth when the chance came, and stayed until retirement.

Dick left in 1974 for the Parnelli F1 team, but he too returned, in 1976, effectively becoming Keith's right-hand man, and his eyes and ears at F1 events. He stayed for 20 years, eventually becoming managing director of Cosworth Racing after Ford bought the company, well after Keith retired.

Having hired some of the best young engineering brains in the country, it made no sense not to give them free reign. But Keith didn't want people going off on expensive, impractical tangents, so he chose designers who were not only bright but able to express themselves vigorously and stand their ground in a debate. That way he could challenge their ideas and satisfy himself they were likely to work, before any metal was cut.

These discussions were not always adversarial affairs. 'Constructive inquisitions' is how John Dickens describes most of them, with everyone putting ideas into the arena and Keith acting as master of ceremonies to direct the conversation to a conclusion. But if someone disagreed with Keith and refused to give ground, the debate could continue for hours – usually in the office, sometimes on the phone, sometimes in the Red Rover after work – because Keith hated losing an argument, even when he was wrong.

After watching Keith in action many times, Bill Brown got a handle on his debating technique. "One of his most favoured strategies was to latch on to any, often quite inconsequential, parts of the discussion which incontrovertibly supported his view. He then refused to entertain any of the other facets and, usually at great length, proceeded to use his great intellect to beat his opponent about the ears with these indisputable facts until said opponent succumbed. Ben Rood once described him to me as an intellectual bully!"

Keith never resorted to bad language – in normal conversation. But in abnormal conversation, when he was angry or exasperated, he could let fly. Geoff Goddard, whose tenacity in debate was probably second only to DKD's, was on the receiving end on more than one occasion.

"One night we had a very long and heated conversation about some engineering detail or other, I can't remember the issue, but it ended after some hours with him exclaiming 'F*** off!' and me saying 'Yes, I'm going home Keith.' But he'd obviously sat there for another two or three hours after I left, musing over what we'd said, because when I arrived at my desk next morning there was an A3 sheet on it, and written in very large block capitals was 'Last night I talked rubbish. DKD.'" (Though the actual language used was distinctly more colourful.)

"That was the way he worked," continues Geoff, "he always wanted to close the circle on any problem. 'Paul Morgan and I loved it, it was education. You'd be learning bits, you knew he was learning bits – although he wasn't going to let on straight away! – and in the end, if you'd argued your case well enough, you'd be allowed to do your own thing ... You learned an immense amount of engineering, and more importantly, the application of engineering.

"All of us younger guys had total admiration for the way he worked. Some came and went, because they couldn't stand the arguments. It was a competition, all those who really enjoyed Cosworth enjoyed that competition. It was a very classless society because in every area you had some superstars. If a man had his job as his surname, say, 'Mick the Weld', that meant he was the best in his field."

Coming from a gas turbine background, Geoff could look at piston engines with fresh eyes. Shortly after he joined Cosworth, he asked Keith why they balanced conrods.

"He gave me all the standard answers you'd find in a textbook, and this started one of these arguments. My case was that the out-of-balance force was only 14kg (30lb), and this on an engine where the firing force is 12 tonnes. So we were talking about 12,000±14kg – who cares? Keith got exasperated with me because I wouldn't back down and called Mike in.

"Mike has a nimble brain, he listened to Keith's learned argument, then listened to me, then stood quietly and thought for a while. Finally he said 'Why *do* we do it Keith?' And Keith threw his hands in the air!" A challenge from Mike was often the quickest way to end an argument.

Some days, however, he was simply too busy to get involved, and could be seen standing in the doorway of Keith's office, unwilling to enter for fear of being sucked into a two-hour discussion. The most risky time of day was late morning, because Keith had probably spent the first half of the morning at home, covering A4 sheets with his small writing, distilling all his thoughts from yesterday's discussions. These sheets, known at Cosworth as 'Tablets from the Mountain', often signalled the start of a very long debate.

If Keith was particularly enthused, he would head straight for Mike's office. Sometimes he'd leave the Tablets with him to think about. Other times, he'd read them out, at which point, in John Dickens' words, "Mike would roll his eyes a bit and a discussion would start."

Malcolm Tyrrell adds "Keith's telephone bill was horrendous, because if he got on the phone he'd run one of these arguments for what felt like the next ten hours and you'd think, I wonder if they ever wanted to go to the bathroom, because they'd never have got the chance! He'd have people stuck on the phone and would be writing and calculating while he was talking."

Since one of Keith's dictums was that intelligent debate required some thinking time before each response, conversations could be disconcerting if you were on the other end of the call. Malcolm remembers wondering "Has he walked out the room, has he put the phone down? ... The conversations were always very, very difficult because of his ability to just shut himself off and think about things."

"At Cosworth," says Geoff, "you could ask us a question on anything and we could do a sum that would try and work it out. What made Keith unique in my experience was that he'd try 100 ways of doing that sum, he could think for three or four months about that one sum. Anybody else would have about half a dozen goes and think 'Yeah, that'll do', and put a big variable constant in to correct the error. But he would be trying for the ultimate answer."

Malcolm concurs. "Keith would do a design, then go away, think about it, come back, rip it up and start again. Completely start again. There could be four or five iterations before he settled on a final design – with long conversations in-between with Mike Costin and Ben. Mike had a fantastic ability to look at a design and say 'That won't work, that will break, and it will break *there*.' And he'd be right. Years later, Keith and I frequently travelled to the USA for the Indy races and we talked a lot on the planes. He described Mike as an 'imagineer', he could use his imagination to foretell if something was going to be reliable, what the weakness was going to be.

"The brilliant thing about both of them was that you could be on the receiving end of a real bollocking, but the minute it was done, that was it, there was no permanent black mark, you weren't written-off. And both of them freely divulged their knowledge ... they were there to educate you. My university education was at Cosworth, the amount that you learned from everybody was phenomenal."

How did Keith manage to tell people they'd got it wrong without appearing boastful or arrogant? "He would be able to explain why you were wrong. I think that's the difference," says Malcolm.

"He would much prefer an engineer to admit he didn't know the answer to a question than to make up a story to satisfy his ego. In fact, at one stage the Duckworthism 'It is better to be uninformed than ill-informed' actually manifested itself as an instruction printed on the engine mileage card, affixed to the Lucas spark box in the centre 'V' of every DFV. Everyone at Cosworth knew what it meant, but some team mechanics took exception to it and left the card blank!"

The 1960s and 1970s are known as a period of industrial unrest in Britain, but the company's egalitarian ethos, and the fact that the management was nothing if not accessible, meant that most employees felt no need for trade union recognition. The furthest it ever got was when, as Jack Field recalls, "about seven hard-core blokes wanted a union, around the early '70s; they used to have a meeting in a van."

Eventually Keith got wind of this and called a meeting of all employees, saying "you can have a union, but the day we have a union, I walk out the door." No one wanted to run even the smallest risk of that, so the idea died on the spot.

Sackings were extremely rare. John Given's wife Val, who worked as secretary to the directors for five years, can only remember one dismissal. Keith didn't shirk difficult decisions, but neither did he relish confronting people with the results of those decisions, so once he'd decided an employee wasn't going to make the grade, he usually shifted them sideways into a boring job and hoped they'd leave of their own accord. On the very rare occasions when more immediate action was necessary, it would fall to Mike, not Keith, to bear the bad news. Explusions were the headmaster's job.

"I liked Mike," says Jack Field. "You wouldn't cross him though, he'd come down on you like a ton of bricks."

Despite his command of his job, Jack's relationship with Keith didn't always run smoothly, and around 1968 he confronted Keith, unsuccessfully, about his concerns regarding salary, car and office support.

"Keith said to me 'The storekeeper out in the machine shop is far more valuable than you,' and I replied 'I know he's a good bloke, but I don't think he's more valuable than me. I'm one of the reasons he's getting all those bleedin' tools out.'"

So Jack resigned and became an agent for carpet magnate Cyril Lord, selling door to door. Bill wanted to lure him back, so to keep him involved he found him some costing work to do during the daytime, and kept his BUPA subscription alive. After about a year, when the pile was wearing thin on the carpet business, Bill persuaded him to return full-time with a much improved deal. Cosworth, including Keith, was glad to see him back. The customers were too, as was Jack, who stayed for the rest of his career.

Then and for many years afterwards, the board would review each employee's pay and perks every year. There were no pay grades, everyone was assessed individually. Sometimes people got more than they expected. Jack remembers: "Keith used to do some kind things. For instance, once I was about to buy a new suite of furniture, and he must have got wind of it, because I got a personal cheque from him, his own money."

The camaraderie among the workforce was strong, with an interdepartmental cricket match every summer and the stag ritual of 'the Chair' played out in a grassed area near Factory 3. There, an employee about to get married could find himself tied to a chair and then anointed with shaving foam, shampoo, after-shave and whatever other cosmetic potions his colleagues could find.

In the mid '70s the company regularly entered a team for the Northampton Rotary Club's raft race, using a four-man pedal-powered paddle-driven machine penned by Graham Dale-Jones and John Hancock. Their design proved so effective that it was eventually banned – to give other participants a chance!

At Christmas time, Father Christmas would arrive for the company party – by helicopter of course – loaded with a gift for every employee's child. There was free drink and food and, for the adults in the evening, a minibus to take you home.

Parties were all paid for by sales of the company's scrap, an idea instituted by Bill Brown as soon as the firm moved to Northampton. Receipts for this went into a 'beer fund', which was administered by Bill Pratt, one of the firm's longest-standing employees, and by this time foreman of the engine building shop.

At party time Keith's sense of fun would come to the fore. "He hadn't always got his engineering hat on," says Malcolm Tyrrell, "with a pint of beer in his hand, he was a great guy to be around. He had a great sense of humour and a truly infectious laugh. But when the face started to redden, the cheeks puffed out and the eyes bulged, then look out!"

In the weeks running up to Christmas, rumours would abound as to whether or not there would be a Christmas bonus that year. There always was, but nevertheless there were sighs of collective relief when DKD arrived for work earlier than usual, a sure sign that the goose was about to lay its golden egg. Each employee was called to Keith's office, in alphabetical order, to receive a cash bonus (for many years, all wages were paid that way). "It may have been a bit Victorian," says Malcolm, "but there was something very satisfying and rewarding about Keith shaking your hand, thanking you for all your efforts and placing a bundle of notes in it."

Cosworth paid 9-10% on top of each employee's salary into a pension, an arrangement which was rare then. Some employees would have preferred the extra in their wage packet instead, but Keith had strong views on the matter, believing that most people are too short-sighted to see where their true interests lie. It was paternalistic, but those who thought about it appreciated it – especially as they grew older.

"You just don't see that level of employee care very often," says John. "What Duckworth had was a supremely happy company."

One unsung hero of that company was Mike Hall, an invaluable lieutenant during the DFV's design phase and later designer of many Cosworth power units in his own right, of which the BDA was the first. Mike Costin in particular rates him highly. "When Mike Hall designed an engine, you could rely on it going together properly, first time." Mike Hall was also popular with the staff, who found him personable, approachable and – if Keith was having a bad day – easier to deal with than the boss.

"There were very few problems with any of his design jobs," says John Dickens, "and he was good at sorting the development niggles."

The job Mike Hall was most proud of in his career was the GA V6, which was conceived in 1972 and was entirely his design – Cosworth's first ever six-cylinder engine (or to be precise, the first to get off the drawing board). The idea was to do for Ford's 3-litre Essex V6 what the BDA had done for its crossflow Cortina unit. Ford

Germany's unrelated Cologne V6 was running out of tuning potential and Walter Hayes wanted a four-cam engine suitable for taking on BMW in the European Touring Car Championship (ETCC).

Many features from the BDA found their way into the GA, including the use of toothed belts and the basic layout of the cylinder head (identical for both banks), with its 40° valve angle and central sparkplug. The bottom end needed a lot of strengthening, because Ford's target output was no less than 400hp, F1 territory just a few years before. To help achieve this, the racing engines were to be bored out to 3.4-litres.

Theoretically the iron blocks had enough meat in them to take the 6.3mm overbore required. In practice only a few per cent were good enough, because the products of Dagenham's foundry were, dimensionally, highly inconsistent. Keith found this absolutely infuriating and, given half a chance, would have marched into Ford's factory and told the foundrymen what he thought of their quality control. Nevertheless, enough good ones were found to complete the 100 engines required for homologation and on the dyno the GA gave 420bhp, enough to take it to a number of wins, though not the title – that went to BMW in both 1974 and 1975.

Interest in the ETCC waned in the wake of the 1974 oil crisis and when new rules came in for 1976 the works teams called it a day. But the GA's career was not over, for it was later used with considerable success in F5000 racing by Alan Jones, David Purley and Tom Walkinshaw, to name but three. By this time its power output exceeded 450bhp, enough to worry the Chevy-powered opposition with their pushrod 5-litres.

The GA never underpinned Cosworth's balance sheet like the DFV or BD, but it did prompt two changes at the company, both with long-term implications.

First, its cylinder heads were machined between centres – a commonplace technique now, but new at the time. Second, the need to produce 200 of these heads and assemble 100 complete engines within a fairly tight schedule was, by Cosworth's standards, nothing short of mass production and Keith, fearful of running late and damaging his excellent relationship with Ford, decided to hire a production consultant to gear the factory up for the job. The man he chose, Alf Vickers, would go on to play a major role in the company's development.

But first, machining between centres – a classic case of necessity being the mother of invention, as Geoff Goddard, who designed the jigs and fixtures, explains.

"The only spare machines Ben had available were Moog machines, which were like a converted Bridgeport with an air-control system for positioning. But we realised that a GA head would just fit on the Moog between centres and that the carousel would hold enough tools to machine it, so the operator wouldn't have to keep reclocking it at each stage, just set it up once. The traditional way to machine cylinder heads involved using plattens, which took hours to set up, and then machining one face at a time.

"Also, by machining between centres you can remove the head between operations, for example to fit seats, and know it will still be in the same place when you put it back. Moreover, all the tolerances are built from just one master axis."

Jane Rood relates what happened next. "Ben told Keith of his idea, but Keith didn't think it would work. He argued with Ben for a whole week about it. We were going on holiday after that week, and the disagreement really upset Ben, it was on his mind the whole time – he didn't settle down for the first week of the holiday."

Having worked with Ben to develop the technique, Geoff Goddard too came in for some stick: "Keith's currency was the C-badge and the Mars Bar. If you'd done something outstanding, he'd say 'I think you might be worth a Mars Bar.'[3] You very rarely got it, but there was a promise of one.

"The opposite of a Mars Bar was the C-badge 'for extreme incompetence in the line of duty'. Everybody in Cosworth was awarded a C-badge on occasion, sometimes a C-badge and bar. I got awarded that for machining heads between centres. I was told we'd never do another head like that, we'd use plattens in future." Nevertheless the system did become widely used, both in Cosworth and elsewhere.

The C-badge was a notional award, but it had a physical counterpart in the Cat's Arse Trophy. "That got put on your desk," says Geoff, "if you'd done a magnificently executed piece of work – that didn't!" – for instance if you'd sweated blood over a super new manifold that turned out to give less power than the old one. "That was one of the great things about Keith, he never bore any grudges.

"Bollockings were lovely. We'd see Keith disappear into the machine shop. Some time later he'd come steaming back and you knew he was angry because he'd walk back [to his office] slamming doors behind him. He'd sit there for 20 minutes, then the office door would open and the dulcet tones would come bellowing upstairs.

"So the guilty party would go down, and the opening 30 seconds would be a dressing down, and then he'd say, 'why did you do it that way?' and then you'd start defending what you'd done, saying it wasn't what it appeared and might actually be a good idea, and the meeting would evolve from bollocking into educational discussion leading to real engineering decision. By the time you got to the other end it was 'you're great, good thinking.' You could go from C-badge to Mars Bar in one conversation.

"Cosworth was a design-led company," continues Geoff, "but the design was very much embedded in 'Could we make it?' because Keith wanted to be able to make everything properly. The machine tools of the time didn't lend themselves to that – even the early CNC machines weren't accurate. That was Ben's strength: if you told him you wanted to hold two-tenths of a thou on something and keep everything in line, he would give you a machine that did that."

Malcolm Tyrrell was another who admired Ben's resourcefulness: "Keith was always extremely keen on getting the very latest machine tools, and Ben played a huge role in this. He'd say 'Right, I've looked at all the existing machine tools, there's nothing around that will do it to the quality I want, so I'll make one.' He'd go to a machinery sale, buy an old grinding machine or something, and turn it into a bespoke machine."

Jane Rood adds "He did that time and time again, he just loved his job. 'Work is not work, it's play,' he'd say. Ben must have saved the company millions." Certainly, as the years went by, Keith became ever more conscious of his huge debt to Ben.

Returning to the GA, its other major effect was to introduce Alf Vickers to Cosworth. Keith's misgivings regarding the production efficiency required for the GA were understandable. No one in the entire company had organised anything resembling series production before – the expertise simply wasn't there. Maybe – aided by the efficiency of machining heads between centres – his fellow directors and the staff could have risen to the occasion. But Keith was worried, and decided he needed outside help.

One day Keith said to Mike: "I met this fantastic bloke at Thursday Club."[4]

The 'bloke' was much older than the average Cosworth employee; in fact he was approaching retirement age. His previous post, as MD of Jensen, had ended following the company's takeover by Kjell Qvale in 1970 and, as he had recently suffered a heart attack, he was in no hurry to swap unemployment for the pressures of the engineering industry. But for reasons which Keith's colleagues never quite understood, DKD took to him immediately. Convinced that he had finally found the answer to Cosworth's managerial problems, he nailed his colours securely to Alf Vickers' mast and persuaded him to take the post of production consultant, starting in March 1973.

A 'Cosworth man' was open, straightforward, creative and modern. Alf was none of these, and staff and directors alike were bemused by the arrival of this small, middle-aged chain-smoker. Imaginative design was not his strong point and his knowledge of machine tools was, by comparison with Ben, well out of date. He was at his best negotiating deals in smoke-filled rooms. But – more importantly from Keith's point of view – he had the ability to make a factory hum.

He had made his name in wartime when the Government pressured Ford into mass producing Rolls-Royce's Merlin engine. Alf, then a young Rolls-Royce engineer, was seconded to Ford to act as liaison. He clearly made a mark, because he went on to manage Rolls' Scottish operation after the end of hostilities.

Alf was inclined to portray himself as the linchpin of WWII Merlin production, a role which, Mike and Ben suspected, he had rather embellished over time, but there was no point in expressing these doubts to Keith. From the moment Alf arrived at Northampton, Keith would brook no criticism of his new appointee.

Bill's opinions were much stronger, and best left unprinted. To him, Alf was everything Cosworth had always prided itself on not being; he simply couldn't understand what had possessed Keith to get involved with him.

Initially, Jack Field agreed with Bill. "Alf came as a consultant with another bloke, who was supposed to be running the machine shop. After they'd been there about a month I bumped into Keith in the car park. I said 'I don't know why you're bothering with them, they're a couple of f***ing tossers. Get rid of them.' Keith replied 'The other one can go, I agree with you, he's useless, but I'm going to keep Alf Vickers.'"

The 'other one' must indeed have been ineffectual, for hardly anyone interviewed for this book could remember his name. His duties were taken over by production engineer Phil Kidsley, who went on to do sterling work for the company and became Ben's right-hand man.

Meanwhile Alf proved his worth as regards the production of the GA and over time the staff came to respect him. Liking him though, was another matter. "Very few people took to Alf as a man," says Mike, "though I never had any altercations with him."

Like him or not, Alf Vickers was now a fact of life at Cosworth, one who would radically reshape the company.

Footnotes

1 Paul Squires worked on the BD series of engines, among others, and in conjunction with fellow Cosworth employee Phil Kidsley hillclimbed a Brabham BT28 with great success. The car was fitted with BD-series engines that were supercharged, turbocharged, and finally both; the noise of the car was a major factor in silencing regulations being introduced into hillclimbing.
2 A Morrisflex is a benchtop motor which, when driving a flexible shaft and grinding attachment, was used for detail finishing of cylinder heads.
3 The Mars Bar award was a hangover from the Edmonton days, where the fridge for everyone's lunchboxes also contained the company stock of Mars Bars. To be allowed to consume this corporate delicacy, moreover in the firm's time, was the highest accolade Cosworth could bestow.
4 Thursday Club was an informal totally off-the-record dinner organised weekly in the Midlands by Autocar journalist Ted Eves – networking, in modern parlance. All the top engineers from industry were invited – for instance Derek Gardner, Walter Hassan, and Spen King were all regulars – on the understanding that they could speak frankly and no one would break any confidences.

Chapter 10

Stress and de-stress

Keith and Mike had always been quite open about the fact that they'd never wanted Cosworth to grow into a big operation. "When we started we expected to become a company of 10 or 15 blokes!" says Mike.

Keith loved the fact that Cosworth had succeeded beyond his wildest dreams, but was much less at ease with the day-to-day implications of that success. In fact he coined a Duckworthism on the subject:

I THINK I AM, ALWAYS WAS, UNSUITABLE TO BE IN CHARGE OF A LARGER COMPANY. THE WHOLE OF MY NATURE, ANYHOW, WAS THAT I WANTED TO DO A FEW THINGS VERY WELL INDEED, RATHER THAN A LOT OF THINGS FAIRLY WELL.

So as soon as Alf Vickers arrived in March 1973, carrying the title Production Consultant, many of the staff suspected that it was only a matter of time before he became Managing Director.

In fact, before Alf ever set foot in the door, Keith had discussed exactly that possibility privately with Mike. Cosworth had never had a managing director, but as the company had grown, the absence of one became more and more obvious to DKD, and it worried him. What would happen to Cosworth if he fell ill or died? Keith no longer wanted to be in his office all day and every day, but someone needed to be.

There were sound practical reasons behind Keith's decision to look outside for an MD rather than appoint one of his existing co-directors, for none of the existing four directors had experience of running the size of operation that Cosworth had now become, let alone what it was growing into.

Mike and Ben were doing a fine job in their present roles: Keith had no desire to burden either with administration. That left Bill, who had the limitation of not being particularly interested in financial matters. "I'm even worse than Keith in this respect," he acknowledges, "I actively dislike dealing with money, not a very good thing for a general manager perhaps."

Even if Bill had enjoyed crunching the numbers, promoting him was a non-starter in Keith's eyes, because as the '60s turned into the '70s, the relationship between the two men slowly started to deteriorate. There was no massive falling out – perhaps it would have been healthier if there had been – just a gradual perception by Keith that Bill's passion for powerboating and his desire to keep things calm and simple at Cosworth was leading him to take too much out of the company and put too little in.

"Keith and I were best mates when we first met," says Bill, and the two men stayed on very good terms for the next decade. The rot set in when Keith started to diversify: Bill believed projects like the 4WD car and the automatic transmission (discussed in the next chapter) were expensive blind alleys, and that the firm should stick to making engines. "So Keith came to see me as a brake on his ambitions, the person forever pouring cold water on all his schemes."

Naturally, Bill objected to any suggestion that he wasn't pulling his weight, feeling that he deserved some of the credit for the growth of the company, whose turnover, incidentally, topped £1M in 1973. Moreover, he could justifiably claim that his end of things ran smoothly because he organised it well and made sure the staff under him could function successfully. "Keith was probably miffed that I kept so unruffled while he struggled valiantly with ever-increasing problems. Towards the end of my tenure he said that he could not fathom what I did all day!"

Even if Keith had no reservations about Bill's work ethic, any attempt to groom Alf for the post of MD would inevitably have raised questions about Bill's position. Compared to the sometimes crazy hours put in by his fellow directors, his workload was relatively light and included many of the tasks typically undertaken by an MD. If Alf were made MD, Keith mused, Bill would have so little left to do that his employment couldn't be justified.

In the early days, Keith couldn't have managed without Bill. Now it seemed that he couldn't manage *with* him.

But it didn't feel right simply to sack him – Bill was, after all, one of his oldest friends. In any case, it would be very hard to make any contractual basis for dismissal, because Keith couldn't point to anything specific that his fellow director had done wrong.

Once he had made a decision, Keith almost invariably stuck to it, but before reaching that point he was inclined to vacillate, especially over a serious issue like this. Normally, it fell to Mike to help him make up his mind, or in extreme cases to do it for him, but here was one decision that had to be his, and his alone. Mike and Bill were equals in the company hierarchy, the only person who could determine Bill's future at Cosworth was the chairman.

Keith ducked the decision, choosing instead to let things slide. At this stage Bill was still a director and Alf a mere consultant, so he let both get on with their jobs, without properly defining what they were, keeping his fingers crossed that they would reach some kind of accommodation, or that Bill would see the writing on the wall and leave. Maybe, somehow, goodwill and flexibility would win out, in the time-honoured Cosworth way.

In the circumstances, that was a forlorn hope, and even the ever-supportive Mike, who always couched any criticism of DKD in very measured terms, was later moved to observe that "Keith didn't define Bill's new role very well."

Mike and Ben were not directly involved in these machinations and continued to enjoy a good relationship with Bill, though they did understand where Keith was

Continued on p137

The directors in cheerful mood in Keith's office in Factory 1, around 1968. Keith is seated; standing (l-r) are Mike Costin, Bill Brown and Ben Rood. The photos on the wall of the veteran car are now in his son, Roger's, house – one of them is reproduced in Picture gallery 1. *(Courtesy Ford Motor Co)*

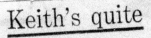

Keith's quite a flier too

IN the world of motor racing, **Keith Duckworth** is a Very Important Person. He is the 34-year-old engine designer who was responsible for the power which pushed **Jim Clark** to victory in this year's Dutch Grand Prix.

Perhaps that is why his new £10,000 Brantly B2 helicopter has the registration lettering— G-A V I P.

After the office, the pub: The Rover (formerly Red Rover) as it looks today. There are several hostelries near the factory, but this was the directors' favourite. *(Courtesy Norman Burr)*

Newly qualified helicopter pilot Keith alighting from the Brantly in his brother's garden in Blackburn. As the above cutting from a 1967 mainstream newspaper shows, it wasn't just the motorsport press that took an interest in Cosworth and its chairman.

Mike Hall poses with the favourite of all the engines he designed for Cosworth, the GA, surrounded by his other creations. His daughter, Maxine, created this montage as a birthday present. *(Courtesy Maxine Hall)*

The Hezemans/Glemser Ford Capri RS3100, sister car to the Lauda/Maas Capri, in ETCC action at the Nürburgring in 1974. *(Courtesy Ford Motor Co)*

Oliver and Keith watching the Cosworth entry in the 1973 Northampton Rotary Club Raft Race. Keith wasn't feeling too well and not long after this photo was taken, he suffered a heart attack.

Family snaps. Left: Roger, Tony, Trish and Julie Duckworth, on holiday in Swanage around 1971, and (above) Keith and Brian with (l-r) Antony, Julia, Trish, Roger and Alison.

The victories kept on coming for the DFV – this is Jackie Stewart on his way to number 56, the 1973 Belgian Grand Prix at Zolder. In just four years the magic 100 would be notched up. *(Courtesy Ford Motor Co)*

The Glastron and its Boss Mustang engine.

First Principles

TEAMWORK! Cosworth staff gather in the car park at St James Mill Road for a commemorative photo following the DFV's 100th win. With apologies to those whose names are partially or wholly lost to posterity, they are:

1 DKD (guv'nor); 2 Mike Costin (engineering director, aviator); 3 Ben Rood (manufacturing director, aviator, motorcycle racer, engine designer et al); 4 Alf Vickers (managing director); 5 Mike Hall (chief designer and drawing office manager, IoM racer); 6 Bill Pratt (assembly and production manager, budgie breeder and fuchsia expert); 7 Gordon Roberts (machine shop manager, ex Cobbler's footballer); 8 Ron White (broddler); 9 Sid Cave (engine build clerk/first-aider, dispenser of salt tablets in summer of '76); 10 Sam Hayes (machinist, part-time barber, infamously cut DKD's hair, once, badly);

11 Bob Going (machinist); 12 A N Other; 13 Frank Webb (assembly shop foreman, ex-HWM race team and Nerus Tuning); 14 Harold Antcliff (machinist); 15 Dick Scammell (development manager, one of Jim Clarke's mechanics); 16 Geoff Goddard (designer, later Prof in Motorsport Engineering Design, Oxford Brookes University); 17 A N Other; 18 Les Howells (accountant); 19 John Bush (personnel, moved to foundry in Worcester); 20 Gloria Fitzhugh (telephonist/receptionist);

21 Mick Hobbs (machinist); 22 Pete Morgan (machinist); 23 Geoff Roper (piston designer and manager, ex Hepworth & Grandage); 24 Sid O'Dell, maintanance electrician); 25 Roy Peasland (sub-assembler, puppy-walker for Dogs for Blind); 26 Roy Finch (engine builder in development shop); 27 Dennis Farndon (engine builder / works engineer); 28 Cliff Charlton (machinist, dancer); 29 Phil Hughes (crank grinder); 30 Dave Shortland (machinist);

31 Gary Toseland (dyno shop engine tester); 32 Malcolm Tyrrell (development tester, cricketer, rugby player, later powerboat and Indycar engine specialist); 33 Paul Squires (development tester, hillclimber of 1100cc supercharged BD-engined BT8 Brabham); 34 Ted Fuller (planner / expeditor); 35 Ian Harris (engine builder in development shop); 36 Pete Chillingsworth (production engineer); 37 Don Atwell (sub-assembler 'Don the Bomb' because he assembled DFV Lucas metering units); 38 A N Other; 39 Ron Sproston (inspector); 40 Frank Pearson (welder);

41 Roman Tolaga (crank lapper); 42 Alan Turner (engine builder); 43 Harry Turner (head storeman, affectionally known as 'H' to engine builders); 44 Derek Hudson (lapper); 45 Mark Wilson (grinder); 46 Bob Crouch (sub-assembler / engine builder, engine build records); 47 Ron (machinist; GI inspection, Filtron); 48 Arthur Robbins (sub-assembler, built DFV water and oil pumps, received A Robbins Award – monies for most promising youngster); 49 Mick Goodman (sub-assembly); 50 A N Other;

51 Mick McDonald ('Mick the Weld', highly skilled TIG welder, welded up Mike Costin's aircraft exhaust, etc); 52 Dave (cleaner); 53 Bob Maule (machine shop, later NDT operator); 54 Bob Merry (maintenance engineer); 55 Keith Labraham (inspection foreman); 56 Ray (inspector); 57 Chris Williams (production engineer); 58 Lawrence Griffiths (quality engineer); 59 Paul Morgan (development engineer, joint founder of Ilmor); 60 Tony Cosford (machinist);

61 Roy Gardner (machinist); 62 Jonathan Morgan (machinist); 63 Mike (grinder, known as Prince or 'Mick the Lick'); 64 Chris Cottrell (production engineer); 65 Malcolm Maskell (works engineering); 66 Steve Tillbrooke (piston shop fitter); 67 A N Other; 68 A N Other; 69 Barry Buck (jig borer operator in prototype machine shop, self-employed manufacturing consultant); 70 Ian Davison (horizontal borer, prototype machine shop, self-employed manufacturing consultant);

71 Dudley Chapman (machine shop inspector); 72 Ian Hawkins (engine builder, later development general

manager at Ilmor); 73 Ted Yates (chief broddler, hand fettled most DFV chambers and ports); 74 Pete Rogers (engine builder in development, joined Ilmor); 75 Jim (machine shop fitter); 76 John Blood (inspection foreman in machine shop); 77 John Phelan (piston-shop fitter, machinist); 78 Alan Baulch (piston-shop fitter, machinist); 79 Alan Sturgess (piston-shop fitter, machinist); 80 Ron Rands (machinist);

81 A N Other; 82 Ray Cory (inspector); 83 Jack Dunkley (cylinder block honer par excellence and classic bike enthusiast); 84 George Fairfield (sub-assembly foreman, farmer); 85 A N Other; 86 Chris Coe (manufacturing planner, very keen bird-watcher); 87 Dick Sharpe (production engineer); 88 A N Other; 89 Reg Florence (engine tester, then engine builder); 90 Bob Osborne (development engine builder, later Snap On franchisee);

91 Geoff Green (piston shop foreman); 92 Pete Rogers (inspector); 93 Ted McKenzie (machine shop manager); 94 Matt Service (labourer in engine shop); 95 A N Other; 96 Paul Skelton (engine builder, joined Ilmor in 1988); 97 Alan Lucking (machinist / buyer); 98 Norman Read (inspector); 99 Ian McKenzie (machine shop foreman); 100 John Davies (inspector / night-shift foreman);

101 John Swinn (inspector); 102 Ron Brind (machinist); 103 Mary Smith (tea lady / cleaner); 104 A N Other; 105 Brenda Smith (draughtswoman / tracer, married Tom Deacon); 106 Alan Borrrell (machinist); 107 Derek Curtis (storeman and musician); 108 Jack Field (sales manager); 109 Bill Hulme (cost accountant, later bought vineyard); 110 Pat Garrod (typist / NC tape maker);

111 A N Other; 112 A N Other; 113 A N Other; 114 Tony Wiltshire (engine builder in development, then NC electronics and Indycar electronics); 115 Andy Beasley (grinder, retirement home owner); 116 Dave Stratton (production planner); 117 John Walker (machinist, known as Grandma); 118 Alastair Lyle (designer of most BD variants and 4WD gearbox, later Tickford designer); 119 Ted Summerton (parts finisher); 120 Kees Mense (production engineer, later founded fabrication company, ey3 Ltd);

121 John Adams (honer in machine shop, rod section and gears, known as Johnny Liqourice); 122 John Hancock (production engineer, chief designer road engines, later consultant, keen sailor); 123 Alan Morris (machinist, later smallholder in New Zealand); 124 Dave Sibley (production engineer, worked closely with Ben Rood); 125 George Hartgroves (lathe machinist, prototype shop); 126 Geoff Oliver (design draughtsman, joined Ilmor as designer); 127 Paul (piston-shop machinist); 128 Jim Bromley (inspector, piston shop); 129 John Underwood (engine build labourer); 130 Len Newton (salesman, later sales office manager);

131 Deryck Norville (production engineer, later founded Filtration Control); 132 Cecil Schumacher (transmission designer, later founded model engineering company Schumacher Racing); 133 Bob Braines (turner, prototype shop); 134 Pete Mayes (engine builder); 135 Roy Jones (chief draughtsman); 136 Judy Mayes (sales office secretary, married to Pete Mayes); 137 Krista Pead (directors' secretary); 138 Neil Lefley (project engineer for prototypes, machine shop manager, supercar enthusiast); 139 Jack Shrive (inspector); 140 Ivor Rogers (machinist);

141 Gary Jolley (works Engineering, electronics); 142 Terry Botterill (engine build foreman, moved to electronics); 143 Don Beaumont (piston forge operator); 144 A N Other; 145 Alan Clarke (piston forge operator); 146 Charles Salisbury (cost accountant); 147 John Wilsher (buyer); 148 Ray Buckley (engine builder in development, 4WD car build, later managed Hesketh Racing engine build); 149 Ian Fitzhugh (jig borer operator, built up forge with Jeff Roper); 150 Charlie Day (broddler);

151 John Dickens (chief quality engineer, became director, later involved with Mechadyne, Antonov Transmission, Diesel Air, Dimuba); 152 Pete Mackenzie (broddler, father Ted was van driver, not in shot, probably on the road at photo time); 153 Ray Barber (sub-assembler).

First Principles

Top right: After the 100th GP win for the DFV, Keith commissioned a model engine, made from pewter and mounted on a wooden base. Each had a numbered plaque, signed by Keith, numbers being by chronological employment. Every employee was called in turn into Keith's office and presented with a model engine and £100 in new pound notes. Ten years later, a similar model was made of the DFX, to celebrate 150 Indycar wins. *(Courtesy Neil Lefley/Cosworth Engineering)*

Following the DFV's 100th win, Ford presented Keith with a superb commemorative book (cover above, introductory page right). Walter Hayes signed the first page, after which there is one opening for each of the engine's years of competition, with a photo of every winning car; the entry for 1973 is shown. At the back are page after page of congratulatory signatories. *(Courtesy Norman Burr)*

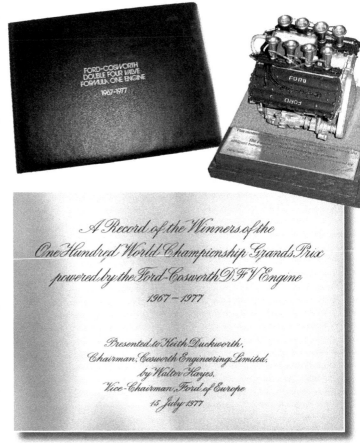

A Record of the Winners of the One Hundred World Championship Grands Prix powered by the Ford-Cosworth DFV Engine

1967 – 1977

Presented to Keith Duckworth, Chairman, Cosworth Engineering Limited, by Walter Hayes, Vice-Chairman, Ford of Europe
15 July 1977

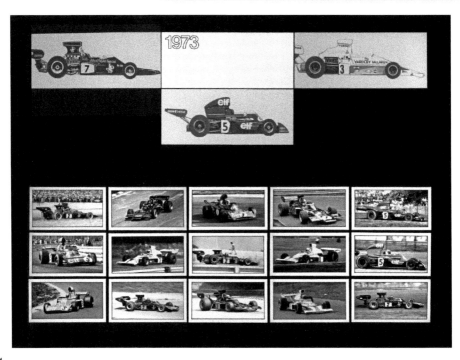

Monaco Grand Prix 1977, Jody Scheckter gives the DFV its 100th win.

Above: To celebrate the DFV's 100th win, everyone at Cosworth was invited to a dinner. Guests included (l-r) Ken Tyrrell, Jack Brabham, Walter Hayes, Ursula Duckworth, Jackie Stewart, DKD, Sally Mayer, Emerson Fittipaldi, Elizabeth Hayes, Teddy Mayer and Teresa Fittipaldi.

The accolades kept coming – Left: receiving the *Autosprint* award in Italy on behalf of Cosworth, December 1974 and right: Keith at the Design Council in 1979, receiving an award from Prince Philip. *(Courtesy Design Council)*

James Hunt in his McLaren in the Belgian GP of 1976, before retiring with gearbox failure. *(Courtesy Ford Motor Co)*

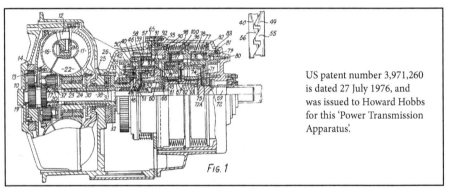

US patent number 3,971,260 is dated 27 July 1976, and was issued to Howard Hobbs for this 'Power Transmission Apparatus'.

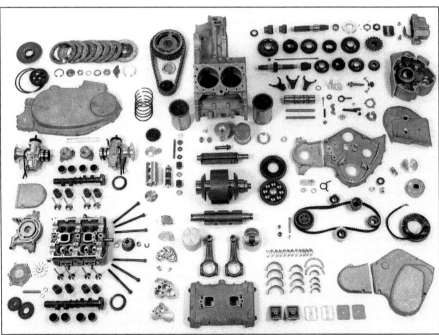

Components of the JA engine. The first Cosworth design to use an integrated cam carrier, it shared a number of parts with the DFV. *(Courtesy Ford Motor Co)*

coming from – particularly on Monday mornings after weekend powerboat races, when they would like as not find the Toy Shop strewn with parts and tools following a frantic panic by Bill and his helpers to ready the boat! To Mike, schooled in an aviation discipline where components and equipment are meticulously stored and organised (in severe turbulence a loose spanner in the cockpit can snag a control cable or hit the pilot, to disastrous effect), this was an anathema.

Alf was just getting his feet under the table when fate took a hand. One day in October 1973 Keith felt ill and was rushed to Northampton General Hospital, where it was found that a blood clot had brought on a heart attack. It was not a particularly severe attack – Keith had managed to walk into the hospital – and at the time Keith didn't think it had done much damage, but it made him even more determined to 'future-proof' the company against the day when, voluntarily or otherwise, he might no longer be part of it.

From his hospital bed, Keith immediately turned to Alf Vickers to hold the fort, and Alf not only obliged but also provided a sympathetic ear, for he had suffered a coronary himself not long before.

In the 1970s recovery from heart attack involved a lot of bed rest followed by quite lengthy convalescence. So suddenly, the need for someone to be in charge day-to-day had become urgent. Even before the attack, DKD had become steadily more reliant on Alf; now seemed a good time to make the promotion Keith had always had in mind. Before the month was out, Alf Vickers was a director of the firm.

Alf's elevation to the board would, Keith hoped, send a reassuring message to everyone at Cosworth, that the company was in safe hands. It was also his way of saying thanks to Alf for stepping into the breech.

By the early 1970s the connection between smoking and lung cancer had become widely accepted, but the public was much less aware of its link to heart disease. In Keith's case, Ursula assumed that heredity was the major factor. DKD was now 40; his grandfather had died at 39 and his father at 43. "Frank had influenza and chest pains and they turned out to be a heart attack," she recalls. "It didn't occur to me that Keith's heart attack was caused by his lifestyle."

It is not certain when Keith acquired the tobacco habit, though National Service was the starting point for many. He was certainly a regular smoker by the time he got together with Ursula at university. "But when I met him I wasn't so aware of it, as everyone smoked back then. He smoked very heavily, at least 20 a day, the first thing he did when he got up in the morning was to have a cigarette – even after the heart attack."

Keith spent a few days in hospital, after which he was allowed home on condition he spent a month in bed – he was only allowed to get up once a day. He was prescribed valium to calm him down, but his mind remained as restless as ever and visitors from Cosworth would arrive in the evenings to discuss all manner of company matters. Shortly after the attack, one visitor arrived to find Mike and Keith deep in discussion about designs for heart pumps! During this period, Keith also amused himself by designing the HA, a 2-litre V6 for F2, and doing preliminary work on a 2-litre V8, but neither project went any further because there seemed no likelihood of any manufacturer agreeing to fund them.

Mike was not the only regular visitor to the house, for in the evenings Margaret Craddock would sometimes arrive.

Margaret was the other woman in Keith's life. Given that fact, it might seem odd that she would feel able to visit the family home, but the relationship had been ongoing for several years and a working arrangement had evolved between her and Ursula. Every Wednesday Keith would stay with Margaret and, if anyone asked, Ursula would explain his absence by saying he had to visit SRE in Swindon. "She was nervous of me initially, because she thought I would hate her, but eventually we got on well together," says Ursula. In fact she came to value the evenings when Margaret arrived to 'Keith-sit' – it gave her a break, a chance to leave the house.

Family life was relatively unaffected by the relationship, as the children knew of it and Keith and Ursula continued to get on well. Ursula had always known that Keith very much enjoyed bright female company. "I was used to that," says Ursula, "and I thought, well, he always comes back to me. And we are good friends. I just lived with it, that was just Keith. And I went out on my own account sometimes too."

For a long time after the coronary, if the subject ever came up, Keith would decorously say that his secretary took him to hospital, implying that the heart attack happened at work, but the truth was rather different. "It did not occur at work," says Ursula, "but on a Wednesday evening at the house he'd bought for Margaret." It was Margaret who took Keith to hospital; she then phoned Ursula to tell her what had happened and offered to babysit while Ursula went to visit him.

Mike remembers Margaret very well.

"She was daughter of an English army man and a German girl. She spoke fluent German, but she was a very straightforward English girl, a barmaid at the Red Rover where all the Cosworth people drank."

When Keith met her, she was at a low point in her life, escaping from a violent marriage, and he felt sorry for her. "He bought a house," continues Mike, "and set her up in that."

In fact, Keith went further and helped Margaret set up a business in nearby Daventry, where she became manager of a branch of Betaseal, an American process designed to eliminate porosity in metal castings by resin impregnating them under vacuum. This was a good move both for her and for Cosworth, because the latter had long been frustrated by the porosity of its large castings, which at this stage were all bought in because Cosworth had no foundry of its own. Not only can porosity render an engine useless – for example by allowing coolant into the combustion chamber – but its existence is sometimes only revealed after the engine is completed, making it a particularly expensive problem to remedy. Having a local company able to combat it was very handy indeed and from day one Cosworth was one of Betaseal's major customers, remaining so until its own foundry came on stream much later and the problem became less acute.

Jack Field tells an amusing story about Betaseal. One day he was called into Alf Vickers' office and asked to drop what he was doing and try instead to rustle up some business for Betaseal. Apparently Keith was fed up with getting earache from Margaret that she didn't have enough work.

Jack tried a number of small and medium-sized companies, without success, and in the end decided to take the bull by the horns and contact Ford. Keith's name counted for a lot at Ford, and soon a senior buyer arrived in Northampton to meet with Jack. A few weeks later, Ford withdrew a carburettor sealing contract from a Northern Irish firm and awarded it to Betaseal. Margaret was amazed to find an enormous truck – the first of many – arriving outside her modest premises, loaded with thousands of components to be sealed. She had to take on extra staff to deal with all the work.

Not long afterwards, Cosworth staff could be heard muttering to each other: "You know, the turnround at Betaseal's not as quick as it used to be…" But we digress.

Keith's heart attack came as a complete surprise, for although he was heavily built and put on weight easily, he was never obese and always led a very active life. Watersports were his main physical exercise, though he did briefly attempt to stay fit by running, as Jack Field remembers.

"He came to me in the late '60s saying 'Jack, I need some running shoes, I've got to lose weight.'

"So next time the van driver came in, I said 'Tom, nip out and get some running shoes, then leave them in the bag on Keith's desk.'

"Next morning Keith comes in with this terrible limp. I said 'What happened?'

'I wanted to do some running, there's a field opposite me, so I thought I'd run round that. But there's a five-bar gate, I thought I'd hop over that, and I did my ankle. So that's it.' I don't think he ever ran again!"

Water-skiing was more to Keith's liking. It was the trendy sport in the late 1960s, and while living in London both Keith and Ursula had tried and enjoyed it. So around 1968 the Duckworths bought into a leisure facility near Little Billing on the outskirts of Northampton. Billing Waters Lake was (and still is) privately owned and enjoyed by some 15 families. Formed from some disused gravel pits, it was long enough for a slalom course and included a water-ski jump.

The Lake rapidly became a central feature in the Duckworths' life. When the family moved from London, almost the only people they knew in Northampton were the employees who'd moved there with them – practically everyone in their lives had a Cosworth connection of one kind or another. The Lake, along with Trish's and Roger's school friends, added a vital balance to the family and enabled the Duckworths to build a social life outside the business. Having said that, they were not the only Cosworth people involved with the Lake: Mike Costin and his family made good use of it, as did Bill briefly, until his powerboats outgrew it.

One of the Duckworths' new friends was a local farmer called Patrick Castell, whose elder daughter Sarah went to the same school as Trish. Both girls loved horses and it was decided that they would share a pony.

"The Duckworths didn't have the land to look after it," says Pat, "but as a farming family that was not a problem for us. So we got the pony, it was jointly owned and mainly looked after by us. Sometimes Trish would stay overnight and, as we were starting a stableyard at the time, it worked out very well indeed. We had some lovely rides around the countryside and the forests."

Even after Sarah and Trish went to different schools, the families remained good friends. "Ursula and Clare [Pat's wife] and the children used to go down to the seaside, and at the weekends Keith and I would drive down and join them. Then one day he dropped in at the farm in his helicopter and took me up, that gave me an appetite for learning to fly. I subsequently got my pilot's licence, which I found easier than expected; I mainly flew Cessnas, Jodels and Robins, but gave it up when senior-school and university fees came along. As an ordinary working farmer I couldn't afford it."

By the late 1960s Keith was quite wealthy – certainly richer than many of his friends – and the gap was widening every month, but he never reminded them of the fact. Pat was not alone in finding this characteristic particularly endearing.

"Keith was a very successful man and I had the deepest respect and time for him.

He was an absolute gentleman: yes, he would put his hand in his pocket, he was very generous, but in a quiet way. He was just one of the boys, an ordinary guy who had a lot of time for a lot of people. If you had a problem, he would talk things over with you and help you out." Pat didn't have a share in the Lake, but was taken there as a guest. "That's where I learned to water-ski," he explains. "It was Oliver who mainly instigated it."

Oliver Achurch was another shareholder at the Lake, a local man involved in the farm machinery business. He too had a young family, and he also had another asset which, from the point of view of Keith's kids, was invaluable – a caravan. The steep sides of a gravel pit can be dangerous for young swimmers, but a safe area had been made for children and they made good use of it, unless it was raining, in which case "... we used to pile into the caravan," says Trish.

The antics at the Lake generated myriad memorable stories, many of which revolve around 'the disc.' Being towed on a ski soon became too easy: once you became proficient you could stay upright all afternoon, which was no good at all. What was needed was a challenge for the skier, and entertainment for the onlookers.

So Oliver cut a disc out of plywood. It was about 1.3m (4ft) across, and the idea was to tow it along at 5-10mph. Roger Duckworth was only about six when this innovation appeared at the Lake, but clearly had already acquired his father's eye for applied mechanics, because he describes it like this:

"The disc was wooden, with feathered edges. You lay on it with a ski rope and held onto it to keep its nose up until you were going at a fast enough speed – you didn't need to go very fast, as it was a huge area. Then you crept up on to it, next you knelt on it, and then if you were feeling brave you could stand on it."

But you had to keep the front edge of the disk above the wake of the boat. "If it touched a wave, it stopped – and you went forward!

"Once you were standing or kneeling, the trick was give yourself a little tug on the rope to spin around, or maybe go backwards for a while – all the normal water-skiing amusement. The next level up was to take a fiddleback kitchen chair, without the back, put your arm through it so you could carry it while you were trying to get up onto the board, and then you put the chair on the disk and tried to climb on it. And there's no friction anywhere because this is gloss-painted wood, and it's wet. Finally you'd try to spin while standing on the chair – that usually results in falling! I wasn't old enough to try the chair, that was dad and Mike and Oliver, but I did try the disk."

Oliver continues: "We started with a chair, but that was too easy, so then we used a pair of wooden steps that I happened to have around. Two of us would be towed, stretching the steps between us, and the idea was for us both to get up on the disc and then for one of us to mount the steps!"

"It was just hysterical," laughs Trish.

Even the less adventurous could come to grief. Oliver remembers "One of the girls, Sharon, was extremely dolly and she and my wife Shirley were out on the disc when we heard this scream and they both fell into the water. It turned out that Sharon's eyelash had fallen off onto the disc and Shirley had thought it was a huge spider.

"We had been known to ski right into the night on a balmy summer's evening, I remember being towed by Keith, we were probably half inebriated, and I said 'I'll take a torch, if I flash, I have a problem.' That was fine until I fell off and dropped the torch. I was waving frantically 'I'm over here,' and in danger of getting entangled in the rope as he circled looking for me."

Pat Castell had more nocturnal success. "It was a harvest moon, the lake was absolutely mirror finish and, as Oliver was an attentive boat driver, I was able to get out of the wake. We went all round the lake, it was a magical moment for me."

Tow boats naturally came in for attention. Oliver says "Keith had a 13ft Fletcher with a 65hp Mercury, which was incredibly unstable – certainly Mike had it on its side more than once. It was very quick but not the ideal boat for water-skiing."

Much more successful as a general-purpose boat was a Delta with a 1500cc Ford engine, which Keith ran for several years, but for excitement nothing could top the Glastron. Constructed at the factory in 1972 by Cosworth designer Neil Lefley, this was a 16ft Fletcher/Glastron hull sporting a 5-litre Boss Mustang engine with nominally 290hp, driving a Berkeley water-jet unit.

The engine was one of ten which Ford had sent from the US in an attempt to get Keith interested in turning them into F5000 units, but DKD was unimpressed with the potential of the engine, regarding it as big, heavy and thirsty. And although Keith was all in favour of good breathing, its huge ports seemed too much of a good thing. Indeed, he once remarked, on inspecting a similarly over-endowed inlet manifold at Ford's US racing headquarters, that there should be arrows on the inside of the casting. "I really did think the holes were on the large side, and the air might get lost if they didn't indicate which way it was supposed to go!"[1]

He never pursued the F5000 idea. Instead, he decided to try the engine as a marine unit and asked Cosworth engineer Neil Lefley to help.

"I was between projects, so I got the job of doing the installation, liaising with Vic Ems at Fletcher's. Unfortunately, Vic was killed, so I was on my own, and only the one boat was finished. However, most of the other Boss engines found their way into boats of various types.

"After the engine and cooling system were installed, Keith and I were on the lake at Billing to sort out the size of orifice needed to get some reasonable engine temperatures, but the engine wouldn't start. Keith suggested taking off the air cleaner to check that there was fuel; there was, but when I turned the key an almighty sheet of flame came out the carb and nearly took off his eyebrows. Some joker at the factory had swapped all the plug leads around.

"Keith also got a soaking when he tried to see how quickly the boat would stop. Jet boats are odd in that the only steering is from angling the jet, so if you are heading for the bank and can't turn enough, you have to stop, or spin the boat. If you back off, you carry on in the last direction at almost undiminished speed. To stop, you pull the throttle lever back through neutral, this puts a bucket over the jet to direct it forward, not back, and if you carry on pulling the lever back you open the engine throttle again to pump the water."

DKD couldn't resist an experiment, so he went from full-throttle forwards to full-throttle backwards at about 30mph. "The boat did indeed stop pretty quickly," recalls Neil, "but not the following wake, which swamped the boat!" The whole of the bow disappeared beneath the waves and Keith, Neil and Oliver spent ages baling it out.

The Glastron was something of a beast, as Oliver well remembers. "It was alright once it was up onto the plane, but because the c-of-g was so far rearward, as you opened up the throttle you created the most monumental bow wave for the poor skier to ride. The finest driver of that boat was my wife Shirley, she could get it up onto the plane and flick it, sliding the boat in the equivalent of a four-wheel drift."

The craft was used for some years as a ski boat, but was eventually sold through powerboat driver Jackie Wilson, with all reference to Cosworth removed.

When Keith had run out of daft things to do on two skis, he moved on to one, both he and Ursula becoming proficient mono-skiers. "My dad thought that playing on the water was a good idea," says Roger, "because you couldn't really hurt yourself, so anything new on the water he would always try."

After his heart attack, Keith was advised to stop water-skiing, so instead became more interested in boats, particularly when Oliver acquired one of the first Laser sailing boats in the early 1970s.

"Keith thought it looked good fun; he wanted one, too. We used the slalom buoys as the markers for our sailing course, but Keith's hand-eye co-ordination was not the best, so it was never too difficult to win against him."

It would have helped if he'd had some instruction, but "... of course there was no question of having lessons," says Trish. "The approach was 'We can work this one out ourselves.' I was too small for it; I had to have someone sit on the end as ballast, but there was lots of hilarity and capsizing."

One day Oliver was sailing alone when Keith arrived in the Brantly. "He must have thought 'I'll help Oliver sail across the lake, I'll hover to give him a bit of breeze!' As he got overhead, the boom flew across at an alarming rate – how I didn't get decapitated I'll never know – and I remember gesticulating to him to piss off. Then he headed for the water-ski ramp in the middle of the lake, which was angled at about 30°. I thought, he's going to land on it! He did, in fact, manage to hover with the tips of his skids touching the top of the ramp."

Keith loved giving people rides in the Brantly. His old university friend, Noel Davies, came to stay a couple of times with his wife, Sheila, and he took them up. "These things glide, you know," he told Noel, who continues, "... and then he turned the ignition off! Keith behaving like a student again!"

"And making improper suggestions to his lady passengers!" laughs Sheila.

Ben's youngest son, Gerald, also got treated. One day he was asked, "Have you ever been in a helicopter? No? Come on then, come for a ride," and the pair zoomed off from the factory in the direction of the river, the helicopter diving under some power lines along the way. "I never forgot that," says Gerald. Gerald was only at junior school at the time, and as he grew up he got to know Keith well. "He was a very jovial bloke when you got him in the right place: in a pub or over dinner."

After Keith's heart attack, the Brantly was no longer seen at the Lake, because Keith immediately lost his pilot's licence. His helicopter-piloting days were over, and the Brantly was mothballed. But this was far from the end of his love affair with flying, a passion which was to provide him with much pleasure and no little anguish in the years ahead.

As '73 turned to '74 and Keith gradually returned to fitness, his thoughts turned again to the factory, and the whole raft of projects he had been guiding from a distance …

Footnotes

1 Interview with Phil Llewellin in *Car* magazine, December 1987.

Chapter 11

Cosworth takes off

Even by Keith's standards, the early 1970s were a particularly hectic period in his life, a fact which may well have contributed to his heart attack. As well as the EA and GA, Cosworth undertook two other major design projects around the same time: the F1 automatic gearbox and the JA.

Given that the company was already prospering, the effect of this frenetic activity on Cosworth's financial performance was dramatic. Turnover was £1.15M in 1973, but two years later had reached £1.64M. Then it really took off: £1.88M in 1976, £2.23M in 1977, £3.46M in 1978, £4.1M in 1979 (*Cosworth*, p148). Keith observed:

> *WE MUST BE THE ONLY OUTFIT, EVER, TO MAKE MONEY FROM*
> *RACING ENGINES AS A COMMERCIAL VENTURE.*

With healthy profits rolling into St James Mill Road, Keith could comfortably afford a bigger house, and in October 1975 moved just up the hill from Larkhall Lane to a fine Victorian farmhouse called Norwood House.

Norwood House had plenty of room for Keith's growing family – Trish was now 13 and Roger ten – plus a garden easily big enough to land a helicopter.

This last consideration was very important, because although Keith's pilot's licence had been suspended two years earlier following his heart attack, he was determined to keep flying. In May 1976 Cosworth bought G-BDOY, a five-seat Hughes 500C, and hired a full-time ex-RAF pilot, Graham Cox, to fly it. With Graham officially at the controls, Keith continued to have a lot of fun in the air.

Cosworth employees had some fun too. Jane Rood recounts how one year the company was celebrating so many GP victories that Keith arranged for Graham to take some lucky individuals to Silverstone in the Hughes. John Dickens reckons over 100 people were ferried in during the day. "A farmer friend, David Wesley, let Keith borrow his field for the take-offs and my son Gerald helped strap people in to speed things up." John remembers being surprised at how free and easy the access seemed to be, but this would change before long: his daughter was shown around Silverstone air traffic control just a few years later, by which time everything was very tightly controlled with landing slots strictly allocated.

Awards kept coming Keith's way. In December 1974 he flew to Italy to accept the coveted *Autosprint* award on behalf of Cosworth, and in 1977 he accepted the RAC Diamond Jubilee Trophy 'For the design and engineering achievements of his Grand Prix engine.' The latter is a particularly prestigious award and is not given every year: the previous recipient had been BAC, for the Concorde.

"We had to do a short bio for him," chuckles Geoff Goddard, "and in reprinting that, the RAC said that he served as RAF airscrew!"

That same year he also won the Ferodo Trophy for the second time – this time in recognition of the DFV's 100th win. Jody Scheckter notched it up at Monaco, after which everyone in the firm was invited to a celebration in a Northampton hotel, along with a number of GP notables including Jackie Stewart, Emerson Fittipaldi, Mario Andretti and James Hunt. The date chosen was 14 July, as many drivers would then be in the UK for the British GP. On the same day, a celebratory photo of the whole Cosworth workforce was taken outside the factory, showing 150 heads, though according to one 1977 press report the total labour force was actually 170.

Two years later another gong came Keith's way, and with it a handshake from the Duke of Edinburgh, this time for winning the British Design Award.

Despite the proliferation of other projects in the early 1970s, work on the DFV continued almost non-stop throughout the decade. The V8 was very much Keith's baby, and always received his personal attention.

A look at how the engine's power output changed over the years suggests that it was in a much higher state of tune at the end of its career than the beginning, but in reality much of the increase was achieved by progressively raising the rev limit, as confidence in the DFV's robustness increased. Keith did not believe in development for development's sake, so changes in power output were only pursued when the engine was finding itself under pressure on the track. Exhaust systems evolved continuously, but between 1970 and 1975 there were no changes to ports (apart from a small enlargement around 1973), valve sizes or cams.

The DFV was quoted in 1967 as developing 408bhp at 9000rpm, but in 1970 this was raised to 430 at 9500 (thanks partly to a four-into-one exhaust system), then 450 at 10,250 (1971), 465 at 10,750 (1975), and 495 at 10,750 (1977). However, development engineer Malcolm Tyrrell remembers seeing at least one late example give 530bhp on test, and a lot of work was done to track down why some engines produced more power than their supposedly identical brethren, by swapping components between engines and retesting.

Although it is a huge tribute to the soundness of the original design that the engine was able to withstand such a large increase in maximum revs, reliability could not have been maintained, let alone improved, without a constant programme of detail development.

Conrods, for instance, evolved through several variants in an attempt to improve fatigue resistance, aided by subtleties like modified thread forms on big end bolts. Crankshaft failures were an issue during 1970, until it was discovered that faulty machining at Laystall was breaking through the nitriding at the fillets of the bearing journals – a problem that led directly to Cosworth setting up its own crankshaft machining facility.

Another issue was inadequate cooling in the area of the exhaust-valve seats, which was solved around 1973 by machining out the cast-in sparkplug mounting and fitting a thinner HE15TF aluminium plug tube, sealed with Silastic, to improve water flow.

Oil consumption varied considerably between engines, and various cylinder liner materials were tried to combat this – initially steel, then tuftrided steel, grey cast iron, spheroidal graphite iron, and back to grey cast iron. The solution came in 1981 with the adoption of Nikasil-treated aluminium, which was more expensive but had two advantages. First, its rather abrasive surface proved excellent at running-in piston rings, improving engine life; and second, it made the engine a useful 3.6kg (8lb) lighter.

Until 1974, pistons were bought from Hepworth & Grandage (H&G), but as demand from the British motorcycle industry dropped, H&G's forging operation became uneconomic, and Cosworth, fearing that its supplier would disappear, bought the forge (at scrap-metal price!) and constructed a separate building at the back of Factory 3 to accommodate it, so that its mighty thump would not disturb the machine shop. An ex-H&G employee, Jeff Roper, was hired to run the forge along with Cosworth's Ian Fitzhugh. Initially, the forge produced pistons for Cosworth engines only, but before long Jeff was running Cosworth Pistons as a semi-independent business under the Cosworth umbrella, and offering its products to other companies, too. Piston rings continued to be bought in, some from H&G.

Surface treatments also came under the spotlight, as quality manager John Dickens explains. "We started to get keen on tuftriding for a variety of components, eventually buying a tuftriding plant to install in the spare space in Factory 3." The plant was bought because of dissatisfaction with the quality coming from the existing supplier, but it was never installed because the 'spare space' was soon needed for more machine tools. Instead, Cosworth found a supplier offering better quality, and resold the plant.

Most of Cosworth's large castings came from Aeroplane & Motor Aluminium Castings Ltd, and their quality was a long-standing concern at Northampton. John Dickens, Mike Costin and Mike Hall spent a long time at the foundries, "... helping to try and sort the problems," as John puts it, but the real solution didn't arrive until some years later when Cosworth built its own foundry.

When the second-compound quill device arrived in 1971-2, a belt and braces approach was adopted to protect the valvetrain. To increase inertia, weights were added to the idler gears on the front of the heads and to the cam gears, while, in conjunction with Holset, a viscous damper was developed for the nose of the crank. The teams didn't appreciate the extra weight, so, as confidence grew in the efficacy of the quill device, one by one these fitments were removed during the course of the year.

After suitable development and testing, small changes like this were sometimes incorporated into engines at rebuild time without specific recourse to the customer, who might otherwise be tempted to blame the tiny engine mod for a poor day on the track.

Keith was always keen to minimise crankcase windage, and used Morse testing to assess the extent of the problem.[1] These experiments, undertaken around 1974, resulted in a change of sump design. Originally, for strength reasons, all five main-bearing caps were integral with the sump, which had the effect of isolating a chamber of air and vapour around each bearing. The revised sump incorporated only caps one, three and five, the others being of conventional design, to encourage flow.

Fuel supply systems varied, as they were the teams' responsibility, but Keith's preferred arrangement was the Lotus 49 system with a pick-up at the bottom of the tank (so there was never a depression at the inlet) and the electric pump mounted low down where it would stay cool. For most of its life the DFV used two pumps, electric to start and mechanical for normal running, but in 1984 a combined electro-mechanical pump was introduced. Mounted inside the tank to avoid an inlet depression, it was electric at low engine speeds, but as the revs rose, a one-way clutch engaged and connected the armature to a cable drive, an arrangement that was lighter (alloy rather than brass), neater and dispensed with one filter.

The DFV's ignition system received considerable attention, not least because the early versions had an electro-mechanical rev limiter, which was not nearly responsive enough. By the time it cut in, the damage was often done. Early DFVs used the Lucas Opus ignition system, which was found to be very sensitive to pickup positioning, so a strengthened distributor was tried. Next came the Lucas Rita system, using a magnetic trigger, but this was dropped as the unit was in a hot position at the front of the engine, and high temperatures adversely affect the magnetic strength.

The breakthrough came with CDI around 1972, when Walter Scherag introduced Cosworth to his company Contactless Ignition: in a telling test-cell demonstration, he covered the plugs of a DFV with oil and then invited Cosworth engineers to start it, which it did easily. CDI didn't seem to aid power output, but the drivers liked it, reporting improved pick-up from slow corners. Like many improvements, it was first tried on Tyrrell's cars but was rapidly adopted for all DFVs, though supply problems soon prompted Cosworth to substitute an equivalent Lucas system. Marelli CDI and a system developed by EFI Technology (run by ex-Marelli man Piero Campi) were also used.

Engines were reckoned to be good for 600 racing miles, after which they needed a rebuild either at Cosworth or one of its approved service agents. Rebuilders were not encouraged to tweak, but they did anyway – Nicholson McLaren tried an enlarged bore and a shorter stroke at one point, and several builders tried different cams.

Sometimes a rebuilder would come up with a tweak that really worked. The Shadow DN5 of Jean-Pierre Jarier gained pole position in the first two Grands Prix of the 1975 season (Argentina and Brazil), thanks to a short-inlet-trumpet package developed by John Dunn. Mechanical failure in both races prevented him from capitalising on it, but within weeks all other teams were following suit.

By 1975 Ferrari's flat-12 had well and truly caught Cosworth's V8 in the power race. The Italian firm took the constructors championship for three years on the trot between 1975 and 1977, Niki Lauda only missing out on a hat trick of drivers' crowns because of James Hunt's last-gasp effort at the Japanese Grand Prix, and his own decision to retire from the race on safety grounds.

Cosworth had to respond, and Keith reasoned that weight-saving offered an easier route to a faster racing car than wholesale redesigning of what was now a ten year-old powerplant. In standard form, the DFV was not the lightest engine ever to grace an F1 car, Keith having deliberately avoided wafer-thin castings in its design, not only in the interests of easy machining and serviceability but also because the powerplant was a stressed member. So in 1976 he dusted off an idea which he had first experimented with in 1969: the magnesium engine. Back then, he'd shelved the project because there was no competitive need for it. Seven years on, things had changed.

For obvious practical reasons, the magnesium components were cast from the same patterns as their aluminium counterparts and thus had the same sections. This was not ideal, because a magnesium casting is not as rigid as an aluminium one of the same size. Even more of a technical challenge was magnesium's higher coefficient of expansion. This had been clearly demonstrated in 1969, when expansion of the block opened up the main bearings, leading to loss of oil pressure. A positive result emerged, however, as the problem prompted a redesign of the drillings in the crankshaft, to allow it to work at lower pressures. What became known as the low-pressure crank operated at 52psi instead of 85psi and functioned so well that by 1974 it had become standard on all DFVs. It gave a more reliable oil supply to the big ends and as a result big-end failures virtually disappeared.

Second time around, Keith didn't do things by halves, specifying magnesium for the block, heads, cam carriers and sump. It was a step too far, however, for despite the low-pressure crank, inadequate oil pressure was still an issue, even with an uprated oil pump. In an attempt to combat this, engines were built very 'tight,' so much so that at room temperatures the fitter couldn't even turn the crank unless the entire assembly was being warmed by a fan heater. In extremis, if the block got very cold, the nip could increase to the point where the main bearing caps in the sump yielded, so teams were warned to install heating in their transporters. For the same reason, coolant had to be preheated before start-up. It was all very marginal.

Finally, Keith gave up the struggle, and early in 1977 wrote to the teams saying the project was being ended. Instead, hybrid engines were tried, reverting to aluminium for the block and sump while retaining magnesium for the carriers and heads.

Unfortunately, the magnesium head didn't work either. There were problems with valve seats rotating due to the head casting's greater expansion and, more fundamentally, the material proved unable to withstand the normal crushing loads of assembly and would yield as the miles built up, cracking the inlet port and allowing water into the cylinder. This tendency was exacerbated by the fact that the magnesium heads ran hotter, because the material has a lower heat-transfer coefficient than aluminium. The footage of James Hunt retiring from the Monaco GP with strange coloured liquid emerging from his engine shows just such a failure. The colour is due to potassium dichromate, an unpleasant chemical added to the coolant to inhibit corrosion, which nevertheless remained a problem.

Hybrids went only to selected teams – Tyrrell, McLaren, Lotus, and Wolf – but as the programme wound down, leaving the cam carrier as the only surviving magnesium part, the focus shifted to maximising power output. In the short term, this meant paying particular attention to assembly, to the point where the rings were honed with lapping compound. One such blueprinted engine notched up the DFV's 100th victory, at the 1977 Monaco GP, installed in the back of Jody Scheckter's Wolf WR1.

In his search for a more fundamental improvement, Keith was mindful of the uprated 1976 BDG, from which Alastair Lyle had extracted the highest BMEP yet seen at Cosworth: 15.5bar. That same year Keith had produced an experimental cylinder head with larger inlet valves, plus ports which were not only larger but also had revised geometry to promote axial swirl. Airflow test results were good, but power output actually dropped from 465 to 440 bhp at 10,750rpm.

With the magnesium programme winding down, Keith revisited this work in spring 1977 and asked Alastair to incorporate the revised valves and ports, but not the axial swirl geometry, into a revised DFV head. This was fitted on a block with new pistons that gave 12:1 compression, the result being 495bhp at 10,750rpm and almost BDG levels of BMEP: 15.2bar. This engine, DFV 254, then gifted its specification to a series of 'development engines' used by Lotus, McLaren and Tyrrell for the rest of the season, though mainly for qualifying as their hotter cams adversely affected reliability. During this challenging period, it was helpful for the teams to have a Cosworth man in the pits, a role filled by Dick Scammell, who by 1976 had returned from a spell in F1 and taken up an expanded role as Keith's eyes and ears.

The last significant reliability issue was the fuel metering unit in the centre of the vee, which initially was hung from a flange at the rear, with no front support. The mounting tended to fatigue because of the sideways shake inherent in a flat-crank V8, and a temporary solution was applied quite early on. Known in the works as the Frankenstein solution, it consisted of two transverse bolts with their ends ground to a point; these were tightened until the mount was braced against the cylinder head casting – crude, but effective. Eventually, in 1977, a proper arrangement was engineered, known as the Forth Bridge mount.

As the 1970s drew to a close, Keith tried one other radical change: desmodromic valve gear, in 1979. Geoff Goddard designed it, and it got as far as running on a test rig before Keith abandoned the idea – he couldn't see a way to produce it economically.

Quite early in the decade, around 1973, Keith had decided that he needed to clear the decks. He wanted his designers' energies and his machine shop's equipment to focus on the DFV and on other new work, not worry about developments of old designs or manufacture of spares for obsolete engines. On the other hand, Cosworth had always been proud of its customer service and he didn't want to leave customers unsupported.

DFV excepted, in the 1970s Cosworth's biggest single activity was the BD series and much later Keith would admit that at one point, despite its continuing success, he considered selling it off in its entirety, to help keep the business to a size he was comfortable with. Another solution, one which he eventually concluded would have been the best, would have been to create an entirely separate company to look after the older engines.

In the event he did neither and opted instead for a halfway house, creating a separate operation called Cosworth Components (CC) in 1973. Its position in the company structure would be similar to that of Cosworth Pistons – still very much part of the firm, but expected to run its own day-to-day affairs.

Cosworth Components consisted of just three people: Bill Pratt would oversee the stores and organise component manufacture, Jack Field would handle sales, and Frank Webb, a very able and versatile draughtsman and an ex-HWM mechanic, would do any design work that was required. Their principal responsibility was to be the BD series and any Cosworth designs that were no longer current, like the FVA, but they were also at liberty to source and sell other components, including items for engines not made by Cosworth.

Jack remembers being told "You can have Bill Pratt and Frank Webb, you can't have anyone else unless their manager says you can have them. You can't use any of the designers, or the test shops, and you can only have parts made in the machine shop if they've got the capacity to do it. Anything else you have to get made outside."

The three-man team was located 'over the road', in the new Factory 3, opened in 1973 and initially used to house CC, the purchasing department, the machine shop for Cosworth Pistons, a fledgling production engineering department (an Alf Vickers initiative) and, upstairs, a canteen cum social club. There was lots of spare space remaining though, and before long it was filled with two new Milwaukee NC machines.

With design and development staff still located in the original buildings, the new premises lacked the buzz of the old and St James Mill Road soon became something of a divide. This feeling was reinforced in the late 1970s when Factory 3 was doubled in size to allow the main machine shop to move across from Factory 2. "Whenever we had a success," continues Malcolm, "what tended to happen was that everyone got together, but you'd forget to invite the machine shop. Or if you invited them, they couldn't come because they were in the middle of a machining operation that couldn't be stopped. It tended to feel like us and them, so whenever I was involved in something, I tried to thank the machine shop guys personally. Sometimes there'd be a real rush for an upgrade and it would be them who'd deliver. Or the purchasing people, who'd put the push on suppliers – it was always too easy to forget them."

In the circumstances, Jack and his two colleagues could be forgiven for feeling pushed aside, both geographically and strategically. Bill Pratt certainly did. "We've been shit on," Jack remembers him saying. "We've put in all this effort and now we're being sidetracked."

Jack saw things very differently. "I told them 'It's a golden opportunity, we're handling nearly half a million in turnover, probably around a third of the total, Keith himself probably doesn't realise that.' He wasn't a businessman in that sense and he wouldn't have given a stuff anyway – the money was rolling in."

Several BD variants had already been developed in conjunction with outside companies, sometimes with little or no Northampton involvement other than to sell kits of parts once a prototype had been tested, and Jack realised that, in effect, he had the green light to continue that process. He could provide any BD variant he sensed there was a market for, provided he could find a way of getting the job designed, tested and machined.

Moreover, there was a great deal of money to be made from more mundane products like fuel filters, water pumps, oil pumps and scavenge pumps – bespoke Cosworth items which had since acquired wider applications. The fuel filter from the DFV, for instance, sold by the hundred.

The three-man team was nothing if not productive, for the 2-litre BDG, 1300cc BDH, 1100cc BDJ and 1600cc fuel-injected BDM all date from the CC period, which lasted until 1977 when it was reabsorbed back into the main company structure. Keith may not have been much interested in the BD, but it simply refused to lay down and die. One year – Jack thinks 1973 – he went to the SCCA National Championship Runoffs in Atlanta and came back with orders for 47 engines, most of them BD variants.

"Frank Webb was bloody useful, he could run a workshop, he could do some of the designs, draw it, get it made," says Jack. Frank was indeed a hard worker – he did all the design on the CC-instigated Ford-based pushrod Clubman's engine – but perhaps not *quite* as much a grafter as the drawing-office records suggest …

One day, Jack relates, Alastair Lyle came over from the design shop. Several years before he'd taken over engineering responsibility for the BD from Mike Hall. By now Alastair had mainly moved on to other projects, but he happened to have a gap in his schedule and wanted some work.

Jack replied that Keith would "skin him alive" if he started giving Alastair work, and said no, but Alastair offered to keep it all under cover, even offering – only half in jest – to give it ZA drawing numbers,[2] so it would appear to have been done by Frank Webb at Cosworth Components! In due course the 1100cc BDJ was drawn up.

"I did the schemes for the crank and head and Roy Jones did the necessary drawings under my supervision," says Alastair. "We did a quick cobble-up […] that was built and run by John Dunn at SRE and peaked at over 145bhp at 9500rpm. The full-house development BDJ that ran in Northampton in 1976 managed to get to 150bhp at 10,000rpm."

The BDJ turned out to be a real screamer, so free-revving that over-enthusiastic drivers often took it beyond its 10,500 red line, with expensive results. "It got so bad that I suggested to Jack Field that the rev counters on these cars should have a large red dollar sign on their dials at about 10,000rpm, to try and stop the lunatics damaging their engines unnecessarily!'!"

Once Alastair had approved the test results, Bill Pratt and Frank organised manufacture of the parts in-house, where production constraints permitted.

Jack and co were left largely to their own devices, though obviously the board knew – and no doubt approved – of the various projects that were under way. Whether they knew all the details of who was doing what is another matter. Alf Vickers certainly did, despite appearing to take no interest in the threesome for a long time, an absence which only served to reinforce Jack's low opinion of him. "I thought he's never been to see any of us, yet here we are, we're really buzzing, and we're doing it with very few staff. Eventually he arrived on our side of the road. He said 'You know what your turnover is, don't you?'

'Yeah, about a million.'

'Its one and a quarter, that's the same as the DFV.'

'But the DFV is more profitable.'

'What makes you say that? When I look at your costs, I can't see a Keith Duckworth, I can't see a Mike Costin, I can't see any design staff, apart from what you get out of the back door. No test facilities. Your operation is far more profitable.'"

On hearing that he'd more than doubled his turnover in two years, and that Alf had been watching approvingly all along, Jack completely changed his mind about Cosworth's newest director. "He was canny enough to have cottoned on to what we were doing by the back door, but he was also giving me a tick for that. That was good."

When CC was started, Jack was still responsible to Bill and thence to Keith, but partway through the operation, in November 1975, Keith finally did what many had expected from day one and made Alf managing director instead of plain director. That put him, notionally at least, in charge of Mike, Ben and Bill.

Mike explains "Bill, Ben and I, were supposed to work under him, but no way would Bill accept it. We hadn't ever had official titles, there were just four of us who ran the place. But Bill handled most of the admin, so he was the most affected by the appointment."

In theory, this left Jack with a tortuous chain of command – to Bill, then Alf and then finally Keith – but in practice Bill was often out of the picture. Between 1974 and 1976 he made a number of trips to the US to develop Cosworth's Indycar presence. Unhappy at the way things were going in Northampton, he welcomed the new challenge.

One issue in particular cemented his antipathy to the new boardroom hierarchy: the costing system. Bill had long had a straightforward costing system based on material costs and hours spent. It was unsophisticated, but by and large produced sensible numbers, and several years earlier, before Alf's name had ever been mentioned, Bill proposed to Keith that it be refined and extended across the firm.

Bill says "It was time that we had a good system installed and I told Keith I would like to legitimise what I had been practising for years. Keith said he wanted a different costing system, arguing that, under my formal system all we were doing was confirming the current methods of manufacture, whereas if we were to improve we needed to concentrate on what we should be doing, rather than what we had been doing. He continually battered my ears with Henry Ford's saying: 'History is bunk.'

"While I could see sense in using Keith's approach to produce targets to which we should aspire, I could not see its relevance to producing sensible numbers on which to cost, and I told him that, as such, it was a right load of old cobblers."

In the absence of any agreement, Bill had carried on with the existing arrangements, but when Alf became managing director, one of his first acts was to introduce a revised system based on the same principle that Bill had proposed and Keith vociferously rejected. "All this occurred without me being told anything about it. That was the end as far as I was concerned," says Bill.

Although Alf's computerised costing system was based on the same principles as Bill's, of existing costs and machining times, a crucial difference was that it also factored in downtime, overheads and depreciation, rather than relying on the profit margin to cover these items. Also, thanks to more sophisticated computers, it was accessible to a much wider range of staff.

The extra variables in the new system could have a dramatic effect on the final price, and initially some of the numbers Alf's system produced were unrealistically high – in Mike's words, "a load of balls".

Eventually, after various revisions, Alf's system produced sensible numbers, but by that point the damage to Bill's relationship with Keith was irreparable. His status was reduced to consultant and as time went by he found himself with less and less to do. The end came in 1977, when Bill was told at a board meeting that his services were no longer required. He retained a non-executive directorship and was paid a consultancy fee for the next couple of years, but in practice that was severance money – his input was negligible after that point.

Alf's other move shortly after taking over as MD was to call a meeting of all the staff, where he briefed them on his plans for the company. Malcolm remembers the meeting vividly and, like many employees, was shocked by what he heard.

"He told us 'The days of relying solely on motorsport are dead ... we can't build a company around F1 because it could disappear like that.' He turned out to be absolutely right, but at the time this was our world. He was telling us that everything we'd cared about was no longer important, or at least less important. He certainly wasn't popular."

He didn't get any more popular when the implications of the costing system became apparent. Measuring downtime involved introducing timesheets, which wasn't explained well to the staff, who consequently resented them – "It felt like Big Brother," says Malcolm. "Only later did we come to understand that he was trying to bring science into production: until then I'd never given a thought to the fact that what I did had an impact on the cost of the engine. My job in development was basically 'there are the engines, you test them, you make sure they're fit for purpose, then you release them.' We took it for granted that there was going to be money to pay our wages."

Around 1977, the strategic decision was made to reverse Keith's setting up of CC and bring Jack's operation back into the Cosworth mainstream. Unlike Keith, Alf didn't see CC as a sideshow, he knew exactly how important it was to the company, and it is a testament to the level of trust now existing between the two men that Alf was able to persuade Keith to do a complete U-turn. Even Mike would have struggled to do that.

Jack was given overall responsibility for all Cosworth's sales, reporting directly to the board. It was a big vote of confidence in him, but it wasn't the job he'd been expecting.

Bill Brown had been nurturing the Indycar market for some time, and Alf had earlier told Jack he could move with his family to America and run a new Cosworth operation there. Jack recalls "I told the kids, I told the wife, I made sure all my work in the UK was passed over to others. Then Alf said 'Come up and have a word with Keith and me in the office.' When I got there, Keith told me Bill Brown was leaving and I was to take over most of his responsibilities.

'What, from America?'

'No, you're not going to America.'

'But I've told my wife, I've told everyone!'

'Well, if you're out of pocket, we'll sort it out, but you're not going to the US. You can have any Ford car you like, we'll look at your salary, but you're not going to the States.' I was really pissed off."

In due course Cosworth did set up an American operation, and Jack spent long periods working there, but it was always controlled from the UK.

An interesting postscript to Alf's elevation to MD is that before deciding on it, Keith asked his old university friend Noel Davies to take the post. He never seems to have told anyone else about this approach, but he was undoubtedly serious, spending hours on the phone trying to persuade his former housemate. Noel, who at the time was working for the Vickers group, was genuinely honoured to be asked, but was used to the working practices of a big company and did not believe he would fit well in a medium-sized operation like Cosworth.

He declined, telling Keith "There are some projects which you can't accomplish with a small team, and building a nuclear submarine is one of them. And there are others, like motorsport, which you can't accomplish without one." He had personal reservations too: "Good friends don't always make good bosses, especially when both are used to having their own way."

Keith's motive in approaching Noel Davies can only be guessed at, but if he had reservations about Alf, he never let on to anyone. On the contrary, everyone at Cosworth understood that Alf had Keith's total support.

LIFE IN THE TEST CELLS

In 1965, when the test cells at St James Mill Road were constructed, they were placed in a separate building at the back of the main factory to isolate the rest of the site from noise and fire risk. By the standards of the 1960s and '70s, Cosworth's approach to health and safety was up to scratch – and certainly better than many – but the standards of the time were very different from those familiar to 21st century engineers. The recollections below from Malcolm Tyrrell[3] – who, as a development engineer, spent countless hours in the test cells – show just how different.

"We had to work pretty resourcefully in those days, especially when the DFV was at its peak and prior to Cosworth allowing engines to be rebuilt by satellite organisations. There was a staff of just five, including the manager, and at busy periods we ran-in and tested six to eight engines per day which would involve all five of us pitching in. Once we had one engine installed and fired up, we would move down to the next cell to install the next, leaving the previous engine(s) to run-in unattended.

"The actual test was another frantic episode. Instrumentation was nowhere near as comprehensive as it is now – basically an analogue tachometer (later duplicated by a digital readout, after we suffered some spurious power outputs!), plus an ammeter and gauges for oil and fuel pressure, oil and water temperature, air inlet temperature and the Heenan analogue load dial. Additionally, one water and one mercury manometer to monitor crankcase pressure and the pressure difference between head and lower crankcase, respectively. In the early '70s we got very technical and added water and

A more likely reason can be inferred from one of Keith's favourite Duckworthisms:

I THINK WE [COSWORTH] ALWAYS MANAGED TO UNDER-EMPLOY PEOPLE. WE ACHIEVED HIGHER STANDARDS THAN THE OTHERS – IT CAME FROM NOT PROMOTING PEOPLE TO THE LEVEL AT WHICH THEY'RE MAKING A LOT OF MISTAKES. IT'S THE REVERSE OF THE PETER PRINCIPLE.

In all likelihood, Keith was so pleased with Alf's performance as a director that he was tempted to leave well alone.

Coincidentally, Noel knew Alf, because the latter's CV included a spell at 600 Group under its autocratic chairman Sir Jack Wellings. Wearing his Vickers group hat, Noel had had some dealings with the company. Later, in 1984, he would join 600 Group himself and effectively occupy the same seat Alf had warmed some years before. "Jack ran it like his own company, there was never any real debate", Noel recalls. "Before he went home at night, he would expect you to join him for a whisky, and chauffeurs would be waiting for each director who had stayed behind."

A more different atmosphere from St James Mill Road could scarcely be imagined, for Keith had strong views about directors' perks, believing they were a total waste of money. "When he asked 'would you like a coffee?', he had a tray, very old with dents and

oil flowmeters. Tracing electrical gremlins was not helped by the fact that at one point Mike Costin took the opportunity to buy a job lot of brown-sleeved wire at a bargain price – and we had no wiring diagrams in those days!

"Engine removal was also challenging, as there was no time to let engines cool off. Keith reckoned that if you had any nerve endings left in your fingers, then the ¼-inch UNF brass exhaust nuts on the exhaust system were too cool! With three engines running full chat and doors having to be opened to set up ignition and speed limiters, my hearing is not what it used to be either!

"At that time of health and safety naïvety, a number of tasks were done in-cell while the engines were running. These included setting ignition timing at 7000rpm on the DFV; optimising FVA ignition at 7000rpm by rotating the distributor to achieve maximum load; and on the early DFV setting the speed limiter, which meant being in the cell at 10,500rpm while it was run up. Once, when there was a valve-spring failure, the associated shrapnel emerged from the inlet trumpet at extremely close proximity. No wonder I'm follicly challenged.

"Sometimes, when an engine failed under test, fluids would ignite, but these fires usually either extinguished themselves or were relatively quickly brought under control. When a bigger blaze occurred, it was not much fun at all, as the dyno set-up was pretty cosy, to say the least.

"Fire training consisted of tackling a real fire, of which I can remember three big ones, mainly caused by reinforced rubber oil hose perishing through radiated exhaust heat. This resulted in a fountain of hot, pressurized oil spewing forth and igniting on contact with the exhaust primaries. The worst of the three was when the initial fire melted the clear, low-pressure fuel-return hose, bringing petrol into the equation. It took many powder extinguishers (no CO_2 extinguishers or Inergen systems then) to get that blaze under control.

"We eventually took the initiative of replacing these rubber hoses with several hundred pounds worth of much safer, but very expensive, Aeroquip. We were testing the DFX at the time and Larry Slutter from our American operation was with us. There was no purchase requisition system in place then, so the first Mike Costin knew of it was when he was asked to sign off the invoice and nearly experienced a seizure. In the test cells, in front of Paul Squires, Larry and I, he went off on a serious tirade about filling the place up with bloody awful stuff that cost a fortune, held no advantage over good old reinforced rubber hose and, in fact, was badly conceived, because every fitting generated a serious pressure drop on account of its restricted cross-sectional area. He finished with the immortal words: 'See Larry, we Cosworth people are big-hole men,' which can't have translated too well to our colonial brother, as he burst into fits of laughter the moment Mike left the cell.

"There were various other fire sources. In winter, for instance, a ky-gas manual plunger pump was used to charm recalcitrant FVAs into life. Four jets were mounted on a common rail and while the engine was being cranked over by the operator outside the cell, the idiot inside had to hold this arrangement up to the inlet trumpets and squirt fuel into the engine. Typically this procedure would get the engine running, but every so often, the engine would have a lean backfire, causing the fuel in the rail to ignite. If the 'driver' kept calm and continued to crank the engine, it would extinguish the flame itself. If not, the whole thing took on the appearance of the Olympic torch.

"On test, the DFV's secondary tailpipes ran from the engine to the external silencers at a height of around 65cm (26-inches). Fuel adjustment required access to the vee-mounted metering-unit datum pin, and that meant straddling those tailpipes. If, like me, you weren't blessed with long legs, heat damage to sensitive body parts was a very real danger. We wore brown engineering smocks at work: if yours was scorched, you worked in the test shop.

scratches, and he would go round collecting the money for the coffee machine!" These are the words of a young Swiss engineer, Mario Illien, who joined Cosworth in 1979 and would later play a significant part in the Cosworth story. Mario found such earthiness endearing, but it can't have been easy for Alf to adjust to the Cosworth mindset.

Although the 4WD car had not worked well, the idea of gaining performance through novel transmission design still intrigued Keith, and he became interested in an infinitely variable automatic being developed by a company called Variable Kinetic Drives Ltd, believing it had the potential to be used in F1. The company was a fledgling operation, based in a shed in the garden of its founder, Howard Hobbs, but it had considerable pedigree, for Australian-born Howard had been fascinated by the idea of automatic transmission ever since boyhood.

Born in 1902, Howard developed the Hobbs Gearless Drive before World War II. A fully mechanical gearbox, it used rotating weights, plus a ratchet device to act as a freewheel clutch. He was unable to persuade any manufacturer to adopt it, but tried again in 1946, forming Hobbs Transmission Ltd to make his second design. Called Mechamatic,

"For a number of years after its introduction, Keith had a deep mistrust of the accuracy of electronic measuring equipment and insisted on sticking to traditional methods. If he wanted to conduct heat-rejection tests, this posed a serious challenge, as oil and water inlet and outlet temperatures all had to be taken with mercury and glass thermometers – and the water inlet thermometer was pretty close to the glowing exhaust collector. Oil and water flows also had to be directly measured, which meant disconnecting those lines and discharging fluid directly into a measuring device – a bucket held by whoever was unfortunate enough to be in the cell with the engine. We were expected to take readings at 7000, 8000 and 9000rpm, only for higher speeds were we allowed the luxury of extrapolating the data.

"Some incidents were, in retrospect, accidents waiting to happen. On one occasion test-shop manager John Given needed to weld some bracketry on the fuel header tank. He drained it first of course, but failed to notice that some petrol had spilt onto the top of the dyno on which he was standing – and that day he happened to be wearing absorbent suede shoes. When he started welding, a spark from the oxy-acetylene torch set light to his footwear. Poor John was left running around the test shop with extinguisher-carrying colleagues in hot pursuit!

"It seems unbelievable now, but for many years smoking was allowed anywhere in the works, and this led to an 'interesting' incident during the BDA road engine programme, involving my colleague Roy Finch. Prior to the engines being collected by Ford, the oil was drained off and then the engine inverted on the build stand to drain fuel from the 40DCOE Weber carburettors. One afternoon Roy walked calmly into the test-shop and asked, in a very cool and collected manner, did I have an extinguisher handy and, if so, could I bring it to his workbench?

"Lighting in the factory was not up to modern standards – basically fluorescent tubes high up in the roof space and therefore not regularly cleaned – and in addition workstations were shielded by having dark green steel shelving all around, up to head height. But that day, Roy's workstation was beautifully illuminated because, some time after draining the oil and petrol into his drip tray, he'd absent-mindedly thrown his 'extinguished' cigarette stub into the tray!

this was a four-speed epicyclic gearbox with hydraulically operated friction clutches. Unlike most early automatics, the Mechamatic was light enough to be used in small and medium-sized cars. A number of manufacturers experimented with this unit and one – Lanchester – got as far as putting it into a saleable car, the 1955 Sprite. However, only ten were built before BSA, the parent company of Lanchester and Daimler, decided to concentrate on the more glamorous of the two names and pulled the plug on the whole Lanchester marque.

Westinghouse Brake & Signal Co bought the holding in anticipation of Ford adopting the transmission for the Cortina, but when Ford decided against it, Howard Hobbs found himself once again liquidating an enterprise carrying his name.

Despite this disappointment, he set up a third company, Variable Kinetic Drives, and started to develop his third transmission, working with his son John from his home at Napton-on-the-Hill, near Rugby. The new design returned to the infinitely variable principle of the first, but with the benefit of hydraulic, rather than mechanical, operation. It was this combination that impressed Keith sufficiently to persuade him to invest in the company and take on a directorship. He was introduced to the Hobbs by Godfrey Shiner, who also invested and joined the board. A third director/investor was Norman Reeve, a farmer with a strong interest in technical matters. He got on very well with Keith, and by 1974 Norman and his wife Gill could be found at the Lake with their two daughters, Amber and Tina.

Keith's thinking was that an infinitely variable transmission would enable the engine to sit at maximum torque or maximum power, as appropriate, for a much greater proportion of the lap than any conventional gearbox. It would be a bit heavier, and would increase fuel consumption, but provided no fuel restrictions were introduced into F1, he thought it could win.

Scaling up the Hobbs transmission to handle 500bhp was very ambitious, and Keith hired Cecil Schumacher from Borg Warner to lead the design. Cecil had previously worked at Hobbs, so he was doubly suited to the task, and by 1974 was hard at work in Northampton on what became known within Cosworth as the LA.

Two years went by before the redesign was complete, the prototype parts made, and an application made for a US patent. The transmission was nothing if not complicated: being conceived in the era before electronic controls, it had to rely on complex hydraulics. The prototype overheated and repeatedly failed on test as various weaknesses became apparent, the most problematic component being the torque converter. This suffered from cavitation around the blades, exacerbated by the need to cope with the DFV's high idle speed, about twice the rpm of a normal road engine.

The LA project rumbled on for over three years, but in 1978 Keith abandoned it altogether, fearing he was in danger of throwing good money after bad. When faced with serious design problems, Keith's instinct was usually to put the job down to experience and move on, but after the event he could find himself wondering whether he had been over-cautious. In fact he had a Duckworthism about it, commenting:

ONE OF THE THINGS I OFTEN DID WRONG WAS TO STOP PROJECTS AT VARIOUS STAGES OF DEVELOPMENT, BECAUSE I FELT WE COULDN'T AFFORD TO PRODUCE TRIUMPHS OF DEVELOPMENT OVER DESIGN.

The LA was just such a project, Keith later commenting: "I think that, on reflection, the gearbox came to grief, and was always going to come to grief, because it was too complicated – a real bag of tricks in the end – a bit big and too heavy. But maybe I should have gone out, looked for someone to give us some support, and then carried on," (*Cosworth*, p140).

Cecil stayed at Cosworth until the end of the decade, during which time he had the idea which was to transform his life. One evening in 1978 Cecil was watching Cosworth employees running model cars on the helipad behind the development shop and he said "You need a diff, they're skittering." So he designed one, for his son's model. It worked so well that by 1980 he had left Cosworth to start making high-performance radio-controlled model cars, a business which is still very much alive today.

In 1973, just after the EAA programme for GM had wound down, Keith was approached by another company seeking the glamour of the 'Cosworth connection': Norton. Like the rest of the British motorcycle industry, the company had been knocked sideways by the onslaught of sophisticated Japanese machines and was in urgent need of a new product to replace the Commando. Norton proprietor Dennis

Poore reckoned that by farming out the engine development to Cosworth, he could not only shortcut the process but also inject interest and credibility into the new bike. Keith, his youthful love of motorcycles undimmed, enthusiastically agreed and took personal charge of the design, with Mike Hall handling most of the drawing.

Dennis Poore's specification called for a parallel twin, in the classic Norton tradition, as narrow as possible and mounted transversely, low down in the bike. He called it the Challenge, though at Cosworth it was always the JA. The 750cc liquid-cooled unit was to develop 65hp in road trim (JAA), fuelled by just a single carburettor, to aid compliance with the emission regulations which Poore believed were inevitable. The target for the twin-carb racing version (JAB) was 90bhp, though the design also made provision for fuel-injection.

The contract divided the work along now-familiar Cosworth lines: the JAA would be built at Norton while Cosworth would produce 25 examples of the JAB, as well as handle all design work. Of the 25 racing engines, 20 were to go to Norton for US homologation purposes. The remaining five, Cosworth could develop as it saw fit.

Parallel twins are notorious for vibration – indeed, Norton's existing engine was particularly bad in this respect – and Keith paid great attention to minimising it, eventually adopting the Lanchester principle and incorporating two balancer shafts, one each side of the engine. The rear shaft was gear-driven from the crankshaft; the front by the camshaft drivebelt.

Apart from its use of belt drive, the JA's head design drew considerably on the DFV, and there was another parallel in that the engine was to be a stressed member.

The gear-driven balancer shaft was hollow, and through it ran a quill shaft whose other end drove the gearbox via a Hi-Vo chain. The box was integral with the engine; its internals were supposed to be Norton's responsibility, but Keith ended up redesigning it, and much else besides. By the time he'd finished, the engine installation angle, the swing-axle pivot point, and the geometry of the chain movement had all been finalised.

On test, the most serious snag proved to be the water pump, which was driven off the end of one of the camshafts, and proved vulnerable to damage by heat soak after the engine had stopped. Fixing that meant re-routing the water flow, which, in turn, meant changing all 25 sets of castings, so instead a modification was hastily fabricated and welded into place on each engine. Keith told Graham Robson: "When I designed it like that my mind had obviously taken a holiday." (*Cosworth*, p144).

The intention, of course, was to change the casting design before any more engines were built, but in the event only 25 were ever assembled, because in 1975 Norton went broke. Fortunately, Cosworth was paid for its work – some £60,000 according to *Motorcycle Enthusiast* – and retained its five engines, but with Norton gone the JA appeared to have no future. There seemed no point in tackling the various other problems that had revealed themselves, and the engines were left, unloved, in a corner of the factory.

Happily, that is not the end of the story, but the rest belongs in a later chapter.

Footnotes

1 Morse testing involves disabling one cylinder, reducing dyno loading to allow the engine to regain its original speed, noting the load reduction, and then repeating for each cylinder in turn. When all the load reductions are added up, the difference between the total and the engine's power when running on all cylinders at the same speed gives a measure of its friction and pumping losses.

2 The ZA project code was used for a variety of miscellaneous design jobs, including Frank Webb's output at CC – see Appendix for full list of codes.

3 When Malcolm retired in 2005 after 37 years with the company, he was Cosworth's longest-serving employee and, as a farewell, he wrote a long open letter to the staff, summarizing his time with the firm. These recollections are taken from those informal memoirs·

Chapter 12

Of life and loves

In his professional life, Keith was a great believer in disseminating information and expressing his opinions. He would happily spend hours discussing things with friends, family and colleagues, or putting the world to rights; all he asked was that they be prepared to listen and to engage in meaningful debate.

By contrast, in his private life he was much more reticent. Even in the sanctuary of the pub in all-male company, when the banter turned to people complaining – jokingly or otherwise – about their wives and girlfriends, Keith was inclined to keep his own counsel. Mike says, "To Keith, our wives were just ordinary girls, but his Ursula was perfect and marvellous." Keith did indeed have the highest regard for Ursula as a person, and never lost it. But as his relationship with Margaret indicates, under the surface his feelings were much more complex.

The person who came closest to understanding those feelings was neither Ursula nor Margaret, but a lady whose name has so far entered our story only fleetingly – Gill Reeve, wife of Norman Reeve, one of Keith's partners in the Hobbs transmission venture. Eventually, she would become the love of his life, and his second wife.

It was not love at first sight. When they met, around 1974, things were purely social. "Norman had met Keith several times," remembers Gill, "and kept saying 'you must meet Keith, you'd really like Keith.' But I didn't meet him until six to 12 months later when we went to a young farmers' dinner dance in Northampton, and there at a table were Keith and Ursula and Oliver and Shirley.

"Norman said 'Come and meet Keith,' so I did, and [Keith] said 'Come and have a dance,' which I did, and that was all there was to it, for at least two years."

"Keith and I went out for a drink a few times, we always found we had great spark between us, and we fell into a bit of a relationship." Keith loved to argue and debate, and in Gill he had found the perfect sparring partner. It wasn't a question of intelligence – both women are very bright – but they have completely different personalities.

There is no reason to doubt that when he married Ursula, Keith cared more for her than anyone he'd ever met, and genuinely believed she was the girl for him. But as Ursula puts it, "People have different ways of falling in love with people; different levels. I think when he first met me, realising that I was a fairly peaceful sort of person and didn't complain about getting wet in his car, he thought 'Well, she's the kind of girl who can cope with me not being a nine-to-five sort of person.'"

In focusing on the practical merits of the relationship at the expense of the emotional, Keith was far from alone among adults of his generation, particularly in northern industrial towns where life was hard. The Duckworth family was better off than many, but only by dint of many years' extremely hard work by both parents, which probably left precious little time for tenderness. Moreover, Blackburn in the 1930s and '40s was not a place where you wore your heart on your sleeve. The Duckworths were certainly a caring family, but equally certainly, not a very tactile one.

"Keith was very stoic," says Gill. "His mother was a tough lady. She told him when he went to boarding school, where they were very hard, that you didn't complain. And that's why he thought feelings and sex were not part of life, not permissible, you didn't need them. They didn't happen at Giggleswick and they didn't happen at home."

Exactly when Keith started to feel uneasy in his marriage is impossible to say, but as he entered his 40s and began his relationship with Margaret (around 1972), he seemed to be in search of something – emotional fulfilment is probably the best description. Maybe he didn't know what it would feel like, or who it would be with, but he knew he'd recognise it when it happened.

It didn't happen with Margaret, but by 1977 it was certainly well on the way with Gill. The pair were drawing closer and closer, and in January of that year they became lovers. They continued to meet clandestinely for some two years: neither of their marriages was going well and they found they spoke the same language.

Gill says "Norman's father had worked hard and provided each of his three sons with their own farm, so we were comfortably off, but Norman and I were married too young and both felt we'd never had any freedom."

Keith was very good at compartmentalising his activities, and at this point had all three women in his life. Even when Ursula came to realise that she and Margaret had a competitor for his affections, she didn't take the new relationship very seriously. "It never occurred to me that anything would actually come of it, I was a bit blind."

"He was a great one for sins of omission," says Gill. "That summer, when he and I were seeing each other seriously, he didn't tell me that he was taking Margaret away on holiday! When he got back he said it was a big mistake anyway: 'She was miserable all the time and I went windsurfing.'"

Not long afterwards Gill said firmly to him: "Look, you've got a wife, a mistress and you've got me." It was not an ultimatum, but Keith knew she would not be prepared to share him indefinitely.

Things moved on a little in June 1978 when Keith told Gill he had to go to America with powerboat driver Jackie Wilson. Cosworth had just built its own powerboat (see Chapter 14) and he and Jackie wanted to attend an American event to get the feel of the sport Stateside. This meant a change of plan, as Gill's husband Norman was going away that weekend and Keith and Gill had intended to see each other on the Saturday night. "I can't do anything this weekend, I've got to go to Florida," he said, "unless you want to come …" Gill was up for the challenge.

This impromptu trip – which was rounded off in some style by Keith bringing home an underwater unit as hand baggage! – was enjoyable, but it was not a turning point. "Florida was hot, humid and we were all very tired. It was not a lovers' weekend at all," says Gill. But, with a little assistance from the British weather, the turning point arrived a few months later, coincidentally as a result of a second American powerboat-racing trip. In February 1979 Keith arranged to go to Colorado, where the Cosworth powerboat was competing. He asked Ursula to accompany him, but she decided she couldn't. "We'd had a winter with masses and masses of snow and Roger was at school at Oundle, where they'd had to postpone their half term because parents couldn't get there to take the boys home. I thought Roger can't just come home and me not be there."

Ursula's decision to stay home opened up the possibility of Keith and Gill having another US trip. It seemed too good an opportunity to miss, but Gill too had domestic considerations – more so, in one respect, as her daughters were at day school. However, they were not on half-term that week, so with a bit of domestic organisation and some help from her sister-in-law, the way was cleared.

Unlike the previous trip, which was a private visit, this one was being done through the company, so Keith duly informed Dick Scammell, who was making the arrangements, that he would be accompanied after all, but not by his wife. A rather flustered and embarrassed Dick then called Malcolm Tyrrell (who was in charge of the powerboat team) into his office and explained the situation. On no account was he to gossip about this – it was a private matter.

On their return, Keith and Gill had planned to leave things at the level they were, but found they couldn't. "We needed to be together more than just a night or two a week," Gill says. Colorado had proved to be a watershed in their lives.

When this fact became clear, Ursula wondered whether things would have turned out differently if she had gone with him to the US after all. "With the benefit of hindsight, maybe I should have put Keith before Roger. I think Keith realised that something would follow from that trip."

Eight months later, in November, Keith and Gill bought Ashwood House in Marton, Warwickshire: a small house with a couple of acres and some stables, and started building a life together. Divorce would come much later – Keith felt that the least he could do for Ursula was let her decide the date for that – and it was not until 1985 that she requested a legal split.

"It wasn't as though we'd drifted apart," says Ursula wistfully. "I still cared for him when it ended, I was very upset. But unfortunately he just fell hook, line and sinker for Gill in a way he'd never fallen before."

Had she wanted to, Ursula could have made life very difficult for Keith, but she didn't have the heart to stand in his way. Divorces and separations are never pleasant affairs, but in the case of the Reeves and the Duckworths, things were kept on a remarkably even keel. Everyone accepted that the failure of the two marriages was the cause, not the effect, of Keith and Gill's relationship, and of course there were no mysterious unknown lovers bursting into people's lives and wreaking havoc – the parents and children all knew each other, the families were friends before and continued to be friends afterwards.

It helped that no one was obsessed with money. Keith agreed that Ursula should keep the house in its entirety and this, added to her existing share of Cosworth, meant that she was well provided for. For her part, Gill left all her assets with Norman, reasoning that Keith would provide a home and look after her, and that she in turn would keep a good household. She commented later that, had she and Keith proved incompatible at that point, she would have been in big financial trouble. At the time, though, she wasn't worried, completely confident of their relationship as she was.

The same could not be said for either of their mothers, or for Margaret, who was

Continued on p169

Like father, like son: when it came to mornings, the teenage Roger had the same opinion as his father.

Trish in action at Rothersthorpe Riding Club show in the club's field, either summer 1977 or '78.

Roger riding pillion on his dad's CX500, around 1976.

The Stuart no 10 steam engine built by Roger and Keith.

Keith (left) and Roger (right) at Cannock in 1987 for a hovercraft racing event.

Keith with Gill and Tina.

Trish and Keith having fun in the ski chalet.

With Gill and their jetskis, 1983.

Three suspicious characters: (l-r) Oliver Achurch, DKD and Mike Smith wait for a taxi after force-landing their helicopter. Note the wary resident eyeing them through the window!

An ideal home – Buckby Folly, seen here from the back.

Alpine skiing with all the family (clockwise from left, Tina,
A N Other, Gill, Amber's boyfriend at the time, the chalet girl, Amber,
Keith, Bernard (a friend), Trish and Roger.

Keith aboard his Honda CB250 Super Dream, around 1980.

In the mud with a Honda ATV, April 1987.

Geoff Brabham's Penske at the 1981 Indy 500, and (below) a close up of its DFX installation. *(Courtesy Ian Bisco/Cos Inc)*

Chickie Hirsashima (left) and Larry Slutter (right), Cos Inc's first employees. Larry is dyno testing an early DFX (DFV-derived, hence the Ford cam covers) on VPJ's dyno. Lacking the proper dyno manifolds, Larry used DFX items, but exhaust heat set off the fire sprinkler system and, as no one knew how to turn it off; the water flowed for over an hour. "We had quite a mess to clear up," says Ian Bisco. *(left photo courtesy Ian Bisco collection, right photo courtesy Ian Bisco/Cos Inc)*

DKD enjoying the sunshine at Indianapolis in the early 1980s.

A customer DFX at Oregon Court, Cos Inc's first premises in Torrance. This is an early unit, fitted with a Ed Pink throttle bodies and injectors. Note missing first compound gear housing, suggesting a failure of the type shown below. The failure illustrated happened at Indy in 1981 when the first bearing housing came loose; later engines used gears with smaller holes. *(Courtesy Ian Bisco/Cos Inc)*

Al Unser Sr was the first Cosworth DFX-powered Indianapolis 500 winner, in 1978.
(Courtesy Ford Motor Co)

Testing a DFX on VPJ's dyno. *(Courtesy Ian Bisco/Cos Inc)*

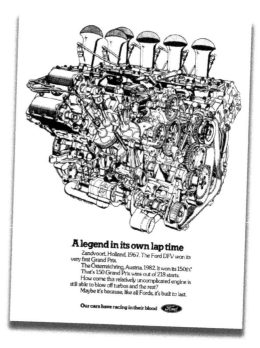

A legend in its own lap time

Zandvoort, Holland, 1967. The Ford DFV won its very first Grand Prix.

The Österreichring, Austria, 1982. It won its 150th.*

That's 150 Grand Prix wins out of 218 starts.

How come this relatively uncomplicated engine is still able to blow off turbos and the rest?

Maybe it's because, like all Fords, it's built to last.

Our cars have racing in their blood Ford

The one that got away: Cosworth histories never say much about the OAA, the company's VW Golf-based offering for Formula Super Vee racing. The basic design, from 1979, was sound enough, but Cosworth never promoted or developed the engine as comprehensively as some of its rivals, notably Judd and Bertil, and interest in it gradually withered away. These photos from the US, where Formula Super Vee was more popular than in Europe, show (top) the OAA in probably its most competitive form, tuned by Cos Inc's Ian Bisco and fitted to Billy Scyphers' Ralt RT5 for the 1980 season, in which form it took one win and three podiums from nine races; (middle) Billy in conversation with sponsor Frank Arciero at Phoenix International Raceway, and (bottom) Billy in the same car in later all-red livery, with his wife Patty kneeling by the car and Ian's wife Anne keeping the sun off him. *(Courtesy Ian Bisco / Cos Inc)*

In the garage at Silverstone, 1981, inspecting the Honda 2-litre V6 F2 engine installed in Mike Thackwell's Ralt: (l-r) Honda CEO Nobuhiko Kawamoto, DKD, Martin Walters, Mario Illien. *(Courtesy Mario Illien collection/Cosworth Enginering)*

Start of the 1982 Austrian GP, at which Elio de Angelis (Lotus no 11), notched up the DFV's 150th win, prompting a congratulatory advertisement from Ford (facing page, top right). *(Courtesy Ford Motor Co)*

Completion of the first DFY in spring 1983: (l-r) development engineer Paul Squires, engine builder Jeff Buttle, Mario Illien, Pete Rogers. *(Courtesy Mario Illien collection/Cosworth Engineering)*

Le Mans 1982, and Gordon Spice in his 3.9-litre DFL-engined Rondeau M382 (co-drivers François Migault, Xavier Lapeyre). An ignition fault ended their race. *(Courtesy Ford Motor Co)*

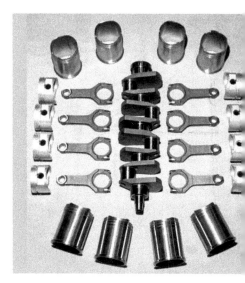

Two photos showing DFV crankshaft evolution. On the right is a DFL crank, with eight full-width counterweights, plus rods, pistons and liners. Rods are the shorter DFX-style items with DFV caps. Note cut-outs in liners to clear crank weights. On the left, George Duckett measures the bearing size on an early crank, recognisable by its thinner intermediate counterweights (arrowed red). *(Courtesy Ford Motor Co)*

Alan Jones and Williams FW07 en route to victory in the 1980 Argentinian Grand Prix. *(Courtesy Ford Motor Co)*

fast fading from Keith's life. Not long before they moved to Marton, Gill received a long letter from her, warning her that she would never be able to hold on to him. "It was a good letter, but it didn't come true."

"Keith and I were both brought up with the ethos that you stay married," says Gill. "My mother was very upset: I'd left a very comfortable, nice farm, to live with Keith, with no security whatsoever. But she supported me all the way and came to see us every Friday when she had done her shopping."

'Mother Duck' was similarly underwhelmed. This was no surprise to Keith, who had not been looking forward to telling her, and rather hoped that Ursula would break the news. But his brother, Brian, dissuaded her from doing so, insisting that it was Keith's job.

Gill says "Em was horrified at first by our relationship," not least because she was worried about losing contact with her grandchildren. Reassured by Ursula that this would not happen, she eventually agreed to meet Gill, and to come and stay with them each summer, and Keith and Gill would sometimes fly to Blackburn and take her out to lunch. Things progressed to the point where she and Gill could function productively in the same kitchen, simultaneously, but they never got to know each other well. By contrast, Gill had always gelled with Norman's mother, and continued to.

The children coped fairly well with the upheaval. Trish, the eldest, had just turned 17 when the marriage ended. Amber was 15, Roger 14, and Tina 10.

"The children were quite grown-up about it," says Gill. "Amber was a bit teenage about it but Tina, being younger, adapted well." Initially, Gill's daughters stayed in the family home, but "Norman had never been a very hands-on father and I realised that it wasn't going to work." Fortunately, Keith and Gill had chosen Marton because it was near to the girls' schools, so they soon moved in with their mother. "Amber was doing GCSEs at Kingsley School in Leamington and went to Rugby School for the sixth form. Tina was also at Kingsley until we moved back to the Northampton area later. She and Keith always had a good relationship, and Keith spent a lot of time with her."

Trish and Roger continued to live with Ursula, though they didn't see much of her, as both were at boarding schools: Trish at Headington in Oxford and Roger at Oundle.

Neither of them saw the break-up coming.

"I was very surprised, says Trish. "I think I was okay with it in general, though I probably felt it inside more than I showed. When you go to boarding school you become pretty self-sufficient. I'd started dating, and I remember thinking that I couldn't imagine meeting someone and knowing that was it for the rest of my life, it's a huge commitment.

"I already knew Gill – we all liked her, because she used to give us shandy! At the Lake she'd have this big cool box full of lovely cold drinks; little things like that mean a lot to kids! I didn't suspect anything, though I think my boyfriend did – he said once he thought there was a spark between them. I can just remember not feeling sorry for myself but feeling dreadfully sorry for my mother."

As with Trish, boarding school insulated Roger. "When the marriage ended I wasn't really old enough to notice that anything had been going on. I was away at school, and when I came back, Mum sat down with us and told us Dad was leaving home. I was upset, but because of his work and my being away at boarding school, I had been semi-trained not to rely too much on parents."

"Trish took it very well, she is very level-headed," recounts Ursula. "Roger never said much, but Keith used to come every Sunday and teach him how to use machine tools and I'd give them Sunday lunch. We didn't really have to work at it, we weren't actually divorced then and I didn't see any point in making things difficult. For the children's sake it was nice for him to see them in a relaxed atmosphere."

Holidays aside, Trish and Roger had never spent long periods in their father's company, so this Sunday routine of being collected from school, having lunch with Mum and Dad, followed by an afternoon of quality time and a lift back with Keith did not represent a huge change, especially as the atmosphere in the house remained convivial.

Roger has warm memories of those Sunday afternoons. "Dad bought a Myford Super Seven lathe and loads of attachments and we built a Stuart number 10 steam engine from a set of castings. He did that because he wanted me to understand something about machining. So he'd come home and we'd go into the workshop for a couple of hours at least and make the next bit. If it was the crankshaft, for instance, we'd set up the four-jaw chuck for the offset to machine the pin. We didn't have a miller, so for milling we'd put the job in the four-jaw chuck and use the milling attachment on the cross-slide. That was a great project.

"I don't know how many hours we put into making all the bits for it, but considering the value of his time, our Stuart number 10 must have been the most expensive engine ever made! That thought rather amused me at the time."

Sharing quality time with Trish was a little more difficult, as she was by now a committed horsewoman – to the point where any prospective boyfriend had first to prove his suitability by getting in the saddle!

Keith had no interest in riding, saying he didn't want another set of brains involved when he was trying to control something, and in fact viewed the entire rider-horse combination as an accident waiting to happen (which with Keith in the saddle, was perhaps correct!). "The centre of gravity is much too high," he opined.

Trish is perfectly capable with mechanical things, but for her, inspiration comes from living creatures. Riding is her life, a passion she shares with Gill. The incongruity of her father falling in love with a woman who is devoted to creatures with which he felt no affinity whatsoever was not lost on Trish. "First thing I said when my mother told me Dad was moving in with Gill was 'How's he going to cope with the horses?'

"Dad was known to do the odd horsey thing for her – he was known to change the odd rug, though when she actually saw him do it, she said she couldn't imagine how he'd managed it, with this horse running round the stable and him running after it, trying to throw it over!" (This incident happened in 1990, when Gill was recuperating from an operation on her hands and Keith was 'helping out.')

So what kind of childhood was it that had nurtured these two well-balanced and independently-minded teenagers? Let's turn back the clock and catch up with their lives …

Trish, the 'Little Sprog,' thought her father "a bit strict" when she was little, but became more and more fond of him as she grew up. By the time she reached adulthood she could sum him up in just three words: "He was super."

She learned early on though, while she was in junior school at Quinton House, that it was a bad idea to ask him for help with homework.

"His opinions were absolute. Everyone knows his pat phrase: 'It is better to be quiet and be thought a fool than to open your mouth and remove all doubt.' You'd be talking to him and you'd think, is he actually going to answer? And that's because he never just came out with something, he'd always have a think about it first, whereas most of us just babble."

IT IS BETTER TO BE QUIET AND BE THOUGHT A FOOL THAN TO OPEN YOUR MOUTH AND REMOVE ALL DOUBT.

Trish went to boarding school at Hawnes in Bedford at the age of ten. "Dad thought the local schools weren't good enough and that if you wanted a good education you had to pay for it. Boarding was no trouble for me. I remember my first night, everyone was crying and I was wondering why. I often used to go and stay with friends, being away wasn't a big deal for me."

Trish boarded at secondary level too. "When you go home, everyone thinks you're a snob. When we moved from Larkhall Lane to Norwood House, up the hill overlooking the village, almost overnight I got accused of turning into a snob."

She didn't like that, but was not about to sacrifice her identity just to fit in. "I retained one friend from the village and when we were about 15 we used to go to the local disco. She'd say, 'You've got to drink lager like everyone else,' and I'd say, 'No, I'm going to drink bitter.' Just to be awkward. And they tried to get me to smoke, and I said 'No, I don't want to be the same as everyone else.' So they did me a favour!"

Trish has the impression that her Dad didn't really know what to make of her. "But he obviously thought I was thick, because he bribed me a lot of money to pass my O-levels and then was absolutely gutted when he had to shell out about a hundred quid! But then he was disgusted because I chose religious studies as an A-level, he really thought that was a bad thing.

"Mind you, I came to agree with him. The teacher we had at O-level was fascinating, she was a lovely lady and she made it interesting. Unfortunately they changed the teacher to this pious little woman who we all hated, she would only do the Bible, so it was very boring."

Keith's scepticism about Christianity had not altered since his run-in with the Giggleswick headmaster 30-odd years before, but despite this, both children were christened. "The idea was that it would give us the opportunity to make up our minds when we were older. And my brother and I went to Sunday school for a while.

"Dad definitely thought there was room for manoeuvre on Christianity. He did think there was someone out there who thought we were all idiots, some very bright person who thought we were all going to kill each other and needed some rules to keep us under control, and therefore issued a story that supported those rules.

"Dad never was confirmed. Most of the people who got confirmed at my school did it because they got a nice tea afterwards. But I never bothered."

When he was very young, Roger did slightly better than Trish in the 'time with Dad' stakes, for when Keith was closeted in the dining room designing the DFV, baby Roger was watching happily from his bouncer, or crawling all over the drawings on the floor. Like Trish, he started school at Quinton Hall, but then moved to Spratton prep school as a weekly boarder before going to board full-time at Oundle.

"I don't recall Dad helping with homework though! Either he was at work or was in his office at home, undisturbable. He wasn't a doting father when we were younger, but once we became interesting he became more involved. As soon as I was old enough to understand a modicum of the stuff he was involved in, he would happily talk me through a problem he was working on.

"I spent my childhood tinkering. When I was about 11 we built a kit of a radio-controlled car, with a metal box frame. It was designed for IC-engined outside use; to make it suitable for use indoors Dad bought an electric motor and a series of epicyclic gear trains to bring the speed down. We put bits of old neoprene, probably old wetsuit, on the metal things to act as bumpers and we drove it around the house. That was the start of getting into radio-controlled cars.

"We used to do events in the Cosworth social club and various local sports halls. Indoor electric $\frac{1}{12}$ scale with the early nicads and a sweepy-arm resistor board for speed control. It was pretty low-level stuff, but he was amazed that I could control a tailslide when I wasn't sat in the car. He felt that his hand-eye co-ordination just wasn't up to it.

"When people ask me how long I've been in engineering, I say since I was 12, because I got lectures from that point forward. I often went to race meetings with Dad and, because he was a luminary in motorsport, I could wander round the pits and see everything. I got to meet so many people – Jochen Mass, Ronnie Peterson ... Mass gave me a Martini hat! When you're a 12 year-old kid, that's the bollocks!

"By the time I was about 13 he obviously felt I was old enough not to be any trouble if he went into a motorhome for a chat. So I'd sit there with a glass of pop and he'd talk to Frank Williams or Patrick Head or Frank Durney and I'd be sat there for hours, because Dad could talk for England."

Going to race meetings was memorable, but Roger learned far more engineering from working through problems at home. He also learned that there was a pattern to Keith's day.

"Dad was very bad at getting up in the mornings," interjects Trish, "he used to have a whole pot of tea before he'd even think about it."

Roger would often find him doing his thinking in bed, "... with papers strewn all over it. And he'd come down to breakfast with his bits of paper and we'd work through some of this stuff. I remember one conversation about compounding, after Renault introduced the turbo F1 engine and we were considering doing one with compounding and a CVT. I can remember him talking through the various scenarios and explaining that he'd been to Van Doorne to discuss it."

Both children have clear memories of family visits to Blackburn, but none of Carshalton, where Ursula's family was based. "I don't think I remember ever going to the house" says Trish, "Grandmama and Grandpapa used to come to us. As children we were not so keen on them, we thought them snobbish. She was high up at Trinity College school of music in London and at school some of my music teachers had heard of her and were very much in awe of her. She gave me the odd music lesson, she was a brilliant teacher – because she terrified you!

"But we loved Granny [Em] because she was cuddly and she gave us sweets. She was a very forceful character though."

"Keith and Brian were hugely different characters," recalls Roger. "To me, uncle Brian was so much more formal. He used to wear waistcoats with pocket watches ... [he] was quite amusing to be around though."

"You can date family photos by the toys," adds Trish with a grin, who realised early on that taking an interest in technological devices was essential if she wanted to spend time with her dad.

Naturally the Lake has many memories for both of them. "I learned to swim there," continues Roger, "and still have a share in it."

"The windsurfing was fairly disastrous," Trish recalls. "We used to go to Swanage on family holidays, and Swanage has a lovely bay full of boats. Dad would be up on this windsurfer going from one to the next, falling off and getting on – and off, and on …"

Along with Gill's daughter, Amber, Roger raced hovercraft for a while in the early '80s, both in the field and at the Lake, winning a championship one season. Martin Walters, who could often be found helping Keith with various projects, also got involved, and at one point built a test rig for one of Roger's machines. This involvement with Martin, and enjoyment of mutual engineering projects, would last until Keith died.

ATVs – the early three-wheel types – were enjoyed around the same time, but by the mid '80s, karting was the thing. Keith bought two, and would take them to a track at Whilton Mill near Daventry with Trish and Roger and, at various times, Gill, Amber and Tina, too. Jetskis were also in vogue in the Duckworth household in the mid 1980s. Keith bought one, then bought another for Gill as a birthday present, "... as we really needed two to have fun – Keith and I would go in the evening and play at the Lake." He then bought a bigger model, better suited to his weight, and for a short time Roger raced this machine. (Roger's competitive nature would eventually lead to his becoming a championship-winning rally driver, about which his father was extremely proud.)

By the end of the 1980s Keith's favoured entertainment was the Honda Pilot, a machine originally designed as a sand buggy, but offering plenty of fun potential in an English field. Around the same time, he acquired a different form of buggy, a twin-engined Power Turn.

Both devices offered ample opportunity for hilarity and mishap, as related later in this book, but they were sideshows compared to the two enthusiasms which were a constant in his life: motorcycling and flying.

Aviation often provided Keith with a bridge between work and leisure, as in 1976, when the Duckworth and Achurch families linked up for a holiday at Swanage. The idea was that Ursula, Shirley and the children would go to Dorset before the British GP at Silverstone, with Keith and Oliver flying down to join them the morning after the race.

Although Keith had ordered his first Hughes a couple of months before, he had not yet taken delivery, so the agent, Sloan Helicopters, loaned them a machine and a pilot, Mike Smith.

Oliver takes up the story. "It was approximately 7am, a glorious Sunday morning with low-level mist and farmers getting their cows in for milking. All was well with the world, until we were just east of the Harwell nuclear research facility, when there was a most unpleasant noise from the tail-rotor drive. Within a second we decided we should be on the ground and not in the air."

They found a space in a growing crop of corn and put the Hughes down safely. For obvious security reasons, landing near Harwell is prohibited, except in an emergency, and although the terrible racket from the tail rotor definitely fitted that description, no one wanted all the bureaucracy, security men, delays and form-filling that would inevitably follow if their position became known. Much better, they decided, to leave the helicopter radio alone, get the machine as close as possible to the A34, and then phone for a service crew who, hopefully, would be able to fix it on the spot. So Keith and Oliver, bag in hand, climbed out and began to trek across the field while Mike

Smith hover/taxied the Hughes just above the crop to get it closer to the road.

"We were dressed in light summer wear but the crop was soaking wet, so by the time we got to the road and linked up with Mike, so were we. We walked through the gate on to the road where we saw an elderly gentleman on his own in an Austin A40 loaded to the gunwales with flowers. He was on his way to see his daughter and, as we were 3-4 miles from the nearest village, we asked for a lift."

The good Samaritan managed to cram everyone in around the flowers, but as these three wet, bedraggled men who had appeared from nowhere related their tale about a helicopter he had never seen, he started to get nervous. "One mile on down the road he asked us to get out of the car, as he did not believe our story!"

Mike Smith returned to Sloans, who in due course diagnosed the problem as a worn tail-rotor bearing, while Keith and Oliver continued by taxi to Swanage, after phoning their familes from a village call box a mile or so down the road.

At Swanage, the toy of the moment was the Laser, which neither man had sailed in open water before. "Sailing in very close company with two Lasers on the plane, Keith lost it in a big way and shot across my bows and hit me amidships," relates Oliver. "We had to return to shore to assess the damage and buy ourselves a fibreglass repair kit to patch up our boats. It was great sport though, and never at any time did we fall out."

Keith and Gill didn't keep the house in Marton very long – Keith needed to be nearer Cosworth. So in June 1981 they bought Buckby Folly near East Haddon, about 10 miles north of Northampton. Keith had never really been at ease in the Victorian splendour of Norwood House, it was too grandiose for his taste, and in Gill's words "... this one seemed about the right size, not too big." They couldn't move in until Christmas, however, and Gill remembers the intervening months as hectic beyond belief.

"It was a mad life, we had horses everywhere, we were going away to GPs, and to America. Until the house was ready, we moved into the cottage so that we didn't have to travel a long way to get Tina to her new school that September (Northampton High School). God knows how I stood it all: I looked after my children, I did the garden and cooked all the food. I had phenomenal energy at that time, he could never understand how I could keep going."

Once life at the Folly – as the house became known – had settled down, Keith and Gill never thought of living anywhere else, because it proved perfect for their needs. Its appeal lay not only in the house itself, a comfortable but relatively modest Georgian construction, but also in its surroundings, for it has extensive outbuildings and stables, plus some 30 acres of land – ample room for horses, helicopters, motorbikes, cars, workshops ...

Even after things at the Folly had acquired a rhythm, life with a teenage family left Gill few opportunities to pursue her own hobbies, and although she looked after, rode and trained her daughters' ponies and horses, she would not have her own horse again until 1988. Despite not getting into the saddle as much as she would have liked during the early 1980s, much of Gill's skill at eventing stems from this period, thanks to Stoneleigh Riding Club. The club had the use of the National Equestrian Arena on Tuesday evenings and made good use of it, winning a national championship in 1985.

Keith didn't see much of Trish after the move to the Folly, as she went straight to Brighton Poly from boarding school, only returning to Northamptonshire in the holidays. But she didn't need to spend much time there to realise that life at the Folly was very different from Norwood House.

"I'd stay with Mum, but quite often I'd go over and see Gill and Dad. The very first time I went there, Dad offered me a cup of tea, and I nearly died of shock because he never, ever made a cup of tea in our house. Back home, the pot was *there* and his cup was *there* and Mum used to totter about and fill it up again. It was a very traditional sort of relationship."

It would be wrong to say that Keith became a model of male domesticity as soon he moved in with Gill. In fact, she reckons he never once cooked in her presence! But he did learn not to take his wife's homemaking skills for granted. "My father used to expect that, you don't get away with that sort of thing here!" Gill would joke, and Keith didn't complain because her approach squared with his own principles, which Gill relates: "He believed we all had our skills and we owed it to each other to help each other make the best of them. At that stage I was no gifted flyer, but he helped me and encouraged me to get my pilot's licence, and said 'You can do this.'

"Keith admired the fact that I would have a go at most things and make a reasonable job of them. So we had a mutual admiration. The great thing about our relationship was not that he stopped doing what he wanted to do, but that he didn't stop me doing things I really wanted to do."

Keith and Ursula's division of responsibilities between breadwinner and homemaker had never been a matter of principle, merely a lifestyle that suited them. In the early years Keith's workload left little time for anything domestic, while Ursula, who remembers coming home from school to an empty house on account of her mother's career, wanted to do better by her children, and was happy for the family to be her focus.

"Mum used to play squash and help out with the WI and all those villagey things people do," says Trish. "Once Dad left, Mum took up running and got very good."

Ursula did a couple of marathons, a number of half marathons and ten mile races, and many shorter events. She lived alone for five years, during which period she became steadily closer to a man she'd met at squash club some years before: helicopter pilot Don Sissins. In 1984 he moved into Norwood House and the following year, Ursula and Keith were divorced and Ursula sold the property. The couple now live in Bedfordshire, but Ursula retains many friends from her years in Northamptonshire.

Roger, who left school around this time, decided to move in with Keith and Gill and stayed for about eight years. "Keith and I had two skiing holidays with all four children together," says Gill. "Skiing bridges the age gap – we stayed in a big chalet at Christmas and had great fun.

"My girls and [Roger] got on very well. In fact, for a while Roger went out with Amber – she went to London Veterinary School and he went to Brunel.

"I just got the dirty washing every half term!"

Chapter 13

Turbos on two continents

Stuart Turner once tried to persuade Keith that when the DFV won it should be called a Ford, and when it lost it should be called a Cosworth. "He wasn't having any of that," says Stuart, "although he did suggest that if ever one broke, we should both blame the driver!"

They were of course talking about F1, where the DFV and its derivatives were always badged as Ford products.[1] But what is often under-appreciated – at least in Europe – is the enormous impact its turbocharged Indycar derivative, the DFX, had in the US, where it did indeed carry a Cosworth moniker.

Ironically, it was Walter Hayes of Ford who suggested the change. It was in Ford's interests for Cosworth to prosper – quite apart from the valuable sporting kudos, Northampton was a very useful development facility – and Walter knew putting Cosworth cam covers on the US engine would broaden its potential market. No team associated with Chevrolet, Ford's traditional sporting rival in America, would dare consider a Ford engine, but a Cosworth unit was politically acceptable (especially one that had never contained any Ford parts in the first place!).

The DFV family won a total of 155 GPs, but the DFX was not far behind, winning 151. That impressive total includes ten successive victories at the Indy 500 (1978 to 1987), and 11 years of dominance in the USAC and CART championships (1977 to 1987). Yet this remarkably successful project came about almost by accident. By 1974 Ferrari had caught up Cosworth in the F1 horsepower race, and back at Northampton Keith and his colleagues were vigorously scratching their heads. One response was to improve the DFV, but they felt that alone was not enough – in 1974, no one reckoned the engine had another nine years of wins ahead of it. The company believed it needed a new income stream.

In the US in late 1973, Roger Penske experimented with a short-stroke 2.65-litre turbocharged version of the DFV, using a crankshaft designed at Cosworth by Graham Dale-Jones the previous year, but doing all the other development work Stateside. Soon he concluded that major changes to the cylinder head were needed: the cooling system was adequate for petrol and normal aspiration, but was simply unable to cope with the combination of methanol and turbocharging. He lost interest in the project.

However, in mid-1974 the idea was revived by the VPJ team, named after Ford dealer Vel Miletich and Parnelli Jones. Based in Torrance, a suburb of Los Angeles, VPJ was running an F5000 car for Mario Andretti, had just completed its first F1 entrant (the DFV-powered VPJ4 which Andretti debuted in the 1974 Canadian GP) and was running an Offenhauser-engined Eagle in Indycar.

The team was having terrible trouble with the turbocharged Offenhauser engines, which seemed incapable of holding coolant for any length of time, so the idea of substituting a modified DFV seemed worth another look.

Initially, veteran mechanic and machinist Takeo 'Chickie' Hirashima and engine builder Larry Slutter took apart a time-expired DFV of their own volition, and after studying its design persuaded the team to release them from other work and let them develop it. They spent the next 14 months working largely on their own initiative, with only very arms-length support from Cosworth, which merely dusted off one of Penske's short-stroke cranks, assembled, tested and shipped to California a complete 2.65-litre low-compression engine antd then, for the most part, sat back and watched. Testing was done with slave electronics and ignition which were then removed prior to shipping, some three or four engines leaving Northampton in this form.

This low-key approach was more a matter of politics than disinterest. Indycar was at that time run by the United States Auto Club (USAC), a conservative organisation which was patriotic to the point of xenophobia about maintaining the 'American-ness' of open-wheel racing on US oval tracks. As a result, throughout the 1950s and early '60s Indycar had existed in something of a time-warp, using four-cylinder Offenhauser engines and heavy, front-engined roadster chassis. When Jack Brabham arrived in 1961 with a mid-engined Cooper, and (even more so) when Jim Clark's second place for Lotus in 1963 heralded the rapid eclipse of the old order, the Good Ol' Boys of the USAC were not pleased. Even the fact that the winning pushrod Ford V8 was American was small consolation.

By the late '60s, it was grudgingly accepted that most chassis were UK-sourced, but powerplants were still US-made, the rules having been changed by this time to permit turbocharging. This gave the venerable Offy a new lease of life and it won the Indianapolis 500 every year from 1972 to 1976, its only opposition being the V8 Ford, which by that point had been developed into a four-cam.

At Cosworth, Bill Brown had been watching this with interest and was convinced that a proper racing engine could do for Indycar what the DFV had done for F1 – open up the sport to new teams by offering everyone a level playing field and a reliable power unit. Keith, despite openly disliking turbocharging, could not deny the logic, but wanted to tread softly. Malcolm Tyrrell recalls him saying "If we go in all guns blazing, USAC are going to ban this thing, because it's not American."

The first DFX was fitted to the Parnelli VPJ6, basically the VPJ4 F1 car modified to Indy rules. The car appeared at practice for the 1975 Indianapolis but didn't handle well, so Al Unser opted to race the Eagle Offy instead, which rewarded him by throwing a rod. But by the last race of the season, at Phoenix, the VPJ6 had been extensively modified – with the help of John Barnard – to become the VPJ6B, and Al Unser qualified on pole, finishing fifth in the race. The first win came the following year, at the Pocono 500, where the power of the DFX – already 50bhp more than the best Offys – allowed Unser to make up a full lap lost in the pits. Every way you looked at it, the DFX had the edge: it was less top-heavy than the four-cam Ford and more powerful than the Offy, not to mention more driveable. The revolution had begun.

The Parnelli team weren't particularly forthcoming with information about their engine, even to Cosworth, so the following year McLaren developed its own version of the DFX, both for its own cars and as a customer unit for the Penske team. Soon, a brisk trade in tired DFVs developed, as ex-F1 units were shipped to the US and rebuilt locally to DFX spec. This was good business for Cosworth, who were kept busy supplying F1 with replacement DFVs and Indycar with cranks and rods, but by 1976 the board felt confident enough to go a step further and design a full factory version of the DFX. An increasing number of components were already being made in Northampton at the Americans' request: now Keith felt it was time to offer a complete engine. Interested teams were asked to commit in advance to the project by paying Cosworth a non-refundable deposit – a considerable act of faith on their part.

Immediately after this decision was made, a piece of foolscap paper appeared on Geoff Goddard's desk. On it Keith had simply written: '2.65-litre V8, Indy, Geoff, do it.'

"That was the DFX," says Geoff, "that's how much trust there was in the design process. I designed it, Paul Morgan developed it."

Having said that, Keith did not expect his engineers to work in a vacuum; his normal procedure with a project was to generate 'Tablets from the Mountain' – sometimes actual layout drawings, more often a sketch and detailed notes – to show the designer what he had in mind.

After much midnight oil from Paul Squires and Malcolm Tyrrell, the first all-Cosworth DFX was fired up in the test cells in January 1977, and by the time an all-Cosworth DFX powered Bobby Unser to pole position at the Phoenix Indycar round that October, the British engine had acquired sufficient critical mass to see off any political challenges. Keith's strategy had worked beautifully.

In parallel with the development of a factory DFX, Cosworth set up a US facility to sell and service it. Bill, who had been back and forth to the US several times since 1974 to liaise with the teams developing the engine, found a factory at Oregon Court in Torrance, not far from the VPJ premises, and Chickie Hirashima and Larry Slutter were persuaded to jump ship and become Cosworth Inc's first employees. They were joined

COSWORTH FILTERS

When Len Newton returned from the US in 1980, the man who'd been filling his role in the Northampton sales department, Deryck Norville, had to be found something to do. So Jack Field gave him one of the items he'd been investigating as possible sales opportunities – a piece of foam which might make a useful washable air filter – to see if he could make a viable product out of it.

The first version was tried by the local bus company, United Counties, and proved so successful that before long it was standard issue throughout the National Bus group. But apart from some applications in Group 4 rallying it had little impact in motorsport, so when in 1987 the foam manufacturer, Beaverco, suggested a joint project to expand and develop the filter range, Cosworth turned down the idea.

However Deryck, who by this point had been running Cosworth's Filtration Division virtually single-handed for seven years, saw the potential and left Cosworth to join Beaverco and start what became Filtration Control, at the same time expanding the company's reach into motorsport by joining forces with Pipercross. Filtration Control has since grown into a large and successful Northampton company.

in 1978 by Len Newton, who moved from Northampton for a two-year stint to help with sales, and in 1980 by Ian Bisco, an ex-Broadspeed engineer who had moved to California to build Can-Am engines for Shadow and had subsequently been made redundant.

One of Larry's first tasks was to fly to Northampton to bring the engineers there up to speed. During development of the 'Factory' DFX, the engine had a tendency to burn pistons, and Larry was convinced that the cause was twofold: oil finding its way past the rings, and the lack of a separate scavenge pump for the turbo. On the DFV, Cosworth had always struggled to maintain consistency of oil consumption between engines, and adding a turbo made this critical. So, for the definitive DFX, Cosworth reverted to the same American rings that had been successfully used by US builders, and instituted a test requirement that every engine should have its pistons inspected by means of a bore scope after running-in.

Later, it was realised that turbo oil supply was also a factor, as Malcolm Tyrrell explains: "In ignorance, and lacking information from the turbocharger manufacturer, Paul Squires and I ran a line from the main oil gallery to lubricate the turbo bearings. We learned later that the oil pressure should be 2bar (30psi) maximum, rather than the 5.4bar (80psi) we were utilising. Excess pressure forced oil into the compressor and thence into the cylinders."

Keith believed adding a scavenge pump to the turbo was unnecessary, preferring instead an external pipework arrangement not dissimilar to that used in the early days of the DFV. However, results were marginal and Larry had concerns for both chassis packaging and any potential gain when the engine was subjected to the increased head-scavenging demands of banked ovals. So one night after Keith had gone home, Larry and some helpers test ran the engine with a temporary electric scavenge pump added, to prove their point – which it immediately did.

Keith never liked being proved wrong and grumped about this for quite a while, but he couldn't argue with the results, so the scavenge pump was redesigned with larger Roots-type rotors. A rotating centrifuge wall was also incorporated – a clever innovation which lessened the effective impact speed of the oil droplets and greatly reduced aeration. The new pump had a dedicated turbo scavenge pump mounted on its rear and, in a useful piece of cross-fertilisation, soon found a home in the DFV. For F1 applications, the turbo scavenge pump was removed and replaced by a blanking plate, leaving a compact powerful pump which helped reduce the engine's footprint in ground-effect cars.

Meanwhile back in California, Cos Inc – as Cosworth Inc became known – was taking shape, though not as quickly as everyone wanted. The exchange controls then in place in the UK delayed the transfer of the money for the premises, so, in Jack Field's words "... we started it off in a granny cottage that Larry had out the back of his house in Redondo Beach."

"But by '76 the place was ready to go," says Bill. Getting Cos Inc up and running at Oregon Court and the DFX established would turn out to be his last significant contribution to Cosworth, and one of the most important.

By 1978 the DFX was becoming widely used, but the racing politics were far from over, and that year team owners became so exasperated with USAC that they formed themselves into an entrants' association, Championship Auto Racing Teams (CART). The USAC line was that CART represented the big-money teams who could afford expensive imported pure race engines, whereas USAC was trying to look after the little guy who couldn't afford to compete unless normally-aspirated stock-block Chevrolet

V8s remained competitive. To achieve this, USAC announced a drastic reduction in allowable boost for turbocharged engines for 1979, from 80-inches of mercury to 50, falling to 48 in 1980. As a sop to the turbo Offy, four-cylinder engines were allowed 60-inches, but even that was not enough to keep it competitive. By mid 1981 all Indycar races were being run under the auspices of CART, except for the Indy 500 itself which remained a USAC-sanctioned event.

The early DFX engines, running at 80 inches of boost, were good for 900bhp, with 1000bhp available in short bursts, but when boost dropped to 48 inches, output fell to around 585bhp, only 90bhp up on the 495bhp quoted for the DFV at the time. So over the winter of 1980-81 Keith put his thinking hat on and the decided that, since the DFX was now effectively a lightly blown DFV rather than a full-on turbo, its breathing, combustion and exhaust should be reworked to take advantage of the latest DFV thinking, including tuned pipe lengths. The result was an immediate gain of 90bhp, and only a modest development effort was needed to lift the figure for the 48-inch DFX to 700bhp at 11,000rpm – some 235bhp more than a DFV at the same revs and with the same cams.

The boost reduction did help the Chevrolet-powered contenders, but it didn't stem the DFX tide: ironically, reducing the boost pressure gave the engine a much longer working life: up to 800 miles between routine rebuilds and 3000 miles for blocks, cranks, heads, liners and valves. This in turn made it more affordable.

Naturally, some teams pushed for special engines, or preferential treatment in some other way, but Cosworth's response was the same as it had always been in F1: No. Sometimes Jack Field got offered bribes in the belief that he could pull strings. "The offers I've had are unbelievable," he says, referring not just to the US but to racing generally. "But they only try once. Bill Brown always said 'A bottle of wine is a gift, a case is a bribe.' For instance, I had two big very expensive waterproof watches given to me. Bill said 'Keep one for yourself,' the other we raffled in aid of the beer fund for the office party. Sometimes I'd find cash left on my desk and I'd ring them up and say 'I'm banking it to your account.' A gun-runner left a big Jiffy bag full of notes once, I took them home and dumped them on Sue's [his wife's] lap as a joke. She said 'Where did you get all this?' and I said 'Don't get carried away, they're going back in the morning!'"

Even when the pressure for special engines was completely above board the response was exactly the same. When Keith received a request from Roger Penske for a special engine in 1983, he expounded his attitude in a reply entitled 'Vested interests.' Malcolm Tyrrell saw the letter and sums up Keith's words like this:

"If I make a special engine for you, everyone else will want one, you'll all start spending huge amounts of money, it'll get unreliable, and you'll all still be racing each other just as you did before. It'll be going nowhere. The whole essence is in the chassis and the aerodynamics. I'm not interested in making one team the dominant force, because it will lead to the ruination of the sport."

The combination of rule changes and race experience meant that the DFX steadily evolved. Compared to the DFV, pistons, conrods, gudgeon pins and main bearings all had to be redesigned to deal with the higher loads, Cosworth settling in September 1977 on an H-section rod in the style of a Carrillo and designed by Alastair Lyle. This was, usefully, lighter than the actual Carrillos commonly fitted up to this point, and crankshaft life improved accordingly. Much beefier intermediate main-bearing caps had to be designed, dowelled to the block.

Sometimes, when the DFX exhibited a problem which had never occurred with the DFV, Cos Inc found that Northampton, frustratingly, was not convinced there was anything wrong. "One of the first problems," says Ian Bisco, "was that when drivers spun out on the ovals, it very often forced the engine to run backwards momentarily and hence broke all the little quills in the second compound gear. The UK finally designed and made thicker, stronger ones and this really helped.

"We also had a lot of trouble with the steel first bearing housing in the front magnesium cover, whose location was compromised by the need on early engines to clear the front crank damper and was thus held on with two regular allen screws on top, but two countersunk screws for the lower housing. On long oval races the countersunk screws had a bad habit of coming loose, and on several occasions allowed the gear to move forward, disengage and damage the rest." Cos Inc replaced them with conventional hex-headed bolts, wired in place, and after some persuasion the fix was eventually adopted for the DFV as well[2].

Cylinder-head sealing also came in for radical attention, Paul Morgan and DKD developing a system based on that used for high specific output aero and LSR engines. The ignition system, a Mallory magneto on the American specification, was changed to a CDI arrangement similar to that already used on the DFV.

The biggest challenge was the cooling system. Larry Slutter had dealt with the turbo's vastly greater heat output by increasing the water flow rate from 140 litres/min (38 US gal/min) to 340 litres/min (90 US gal/min), but this was only a partial solution. What was needed was Geoff Goddard's revised head casting, which increased the spacing of the exhaust valves to that of the inlets, thus allowing water to flow around their seats. "We went without that luxury for the first season," said Larry, "but at the time it was still cheaper to run a new cylinder head and throw it away after every race than it was to run an Offy!"[3]

Geoff's revised head was itself improved, Paul Morgan trying a variety of seat diameters and depths to dissipate the heat and overcome the seat distortion that had previously led to significant cylinder leakage and potential engine failure. At one juncture, Paul and Mike Costin experimented with sodium-cooled exhaust valves, but thanks to the effectiveness of the revised head design, there was no need to pursue this.

The other major development issue was the fuel-injection. Small improvements were made to the mechanical Hilborn system used by VPJ, but Cosworth was never happy with its crude mixture control – it worked satisfactorily in steady-state conditions, but when the engine was suddenly loaded up, for instance after a spell under yellow flags, mixture could not be accurately matched to speed, boost and throttle opening, so it was all too easy to run weak and melt or scuff a piston. Eventually a new system was designed from scratch by Paul Morgan and Martin Walters; it was still mechanical, but controlled by a three-dimensional cam which responded to intake and plenum pressures. The throttle pedal operated a single butterfly (the Hilborn had one per intake), mounted downstream of the compressor and connected in turn to the cam. "Our system was a bit like the Bosch Jetronic," explains Malcolm Tyrrell, who took over DFX development from Paul Morgan around 1983, "and worked very well."

Other differences from the DFV included a mechanical fuel pump (the inner and outer rotors from the original Hilborn injection system were retained), rather than the DFV's combined electro-mechanical device, and the absence of an onboard starter. All in all, considering the huge increase in power output, the evolution from DFV to DFX went remarkably smoothly, and is a testament to the strength of the DFV's bottom end.

When Bill left in 1977, Jack picked up the US operation, which rapidly became a good platform for all sorts of products. But Torrance at that time was sales, rebuilding, technical liaison and a small stock of spares; no manufacturing or testing. The latter was subcontracted to VPJ, despite – or perhaps because of – that company being very unhappy at the way Cosworth had picked up the DFX ball and was now running hard with it, to the detriment of those who had developed the concept. And, of course, it had lost the services of Chickie and Larry

As it turned out, within a few years Cosworth too would lose them.

"Chickie was a heavy smoker," Jack recalls. "He contracted cancer and eventually died from it, but wouldn't stop smoking and refused all painkillers." Chickie died on Christmas Day 1980, aged 68.

Larry left the company in 1986, in circumstances which those in the know at Cosworth declined to elucidate – and still decline, to this day. Jack understood the decision but regretted the need for it, as it was a big blow to the American operation. "Larry is Mr Cosworth as far as Indy is concerned," Jack told Alf, "we've just got the Queens Award for Export Achievement and that's all down to the DFX. Have a word with Keith."

Keith's answer was uncompromising. "No, he's got to go, and you've got to go and find a replacement."

Officially, Alf was president of Cosworth Inc and Jack vice president, but Jack ran the operation. "Initially I'd go out for a month at a time, when Northampton was closed for factory fortnight, which meant that I was only away from work in England for a fortnight. I'd rent an apartment and take my wife and daughter with me. Later, I stayed out a lot longer: when I was in England I ran America from England, and vice versa. On this occasion I reckoned I'd need at least six months to find someone to run the place."

Jack settled in at Torrance and put out feelers. A couple of high-flying American candidates were approached but rejected as too expensive, and eventually he turned to Ian Bisco, who had become more and more involved as Chickie's health deteriorated and knew his way around the operation very well. Ian was put in charge, backed up by Penny Storch, the existing administrator, and the two went on to run Cos Inc successfully for many years. But until the decision was taken to divide the work in this way, Jack remained in the driving seat.

"So I'm there running the company: the place was humming nicely. Nothing for me to do, sales department taking calls, engines being built. So I said to Penny, give me a list of slow payers, I'll chase some money."

The biggest outstanding account was $80k, owed by Frank Arciero. "I'll have a go at him first," said Jack, but Penny's face fell at the suggestion – this was clearly a phone call she'd been putting off. Frank, she explained, was a tough customer, a classic rags-to-riches Italian immigrant who had made a fortune in Californian construction and real estate, owned a fine vineyard and was a passionate racing enthusiast. He hadn't achieved all that by taking kindly to being lectured about credit terms.

Cosworth in the UK had always been very firm as regards payment terms, but Cos Inc seemed to have been more lenient – Frank usually paid in person. "Frank had two engines on order," recalls Jack, "about $60k each, to be fitted to March cars, and he hadn't put any deposit down. I'd always insisted that if they didn't put 25% down, I didn't take the order. And he owed $80k already."

Jack gave him a call, and a husky voice came on the phone ...

"Is that you Jack? I heard you were coming over here, how's things?"

"Very well, thanks."

"We'll have to have a meal together. How about next Tuesday?"

"Yeah that'll be fine."

"We'll call back and tell you where and what time."

But on the Thursday before, Jack got a phone call from Cosworth: March was asking for the Arciero engine. Jack recalls: "I told them it can go to March, it can go in the car, but the car mustn't be shipped – that was a technique I quite often used. But on Friday night I got another call from England." March wanted to ship the car.

"Tell them they can't till I say so," said Jack. Five minutes later, his phone rang. It was Frank Arciero's secretary.

"Frank wants to know if you've got a problem."

"No, I haven't got a problem, Frank's got a problem. What with the money he owes us and another engine in a car, that's another $60,000."

"Right I'll have another word with Frank and he'll ring back."

Frank did ring back. "Jack, didn't we have a conversation the other day? And what did we decide?"

"We decided to have a meal on Tuesday. Your people were going to tell me where and when."

"What did you expect was going to happen on that Tuesday?"

"That you would pay me $80k. But Frank, it ain't Tuesday. It's still only Friday. You owe $80,000 and there's $60,000 of ours sitting in that car. You've got another engine on order and you haven't paid any deposit on that."

"Right, I tell you what, you call England and get that car shipped tonight with your engine in. And if I don't pay you the $80,000 and the $60,000 on Tuesday, I'll allow you to come in here with a gun, past my boys, and blow my f***ing brains out."

Impressed as he was by the fervency of this offer, Jack didn't fancy taking him up on it. Being tough on credit was one thing, but he drew the line at shooting debtors in cold blood. It was time to back off: "Okay Frank, it's on its way."

Jack never did get his lunch, but next Tuesday Frank paid the bill, and in due course paid for the second engine, too. However, he never spoke to Jack again. Later, when Jack told Keith about the incident, his response was: "You let it go? I wouldn't have!"

Apart from one impromptu visit in the mid 1980s, Keith never went to Torrance, despite Cos Inc being a major investment for the company. In truth, he was always more at home in the F1 scene than Stateside. Nevertheless, the success of the DFX inevitably drew him to America and he made several visits to Indianapolis in the company of either Paul Morgan or Malcolm Tyrrell to meet the teams and assess development.

Travelling with Keith was never dull, and Malcolm's account of their visit to the 1986 event gives a good idea of what a trip with DKD could involve.

"He always travelled very light, with just a small attache case for a week. He wanted to be straight off the plane at Chicago with his hand baggage and on to a connecting flight to Indianapolis. When he saw me pull up at his house with a suitcase he gave me a bit of a dressing down for slowing up the journey. Despite the pre-booked itinerary, he always wanted to catch the next available plane, he didn't like hanging around airports.

"But in Chicago, thanks to my impedance, the next available flight was some time off. 'There's no alternative,' he said, 'we'll have to go and have a beer.' So he put his briefcase in a left-luggage locker and we talked shop over a beer or two. He took his handkerchief out of his pocket to sneeze.

"Keith tended to become oblivious to time when deep in engineering conversation and my attempts to get us to the departure gate fell on deaf ears. When we eventually went back to the locker he couldn't find his key; I wondered if it had dropped out of his pocket when he withdrew his handkerchief, so I rushed back to the bar, found the keys, rushed back, got the attache case and rushed to the gate. It was shut, but we managed to talk our way through – this was pre-911 – and get on the aircraft. We'd made the flight late and everyone in tourist class was looking daggers at me. Keith didn't give a damn – and anyway, he was up front in business class!

"We went down to the circuit early Sunday morning, it was raining and the jet dryers were going round and round. Keith went to speak to some of the teams – he always enjoyed being around Carl Haas and Newman/Haas Racing, especially as they were running Mario Andretti at the time, a driver we all had a lot of time for. DKD was fascinated by the technical aspects of differentials, locked diffs etc, at banked ovals, and I remember one debate, with Mario Andretti, Eric Broadley and Nigel Bennett going on for at least two hours.

"A J Foyt was good company too, but Keith wasn't so keen on U E 'Pat' Patrick, who was an enthusiast of all things American and a great USAC team player. I'm sure he lamented the passing of the Offenhauser – he was always ready to give Keith's ears a bashing over prices and deliveries.

"The rain continued, and it became obvious that the race wasn't going to happen – it was eventually run the following weekend. So we decided to go home. At the rental desk in Indianapolis, I'd originally asked for a mid-size car, but Keith reckoned that was too flamboyant and insisted on a small Chevette. Now he had this notion that we wouldn't catch a plane: we'd drive back to Chicago in this fairly insignificant piece of hardware and catch a flight there. 'You drive, I'll map-read,' he said.

"But as the race had been postponed, everyone was trying to leave and everything was totally gridlocked, except for the emergency lane, reserved for ambulances etc.

'Get in that lane,' he told me.

'But we can't …'

'*Get in that lane!*'

"And so I nudged into this lane, but a USAC guy placed himself firmly in front of the car, saying 'You can't go down there.' DKD elected to get out of the car and discuss at some length with the official the error of his ways, and the futility of amateurs attempting to control traffic. As Keith continued to engage with the guy, I spotted a six and-a-half foot cop walking towards him. Keith was unaware – he had his back to him.

"If only I could have captured the next minute on film! Basically, the police officer taps Keith on the shoulder, which is initially ignored. The cop taps harder, which gains Keith's attention. He swings around expecting to see another elderly USAC official; instead he is staring at the cop's chest! Keith is instructed to shut up and 'get in that goddamn car and just sit quiet with everybody else,' or risk arrest. Wisely, he opted for the former.

"We eventually got moving, and I told him I was unfamiliar with the route and could do with some navigational assistance. Keith agreed, but then fell asleep as we approached the mayhem that is Chicago on a Sunday evening. Eventually we got to O'Hare where Keith had a further animated discussion with the Hertz attendant, on learning that there would be a surcharge for returning the car to Chicago rather than

Indianapolis. Finally we made our way to the check-in desk, where he presented the staff with a USAC pop-off valve as hand luggage. The airline didn't like the idea of this pretty substantial chunk of metal flying around the cabin in turbulence and insisted it be wrapped and checked in. Under protest, he did so, and we made the plane."[4]

Sometimes, Malcolm felt more like Keith's minder than his employee. "He was on a different stratum. But an entirely likeable guy, though desperately infuriating at times."

Had Keith known, when the DFX was mooted in 1974, that the DFV was still less than halfway through its F1 career, he might never have authorised the project.[5] But rather than challenging the wisdom of that decision, events in the next two or three seasons seemed only to confirm it. Admittedly some challengers, like Matra's V12 and Alfa Romeo's flat 12, never fulfilled their promise, and another faded away – the famous name of BRM leaving F1 for good during 1976 – but Ferrari was a different matter. When the Italian company won three consecutive titles from 1975 to 1977, it seemed as though Cosworth's fears were being realised. Moreover, it became clear in 1976 that a new threat would soon emerge, for Renault was busy turbocharging its 1.5-litre V6 F2 engine to make an F1 power unit, the Renault RS01 making its debut at the 1977 British GP.

The intention had been for the car to make a patriotic entrance two weeks earlier at the French GP, but it was not ready, and its debut at Silverstone showed how far the concept still had to go, Jabouille qualifying 21st out of 26 starters and dropping out with turbo failure on lap 17. Nevertheless, F1's turbo era had begun.

When the rules of the 1966 3-litre F1 formula were written, they called for normally-aspirated engines, but 1.5-litre supercharged units were also permitted, so that teams wanting to avoid the expense of developing a 3-litre power unit could continue to compete by blowing their 1.5-litre engine from the previous formula.

In the event, no one made use of the concession, but it remained in the rulebook and ten years later Renault interpreted it to mean that turbocharging was also allowed. Keith was convinced that it was not, and said so publicly and repeatedly, so much so that a Duckworthism developed on the subject:

TO MY THINKING, TURBOCHARGERS IN FORMULA 1 ENGINES WERE ALWAYS EXPRESSLY AGAINST THE RULES.

However, FISA never challenged the legality of Renault's move and Keith could see the writing on the wall. He knew that the 2:1 capacity ratio between normally-aspirated and turbocharged – a historical anomaly without any serious technical basis – actually favoured the latter if boost pressure was unrestricted, and that a turbo victory was probably only a matter of time.

Fiat money had come into Ferrari as long ago as 1969, now the entry of Renault meant that Cosworth was competing against the resources of not one, but two major manufacturers, plus a third, smaller, operation – Alfa Romeo. If other big companies followed Renault's lead and started pouring money into the development of ever more powerful engines, a power race would begin that a medium-sized company like Cosworth would struggle to match, and the level playing field which had done so much to help both F1 and Cosworth thrive would rapidly be eroded.

Keith had never been a big fan of turbocharging, calling it 'screwdriver engineering.' To him, it seemed too easy: all a team had to do to gain extra power was turn up the boost and hope that the engine held together. If a powerplant was made of sufficiently robust materials, and if the team manager had the nerve, it could win – even if it was not the cleverest piece of engineering on the grid.

He also had a more fundamental objection to FISA's position, arguing that once you have a turbine in the exhaust, it would be easy to ensure that unburned fuel found its way into it – in extremis could even be injected – so that the turbine developed power in its own right rather than merely pressuring the charge for the engine. Then, if the outputs from turbo and engine were both coupled to a compound gearbox, the car would in effect have two engines, something which the rules definitely did not allow. Once the rules have been circumvented in this way, he argued, what was there to stop a team using the turbo as the main power source, by coupling a huge turbine to the engine exhaust and relegating the reciprocating engine to little more than an air pump? Horsepower outputs would soar well into four figures, yet according to FISA's logic, everything would still be legal.

Renault's 1977 debut was followed by two years of failures and disappointments, but dogged development work and a very large pot of Renault money finally produced a result when Jean-Pierre Jabouille and René Arnoux took first and third at the 1979 French GP. From that point on, turbo power became more and more necessary for any team wanting to win.

Those two years gave Cosworth some breathing space, during which Keith pursued a two-pronged strategy. The first prong was obvious: to improve the DFV, and to develop new variants of it. The second prong was more subtle.

In February 1978 he proposed to FISA that it adopt a fuel-flow formula. Under it, all capacity and aspiration limits would be removed and a limit of 34cc per second be substituted (27cc/s was later mooted), starting with the 1982 season. Cars could carry any quantity of fuel, supplying a large normally-aspirated engine, or a small highly boosted one, or anything in-between – the sole aim being to extract the most power from a given fuel flow. The idea was also environmentally sound, for the oil crisis of 1974 was still fresh in the public's mind and any formula which encouraged efficient use of what was now acknowledged to be a finite resource had an obvious appeal.

However, it did not appeal to Ferrari, Renault and Alfa Romeo, all of whose engines were thirstier than the Cosworth, and the Fédération Internationale du Sport Automobile (FISA) rejected the plan (having first got Cosworth to make up a prototype control valve, at its own expense). Any further pressure to change the rules then became swamped by the more general dispute that was brewing between FISA and the teams' representative body, the Formula One Constructors' Association (FOCA), as the latter fought to have greater control of the sport and of its increasingly large revenues.

Broadly speaking, FISA was seen to support the French and Italian manufacturers, while most FOCA members were Cosworth customers. However, as Ferrari, Renault and Alfa Romeo were also in FOCA, the situation became very confused and was not helped when Lotus began experiments with ground effect, starting with its 1977 Lotus 78 and going on to win the championship the following year with Mario Andretti and the very successful Lotus 79. The DFV was slimmer than rival power units and better able to take advantage of this new aerodynamic knowledge. As other teams followed

Lotus' lead, the effects of airflow beneath the car became better understood, and in 1980 to Cosworth redesigned the DFV's auxiliaries to reduce their footprint and thus enable its customers to push home their aerodynamic advantage.

The aerodynamic arguments came to a head in early 1981, when FISA suddenly banned movable sideskirts. The matter ended up in court and UK politicians started weighing in with jingoistic statements about plucky Brits and cheating Frenchmen (chief villain, in their eyes, being FISA chairman Jean-Marie Balestre). Peace, in the form of the Concorde Agreement, was regained shortly afterwards, but as a result existing regulations were effectively frozen for several years, so it was not until 1987 that the turbo power race was reined in.

As a result of this legislative hiatus, in the early 1980s engine makers jumped one by one onto the turbo bandwagon, including Ferrari (1980), Matra (1982, though the engine never raced), BMW (1982), Alfa Romeo (1983) and Porsche (badged TAG, 1983). The only consolation for Cosworth came in 1982, when rotaries, diesels, sarich orbitals and gas turbines were banned. This ruling put an end to Ferrari's experiments with injecting fuel into the turbocharger, a move intended to reduce turbo lag but which could otherwise have led down the very compound powerplant path that Keith had warned about.

Even without the complication of the FOCA/FISA power struggle, it is not surprising that Keith's fuel-flow formula did not find favour. His views were sincerely held and had considerable technical merit, but they coincided with what was commercially advantageous for his company, something his rivals were not slow to point out. Moreover, the fact that by 1978 Cosworth was making very good money selling turbocharged DFXs to the US smacked of double standards.

Keith put the idea forward again in 1979, this time in an attempt to revive what was then becoming a moribund sector of racing: sportscars. He was partially successful in that Group C, which successfully revived the sector from 1982 onwards, did indeed include a fuel limitation, but not of flow, only capacity (100-litres for C1, 55 for C2), with refuelling permitted.

A sports car version of the DFV, the DFL ('L' for long-distance), was produced by agreement with Ford for competitors in this category, and came in two sizes: 3.9-litre for Group C1 and 3.3-litre for C2. The larger engine was not very successful: the DFV had always been regarded as 'a bit of a shaker,' and increasing both the bore and stroke exacerbated this characteristic to the point where the engine became unreliable and disliked by the drivers. The smaller unit, however, achieved many class victories during the '80s, and was especially popular with privateers in chassis like Spices and Tigas.

As far as F1 was concerned, Keith was determined to squeeze every bit of life he could out of the DFV concept – for which, incidentally, Cosworth was awarded the Ferodo Trophy – for the third time – in 1981. Weight-saving efforts continued, titanium being adopted for valve spring retainers and, from around 1982, for inlet valves. About the same time, cam design received attention: various engine builders had tried higher lift cams and found them beneficial, now Cosworth produced its own, dubbed DA12, replacing the DA1 of many years' standing.

Lots of work was done to minimise crankshaft windage, Keith working closely with Mario Illien, a Swiss designer who had joined the firm some two years earlier. Windows were cut in test cylinder blocks to see where oil was moving in the crankcase, the result being a modified crankcase which gave better oil collection and a small power bonus.

Although Mario only stayed at Cosworth for a little under five years, he had a disproportionate effect, so it is worth introducing him in more detail.

Working for Hans Funda in Geneva, his first contribution to race-engine design was an F2 engine based on the four-cylinder Chrysler 180 block, undertaken in 1971-72. Swiss engine builder Heini Mader got to hear of his abilities and, as Heini was a good Cosworth customer, an introduction was made.

"In late 1978 I came for an interview. Keith's office was full of bits. When he had visitors or potential customers, there was no room – every surface was covered. The interview went on and on and on, and by four or five o'clock in the evening I was still in his office. It was very revealing, how open he was, the way he was thinking, he was definitely a very interesting person. My English was very limited, it was not easy to follow him and give him intelligent answers. But at the end of the day he offered me a job. I was 30 at the time; I joined Cosworth in April 1979."

Keith and Mario formed an immediate rapport and before long DKD had come to regard Mario as his heir apparent, the designer whose thought processes most closely mirrored his own.

"He decided that I should report direct to him – that upset a lot of people. I didn't mind that though, I liked working under pressure. Keith would call me to his office, or to his house, just to bounce off some ideas: he wanted the challenge and the argument. To Keith, the job was life. And in those days I was single, I could work all hours of the day and night. We ended in the pub once in a while!

"The interesting thing to me about Keith was that once he trusted you, you had all the freedom in the world. And he would be very loyal to you.

"But he was quite tight in many ways! One day, when he was proposing the fuel-flow formula, we arranged to fly to Zurich to discuss the idea with a professor at ETH University. Keith took me along to help with translation etc. As it was a very early flight, we went down to Heathrow and stayed the night. Keith insisted we share a room! We ended up spending quite a lot of time at the bar – he would spend money on things he liked."

'In 1981 I had go back to Switzerland to do military service – I committed to that before I joined the firm. It was good in a way, six months army service: having a project in mind, I had plenty of time to think and came back refreshed. I think I went straight on to the DFY."

The DFY was a last throw of the DFV dice and was authorised by Keith in 1982. Around this time various outside builders were experimenting with short-stroke DFVs, and Keith had earlier authorised Geoff Goddard to develop Cosworth's own, the DFVss, using the 90mm bore of the 3.9-litre DFL. But its output was little different from the standard DFV – at that time officially 495bhp, though in reality more like 510bhp.

So the focus shifted to Mario's DFY. This used the same short-stroke block as Geoff's engine, but mated to an all-new cylinder head. In Mario's words "It was a bit of an orphan," and was still under development as the 1983 season loomed.

For 1983, Keith had committed to McLaren, Lotus and Williams to deliver an improved DFV, and had agreed that the teams would not be obliged to buy the new engine if it didn't deliver a useful performance increase. Knowing that the 'proper' DFY was not ready, he asked the man sitting at the next drawing board to Mario, the by now very experienced Geoff Goddard, to develop the DFVss into a 'stopgap DFY.'

He then urged Mario to speed up development of his engine. "At Easter 1983, two weeks before they were due to deliver the engines, Keith phoned me and said 'Would it be a challenge to fast-track the remaining work on the DFY?' So I took it on, but I said 'I want to have the freedom, once the DFY works, to get it into a car!' He said, 'Okay, but you find your own team!'"

Mario and three colleagues – development engineers Tim Whiskerd and Paul Squires and engine builder Pete Rogers – "worked more or less day and night for a couple of weeks."

Keith had thus created a rivalry between two designers with very different modi operandi – Geoff tended to visualise a concept and make a prototype incorporating several ideas in one go, while Mario was inclined to painstakingly explore one avenue at a time – but he managed to harness this 'creative tension' productively and as a result two new DFV variants made their appearance.

Geoff's developed DFVss gave 520bhp, thanks mainly to some reworking of the ports and larger inlet valves. It was quickly followed by Mario's DFY which, once the cams had been changed to get the best out of the new head, achieved another small power increase, output being around 530bhp. More significantly, it offered greater torque and was substantially lighter. In a break with DFV tradition, the DFY's cylinder head used a 22.5° valve angle instead of 32° and had its head and cam carrier cast as one component. Its inlet manifold was made of magnesium alloy (double-skinned to keep the charge cool) and the inlet trumpets were shorter, as was the exhaust system. A standard DFV weighed 159kg, the DFY only 132kg.

The DFY was genuine progress, and Mario got his team when Ken Tyrrell agreed to buy the new unit. But it was not enough to turn the turbo tide and won just one Grand Prix, when Michele Alboreto took victory in the 1983 Detroit race. It was the 155th and last win for any DFV variant in F1, the other 154 all going to the DFV proper.

Although its days of powering drivers to the top spot on the F1 rostrum were now over, this now venerable concept still had a remarkable number of years' life left in it. Not only was its Indycar career far from over, but as we discuss later, other variants continued to compete in F1 and were also used in lesser formulae.

The upshot of this longer-than-expected lifespan for the DFV family was that, far from replacing it as an income stream, the DFX supplemented it. As a result of this, and of road-car projects, another era of expansion at St James Mill Road became unavoidable. But first we must make a nautical diversion …

Footnotes

1 There was one exception to this: during its six-year period of Saudi sponsorship (1978-83), Williams ran F1 cars with Cosworth cam covers to distance itself from Ford's US roots and America's support of Israel.

2 Interestingly, Mike and Keith were never very keen on countersunk fittings, having satisfied themselves through experimentation that the accuracy of fit, and hence of security, was much less predictable than with flat contact faces.

3 p170 of *The Power to win*, John Blunsden (Motor Racing Publications Ltd, first edition 1983).

4 Keith's interest in the pop-off valve was understandable. It was a standard-issue component on any turbocharged Indycar to limit manifold pressure and hence power output, and getting the best out of it was vital to a team's chances of success. An air tube connected the valve to the driver's helmet, who could thus hear the valve working and keep the turbo boost at the optimum level, where the valve was just about to pop. Teams tried all sorts of political and – when no one was looking – technical ruses to get a little extra pressure. It was not unknown for USAC officials to be cajoled into increasing the valve spring preload a little, to keep a crowd-pleasing driver content.

5 For a more detailed description of the DFX's history and development, see the excellent article in *Motor Sport*, February 1978, p143.

Chapter 14

The marine adventure

In Keith's ideal world, everyone in motorsport would behave reasonably and logically, and there would be no need for politics and backbiting. The best drivers and equipment would naturally rise to the top.

But in the late 1970s, motor racing, both in Europe and the US, was moving in the opposite direction, with disputes growing between FOCA and FISA in the Old World, and CART and USAC in the New. Add to that Keith's antipathy to the use of turbos in F1 and USAC's dislike of foreign engines, and it's easy to see why he became rather disillusioned with motorsport around this time and amenable to a new challenge.

That challenge, powerboating, developed following Bill Brown's departure from Cosworth in early 1977. Bill had been a passionate powerboat builder and competitor for well over a decade by that point, and had collected around him several like-minded folk, from within and without the company. This informal 'Team Brown' could often be found in the Toy Shop after hours, and naturally other employees followed the group's fortunes and creations with interest.

Mike and Ben, who were much more interested in flying, kept well away from Bill's hobby, and despite his long-standing enjoyment of watersports, so did Keith. This greatly disappointed Bill, but was probably for the best. When two strong-minded individuals have professional differences, it makes no sense to open up a whole new field of potential friction.

As a result, Bill was left to do his own thing, and there was never any technical connection between his Cosworth-powered boats and the all-Cosworth designs which the company subsequently campaigned under its own name. Bill had access to Cosworth's stores for fasteners and some fittings, but the hull and all the major parts were self-financed, assisted from 1976 by some sponsorship.

However, there was certainly continuity as regards the people involved. Malcolm Tyrrell played a pivotal role, and this chapter draws considerably on his memoirs.

Bill got into powerboating through Roger Hook, son of Harry, who found Cosworth its site on St James Mill Road. His first boat was a wooden, deep-vee, Worbold monohull powered by a Lotus twin-cam engine: "... a simple, straightforward craft," but good enough to take him to several British championships.

He sold it in 1974, his eyes now on racing catamarans – tunnel hulls, as they are known in the sport. The works teams used either Mercury or OMC (Johnson) factory-tuned V6 two-strokes, but these were not available to privateers, so Bill opted for a BDA, soon upgraded to a BDG with rally cams.

"My first tunnel-hull, with a wooden Burgess hull, drove through an inboard-outboard Mercruiser racing unit from Mercury Marine. It was initially raced in 1975. But Mercury could not get it to last at our rpm, so my friend Tony Westaway and I took on the rebuilding, first getting it to actually finish a race, and then to win."

In addition to Tony, Bill was assisted by Pat Castell, Chas Ridal Shooter and Malcolm Tyrrell, and was friendly with another racer, Jackie Wilson, who built a similar boat with their help.

Bill was strictly a privateer until 1976 when, no doubt with one eye on his by-now inevitable exit from Cosworth, he left the amateur ranks and turned Team Brown into Team Carlsberg, thanks to the sponsorship he'd negotiated towards the end of the previous year. David Mills[1] was appointed manager and Doug Simpson from Shadow F1 became the mechanic.

That same year, Bill and Jackie had a collision at Lake Windermere during Speed Week. It was an accident – each driver was concentrating on what he was doing and failed to see the other – but it left an acrimonious aftertaste and Bill and Jackie subsequently went their separate sporting ways. Bill was thrown from his boat and spent the next six months recovering from hypothermia, a broken scapula and a frozen shoulder, while Jackie lost his boat, which broke up. The engine was thought lost, but three weekends of dragging the site with a magnet found it and the unit was eventually returned to Malcolm for rebuild.

Before long Bill was finding technological advancement more satisfying than pot-hunting, and was putting increasing amounts of effort and sponsorship money into his "... beloved revolutionary composite catamaran." This, too, was powered by a BDG/Mercruiser combination, but the hull had an aluminium centre section onto which different sponsors, made from glued and riveted aluminium/balsa sheets attached to aluminium mounting tubes, could be bolted to suit different conditions – "A pretty far-reaching idea," in Malcolm's words.

Construction was started in late 1976 by John Thompson who, after helping build the 4WD car, had left Cosworth to start his own fabrication shop in nearby Wollaston, called Auto Racing Technology. "Unfortunately," says Bill, "the resins then available set too rigidly and cracked. So the boat constantly took in water [and] rarely realised its potential. When it did, it was the fastest thing on the water in the 2-litre class."

Meanwhile, towards the end of 1976 his estranged former co-driver Jackie Wilson had been looking at the rule changes proposed for 1977 by the sport's controlling body, the Union Internationale Motonautique (UIM). Hitherto the top European class had been the 2-litre ON category, and in the US the unlimited OZ class – but from 1977, Europe would align with the US. So Jackie called Malcolm and asked his advice on the most economic way to acquire a competitive OZ boat.

"I recommended the Cosworth GA. Cosworth's contract with Ford had called for a total of 100 engine kits to be manufactured, but Ford's decision to quit the European Touring Car Championship in 1976 meant that many of these kits were still in storage. The asking price was just £7.5k per kit, it seemed a real no-brainer to me! Jackie had a Mercury dealership on the South Coast and early in 1977 came up to sell Keith a boat. He told Keith about my proposal.

"To Keith, the idea of using a GA was a red rag to a bull, as he didn't like six-cylinder engines in general and he was a bit brittle about this particular one, because in F5000 trim it gave some 450bhp from 3.4-litres, similar to the 3-litre DFV at that time, which was of course much more expensive. So he phoned me at home.

'I hear you've had this stupid idea of putting a V6 in a boat for Jackie. Why are you doing that?'

'Well, it's available, and it seems to fit the bill, Jackie's funding it himself and he hasn't got a lot of money.'

'Why don't you use a DFV?'

'A, the initial cost of buying one, and B, the rebuild cost – it would be prohibitive.'[2]

'What if I gave you one? In fact, why don't we set up a boat division and you run it? Why don't we go for a drink?'

"So we went to the pub in Kislingbury and we talked about it over a pint or two. By now it was July and he'd just come back from Silverstone where Renault had debuted the turbo engine, which Keith regarded as completely against the rules. He was getting really disillusioned with F1 and all its antics, so the idea of building a powerboat was a bit of light relief." The upshot was that by August 1977 Malcolm had left the development department and been put in charge of Cosworth's new boat division.

Earlier that year, Bill had said his final goodbyes at Cosworth. His exit didn't leave a hole managerially, but as an individual he was missed. "Apart from shouting at us in the car park when we used someone else's slot, Bill was a really friendly, good bloke," says Geoff Goddard. "He was always doing mad things – he had an old Capri 3-litre and he bent it quite often, as he had a habit of arriving at traffic lights at way beyond the velocity from which you could stop. And when his wife Irene told him to get the grass mowed, he borrowed some sheep from Oliver Achurch, only to have to rush back home when it turned out they'd all jumped over the fence and were eating the neighbour's prize garden. When he got back to the office he had us all in stitches!"

Bill was affronted to learn that, having ignored his own powerboating efforts for years, Keith should decide to build his own within months of his departure. Team Carlsberg and Team Cosworth never raced head to head – they were in different classes – and Malcolm is sure it was timing rather than spite that got Keith involved when he did. Nevertheless, Malcolm reckons DKD took private satisfaction from the contrast in resources and machinery, the Cosworth boat boasting a factory standard of preparation and engineering plus a custom paint job that would have looked at home on an American dragster.

Team Carlsberg's star faded in the next couple of years, as Bill explains. "Unfortunately Carlsberg got impatient and felt I should have bought a competitive two-stroke outboard and concentrated on racing. In 1979, before we had time to solve the resin problem, they pulled the rug out and we didn't have enough funds to continue."

This was the end of Bill's career as a constructor, though he remained very active in the sport. He was already chairman of the UIM's international technical commission and a member of its central committee. In the ensuing years he strengthened his links with the administration of the sport, working initially from Singapore, where he moved after disbanding his team. He also made a significant contribution towards the development of the demountable cockpit, a valuable safety aid. Bill now lives in Thailand with his second wife and their daughter.

At Cosworth, meanwhile, there was positive movement. "Jackie had already instigated Chris Hodges to build the hull," says Malcolm, "I did all the marinisation of the DFV, Mike

Hall designed the bellhousing driveshaft and the modifications for the Mercury upper sterndrive which mated to the DFV, while I made the spaceframe and with assistance from Ian Hawkins and Tim Whiskerd fabricated the oil, water and fuel systems.

"We had some help from Mercury, who were interested because there was a big lobbying group in the US saying two-strokes were bad for the environment and the sport should be moving to four-strokes. Therefore Mercury gave us a lot of help with underwater units and some of their technology." In return, Cosworth supplied a DFV to the US for Mercury to install in a hull of its own choosing, so it could evaluate a four-stroke powerplant. Malcolm helped from a distance, providing advice and support, and their boat showed promise, taking a victory not long after its completion.

"So we did it, we went racing, and Keith really enjoyed it."

He wasn't the only Duckworth enjoying it, for Roger also got involved. Keith got Chris Hodges to design a miniature version of the new Cosworth hull for Roger to race in the Junior category, where the rules stipulated the use of a standard Yamaha 9.5hp outboard engine. It was put together at Norwood House and finished in the same custom paint job as its big brother – an amazing toy for a 13 year-old.

"It's a shame," says Roger, "but I cannot recall any pictures of it despite the fact that it sat in our garage for quite some time before Dad had a little time and decided we should go and test it at the Lake. So we bolted the engine onto the back and, because it had no seating, Dad borrowed one of the seats out of the Brantly helicopter and somehow jammed that into the wooden structure of the base of the boat, and off we went.

"As I wasn't considered competent (or Dad feared things were likely to go wrong), we lowered the trailer down the ramp and pushed the boat off into the shallow water. Dad got in, despite being way too large for it, started the engine and set off tentatively across the water. He didn't go far before trying to speed up a bit, perhaps to see if it had any chance of getting on the plane, but it wasn't responding well – probably because it was overloaded – so he shut down the throttle.

"At that point the boat nose-dived and, as it was virtually blade-shaped at the front end, this immediately submerged the nose and swamped the deck. The boat then began to sink, which it continued to do while Dad rescued the helicopter seat and swam back to the ramp. I can't recall how we salvaged it but I never did race that boat. Instead he bought me a Dart, a conventional vee-hulled fibreglass boat, onto which we attached the same engine. It was with the Dart that I went racing, with Dad encouraging me and trying to do little tweaks within the very limited regulations. Races were often at the same places as the normal national events, such as Iver Heath near Uxbridge, Stewartby in Bedfordshire and Holme Pierpoint in Nottingham. This boat was still in the workshop at the Folly when Dad died."

But back to the serious machinery, where Malcolm again takes up the story. By now it was spring 1978, and the Cosworth Hodges boat was ready to run.

"The class we were competing in was for outboard-engine race boats. The UIM rule book stipulated that an outboard engine should be able to be lifted from the hull, complete with its propulsion system, so that by connecting the power plant solely to battery and fuel it would be able to run.

"Our design used spaceframes at the front and rear of the DFV to mount the engine to the marine-ply hull. The front spaceframe contained the mounting points for the dry-sump oil tank, while the rear provided the mountings for the stern-drive and oil cooler. A cast bell-housing carried the Lucas 3M100 starter motor, while a quillshaft and twin constant-velocity joints took the drive from engine to the stern-drive. Additionally, Keith came up with a design for an automatic clutch-release mechanism, basically utilising a steel Belleville washer and a sprag clutch. It was activated through oil retained by a rubber diaphragm and centrifugal force. Naturally, it worked first time, achieved the designed clutch engagement criteria, and never let us down!

"The Cosworth Hodges boat ran a total-loss cooling system: we picked up water from the underwater leg and fed it into the engine, where it was directed by an automotive thermostat, either into the engine or to a spill-off. We had spill-offs with different orifices so we could control the block pressure. Keith said, 'We've got no idea what block pressure we're running, we ought to go up to Chasewater, run it and see where we are.' So I put a pressure tapping on the filler standpipe connected to a pressure gauge.

"We sent Jackie off and he came back saying that the gauge hadn't moved. So we installed smaller orifices and sent him off again.

'No, still hasn't moved.'

'Really? Must be a faulty gauge.' So we put on another gauge and sent him off again.

'No, still hasn't moved.' So we put even smaller orifices in.

'Still hasn't moved.'

"Keith couldn't believe this, so I stripped the gauge assembly and immediately saw the problem – my fault entirely. I'd given the ⅛-inch BSP union to our welder and asked him to silver-solder it on. He'd done so, but hadn't drilled the hole through the middle – which I assumed he'd do."

It was an easy matter to remedy this and set up the cooling system, but not before Keith had delivered a vintage rollocking to his marine division supremo. As DKD's long-time confidante, Martin Walters would have said in his Welsh accent, "Never assume."

"Underwater gearcases were a big issue," continues Malcolm. "We used essentially the same gearbox as Mercury and they used to suffer from the same problems. You had a single input shaft and a pair of helical spur gears which used to attempt to split the drive. These gears were very small, to keep the gearcase narrow, so they were connected to two further vertical shafts and thence to two bevel gears which split the drive to the horizontal shaft to the prop. Keith, like most engineers, would say that there was no way you could effectively split the drive with such a mechanism – one gear is bound to take the drive before the other. It just can't work, so we had to do the best we could.

"One thing we did was to preload the input by providing them with a micro adjustment, so we could find the point where they would just slip on to their splines.

"Our first outing was at Chasewater near Birmingham in 1978. We did okay, managing a top-three position in heat one, but then had an underwater failure, which wasn't unusual because even Mercury was having them at that time. Then we went to Fairford and won a British Championship race there."

The next event on the calendar was at Bristol, but before that the team decided to check the boat's longitudinal centre of gravity. Malcolm explains: "We knew the works boats arranged for their centre of gravity and centre of lift at terminal velocity to be fairly coincidental, so that the boat's attitude didn't change much between power on, when you lifted it up off the water, and power off, when it sat back down and you could scrub off the speed.

"Mercury reckoned that the 'ideal' longitudinal centre of gravity for a tunnel hull was just rearwards of the driver's seat. The reasoning was that to minimise drag when running flat out, the boat needed to run on a cushion of air, with only the rearmost area of the twin hulls and the surface-piercing propeller shaft in contact with the water. When the driver lifted to negotiate the single-buoy turn, the boat needed to quickly settle itself back onto the water to scrub off speed.

"On most boats, set-up could be trimmed by moving the combined engine/ underwater drive unit with hydraulic rams, to balance the hull, or lift the nose when accelerating. On our boat, the engine was fixed and just the stern drive/underwater unit could be trimmed out or in. When we checked our longitudinal c of g, it was way back because of the weight of the engine. I tried moving things forward, like fuel tanks and batteries, but Jackie said he didn't like any of that, so Keith said 'The engineering solution is to put a wing on it,' to give lift to the rear of the boat.

"So Keith and Geoff Goddard selected an appropriate NACA wing profile and we got Bob Sparshott (an ex-Team Lotus fabricator) at BS Fabrications to do a wing for us, mounted it on the back, turned up at Bristol, and the scrutineer Doc Shepherd said 'You can't have that.' Keith took issue with him, saying, 'There's nothing in the regs to prevent it, it's perfectly safe.' Unfortunately, we had no time to test the wing and when a bolt came out of the lower mounting it nearly came off, so it was banned for the second heat."

The wing never reappeared, its Bristol reputation preceding it to future events, so Keith opted instead to fit brakes to overcome the boat's tendency not to 'settle' on the water, and hence to run past turn markers. The brakes consisted of a 63mm-dia (2.5-inch) spherical-ended aluminium bar some 10cm (4-inch) long, mounted on an upper and lower wishbone arrangement on the rear of each sponson, sprung-loaded in the raised position. A bowden cable connected it to the brake pedal, which the driver could push to lower the brake into the water. This caused the hull to pivot about that point on the longitudinal plane, thus lowering the front of the hull. It was not a new idea: a similar mechanism had been deployed on Donald Campbell's record-breaker, *Bluebird*, while the works boats were experimenting with nitrous-oxide activated brakes.

Malcolm continues "Despite protestations by the pilot, we were never convinced that Jackie ever used the mechanism – maybe it was the *Bluebird* connection! Or possibly the fact that Renato Molinari was reputed to have run brakes at the British Grand Prix at Chasewater (no one knew for certain, as the works teams always kept their hulls covered when out of the water). Renato's boat 'exploded' on the first lap as he approached a turn buoy!

"In September 1978 we went to race in Amsterdam in the docks, a very similar environment to Bristol and well suited to our boat. The support crew was Tim Whiskerd, Ian Hawkins and me. Mercury, Johnson and all the usual OZ crews were there because it was a European championship race. The entry list was huge, but Jackie had gone well in practice.

"The method of starting the boats was to line them up against moored barges – difficult in calm water, almost impossible in rough water, as at this event. Jackie set off, all askew, but he righted it and soon he was flying up to third on the first, standing-start lap. Conditions were very choppy and as the Cosworth boat was built to an endurance specification, it had the edge on the sprint boats, which were struggling. But then he came round the turnbuoy near the startline and Ian and I thought, that looks low in the water, he's been holed! Jackie had split the starboard sponson trying to negotiate his way through heavy water and traffic.

"For problems during the race, the marshals have a big net that drops down in the pit area; the boat goes over the net and then a crane lifts net and boat up out of the water. Unfortunately our incident happened so close to the beginning of the race that they hadn't had time to get this organised, so Jackie kept going round and round. All the boats had little built-in self-baling devices which removed some of the water, but these had their limits and eventually he had to come in.

"When you crane-launch a boat, you use a rope device which hooks on to two points inside the cockpit and two points at the back. When Jackie arrived, he immediately started to sink and they couldn't manage to get these hooks on; moreover, with the race still going on, all the rescue divers were on race duties. Dick Scammell, who had just been to Sweden to Ronnie Peterson's funeral, had stopped by to see how we were getting on and became the hero of the hour when he suddenly dived fully clothed into the Amstel from a height of about 15 feet to connect the front two hooks. This was enough for the crane to lift the boat partially out of the water and prevent it from sinking completely. Eventually a diver from the rescue team came along and connected the other two.

"Despondently, (we were definitely going to win that one!) Tim, Ian and I busied ourselves draining off as much water as possible and inhibiting the cylinder bores etc in readiness for heading home. By this time the first heat had finished and Gary Garbrecht, the head of Mercury racing, came up. He and Keith had developed a pretty good banter during the year and a half or so we'd been racing. Gary said 'Well, that's the trouble with four-strokes, immerse them and that's it, your weekend's over. With two-strokes, all you do is take the plugs out, evacuate the water, put fresh fuel in, spin them over a few times and they run.'

'Keith said to me, 'Malcolm, we're going to start that engine.' So we had to take all the exhausts off, drain the water out, remove all the scavenge pumps and pressure pumps, take the oil tank off and drain all the oil, pump the fuel tanks dry, change the fuel filters and spark-box, then drain the intercooler – a real old mission. Meanwhile Gary got his support team to do a brilliant carpentry repair on the big hole in the back of the boat.

"After about an hour we fired it up and let it run to boil off any remaining water in the oil. Keith nodded at Gary as if to say 'See, I told you!' We were ready for the second heat. But they got the boat hovered and just as they were ready to lower it into the water, the engine coughed and stopped. No amount of coaxing would cajole that DFV to fire up – until we got back to the UK. Perhaps it was homesick, or perhaps it had simply decided that it had had enough of being submerged for one day.

"In October, we took the boat to Windermere to go record-breaking, including a crack at the unlimited record for inboards (we were technically an outboard, but that was boat racing in the '70s!), which on 19 October we raised from 76mph to 123mph. I believe we exceeded 130mph on one run but, as with all speed attempts, the record is set by the average of two runs in opposite directions. Due to the blustery conditions, Jackie had a 'big lift' on the upwind run. It's sad to think that nowadays there is a 10 nautical mph speed limit on the lake …

"But the most impressive result, to my mind, was our success in February 1979 at the Parker Dam 7 Hour Endurance Race on the Colorado River. Jackie had been desperately wanting to run the boat in America and this event seemed the perfect opportunity as the cream of the sport would be there, including all the Mercury and OMC works boats and drivers such as Renato Molinari and Billy Seebold.

"This one's a real racers' tale, as at one point we were third overall and heading for overall victory. However, it was not to be. The Achilles Heel of our boat was the Mercury underwater unit. Despite resin sealing the gear casings and very careful assembly, every so often we would suffer bevel-gear failure through one of two mechanisms. First, and more likely, water ingress – possibly caused when the gear housing cooled during refuelling, resulting in negative pressure inside the casing, which drew water past the lip seals. Or, second, the inherent mechanical limitation of the split-drive Mercury unit.

"So to successfully navigate a seven-hour endurance race we reckoned we'd require at least two changes of the complete underwater unit during refuelling stops, a process we estimated would take just ten minutes. To warn the driver of impending failure, we connected a pressure gauge to the gearcasing, as we knew the oil temperature, and hence the internal gearcase pressure, tended to rise when the gears were about to fail.

"Initially, I got sent down to the far end of the course with a couple of Mercury guys, in radio contact with the pits. It soon became clear that the conditions on the Colorado River were pretty choppy, because boats were running in one direction, doing a 180 near where I stood and running back to the start/ finish line. This suited our boat – we were running well.

"Some two hours into the race, Jackie arrived for a refuelling stop, by which time I'd made my way back to the pits. We had three carefully assembled and run-in gearcases at the ready, which we had run on the boat at the Lake Havasu shakedown and then stripped and inspected the night before the race, but the driver reported that the telltale gauge had not flickered, so we elected to continue. Two hours later again, the co-driver, Brett May, also reported no gauge movement. By this time we were getting concerned: perhaps the gauge had failed, or maybe the line between gauge and gearcase was blocked or damaged? So we elected to change the unit.

"However, the propeller was seized on the driveshaft. We only had one 'demon' prop that matched the water conditions and full-tank boat weight, so we spent ten minutes attempting to remove it, standing up to our thighs in cold Colorado River water. But it just would not budge, so I decided to replace both unit and prop. This cost us some 20 minutes, and in addition the boat lost some performance due to the change in prop, so we finished the race sixth overall."

At this point, politics kicked in. The headline 'Britannia rules the waves and America waives the rules,' was originally used in reporting the failed attempt by the British yacht *Endeavour* to lift the America's Cup in 1934. But it could just as easily be applied to the nationalistic farce that was about to unfold.

In their 2-litre boats, Bill Brown and Jackie Wilson had used a spaceframe containing the engine and gearcases, so that the team could lift out the spaceframe, put it on the dockside, connect a fuel line and fire it up, thus qualifying the boat as an outboard. The Cosworth powerplant was similar in principle except that, as the DFV block was designed to be load-bearing, it only needed two small spaceframes – one each end.

Before the race, the Cosworth team had been told by the organisers that, although their boat satisfied all the UIM regulations regarding the definition of an outboard, its spaceframe-supported powerplant was not in their view an outboard. Team Cosworth would therefore have to race in the inboard class, against craft with monster engines like big-block Chevys, etc. Unfair as this seemed, there was nothing to be done about it, so the British contingent had put the disappointment behind them and concentrated on winning their class.

They achieved this in style, for although their 20-minute stop had pushed them down to sixth overall, behind the factory outboards, they'd come home some 80 miles ahead of the next inboard. This was a real vindication of both boat and team – or so it seemed …

Back to Malcolm: "We were obviously elated and went along to the prize ceremony full of beans. Imagine our disbelief then when the organising body announced that we had been disqualified from the inboard class as the engine was not of American manufacture. They'd just created a new rule! Question: when is a Ford not a Ford? Answer: when it has Cosworth on the cam covers!

"At this point DKD took the microphone and elected to make one of his famous speeches, reserved for when governing bodies (or careless engineers) caused him personal upset. He really gave it to them with both barrels, going on for several minutes, with alarming fervour and tremendous zeal, about the xenophobic characteristics of the typical American, the state of their nation, and much more besides.

"The buzz in the crowd suggested they were none too happy about being lectured in this way and, bearing in mind the girth of the average American redneck racer, I was getting a little uneasy at the prospect of being thrown into the Colorado River, or far worse. At one point I thought, we're going to be lucky to get out of this place alive! Thankfully, we did escape, but in later years, when travelling with Keith to Indy, I often wondered if he would get refused entry, due to his name appearing on a blacklist as an undesirable alien.

"The sad postscript to the episode is that when we got the boat home and stripped down the first gearcase, it was immaculate. With hindsight, if we had trusted both the gauge and our assembly skills, we could have left it alone and achieved an even better result."

Despite falling foul of the same nationalism that he and Bill had so carefully circumvented in Indycar just a few years previously, and despite knowing that the commercial potential of the powerboat project was inevitably limited compared to the opportunities in motorsport, Keith was keen to carry on. When he was enjoying himself, he often allowed his curiosity to steer his design focus, provided he felt that a project had at least a modest prospect of generating a return. In the case of the powerboat, the plan was to offer teams a marinised version of the DFV, but it soon became clear that in powerboating, Cosworth was up against the same problem that was developing in F1: teams being given engines. For Mercury and OMC, the dominant names in the sport, OZ class racing was part of their marketing budgets and top independent teams received free engines.

"Nevertheless," recalls Malcolm, "Keith had spoken about getting me down to the boat tanks at Southampton and doing some research on hull design with Chris Hodges; he'd also thought about different engines, including turbocharging. But Gary Garbrecht said to Keith 'Look, we're designing a 3.4-litre V8 outboard which is going to destroy you, don't go down that route.'"

Instead, Gary convinced Keith to build a tunnel-hull design to compete in Unlimited Hydroplane racing in America, which attracted considerable TV coverage, sponsorship and spectator interest. At that time, tunnel hulls were unknown in the category, so the boat would be a first. Moreover, Keith was excited by Gary's comment that the Allison aero engine from WWII was still a popular powerplant for top-class hydroplanes. The Allison was similar to the Rolls-Royce Merlin used in the Spitfire, an engine that Keith revered (in fact some details of the DFV are clearly inspired by it), and the idea of developing a successor really appealed.

So Keith started doing some homework. Mercury didn't produce complete boats, only powerplants, which in the late '70s it installed in Seebold hulls. Mercury Racing would therefore provide a Seebold hull, scaled up from an OZ-style design to one suitable for Unlimited Hydroplane events, and Cosworth would install two DFX engines in it to create the first tunnel-hull to compete in the class. This was serious stuff: the driver would have around 1500bhp on tap!

The 28ft hull was delivered to Mercury's premises in Oshkosh, Wisconsin during the winter of 1979-80, and Malcolm was seconded there to take initial measurements for the engine installation. He found travelling on Keith's behalf no more luxurious than travelling with him – "Oshkosh was not a pleasant experience in mid-winter, especially with extremely limited expenses and no company credit card!"

Next, Keith and Malcolm visited Don Aronow, the Miami-based constructor who built the famous Cigarette hulls which, on account of their speed, were particularly popular with drug runners. To have any hope of catching them, the US Customs Service needed the same craft, and Aronow thus found himself with a nicely self-perpetuating business – until he was murdered in 1987.

Gary Garbrecht had suggested Don in the belief that he would have the manpower to assist with the installation, and because he knew all about seagoing craft, whereas Seebold concentrated on circuit racing, but he was too busy to do the work. So Gary then suggested Bob and Jack at Custom Marine, also in Miami.

"While we were there, Gary arranged for us to follow the Bimini Offshore Powerboat Race from the 'comfort' of a light aircraft. Keith was not a fan of light aircraft, and just 30 minutes of observing the antics of other light aircraft and helicopters, flying with little apparent regard for fellow airspace users, was enough for Keith to ask the pilot get us back on the ground. However, Keith was impressed with the money that was being spent on engines, with powerplants such V12 Lamborghinis being installed. So much so, that he asked Mario Illien to scheme a large-capacity engine of around 7-litres, as a project.

"We then moved the Seebold hull to Custom Marine and I flew out and spent a month fitting out the boat," recalls Malcolm. This was a more pleasant trip: not only was the weather far better, but he now had the luxury of travellers cheques, "... though Holiday Inn must have thought I was a bit of a flake, as they asked me to hand over a considerable amount of them as surety."

Before he went, he constructed a mock-up of the hull at Cosworth to facilitate the design and installation of the two DFX engines, prior to them and the accompanying kit of parts being shipped to Miami.

"Because of our experience with the DFV boat, we'd decided to install the DFXs way, way forward. Keith said 'We'll have these really long driveshafts, about eight feet long.' I said, 'What about the whirling?' but Keith came up with a cunning scheme, using aluminium tubes which were slotted to accommodate a clip to which a bearing could be attached. This arrangement was schemed by Keith but detailed by Cecil Schumacher, who also drew out a 2-D layout of the entire exhaust system and turbocharger mounting, which I then fabricated. Typically for Keith, it all worked perfectly."

But then, DKD had a Duckworthism on this very point, and would proudly tell visitors to St James Mill Road that:

We [at Cosworth] are the only people who expect a prototype to go together straight away, without fitting.

By spring 1980 the Cosworth Seebold boat, named *Aronow-Halter Special* in recognition of Aronow and Custom Marine's input, was finished, and Malcolm had arrived home. Keith wanted him to go back to America to run it, "... but that meant months away at a time when we had a young family. Having already been away for long periods doing the installation work, I just couldn't commit myself to that, so Paul Morgan agreed to take on the challenge, with Ian Hawkins. Paul was project leader for the DFX and, with the Indy programme now running well, he could afford to diversify a bit.

"Two significant problems emerged. First, as we had learnt from the DFV exercise, a boat requires a significantly different power curve to a race car. With the boat at rest, there is a major wetted area, and to break free from this the boat requires significant torque at low engine speed, something not available from a turbocharged engine with its inevitable turbo lag.

"The second problem concerned the starting procedure. Because methanol has low volatility, it can give cold starting problems, and with twin engines turned over by starter motors with inertia bendix drives, the problem was exacerbated. Once you'd got one running, you couldn't hear what the hell was going on with the other one!

"Fix one, to overcome lag, was engineered by Paul Morgan and consisted of fitting the engines with a nitrous oxide supply, engaged by a driver-operated solenoid. We ran this system on the dyno and the resultant torque multiplication was impressive to say the least!

"Fix two was to engineer pre-engaged starters, which kept the engines rotating until they eventually fired, along with an LPG system which was used purely to fire up the engines."

Aronow-Halter Special now worked, and, in fact, the terminal velocity was so high that when Mercury took the boat to its test base at Lake X in Florida for Earl Bentz to try – Jackie having left the project following the switch to hydroplane racing – the marine-ply hull started to delaminate. So Seebold and Mercury decided to clad the underside in sheet aluminium.

"The project was rather getting away from us at this stage," recalls Malcolm, "as the aluminium increased the boat's weight, which had been one of its advantages over the opposition."

The other supposed advantage of a tunnel hull had been manoeuvrability, but one of Keith's favourite sayings was that "First ideas usually turn out to be complicated," and the truth of that was about to be demonstrated.

FIRST IDEAS USUALLY TURN OUT TO BE COMPLICATED.

"Although our boat was undeniably fast," continues Malcolm, "we'd been led to believe that its main advantage would be its cornering capability. A typical unlimited hydroplane hull was of true hydroplane form, what is called a three-pointer, rather like *Bluebird*. Such hulls are very quick in a straight line, but hopeless at turning, as there is little hull to anchor the boat and prevent longitudinal drift, or slide.

"Dick Scammell got asked to go out to San Diego to witness one of these races, and was soon on the phone saying 'Where have all these single-point turns gone, everything is marked out as 50-yard radius turns!' The organisers, knowing the limitations of the three-pointer hull, had designed the course accordingly. At a stroke, the principal advantage of the Cosworth boat's tunnel-hull had been lost.

"We'd been sold a bum steer, which brings us back to 'never assume' – always do your market research rather than relying on what others tell you, as they probably have a vested interest!"

Aronow-Halter Special entered just one event in its original form, the APBA Gold Cup Madison Regatta on 6 July 1980, Earl Bentz qualifying with a best lap of 113mph, 12mph off the pace of the lead boat, *Miss Budweiser*. But somewhere in the frantic preparations for the race itself, an oil line got left undone and an engine got destroyed, so the boat never made the start line.

An interesting, but totally US-centric, viewpoint on the project was published in the April 1982 edition of *Powerboat* magazine,[3] from which the reader would get the impression that the boat was entirely a Garbrecht-Aronow idea, and that Cosworth's only input was the loan of two engines, soon rejected because of lack of torque.

Had that been the true extent of Northampton's involvement, Alf Vickers might not have worried about the project. What actually happened was that around this time, Alf took a long hard look at the whole marine adventure and said to Keith "You've got to forget all this, it's not earning us any money, we're haemorrhaging cash just so people can go and have fun." So the plug was pulled, ending what Malcolm regards as the most exciting period of his entire career at Cosworth.

Could the hydroplane or its powerplant have made money? "Possibly," says Malcolm. "There weren't a lot of Allison-Merlins around, there was a need for something new. But you've got this protective xenophobic culture working against you."

By way of consolation, at the Boat Show in 1980, Cosworth's efforts with the DFV-engined craft received recognition when the K7 Club presented Keith with its K7 Award – ironically just as the boat's career was winding down – 'For the person the club considers to have done most to further British endeavour.' The Cosworth Hodges was subsequently put on display at the National Motorboat Museum at the Watt Tyler Country Park, close to Basildon in Essex. When that closed, Cosworth was asked if it wanted it back, but this was long after Keith had retired and the management of the day was not interested. At the time of writing the boat is in Florida, where Jackie Wilson's son Mark, himself a successful boat racer, is hoping to restore it for his father to drive in an American Old Timers event.

Cosworth had no further involvement with *Aronow Halter Special*, which was subsequently re-engined with twin supercharged Keith Black Chryslers and renamed *Aronow Unlimited*. Its fate is unknown.

Footnotes

1 David Mills had earlier tried unsuccessfully to help Great Train Robber wheelman Roy James restart his driving career.

2 The GA did get used for powerboating, but not by Cosworth. Malcolm Cole bought two for Class II Offshore racing. See p21 of *Powerboat & Waterskiing* magazine, January 1983.

3 *From Drawing Board to Tunnel Vision*, by David Speer, pages 47-48 of *Powerboat* magazine, April 1982.

Chapter 15

New openings

The 1980s were, in many ways, the most fulfilling years of Keith's personal life. After he moved in with Gill in 1979, there was a new spring in his step, and a greater willingness to indulge in leisure and look outside the workplace for intellectual stimulation. The rate of expansion at Cosworth was unrelenting, but Keith was increasingly willing to put his faith in his colleagues, who continued to prove themselves well up to the task.

Holidays began to become less of a rarity. In 1982 the couple purchased a very desirable apartment at Arenal in Menorca, on a hillside overlooking the bay. Keith liked the place so much that he even coined a Duckworthism about it, observing:

> *I HATE GOING ON HOLIDAY, AND I'LL TELL YOU WHY – I'M PRETTY SURE THAT I COULD GET TO LIKE IT!*

"We had a great time," says Gill, "I dragged him off to places he didn't want to go, it did broaden his world."

Naturally, no home of DKD would be complete without some toys, and sometimes he invited a playmate along, Oliver and Shirley Achurch accompanying them to Menorca on several occasions. He and Gill would also meet up with Rex Bryan (the architect who designed Factory 1), and his wife Vee, who had a house in Menorca. (In fact Gill is still in touch with them – they meet at least once a year for lunch.)

"We bought a couple of windsurf boards for Keith and Gill, plus a Tinker inflatable dinghy, which could be rowed, sailed, or fitted with a small outboard. We tried all three," says Oliver.

They also had a lot of fun with an Aquascooter, though only after a less-than-successful trial run at the Folly – described later! "Most of these nautical toys were purchased following Keith's and my annual visit to the Boat Show," says Oliver. "Once he came away with one of the very first Sony Pixus portable GPS units."

Keith was first and foremost a mechanical engineer, but there was no denying the increasing importance of electronics and any new gadget had an appeal. "People used to give him watches," remembers Gill. "He had one of the first digitals: it had a red face but was blank unless you pressed a button; even so the batteries only lasted about two days!"

"But he wasn't interested in buying clothes, that was a nightmare. He'd buy pinks and reds which looked horrible with his blue eyes. I ended up buying stuff for him, he looked fabulous in blues and greys. I think I did smarten him up a bit!"

Although Keith never became a celebrity in the sense of being a household name, he did become known outside engineering and motorsport, and was a guest on the very popular BBC radio programme *Down Your Way* in the early 1970s. He also took part in *Desert Island Discs* in 1982, and, asked to select some music, he chose the jazz clarinet classic *Petite Fleur* by Sidney Bechet. In general though, music didn't inspire him. "His taste in music was non-existent," says Gill. "He'd listen to country and western or jazz on the car radio, but left to his own devices he wasn't really interested. But he was very diverse in other ways, he would always sit and listen to people on their subjects, he would be attentive and try and analyse what you were doing. He didn't go out and be bored by people."

Keith and his company received many awards over the years, but it was not until June 1984 that he received a truly national accolade: the OBE. It was a proud day when Keith went to Buckingham Palace to receive his award from the Queen, but privately, many of his friends and colleagues felt he deserved more. Certainly, many of the new knights ennobled in the same honours list had contributed vastly less to national life than David Keith Duckworth.

From childhood, Keith had always enjoyed birdwatching, for which the Folly, with its big French windows overlooking open farmland, was ideal. He and Tina each had a pair of binoculars in their bedrooms, and books to identify birds, and would trade notes on what was going on in the bird world at different times. But he was less keen on larger creatures, particularly those which lived in stables …

"He did struggle with horses." admits Gill, "though latterly, when he tried to do a few jobs for me, he got a great appreciation of how hard I work with them!"

His niece Julia who, as the Blackburn end of the family, only saw Keith occasionally, noticed the change in him. "In his early married life to Ursula, he spent a great deal of his time working and probably being intolerant of others' ineptitude, as he would have seen it. Later […] he mellowed considerably. I remember Keith getting hold of a book and finding it had been bound incorrectly. Dad was very surprised to see that he was quite nonchalant about it: a few years before, Keith would have been jumping up and down about it."

In 1985 Ursula asked for a divorce, prompting Keith to comment to fellow director Bob Graves: "You know Bob, Ursula didn't deserve that. Gill and I are designed for each other, we're both ambitious, we're both driven."

Keith and Gill, who had made their home together seven years before, were now free to make everything official. In a decade which generated many happy memories, 18 April 1986 stands out as a high point, because that was the date when Keith and Gill finally tied the knot. It was a deliberately low-key event, a registry office ceremony held on a Friday afternoon at Northampton town hall, with just Roger, Amber, Tina and Gill's mother present. There was no fancy reception, no official photographer and no honeymoon. In fact, Gill cancelled it three times because Keith was too busy. But none of that made the occasion any less joyful. It just felt right – very, very right.

Happy though his home life undoubtedly was, Cosworth was never far from DKD's thoughts, and throughout the late 1970s and the 1980s there was certainly plenty to think about. Alf's policy of promoting the firm to the mainstream motor industry was paying off, and when Cosworth opened its own foundry in 1978, its credibility rose another few notches. The inconsistent quality of bought-in castings had irked the engineers at Cosworth since its earliest days. A number of foundries were tried and, as John Dickens observes, "I spent many hours at all of them, wearing my 'quality manager' hat!" Two became the preferred suppliers: Aeroplane & Motor Aluminium Castings in Birmingham was used for complex jobs, and Roseblade in London cast most of the smaller items, but 'preferred' is not really the right adjective, because in Keith's view none of them was truly up to scratch.

It seemed to Keith that casting was too much black art and too little science, and he concluded that the problems arose not only because the alloys were sometimes inconsistent but also because the atmosphere to which the molten metal was exposed was itself variable. A skilled foundryman could adjust the process to mitigate these factors, but Keith wanted to eliminate what he called 'By guess and by God' methods.

Around 1976, through a contact of Alf, DKD found a kindred spirit in John Campbell, a physicist turned metallurgical engineer, and with his assistance Cosworth set about painstakingly developing a system in which molten alloy of consistent composition was moved by enclosed pipes into enclosed moulds.

Traditional sandcasting involved pouring metal into the top of the mould, from where it would cascade down, carrying impurities such as dross, mould fragments and air bubbles along with it into the mould cavity. As the mould cooled and shrank, there was the risk of defects in the finished casting due to gas coming out of the solution, trapped air bubbles, and other faults.

In Cosworth's process, metal was degassed with argon and stored under a nitrogen blanket to minimise impurities. It was then drawn from the cleanest, mid-level sector of the holding furnace and gently pumped into the base of the mould using a computer-controlled electro-magnetic induction pump similar to those used in the nuclear industry, with no moving parts. Pumping rather than pouring produces a far more homogeneous casting than traditional foundry techniques.

Other aspects of the casting process also received a critical eye. For instance, zircon sand was used for the mould, rather than silica – zircon is rounder and of more consistent shape and size, as well as having a coefficient of expansion closer to aluminium, all properties which improve accuracy and stability. To minimise sand wastage, a thermal recycling system was built-in. This proved so effective that the recycled sand was actually cleaner and more regular than the original material. Core location and shape were also rethought to improve accuracy and consistency.

These ideas sound simple in principle, but they proved anything but to put into practice, as John Dickens recalls. "We made the first Cosworth-process casting – later patented as Coscast – offsite at a development foundry, from cores that I took from the current supplier and modified in my kitchen overnight. It was a cam-carrier casting, and it turned out well enough to encourage us all to go ahead properly. It then was a long hard slog to get it to work consistently."

By 1978 Cosworth was confident enough to scale up its pilot project into a proper production facility, but there was no room at St James Mill Road, the intended location in Factory 3 having been filled with machine tools by this point. So as John Dickens explains "I spent time with John Campbell looking for a new foundry site near Northampton, but eventually John Campbell and Alf settled on Hylton Road in Worcester – far enough away not to divert everyone's attention at Northampton, yet accessible. It also had a famous choir, which was important for John and his original two cohorts!" John Campbell, now Prof John Campbell, has since become a world authority on casting technology.[1]

A new company, Cosworth Research & Development, was set up to run the foundry, and one of the first castings produced by its Worcester foundry was the head for the DFX, for the good reason that the combustion pressures involved with a turbo engine place a premium on casting integrity. The reduction in porosity was marked, as was the improvement in dimensional accuracy – an outsourced DFV head, for example, was typically cast 5mm oversize, the in-house product just 0.5mm over.

Keith didn't spend a lot of time at Worcester, but even with staff he scarcely knew, his reputation preceded him. One day, he arrived in the Cosworth helicopter, which landed in its usual spot, on a cricket pitch on the opposite side of the river from the foundry. They were flying five-up, but the only car available to give them a lift to the factory had five seats including the driver, prompting the receptionist to quip to Mike: "Never mind, Keith can walk across the river!"

Meanwhile, the motor industry had been steadily becoming more aware of Cosworth's abilities. There had always been a trickle of contract machining jobs – for instance, in the early 1970s a batch of experimental four-valve heads was machined for Saab[2] – now it started to become a flow.

In 1978 an enquiry arrived from Vauxhall, which back in 1976 had homologated a rally version of its Chevette – the HS – using its iron slant-four engine mated to a 16-valve head from an alloy Lotus Type 907 engine – an easy conversion, as the two engines were related and shared the same bore centres. Getting the car homologated had been something of an achievement, given that the engine in that form was not a production entity, and Vauxhall's intention was to substitute its own 16-valve head as soon as possible. However, internal production constraints and the failure of an arrangement to have the heads made under subcontract at Jensen meant that as late as spring 1978 there was still no Chevette HS on sale to the public.

As a result, the car was excluded from that year's Rally of Portugal, and Vauxhall turned to Cosworth to extricate it from an embarrassing hole by machining 400 HS cylinder heads in double-quick time. There was no Cosworth design involvement, this was simply a manufacturing contract, but it was good business and cemented the company's reputation for being able to make medium-sized quantities of components with an efficiency and consistency normally associated with mass production. The difference, needless to say, was having Ben Rood heading the manufacturing team. Talking to Graham Robson, he commented: "Anyone can make two, and anyone can make a million. With two you can do it by hand, and to do a million you can afford to throw so much money at it that you can solve any problem. But between 500 and 10,000 of anything, that's the most difficult production problem, where you can't afford to get anything wrong. I like to think that Cosworth is in that market," (*Cosworth*, p155).

In period, the Chevette work was not attributed to Cosworth, perhaps because of the awkward circumstances under which it had arisen. Indeed GM, unlike Ford, tended to reveal – or otherwise – its association with Cosworth on a case-by-case basis. Only occasionally, such as with the Chevrolet Cosworth Vega, was its marketing value fully exploited. The public undoubtedly associates Cosworth principally with Ford, but as far as road cars are concerned, until around 1985 Keith's company had actually done more work for GM. "But no one ever knew what we did," says Mike. "We all had to sign a confidentiality agreement." Writing over a quarter-century later, it is not easy to piece this GM jigsaw together, but the Appendix includes the known projects.

Despite both being owned by GM, Vauxhall and Opel operated independently in the 1970s, but it's probably not pure coincidence that also brought Opel to St James Mill Road. In 1975 the Rüsselsheim firm had announced a DOHC four-valve version of its Ascona/Rekord engine, the aim being to dislodge BMW from its dominance in F2 and also to go rallying. But once on the stages, the unit suffered some very public blow-ups and Opel asked Cosworth to make it reliable. Mike Hall became Opel's point of contact at Northampton, where the engine was known as the KAA, with Alastair Lyle and Geoff Goddard doing much of the design work.

Their options were limited, as the narrow valve-angle head (only 20°) and chain-driven valvetrain could not be altered, but changes to ports and camshafts, and a lot of detail development work, finally produced a 2.4-litre Weber-fed power unit capable of producing the required 240bhp reliably. Cosworth also advised Opel on improvements to the fuel-injected mass-production version of the engine.

Northampton's reward for all these efforts was a contract in 1978-79 to machine and assemble 400 of these DOHC heads for the Ascona 400 saloon, using castings supplied from Germany. Another 400 head assemblies were produced the following year – this time for the Manta 400 coupé – total cylinder-head production eventually topping 1000.

In addition, Cosworth continued to develop the rally version of the power unit (extracting 280bhp from it by the end of production) and, in conjunction with SRE, to supply Opel with complete competition engines. Opel never advertised the fact, but in Mike's words, "… when Opel was winning the World Rally Championship, the engines never went anywhere near Rüsselsheim, they went straight back to Northampton."

Alf's drive to keep the spindles turning convinced him that Cosworth needed a manufacturing director; someone who could double as his deputy but whose main role would be to sell Cosworth's skills to a wider audience right across Europe, and thus maximise machine-shop productivity. Thanks to the forge thumping away at the back of Factory 3, the motor industry already knew of Cosworth's ability to design and make pistons for all sorts of applications, right down to small batches for restoration work. Now it was time to build on that foundation, because by the late 1970s Cosworth was in the enviable position of being able not only to design an engine, but also manufacture medium-sized quantities of it, including any necessary alloy castings – a rare combination. The successful candidate, Harvey Fox, was tasked with making that point to the world's motor manufacturers.

More mundane work was also welcome, and all sorts of subcontract machining appeared at Northampton as a result of Harvey's efforts – including gearbox parts for the washing equipment used to clean out oil-tanker tanks; cylinder heads for Jaguars; inlet manifolds for Rolls-Royce; overdrive gearbox mainshafts for export versions of British-built Ford Transits; special blocks for the Ford 2.4-litre York diesel; air intakes for Lynx and Sea King helicopters (to a very high spec) and a suite of steering gearbox housings for the combat recovery vehicle version of the Challenger tank made by Vickers.[3]

The foundry, too, soon acquired an enviable reputation, and pallet-loads of parts could be seen leaving Worcester for all sorts of surprising destinations, including cylinder-head castings for the Chrysler TC by Maserati and V6 two-stroke blocks for Mercury Marine[4] (which, incidentally, were an incredible 28% lighter than the porous sandcast American originals).

In 1980, not long after he took the job, Harvey hit the jackpot. He visited Mercedes and to his surprise was asked if Cosworth could design a four-valve rally engine based on the company's new SOHC 2.3-litre M102 engine. Some work had already been done in-house, but the company was not satisfied with the result. Cosworth was given a completely free hand to come up with something better.

Without any disrespect to Ford or GM, being trusted by Daimler-Benz to design a competition engine for Mercedes' new C-Class saloon was a huge accolade. The news sent a buzz of excitement around the works – even though the wider public could be told nothing of the deal because of Mercedes' desire for confidentiality. What became the WAA used a one-piece cylinder head – ie with integral cam-carriers – thus taking full advantage of Cosworth's new-found ability to cast complex shapes. It was mated to Mercedes' existing block and, like the parent engine, employed chain drive to the camshafts. The target for the rally engine was 270bhp, while the racer had to produce 300bhp, both on Kugelfischer injection.

Cosworth didn't have the luxury of being able to test the first engine in private. Although the engines were assembled in Northampton jointly by Cosworth and Mercedes fitters, they were sent to Stuttgart for test, so it was with considerable satisfaction that Mike Hall saw 267bhp on the Mercedes dyno the first time the WAA was fired up. Everything looked set fair for a homologation run of several hundred cylinder-head assemblies – until Mercedes abruptly cancelled its motorsport programme in 1981, following a string of disappointing results with unrelated larger models.

Happily, this cloud had a silver lining – in fact, a golden lining. Rather than waste the effort expended in creating the WAA, Mercedes decided to produce the design and fit it to a top-of-the-range C Class, the 190E 2.3-16. Instead of a homologation run, Cosworth was asked to produce 5000 head assemblies a year! It also paid Cosworth the biggest possible compliment by abandoning the confidentiality agreement. The 190E 2.3-16 reached the showrooms in 1984, followed by an enlarged 2.5-16 and Evolution I and II versions, all very successful. Today it is a sought-after classic, not least because Ayrton Senna used one as his road car.

There was no way such quantities could be produced at Northampton, so a new factory was built at Wellingborough in 1984, not just for the Mercedes job, but for other volume contracts, discussed in the next chapter.

For the same reason, the foundry at Worcester had to be augmented by a much larger second plant, Foundry 2. The decision to build this was taken as early as 1981 – a brave move at the time, as the Mercedes contract was not yet a certainty and the first plant was relatively small. To date, it had not attracted much work from outside Cosworth and had little credibility with the wider engineering industry. However, Keith and Mike felt it was all or nothing: they reasoned that the best way of telling the world they were serious about revolutionising aluminium casting was to build a fully-operational scaled-up plant.

They struck a deal with GKN Contractors, part of the large engineering group GKN, to provide extra investment and to licence the process worldwide, but the group closed down its contracting arm in 1983 before any licences had been signed, leaving Cosworth to go it alone.

By this point, Bob Smith had been hired as foundry manager. He had no experience of the engineering industry, but was recommended by Peter Michael, chairman of the UEI group, which was by then heavily involved with Cosworth (as discussed later in this chapter). Together with Simon Wilkins and David Tomlin, two of the redundant GKN engineers, he set about turning Cosworth's Worcester enterprise into a viable business.

Crucial to that was finding a way to improve Foundry 1's reject rate, which, though good by the standards of traditional casting, remained higher than ideal. The key breakthrough came when Mike, who as a glider pilot had a keen eye for convection currents and their effects, pointed to the bubbles rising in an electric kettle as it boiled and said: "That's what's spoiling some of our castings, we need the hottest material at the top, not the bottom." This, as John Dickens puts it, "... was a Eureka moment." Mike and Simon Wilkins realised that once the mould was full, the feed pipe needed to be disconnected and the mould inverted, a process they named 'roll-over.'

The engineering challenge of isolating a feed of molten aluminium and then rotating a hot, heavy mould, weighing several times as much as its contents, was considerable, but it was overcome. Thus modified, the Coscast process proved hugely successful, and has since been widely adopted.

To finance Foundry 2, UEI's coffers were raided to the tune of £750,000, though by the time the new plant opened in September 1984, the final bill, according to *Autocar*, was a full £1M[5].

Scaling up the process to such a degree was not without its problems, especially as, by this point, Mercedes head production was under way and Cosworth was keen to shift it to the new, much more economic, plant. John Dickens, who was appointed contracts manager around this time to look after Cosworth's growing portfolio, spent several months at Worcester sorting out problems which could otherwise have led to cancellation of the Mercedes contract. Once the plant was fully up to speed it was capable of producing 30,000 castings per annum, using one shift of 16 people.[5]

Back in Northampton, an interesting aside from the company's mainstream operations had been initiated by Keith, bearing the previous alphabetical code to the Mercedes job – VA. The VA was a driver-controlled rear axle intended for F1, Keith's idea being that the driver could uncouple the inside wheel on corners and transfer all power to the outside wheel. It used a crown-wheel and pinion but no conventional diff, the latter being replaced by a hydraulically controlled lockable clutch on each wheel, operated by fingers and Belleville washers, and controlled by paddles on the steering wheel. It was a good example of a Duckworthism in action:

I HAVE A VAST NATURAL CURIOSITY, AND THIS TRAINS ONE TO BE INVENTIVE.

Cecil Schumacher designed it in 1978, and Keith tried to interest Patrick Head at Williams in the idea, which got as far as one (very heavy) prototype, before FISA stepped in and banned driver-controlled traction devices. But Keith was disinclined to ditch a promising idea simply because a rule-maker had taken a dislike to it, and revisited the idea years later, after he retired.

While there was no doubt that Alf's appointment as MD in 1975 had hugely lessened the burden on Keith's shoulders, ensuring that the day-to-day management of the firm was in safe hands was only half an answer to the question of future-proofing

Continued on p217

The Cosworth Hodges briefly sported a wing – here it is under test before its Bristol debut.
(Courtesy Malcolm Tyrrell/Cosworth Engineering)

First event for the Cosworth Hodges at Chasewater, Birmingham. *(Courtesy Malcolm Tyrrell/Cosworth Engineering)*

The busy pits area at Bristol in 1978. The Cosworth boat is on the extreme left. *(Courtesy Fast On Water)*

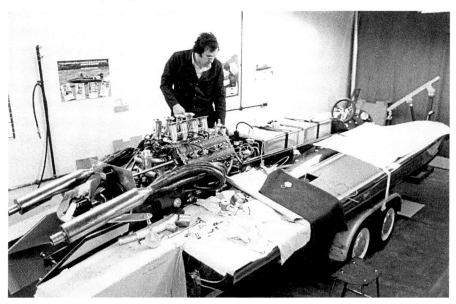

Ian Hawkins on the initial build of the DFV-engined boat at Cosworth. *(Courtesy Roy Finch/Cosworth Engineering)*

The Cosworth Hodges boat in the National Motorboat Museum in Essex (since closed). The number 22 ET is the one it carried on its last successful race, at the Parker Dam Enduro Event. *(Courtesy National Motorboat Museum)*

The Cosworth Hodges' DFV engine, mounted on its subframes ready for installation. The picture, taken on 11 May 1978, illustrates how the complete marinised DFV powerplant could be removed from the boat and run independently. *(Courtesy Malcolm Tyrrell/Cosworth Engineering)*

Left: First outing for Bill Brown's wooden BDG-engined boat in Carlsberg livery, at the GKN Powerboat Sprint Championships in September 1975 at Bute East Dock, Cardiff. Bill came second and first in the heats and second overall, and won the concours d'élégance. Right: The last powerboat raced by Bill: his troublesome, aluminium-skinned, BDG-engined machine. *(Courtesy Bill Brown collection)*

The *Aronow-Halter Special* ready to travel to its first race. *(Courtesy Ian Hawkins/Cosworth Engineering)*

First blood: a heat victory at Fairford. Jackie Wilson climbs out of the Cosworth Hodges while Malcolm Tyrrell celebrates in time-honoured style.
(Courtesy Malcolm Tyrrell/Cosworth Engineering)

Overview of the *Aronow-Halter Special*'s engines and driveshafts. *(Courtesy Ian Hawkins/Cosworth Engineering)*

The Cosworth team arrives at the Nautical Inn at Havasu City, Arizona, prior to the Parker Dam race. *(Courtesy Ian Hawkins/ Cosworth Engineering)*

Getting the *Aronow-Halter Special* up onto the plane. *(Courtesy Ian Hawkins/Cosworth Engineering)*

An impromptu ride in a hot-air balloon near Andover, arranged courtesy of a UEI employee. Keith and Gill flew to the take-off site by helicopter.

A proud moment as Keith poses with Trish and Roger after receiving his OBE at Buckingham Palace in 1984.

Keith was not the world's most talented windsurfer but he had a lot of fun trying. This photo was taken around 1988 in Menorca, where he and Gill also kept a Tinker dinghy.

Keith and Gill bought a holiday home in Menorca in 1982 and enjoyed it for many years. This photo was taken in 1994.

Keith and Gill signing the marriage register at Northampton Town Hall on 18 April 1986.

Keith gingerly stroking a horse at the Folly. This was about as close to a horse as he felt comfortable!

Cylinder-head manufacture for the Chevette HS represented Cosworth's first involvement with the European end of General Motors and ...

... was followed by design and manufacturing work for the Opel Manta 400. *(Courtesy GM)*

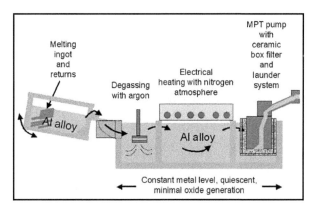

A modern diagram of the Coscast process, taken from the website of Mahle Powertrain, which now owns the rights to the technology. The operating principles have changed little since the process' development in the 1980s. *(Courtesy MPT)*

Victors pose after the Daytona win. *(Courtesy Bob Graves collection)*

The Quantel Cosworth JAB in its 1986 form.
(Courtesy Bob Graves collection)

World record drive of the Mercedes-Benz 190 E 2.3-16, on the Nardò high-speed track in Italy, 11-21 August 1983. The car covered 50,000km, and set three world records and nine class records. *(Courtesy Mercedes-Benz UK)*

Ayrton Senna takes the opening race of the new Nürburgring, 12 May 1984 in the Mercedes-Benz 190 E 2.3-16. (Courtesy Mercedes-Benz UK)

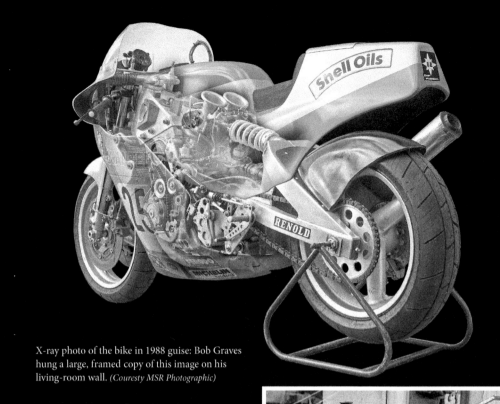

X-ray photo of the bike in 1988 guise: Bob Graves hung a large, framed copy of this image on his living-room wall. *(Couresty MSR Photographic)*

The JAB was originally designed for a twin-shock frame. *(Courtesy: www.accessnorton.com)*

Daytona BOTT, 1988: Roger Marshall being chased by a Honda. *(Courtesy Bob Graves collection)*

ROGER MARSHALL on the QUANTEL COSWORTH winning the grand prix class of the "Battle of the Twins" Daytona 1988 – first win by a British motorcycle since 1971

This poster had pride of place for many years in Keith's study. The caption reads: "Roger Marshall on the Quantel Cosworth winning the grand prix class of the Battle of the Twins Daytona 1988 – first win by a British motorcycle since 1971." Bob Graves' dedication adds: "With many thanks to many at Cosworth."

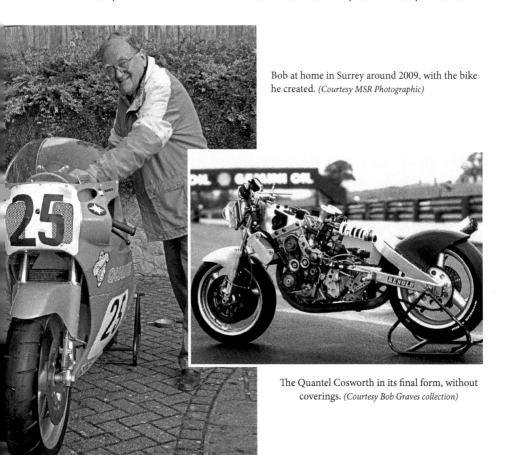

Bob at home in Surrey around 2009, with the bike he created. (Courtesy MSR Photographic)

The Quantel Cosworth in its final form, without coverings. (Courtesy Bob Graves collection)

Cosworth. The ownership of the company also needed to be addressed and, as Gill comments, "Alf had made it possible to sell Cosworth."

Back in 1966, Keith had given five per cent of the shares to each of his three co-directors, and kept the remaining 85%, the shares being in their wives' names to guard against death duties. Keith was uncomfortably aware that if he were to die or become incapacitated, managing the company under such an arrangement could be problematic. "Keith decided he needed to clear up his affairs," says Gill. "The company structure needed to be made coherent. He also wanted to pay Mike and Ben out – he felt they should not be too old before they got the benefits."

So towards the end of the 1970s Keith began the hunt for a buyer, a benign investor who would purchase the Cosworth shares but have the good sense to leave the existing management in place, so that life at St James Mill Road could continue more or less as usual.

A contact of Keith's who raced Aston Martins had successfully dealt with a similar problem by selling his firm to United Engineering Industries (UEI). This group, he explained, was a hands-off management which loosely controlled a number of small and medium-sized companies: each part of the group submitted its figures every month and, if they looked okay, their management was then left pretty much to its own devices.

This sounded exactly what Cosworth needed, and in due course Alf negotiated a deal on Keith's behalf, Cosworth being sold to UEI in March 1980 for £6.2M. Of that total, 85% went to the Duckworth family: Ursula got five per cent, another 28% went into a trust for Trish and Roger, and Keith retained the rest. UEI directors Len Jagger and Ian Skipper joined the Cosworth board, followed shortly afterwards by Harvey Fox, while Ursula (by now living apart from Keith), relinquished her directorship, as did Bill Brown. At the same time all four of Cosworth's founding directors sold their shares in SRE to the fifth man in the partnership, John Dunn, who thus assumed full control, although Keith retained personal ownership of the premises.

None of Keith's three original co-directors had wanted to sell their Cosworth shares, but in the event they all parted with them. Practically everyone thought the company had been undervalued – according to Mike, Cosworth's cash reserves alone amounted to £1.2M at the time of the sale – but Keith was not bothered. Neither was he interested in offshore finance, or other tax-efficiency schemes. In fact, he expressed his views on wealth often enough for them to become immortalised as a Duckworthism:

IT IS THE YEARS OF SOCIALISM, AND THE HIGH TAXATION THAT WENT WITH IT, THAT WAS THE DEATH OF ALL THE MORALS AND ETHICS OF THE CITY OF LONDON. I STILL DON'T WANT TO BE SERIOUSLY RICH. I'M STILL QUITE AMAZED THAT SOME PEOPLE WHO HAVE MADE SOME MONEY ACTUALLY SEEM TO WANT A LOT MORE. WHEN I LOOK AT THE KIND OF PEOPLE WHO HAVE MADE A LOT OF MONEY, I DON'T THINK THAT IT IS A GREAT CRITERION OF ACHIEVEMENT IN LIFE. SELF-ESTEEM, YES, THAT DOES COME INTO IT – IT'S REALLY THE ONLY THING THAT COMES INTO IT.

Later, Gill would observe: "Cosworth was sold just a bit early. If he'd waited he could have floated it on the stock-market and made a lot more money. He should have done better out of it but he never griped, he had all the money he wanted. If he liked a motorbike, he'd go and buy it, that was the extent of his indulgence." To Keith, the priority was to ensure that his company stayed in safe hands.

In the short term, the sale to UEI achieved exactly what DKD hoped for, in that Messrs Jagger and Skipper were rarely seen at Northampton, and life at Cosworth scarcely changed. But in the longer term, far from achieving corporate stability, it set in motion a complex series of takeovers and reorganisations which would eventually change Cosworth out of all recognition.

The first change – the replacement of Len and Ian by Bob Graves – happened within a matter of months, and turned out to be a change for the better.

Bob Graves was an electronics man, not a mechanical engineer, but he had a good feel for machinery and a useful knowledge of mechanical engineering, having raced motorcycles in his youth. In 1973 he and a friend, Peter Michael, had started a company called Micro Consultants from the bedroom of his home in Surrey – integrated circuits were in their infancy at the time, and Peter wanted to use the new technology to produce a digital-to-analogue converter that was hugely faster (1MHz instead of 1kHz) than existing equipment, and far smaller (about the size of a cigarette packet).

The company had no pedigree whatsoever, but its fast data-conversion products had enormous potential for media and communication applications, and were so demonstrably superior that, after a shaky start, the operation mushroomed. Within a couple of years it developed a product for the opposite conversion – analogue to digital – and inside four years the speed was up to 18MHz – "... enough for a colour TV," in Bob's words. "We'd grown to a large laboratory at Newbury and had a few hundred people working for us."

Just as Bob and Peter were considering taking their company public, UEI approached them with a takeover offer. But whichever way Bob and Peter manipulated the figures, it was impossible for them to avoid the conclusion that Quantel (the company which Micro Consultants had by now morphed into) was actually worth more than UEI. So although UEI and Quantel did join forces, it was on terms which gave Quantel considerable influence on how the whole group was run – so much so that by 1985 Len and Ian had departed for pastures new, leaving Peter Michael (Sir Peter, by then) as chairman of UEI.

"In 1981, one of the UEI companies I was interested in was Cosworth," relates Bob, "which it had only just acquired – far too cheaply. We felt we needed someone on the Cosworth board and the only bloke who'd raced anything was me, I'd done bike racing for fun as a youngster, with secondhand machines, but I'd won a few things. So I appointed myself to the board and a number of people I knew said 'My God, you're going to be eaten alive by Keith.'"

He needn't have worried. "Keith and I were chatting about something, and the subject came up of a motorcycle called the Dunelt, which had a two-stroke engine with a piston bigger at the bottom than the top, to give a supercharging effect. The fact that I knew about this tweaked his ear, so I didn't get eaten alive. And I knew enough of Keith's reputation to shut up and listen.

"He was very single-minded, and he was very rarely wrong. People in general, in engineering, learned not to argue with him. But once you were in the fold, he wasn't half as obstinate, he would listen."

Bob quickly tuned in to the relationship between the three founding directors. "Mike Costin is a fantastic character and a bloody nice bloke. Keith used to say, 'There's no other guy in the world who can spot a fatigue potential like him, he smells them.' Even though Mike was modest about his abilities, he and Keith were bloody close. They were like *that*." (He crosses his fingers.)

"I went to the monthly board meetings, and I found myself looking at things very much in Keith's way, though not with his depth of knowledge. Keith's approach to business was like mine, straight up and down, and Mike complemented him, not just engineering-wise but also in getting the best answer out of him. Keith would sometimes vacillate – should I, shouldn't I? – and after a while Mike might say 'Well that's all right, we're doing so and so – okay Keith?' And Keith would say 'Oh, er, yes.' Mike had made up his mind for him.

"On more than one occasion Keith said Ben had not got the credit he deserved. He was a machinist, a very good designer (very hot with camshaft design), and developed a lot of big NC machine tools in-house, as well as being into computing right from the start. Ben was bloody marvellous, and a hell of a nice guy."

Bob's genuine interest in, and enthusiasm for, the Northampton company was evident every time he came to the works. People took to him very quickly, and within a remarkably short space of time he was accepted as every inch a 'Cosworth man', so much so that when he died in late 2012, just days after being interviewed for this book, many at Northampton were deeply saddened by the news, even though he had long since retired to Surrey.

One day, while wandering around the works with Keith, Bob spied a row of dusty and forgotten parallel twin engines. "What are these?" he enquired of Keith.

"Don't talk about that, it was a waste of our time and energy, it's the only bloody engine we've ever designed that's never won a race." Keith explained to Bob that he was looking at the JAB, the stillborn competition brother of the JAA, and about Norton's demise. As an ex-bike racer who was still involved with sponsorship here and there, Bob was intrigued.

"Can I have one? I'll wrap a frame round it."

"If you like, but don't come back here for any bits and pieces, we don't want homers here!"[6]

"I'd better take a second one then!"

Despite Bob's position as a Cosworth director, the Quantel Cosworth, as the bike became known, was a purely personal project, involving no company money and virtually no company resources. For a long time, many employees knew nothing of it, but some of the design staff lent a hand out of hours, particularly Geoff Goddard, who often travelled down to Bob's opulent hillside home in Surrey.

"Right from the beginning of his involvement with Cosworth, my wife, my children, all [of us] went down to stay with Bob. With all the projects he ran, he'd call me up and ask if I could do things. Everything I did for Bob was for free, and as a result we were just natural friends. The double garage was actually a machine shop with mills, grinders, lathes, CNCs, wall-to-wall with machines. Up above was the build shop – he had his bike in there and later he built two 1924 Amilcars there, from the original plans."

Keith was not actively involved in the work, but he took an interest. The prospect of the company's black sheep being finally guided into the racing fold was very satisfying, especially as the JA was in many respects 'son of DFV'. Its capacity was one quarter that of the DFV, its head design was very similar, and it used the same pistons and rods: second only to the DFV itself, the JA is probably the Cosworth engine with the most DKD involvement, though Mike Hall handled much of the detail work.

"I had this stupid idea that we should go and win Daytona's Battle of the Twins (BOTT)," explains Bob. The engine had been under test when Norton's bankruptcy occurred, so there was still development to be done, and of course there was a frame to build and develop. But Bob was nothing if not committed, and before long he was spending more time in Surrey and rather less in Northampton. He was also spending a great deal of his own money.

"Just as with the DFV, the engine was designed to be load-bearing, so of necessity Keith had roughed out the whole bike before designing it. However, there were some mistakes in the bike that I couldn't understand. For instance, he designed the swinging arm with a pivot on the engine, which rather fixed the geometry. In the old days when you had only two inches of suspension movement, you could have got away with it, but with 5.5 inches we used to be sitting on the line with the chain dangling. I solved that by using a roller to tension the chain, effectively altering the pivot point, and converting the suspension to pull-push.[7] To help us get away with that we had a cush hub with blocks of rubber, and it worked perfectly. This frame was mainly made of ¼-inch duralumin which we machined in the workshop at my house. Welding was done at Exactweld, aircraft welders."

The finished frame weighed just 6.6kg, including forks. By contrast, the engine was on the heavy side, thanks to its twin balance shafts, and its centre of gravity was higher than ideal. No major changes were made though, aside from boring it out from 750 to 822cc. Development concentrated on the cooling system, which on Keith's own admission had needed work, and on mixture supply. "The junction of the two ports was a separate piece, as its length was critical to engine performance," explains Bob.

"On carburettors, our power figures had never been anything like the 110hp Cosworth claimed – which is odd because Cosworth figures were always conservative. We never managed better than 100,[8] equivalent to 85hp at the back wheel, though we did have a lot more torque. But we couldn't look into it further because the bloke who did our testing work was killed in a flying accident."

The gearbox had a tendency to seize up on the selectors because the oil wasn't getting where it was needed. The fix was simple: a gutter to direct the lubricant. "We did lots of detail development like that, but we knew there was more to do."

It was 1986 by the time this after-hours project was finally ready to compete, and by this stage Bob had gathered a little team around him for the trip to Daytona. He took on Australian racer Gary Flood – "... the only man to win the 250, 350 and 500 motocross titles in a single season" – as general mechanic, and arranged with another Australian, Paul Lewis, aka Angry Ant, to ride the bike. John Surtees went too: he'd heard about the project and became, in Bob's words, "... our mentor."

Paul Lewis was light, brave and accurate, but had acquired a reputation for throwing victories away through impetuousity – a reputation he demonstrated at the 1986 Daytona BOTT.

Initially he led the race from the Cagiva/Ducatis of Marco Lucchinelli and Jimmy Adamo, but Lucchinelli pulled clear and left the others to fight for second. Near the end of the race Lewis had a controversial – and in Bob's eyes entirely unnecessary – run-in with Adamo which caused the latter to crash out at around 140mph (fortunately without serious injury). Lewis cracked a bone in his foot but managed to clinch second.[9]

In this instance, Lewis had come away with a result, but Bob was disgusted with him for taking unnecessary risks and felt that, had Lewis used sensible tactics, first place might had been on the cards. "We came back and licked our wounds, although our second place was very well received."

For 1987 Gary found Rob Phillis, another Australian rider, and the team experienced another disappointment. "One characteristic of the bike was that the torsional vibration frequency of the crank was around 4000rpm. Normally you never notice it, you just drive through it, but it was very sharp and we said to Rob, on no account drive this full bore below 4000."

Rob took the bike out for practice, then brought it in.

"Bloody bike's falling to bits," he said, "it's starting to vibrate, things are coming off it."

"You weren't full-boring it out of that first turn were you, in third?"

"No of course I wasn't."

So, they put the second motor in. Half a dozen laps later he'd done it again. Bob was livid. Gary was very upset too. All that work and effort, and they'd had to come home.

"I said to Gary 'We'll have one more go, because it's a bit expensive!' I bought an analogue fuel-injection system, very mickey-mouse, it didn't have any stabilised power supply, which is ridiculous, you can't produce a consistent output when the voltage is varying between 12 and 14V! Fortunately that was within our powers to put right. We got it working pretty well except that the bottom end was dirty.

"Fuel-injection made an enormous difference. When I got it working properly I got 130bhp, with the same head and porting. So in 1988 we went back for a third try. This year Roger Marshall was riding: seven times British champion, he'd just got the push from Suzuki despite winning the championship. Roger had never ridden the bike before Daytona apart from half a dozen laps at Brands in the pouring rain. We had, in the meantime, had special sets of gears made for Daytona. It's only a five-speed box and of course we needed to keep it over 4000rpm (though that was only ever a problem to one rider!). We were timed at 178mph.

"Roger put in some good qualifying laps, but the organisers were very uncooperative with us, as they usually are in the States.

'You're not going out on the track unless you've got all those wheel nuts locked,' the scrutineers said.

'What about the Harleys, they're not locked!'

'They're experts, they know what they're doing.'

"Now the Quantel Cosworth had no oil breather pipe. Any air that wanted to come out, emerged through a 4mm hole in the centre of one of the sprockets.

'We want to see a proper breather.'

"They called us in and John Surtees said, 'We don't have one.'

'What do you mean, you haven't got one? You have to have one.'

'No we don't, it's part of our patents, and we're not telling you how. If there's oil coming out, we'll do something about it.'

"In the end we screwed on a union with a pipe disappearing under the tank. It didn't bloody go anywhere, but it kept them happy. So it was lovely when we won! Moreover, we'd won against machinery which was practically to works standard – and standards had changed enormously during our three years. We were very lucky because, pushing up to the line, we thought 'that doesn't sound right,' and we rushed back and got a voltmeter. We only had 12.5V: the charging had failed. So during the race we were reliant solely on the battery, and as that weakened, so did the performance. By the end, we were 600rpm down on the straight. But we still won.

"The reception at Cosworth was fantastic. Mike Hall, who designed the engine after Keith's initial work, was very proud of the JA. He made a point of mentioning it at his retirement, at which point Keith jumped up and interjected, tongue in cheek 'Oi, we make car engines not bike engines, keep to the point.' Mike begged to differ.

"After we won, Daytona kept inviting us back, but we weren't interested. I'd done what I set out to do."

The Quantel Cosworth went on to win at Spa and Assen, but wasn't subsequently ridden in anger in Britain, though Bob and Roger Marshall did take the bike to some demos. Keith and Mike allowed themselves a day off and went along to one, at the North West 200 in Northern Ireland. It wasn't a proper race, just a few fast laps, but nevertheless when some of the other riders were just ending their first lap, Roger Marshall was starting his third. Later, back in the paddock, Bob found him "... sitting on the bike looking really strange. He told me 'I just realised I did two laps flat out 15mph faster than the works Hondas!' He was so shaken up."

"Life was different for me at Cosworth after Daytona – I'd achieved something and had some credibility. Several people from Japan wanted to produce a series of bikes and/or engines based on the design, but I wasn't interested in taking it further."

With the factory busier than ever, Alf wasn't either, and neither was Keith. His mind was on other problems, and he knew that the engine needed more development. As a result, the enquiries came to nothing. Geoff Goddard remembers Jack Field "... sobbing on the phone, saying to would-be customers 'It's a museum piece, we haven't got any more!' All the patterns had gone, everything."

So the Quantel Cosworth with its JAB engine remains unique. The entire project, from lifting the engine off the shelf at St James Mill Road to eventual victory, had cost Bob something like £100,000 of his own money, but it had laid to rest the 'never won a race' stigma of Cosworth's only motorcycle engine. The bike now lives in the National Motorcycle Museum at Solihull.

Keith's decision not to disinter the JA was motivated by a desire not to distract his designers, for while Bob had been painstakingly pursuing victory at the BOTT, Cosworth had been busy with a whole new generation of F1 engines, and a car called the Sierra Cosworth was rapidly becoming a motoring icon ...

Footnotes

1 For more information on Coscast, see Complete Casting Handbook: Metal Casting Processes, Techniques & Design, John Campbell, (Butterworth-Heinemann, 2011). The description of roll-over appears on p520.

2 Not listed in Appendix as chronology is uncertain.

3 Other than the Jaguar work, which was done in 1982, these jobs are not listed in Appendix as their chronology is uncertain.

4 Not listed in Appendix as the chronology is uncertain.

5 p29, Autocar, 29 September 1984.

6 By 'homers,' Keith meant private projects, of which there happened to be quite a few in progress at Cosworth at the time.

7 Believed to be a reference to conversion to monoshock.

8 Cosworth's records show the JAB as originally developing 90bhp (see Appendix), which is in line with quoting a conservative figure for a 100bhp engine. The 110bhp was probably a development figure not consistently achieved.

9 There is a short clip of the race, including the accident, at www.YouTube.com/watch?v=tpyWzT7DZeI.

Chapter 16

Icons of the Eighties

Ever since the Escort's rallying heyday with the BDA, Stuart Turner had kept in touch with Keith. For several years the contact had been more social than professional, because Ford's Advanced Vehicle Operations, which he had headed, closed in 1975 and he moved into the company's public affairs division. By 1983, however, Stuart was back as director of Ford Europe Motorsport. The company was once again hoping to raise its profile through competition, not least to boost the image of the Sierra.

Much had been expected of the Sierra, successor to the famous Cortina, but it received a distinctly lukewarm reception at its launch in 1982. The public was decidedly ambivalent about the car's 'jelly-mould' styling, while Ford's decision to buck the industry trend and retain rear-wheel drive (RWD) was leapt on by rival manufacturers, particularly Vauxhall, as evidence that the Sierra was not a truly modern design.

Offering sporting versions of the Sierra was an obvious route to improving the car's appeal. RWD was no disadvantage in competition, particularly when combined with an effective independent rear suspension, the one major technical change which distinguished the Sierra from its live-axle predecessor.

Stuart takes up the story. "Walter Hayes was in America by then and got word that things in Europe were not smooth. He asked me to write a report for him summarising the situation, and a month later I was back in motorsport. But I said, 'If it's going to work I need to have a clean sheet of paper.'"

The resulting wishlist proposed several projects, among them a new F1 engine and a new Group B rally car. Clearly, a trip to Northampton was called for.

"I took the chairman and president of Ford Europe to see this legend Mr Duckworth. 'You'd better come and see a Formula 1 engine,' I told them, and we were walking through the works when we saw a Pinto engine with a four-valve head. We asked 'What's that?'

"Keith said 'Oh, we think we can sell some as tuning kits, maybe a couple of hundred,' and no more was said.

"Then, over a ploughman's lunch – and if there isn't a plaque outside the pub commemorating the event, then there should be – I said 'That engine that we've just seen, if that was turbocharged and put in a Sierra, Rover wouldn't win another touring car race.' And because the top two people of Ford Europe were there, along with Keith Duckworth, that gave the project a bloody good following wind.

"Something Keith appreciated when I told him later, was that there was quite a job selling the project within the company to get it approved. We'd have to find buyers for 5000 to homologate it, complete with this big spoiler, and I remember being at a Ford of Britain meeting pitching to sell this project. I won't say I was struggling, but I was having to work hard, and Sam Toy, who was UK chairman at the time, looked at a picture on the wall of Jim Clark on three wheels in a Lotus Cortina and said 'Are you saying that the Cosworth will do for the Sierra what the Lotus did for the Cortina?' And I said 'Bugger, I wish I'd written that in my paper, because that sums it up!'"

By spring 1983 the project to build the Sierra RS Cosworth, as it was called, was approved in principle, but the ink had hardly dried on the contract when Keith realised the true implications. Mike Costin, talking to Simon Taylor for his *Lunch with …* series in *Motor Sport* (February 2012 issue), explains.

"The 16-valve turbocharged Sierra Cosworth was something that Keith took on with a quick, 'Yes, we'll have a go at that.' Then one morning he came into my office and said, 'We're in the shit with this Sierra project.' Building the prototype, getting the power, then going through all the approvals with Ford, was going to be a massive task, especially as we were in the middle of Mercedes and Opel contracts too.

"Keith said, 'We'll split the company down the middle. You be chief engineer, road engines. I'll be chief engineer, race engines. You'll have to go off and do it somewhere else.' I moved into another building over the road with Mike Hall, the ex-BRM guy who'd been with us since the start of the DFV, as my chief designer. We started again. Then we built a new factory in Wellingborough for production.

"The initial Sierra contract was for 5000 engines a year. Plus there were much more powerful rally specials with a bigger turbo. Later on, the boy-racers could buy third-hand Sierras for very little money, chip them and get massive horsepower. Some claimed 550bhp or more. But the truth is, we had to get 250bhp[1] out of that engine in all types of everyday usage, utterly reliably.

"The book of tests we had to comply with for Ford was several inches thick. One was [that] we'd take a new engine off the line; we were allowed 15 seconds to get the oil pressure up, then we had to run it at 7000rpm from cold, like somebody abusing a cold car on a winter's morning. Then take the hot water out, put cold water in, do it again. Then take it to bits and there wasn't to be any scuffing, anywhere. Then there was the 300-hour test: 24 cycles of 12.5 hours each, maximum power for a set period, then drop to maximum torque, then to tick over, then to maximum power again. For 300 hours. Then strip the engine, and all wear had to be within strict limits. Then reassemble the engine – you're only allowed to change gaskets and O-rings – and the same cycle for another 300 hours. It was all in the Ford contract, but I don't think Keith read the small print when he signed …"

That four-valve head which Stuart Turner had spied in the works was designed by Mario Illien, and at Cosworth was designated the YAA. The first turbocharged prototype was the YAB, and the eventual road car engine the YBB, using a Garrett T03 turbocharger. After October 1983 Mario was not involved, as that month he and Paul Morgan left Cosworth to set up their own company. Draughtsman Geoff Oliver left around the same time, leaving a distinctly overworked Mike Hall to head up the design side of what became Cosworth's biggest ever project. The design target was 200bhp – it actually came out at 204bhp – but the engine was designed from the outset for Group A homologation, so practically every component apart from the cylinder block had to be redesigned to cope with the 400+bhp required.

Cosworth's two biggest contracts to date had been the WAA for Mercedes and the KBA for GM (discussed later in this chapter), both of which involved supplying complete, assembled cylinder heads. As production of these had been ramped-up, Cosworth had to overcome various casting and machining quality issues, but the YBB raised the stakes to a whole new level because Ford wanted Cosworth to build and assemble the entire powerplant, complete with turbocharger, from blocks supplied by Ford. This was a first for Cosworth, and together with the other contracts represented a huge commitment, far in excess of anything Cosworth had signed up to before. An entirely new factory needed to be constructed and equipped, capable of producing up to 30 YBBs per day.

Ford knew – even if Cosworth didn't as yet – that the project would be hugely challenging and quite unlike anything the Northampton firm had tackled before. Had Cosworth not been part of UEI, the financial commitment probably would have been impossible – and indeed Ford might not have sanctioned Sierra Cosworth production at all, for fear of Cosworth overstretching itself.

As it was, a site was found in Wellingborough, about ten miles from Northampton, and construction of a new 30,000ft^2 factory began in 1984, the plant being opened by the Duke of Kent in 1985 and producing its first YBB that November.

Equipping the factory involved massive investment, though some typically innovative production solutions from Ben Rood helped contain the costs. For instance, five Heller computerised workstations were installed, each capable of taking up to 160 cutting tools, but one was specially modified to ream valve guides and cut valve seats, saving the company the huge expense of buying a special machine for the task. During his career at Cosworth, Ben reckoned he built between 30 and 40 special machine tools, including conrod makers and block line-borers.

Close liaison with Ford was essential, a role filled by project engineer Paul Fricker. He went on to specialise in the YB series and at the time of writing runs his own company, Fricker Automotive.

John Dickens was also heavily involved. "Production-related contracts like the YBB had investment and employment implications that were not immediately covered by cash and likely returns – any production hold-up, for example, would probably have a disastrous effect on cash flow and employee relations. This vexed Keith considerably – not to say that others weren't similarly concerned, but with Keith it showed. Additionally there was the issue of how to cover the cost of customer issues in the field. Since we had no experience of such things, the contract negotiations were somewhat one-sided – we were rather short of trust, since we'd already covered more testing costs than we originally envisaged."

The engineering development described by Mike was all new to Cosworth, "... but when it was complete we thought we'd done a reasonable job," says John Dickens. However, that was not the end of the story, because Ford's Production Validation (PV) procedures then kicked in. "PV was a whole new ball-game. Not only had the engine to survive the tests all over again under the surveillance of hard-nosed Ford production staff, headed by the legendary Bill Hayden, but it had to do so in the car, with all its other special modifications from the common rep-mobile.

"Rod Mansfield and his team at Ford's Special Vehicle Engineering were adept at managing this process, but it was all new to us. Meanwhile, we'd built a factory and started employing staff, expecting a given start-date and production build-up. It didn't happen."

The car was previewed in March 1985 at the Geneva show, the intention being to commence sales that September and complete the 5000 production run by summer 1986. In the event, the end date became the start date, with the first cars finally delivered in July 1986, ten months later than scheduled.

In December 1985, with several problems still unresolved and the press launch in Spain looming, the entire project hung on a knife edge, as Paul Fricker recalls. "Hayden wanted to stop the program, and a meeting was held between him, Ford Europe's chief executive Alex Trotman, and Walter Hayes to discuss whether there was any point in authorising the launch.

"Walter rang Keith," Paul recalls, "and asked if the engines were going to fail during the press launch. Keith rang Mike, but he was like a bear with a sore head, having been to a do the night before, and told him to ring me. I said that all the failures had an indicated mileage of over 25,000 miles, so there should be no issues at the mileages likely on the launch. Walter then learned that the cars were already on their way to Spain and that the flight tickets had been given to the German journalists. Keith said the engine would survive, so Alex gave the nod."

Fingers were crossed extremely tightly as the press launch commenced, but it went well, producing the best press reviews anyone could remember for a Ford vehicle. The engine was a gem, journalists reported, and Paul remembers Rod Mansfield adding: "... like a ruby – red and expensive!"

The only snag concerned one of the engine protection systems that Keith had demanded; it was designed so that after max power (6500rpm), the engine management lowered the boost and then cut off the fuel.

Paul continues: "The press were in the cars within ten minutes of landing in Seville, and of course immediately went for Vmax on the excellent derestricted roads. But the cut-off had not been calibrated well enough at Northampton: the cars would do 155mph and then experience fuel cut-off! There was much discussion in the bar each evening on this topic. My view was they should not be going that fast!"

The real issues – the ones which happily did not become apparent at the launch – then had to be tackled. Tappets would wear out (solved by Dave Lee, general manager at manufacturing, who changed the cam manufacturing route), and pistons would scuff (new top ring from piston manufacturer), but the most serious problem was head-gasket failure. "Here Keith did an excellent analysis of the problem, and we worked with Rienz to significantly improve the situation. It was really only closed when we were able to use the three-layer steel gasket," says Paul.

The Sierrra RS Cosworth proved an immediate success and achieved everything Stuart Turner had promised Ford it would, and more. It completely turned around the standard Sierra's lacklustre image, and the Sierra became Britain's best-selling car.

Soon it became clear that demand for the Sierra RS Cosworth far exceeded the 5000 needed for Group A homologation. In no time at all the 'Cossie' became a 1980s icon: no other car anywhere near its price could offer 150mph performance combined with everyday practicality. Before long, it seemed every young man with a Sierra, no matter how humble its engine, wanted louvres on the bonnet top, wheelarch extensions on the sides, and of course, that huge 'whale tail' spoiler on the back.

Like all the best Cosworth powerplants, the engine went from strength-to-strength and took on a life of its own as numerous variants were produced, the first of which was the YBC (280bhpm in rallying spec, up to 340bhp for racing).

The car's reputation was further enhanced when the limited edition RS500 appeared: just 500 of these 'Evolution' Sierras, with uprated 225bhp engine, found their way onto the road, but the strengthened YBD-series powerplant had the potential to produce up to 500bhp in the right hands, and tuners were soon enthusiastically chipping and modifying them. The YBD powered the Sierra to the World Touring Car Championship in 1987 and also notched up many wins in the British Touring Car Championship between 1987 and 1990, particularly in the hands of Andy Rouse and Robb Gravett, the latter taking the title in 1990.

As a rally car, the Cossie never achieved the iconic status of the Escort, but nevertheless it chalked up many successes. Jimmy McRae took the British Rally Championship with it in 1987 and 1988, and the car found many friends among privateer competitors.

With the car continually developing, the testing and PV programmes were ongoing and these produced some very serious ups and downs at Northampton, despite many of the issues not being of Cosworth's making. John's notes from October 1987 record that "4P (a particular PV process) had been stopped due to one engine failure associated with detonation, three bracket failures, a clutch-plate failure, exhaust downpipe joint failures, Recaro seat concerns, boot-opening concerns and a crankshaft oil-leak.

"We calculated various scenarios of start-stop costs, and it all looked pretty disastrous to the total business. Negotiations became more and more anxious and exasperating; Keith grasped the nettle and a meeting was set up at Ford's Mayfair office with Alex Trotman."

John describes those discussions as hard but cordial. "Alex seemed to appreciate that we had all dug ourselves a pretty deep hole; his motorsport and sales people were desperate for the fillip that a successful Sierra flagship programme might bring, so he smoothed the way to what was to become a complex pricing contract which enabled us to survive the lean times of non- or low production while Ford benefited from lower costs when the factory was singing along. Without that meeting, the programme could easily have folded."

As it was, the car went from strength-to-strength and, with demand running at unforeseen levels, it became clear that middle management at Wellingborough needed to be strengthened. This brings us to Bernard Ferguson, who was drafted in from Northampton to help.

Bernard has certain parallels with Keith: he's Lancastrian (from Burnley, just a few miles from Keith's native Blackburn), well educated and blessed with a straightforward no-nonsense approach to life. He is not, however, an engineer, though he spent almost his whole career in the motor industry, initially working in purchasing and supply. His first job was at Rootes, after which he moved to Northern Ireland to work for a DeLorean associate called Trimtech, which was responsible for supplying all the trim for the ill-fated DMC-12 sports car.

"Eventually I got made general manager, but when DeLorean folded, Trimtech went too, so I was looking for a job. Trimtech had been an offshoot of Chamberlain Phipps in Northampton, so I talked to the local training organisation – there were a lot of those in the Thatcher years, everybody seemed to be unemployed – who told me that Cosworth were hiring. This was early 1984.

"Cosworth told me they had a vacancy for a contracts engineer and asked me in to discuss it. As I'm not an engineer, I had no great hopes of getting selected, but as luck would have it, the job consisted of trying to sell Cosworth's services on the road-car side, working for John Dickens and ultimately responsible to Mike. I realised they were all racing people, whereas I came from the industry."

John had recently been promoted from quality control to a sales role roughly equivalent to Jack Field's, but on the road-car side rather than racing. Bernard spent a few months in the contracts department, holding the fort while John was away working at Worcester and on sales trips, and in the office next door was Jack. The veteran sales manager was approaching retirement and on the lookout for a successor.

Jack had become sales manager simply by growing with the firm, but times had changed. He knew the next occupant of his seat needed to be educated, but not at the expense of that common touch which was so vital in the rough and tumble of the racing fraternity. Through the thin office walls, he could hear Bernard's down-to-earth phone technique; a little northern grit would go down well in the paddock, Jack decided. When the time came for Jack's cockney twang to answer the sales-office phone for the last time … well, a Lancashire accent would strike just as good a pitch.

He said as much to Bernard – and to John, who responded with a robust "He's doing fine, keep your hands off him!" – but the discussion was overtaken by events, because Bernard was moved to Wellingborough. Cosworth suddenly had a major issue of supply and manufacture. In Bernard's words "How the hell are we going to make 5000 YB engines quickly enough?"

Bernard worked at Wellingborough for about a year. "Jack," he recalls, "was still looking for a replacement and was still pestering me. Effectively, I was offered the position as Jack's replacement." By now, YB production was rolling nicely and Bernard fancied a change, but nevertheless, for reasons discussed later, he didn't take the job. Instead, he left to become general manager of Valcast, a nearby engineering supplier which numbered Cosworth among its customers.

That turned out to be a mistake – "I got bored and wanted to get back into the motor industry" – and before long the manager at Cosworth's Wellingborough plant, Mark Hunt, suggested he return. "I'd been there about two months when Jack wandered through and saw that I'd come back. Next thing I knew, I'd got his job. It was a great opportunity and I grabbed it."

Meanwhile the Cossie spawned a more subtle notchback, the Sierra Sapphire RS Cosworth. This led in 1990 to what many believe to be the most desirable Cossie of all, the Sierra RS Cosworth 4x4 which, confusingly, retained the saloon body despite 'Sapphire' being dropped from the name. To counteract the weight of the 4WD transmission, the engine (designated YBG with catalyst, YBJ without) was reworked to give a little more power – 220bhp. Sideskirts and whale tail were gone, what remained was a car of subtle appearance and highly unsubtle ability. By the end of production in 1992, total production of all Sierra Cosworth models had reached nearly 31,000.

While the Sierra RS Cosworth is the most famous road car associated with the Cosworth name, and the Mercedes 190E arguably the most prestigious, they were by no means the only road car projects at Cosworth during the 1980s. The advent of the Coscast process, which remained unique for some years, not only gave the company's designers new freedom to create intricate castings, but also secured the associated production contract, as Cosworth was the only company capable of making them. Hitherto, the company's design jobs had generated production runs typically numbered in the hundreds – now the totals could be measured in tens of thousands.

After the Sierra, the most significant job in turnover terms was the Opel work mentioned by Mike in his *Motor Sport* interview. GM called this engine the Family 2 unit, but in Cosworth-speak it was the KBA, the last Opel job having been the KAA. In reality, the eleventh letter of the alphabet was the only connection between the two, because this four-valve head for the front-wheel drive Vauxhall Astra and Cavalier / Opel Kadett and Ascona was a clean-sheet design by Mike Hall and his team. It was one of the most modern mass-production engines of its era and when installed in the later Astra GTEs – the Red Top engines from 1987 on – gave the GM product top spot in the hot-hatch performance race. Like the Mercedes, the KB was cast at Worcester and then machined and assembled at Wellingborough.

There were a couple of other GM projects too. The DB was a twin-cam alloy-head 16V conversion for the Pontiac Iron Duke engine, sold in kit form and fitted to some Fieros, while the EB was a stillborn V6 for Buick-Oldsmobile-Cadillac, which never made production due to internal GM competition from Chevrolet-Pontiac.

Closer to home, Cosworth was involved in the MG Metro 6R4, manufacturing and assembling the heads for the V64V, as its 90° V6 is known, in 1985. The engine was not designed at Northampton – credit for that goes to Austin Rover's David Wood – but Mike Hall did some consultancy for him during the engine's development and David already knew his way around DFVs very well. The familiarity shows: the breathing arrangements are very similar and many of the internals are DFV components. Later, in 1989, Cosworth made parts for the twin-turbocharged 3.5-litre version used in the Jaguar XJ220.

TWR's racing Jaguar V12s also had some Cosworth design and manufacturing input, though it was not widely known at the time because TWR always retained overall control. Northampton became progressively more involved as the engine developed, until, by the late 1980s, only the block was supplied by Jaguar.

Nevertheless, in the motorsport public's mind, it's the Sierra that defines this era at Cosworth as far as road cars are concerned. Its success is the best possible tribute to Alf Vickers' far-sighted policy of diversification, though sadly he did not live to see the end of Sierra production. He was not a young man when he joined Cosworth in 1973: by 1985 he was well past retirement age and his health was beginning to fail. That December he stepped down to the post of non-executive vice chairman, and in May 1986 he retired completely. He died less than two years later, in February 1988.

Alf's retirement was a turning point, both for Cosworth and for Keith. Even those who'd had their doubts when Alf arrived – and there were many – admitted that he had done a fine job for the company and many had personal reasons to be grateful to him.

Malcolm Tyrrell, for instance, who had spent many months abroad on Cosworth business, lobbied that he should be paid more when obliged to live away from home. "I took the issue to Dick Scammell and we tackled Alf about it, who immediately said 'Yes, the time you spend away should be recompensed, including your travelling time.' He was only bringing a normal commercial reality to the company, but it was completely new to us. We'd never even asked Keith about this, because we knew he'd have said: 'Sorry, but that's part of your job, I'm not paying you to sit eating and drinking on an aeroplane. We only pay you when you get there.' Mike would have said the same."

John Dickens spent many hours with Alf in the Cosworth boardroom, mostly at meetings with Ford executives, and came to admire his negotiating skills. "He had a wonderful technique when the conversation got sticky, he'd just pull his cigarette packet off the table slowly, flick it open slowly, offer the cigarettes round then he'd take a while searching for his lighter. There'd be eight or ten of us sitting around this big boardroom table, with his office at the end. He'd disappear in there to find his lighter. By the time he'd got back, laboriously lit his cigarette and taken the first pull, everyone was agog to hear what he was about to say. He'd got the attention of the whole room."

Jack Field was also a fan. "Alf Vickers was a whizz kid, I thought he was wonderful, a hell of a bloke. He was a good accountant, and he understood engineering."

Bernard Ferguson had never known Cosworth in the pre-Alf days, but spent many hours in the company of those who had. His conclusion is blunt, yet is echoed by many: "Alf turned Cosworth from a hobby shop into a business."

No one ever truly understood why the chemistry between Keith and Alf had been so immediate and so strong. Perhaps it was his wartime involvement with Merlin production, an engine Keith revered. Perhaps DKD subconsciously regarded Alf as a father figure. Since losing his father at the age of 12, the closest thing Keith had had to that was his cousin Harry, and he'd seen very little of him since going to university. Alf offered an older, wiser head who could be trusted to be supportive but not obstructive. It is significant that, alone of all Keith's colleagues, Alf had the ability to persuade Keith to do things he *really* didn't want to do. Alf rarely exercised it, but when he did, as with the abandonment of the boat project, it worked. Even Mike didn't have that kind of clout.

Keith and Mike knew that Alf's departure signalled the end of an era. His replacement would not only be of a different generation, but would be running a company whose co-founder, chairman and chief designer would probably also retire within a few years. Before long, the newcomer would have more authority and freedom of action than Alf had ever had.

Yet Cosworth needed to change, and Alf himself acknowledged the fact, observing in 1985 that the firm had grown to a size where it would make an attractive subsidiary for a large conglomerate. He also commented that the Vickers Group might be a suitable home for it.

The man to whom he made these remarks was Richard Bulman, a Hawker Siddeley engineer whom he had known for many years. Alf had long believed that Richard was the right man to succeed him and had been promoting his candidature to the rest of the board. "I had seven years of interviews!" says Richard. Mike liked the fact that Richard had an aviation background, with experience at De Havilland, where he had cut his engineering teeth. Bob was also supportive, and everyone liked the fact that he had experience of engine manufacture.

Keith was ambivalent. There was none of the immediate rapport which he had struck up with Alf. But eventually Bob Graves brought the matter to a head: something had to be done and the time was right, because Richard was known to be unsure of his future at Hawker Siddeley, his own key director having recently died. DKD could find no good reason to object to the appointment, so the deal was done. Richard Bulman became managing director of Cosworth in December 1985, bringing with him his machine shop manager, Dave Gulliford – "... a very capable guy," in John Dickens' words.

Not long after Richard's appointment, Keith bumped into Jane Rood in the car park and asked her what she thought of the new MD. "He's too posh for us, Keith," came the reply, a sentiment echoed by her husband, who thought he wasn't a 'Cosworth man.'

Bob understood these sentiments, but still believed the board had made the right choice. "Richard was a bit stuck up," he says, "but you couldn't argue with his ideas."

For his part, Richard was – and still is – rather bemused by this reaction, pointing out that his background, as regards his family's social standing, his education and his career, is not that dissimilar to Keith's. He is an able and practical engineer, not a grey banker in a suit. But his controlled, urbane manner and southern accent implied a world view far removed from Keith's – much further than it actually was. Perhaps the best way of summarising the difference is to bring it down to basics: while Keith loved his beer, Richard was happier with a glass of good red.

Even before Alf's retirement, Keith had the feeling that his company was slipping away from him. He had never enjoyed day-to-day management but he did like to feel in control of events. Yet following the massive expansion of the road car side of the business, he no longer felt he was. Discussing the cash-flow implications of production stoppages in a Mayfair boardroom was a million miles from the modest race-engineering company he and Mike had envisaged all those years ago – and not nearly as much fun.

The company's payroll had mushroomed. Back in 1983, when the company celebrated its 25th anniversary, he'd given Mike a clock inscribed: 'From the Idealist to the Realist. Together, at Cosworth, we beat the world.' Then he'd called in every member of staff to his office, one by one, to give each a memento, and had been struck by how big the firm had grown. "It took me all morning to see everybody!" he remarked to Stuart Turner. Yet at that point Cosworth only employed 275, of which 230 were at Northampton where the company had 54,000ft² of space over 4.25 acres. That employment total was not much different from the year before, yet by 1988, thanks largely to the road car business, it had leapt to 570.[2]

(Incidentally, it would peak some years later at well over 1000, counting all Cosworth premises including the foundries, the electronics division, Wellingborough, Torrance and a constantly evolving mix of around a dozen factories and buildings along St James Mill Road.)

Many of the new faces at Worcester and Wellingborough had attitudes which, of necessity, were very different from those of a race-engine designer at St James Mill Road, and some of them Keith found impossible to empathise with:

THEY ALL SPEAK IN A PARTICULAR WAY ... LIKE POLITICIANS. IT IS A CHARACTERISTIC OF ME, AND PROPER COSWORTH PEOPLE, THAT IF YOU ASK SOMETHING, THERE OUGHT TO BE A CERTAIN AMOUNT OF DELAY BEFORE ANYONE REPLIES. BUT AS FAR AS I CAN SEE, IN A LARGE COMPANY THE LAST THING YOU CAN AFFORD TO DO IS NOT TO START REPLYING IMMEDIATELY ... WHAT THOSE PEOPLE DO IS LEARN TO WAFFLE. IT IS ACTUALLY KNOWN IN THE DICTIONARY AS 'EQUIVOCATION' – THE USE OF MISLEADING WORDS TO CONCEAL THE TRUTH. I ACTUALLY FEEL MENTALLY ILL WHEN PEOPLE STATE SOMETHING WITH NO MEANING. IT COMPLETELY BUGGERS ME UP, I WORRY ABOUT IT. I DON'T THINK I SHOULD BE PAID TO SUFFER THE COMPANY OF PEOPLE WHO ARE WAFFLING.

With his loyal lieutenant retired, Keith's sense of isolation increased. He said as much to John Dickens on the phone one evening, commenting that it was "… very lonely at the top."

George Duckett noticed it too. The days were gone when everyone knew everyone and felt comfortable chatting to the boss, even if the boss still felt comfortable chatting to them. "In the Cosworth canteen," George recounts, "he would sit down with the lads for lunch and half of them would just get up and walk out because they didn't want to talk to him. I found that very sad. I could never understand their attitude because he was such a friendly person. We often sat together: he liked to be with the lads."

Things were not the same in the boardroom either, where Keith quickly came to rue the day he'd agreed to Richard's appointment, finding that he could no longer bank on his MD viewing things from the same perspective as himself.

"Keith's powers of analysis in almost any problem, providing he chose it, were remarkable – and not just in engineering," comments Richard. But he found Keith's management style rather laissez-faire, and believed the company was now too big to be run that way. His loyalty was to Cosworth first and Keith second, and if the two did not coincide, no amount of anger or oratory on Keith's part would deter Richard from calmly and firmly standing his ground.

"After Richard Bulman had been there a couple of weeks, Keith couldn't talk to him," remembers Mike.

"They had some enormous rows," adds John Dickens, "which were grossly embarrassing to those on the fringes of them, which I tended to be quite often."

It was a difficult mental adjustment for Keith, who for the first time in Cosworth's history was working with a man who was not only his intellectual equal but also in a position to make his ideas stick, whether or not DKD approved. For the greater good of the company, the two men had to find a way of functioning together, which they did, but it was never a happy relationship.

In general, though, the second half of the 1980s was not an unhappy time for Keith, and at St James Mill Road he was content to leave as much corporate planning as he could to others, and concentrate whenever possible on his first love, engineering design. Particularly, race engineering design, for the DFY's sole victory in 1983 had demonstrated that a new F1 engine was well overdue.

Creating it would be his next challenge.

Footnotes

1 The road-going Sierra Cosworth had 204bhp in standard form, but many were chipped and modified.

2 1982 figure from John Bolster in *Autosport*, 2 September 1982. 1983 and 1988 figures from pp214 and 227 respectively, *The Power to Win*, John Blunsden (Motor Racing Publications Ltd,1983).

Chapter 17

"We have to start again"

Keith's long-standing belief that turbocharging was against the spirit of the F1 regulations was the principal reason Cosworth did not test run its first turbocharged F1 engine until 1984, a full seven years after Renault had demonstrated the idea's potential on the track.

However, there was another, deeply personal reason for Cosworth sticking with the DFV, despite it becoming progressively less competitive. Walter Hayes, whose reading of Keith's psyche was better than most, explained it like this:

"I concluded that Keith genuinely thought that he had produced one masterpiece, and he was reluctant to drag himself up to go and do it all again. Keith had already created the one perfect thing in his lifetime and although it was still a great engine, it had been hit hard by regulations, and by the activities of other people. I honestly believe he was resentful that, although he had probably designed the finest engine in the world, he was going to have to try again." (*Cosworth*, p197.)

Keith's policy to counteract the turbos was to do everything he could in engineering terms to maintain the DFV's competitiveness, while consistently lobbying and hoping for a change in the rules. Eventually, he believed, the power race the turbos had unleashed would lead to their being banned on safety grounds.

His prediction was right, but his timescale was not – the changes happened too slowly to help the DFV. By 1984, only a year after the DFV series' final GP victory, safety concerns had already prompted FISA to limit power by banning in-race refuelling and limiting tank capacity to 220 litres. But there were no further engine changes for 1985, and although in 1986 tanks were downsized again to 195 litres, normally-aspirated engines were actually prohibited.

This move was not popular with the smaller teams, so for 1987 the atmos were back, with a 3.5-litre limit to make them more competitive, helped by a 4 bar boost pressure limitation for the turbos. Next year, boost and tank size were cut again, to 2.5 bar and 150 litres respectively. Not until the 1989 season did the turbos disappear completely: now engines had to be normally-aspirated, of a 3.5-litre maximum and have between 8- and 12-cylinders; all fuel consumption limits were removed.

Had this programme of rule changes been fixed in 1983, Cosworth probably wouldn't have bothered developing a turbo engine, and instead concentrated on developing an all-new 3.5-litre atmo unit. But in reality the rules evolved year by year: in 1983 there was no sign of the turbos disappearing, and Cosworth was faced with the choice of engineering an engine for an ever-evolving specification or witnessing the rapid demise of its name in GP racing. Reluctantly, Keith chose the former.

The pressures on him to do so were considerable, and not only from his colleagues at Cosworth. Walter Hayes at Ford also wanted to move on. So did Ken Tyrrell, who, of all the team proprietors, was closest to Keith, having been with the DFV right the way through its career, buying the very first customer engine and notching up the engine's swansong victory in Detroit in September 1983.

Immediately after that race the two of them tackled Keith about the problem, but he was not persuaded until Walter subsequently asked DKD to dinner at his home and applied a little psychology. At his wife's suggestion, they gave him the food he liked best – traditional British cooking like Lancashire Hot Pot – and steered clear of wine, making sure there was good beer on tap instead. It worked: by the end of the evening Keith had come round to the idea of a new Cosworth F1 engine.

Walter had already done his homework and had secured Ford's financial backing for a turbocharged F1 powerplant. Cosworth wasn't the only possible source though, and Keith reckoned Erich Zakowski's Zakspeed concern would actually get the job, as the decision was down to fellow-German Mike Kranefuss, now working in Detroit. But Kranefuss knew Cosworth of old, having been involved with the GA, and opted for the Northampton firm.

Quite separately, but almost contemporaneously, serious matters were afoot in America. Earlier that year Keith had written his 'vested interests' letter, turning down Roger Penske's request for a special Indycar engine, but Roger had refused to take no for an answer. Unbeknown to Keith, he approached Mario Illien and asked if he and Paul Morgan would like to set up their own company to develop a new Indycar engine with Chevrolet money.

It was a tempting offer, but one which put Mario in a very awkward position. "My good relationship with Keith made it extremely difficult for me when I decided to leave. He was upset, and I almost couldn't do it. I suffered a lot, disappointing Keith. I had many sleepless nights. I felt disloyal, not so much to Cosworth but to him personally. He was upset for a long time. We didn't talk for quite a while."

Mario left Cosworth for two reasons. "One was that Keith was hanging on to the normally-aspirated engine, despite the world moving on. He offered me work on the turbo F1 project, but I felt that the chances of the engine being successful, arriving so late on the scene, were small. The other reason was that the company had been sold – Keith was becoming less and less involved – and I wasn't sure what my future there would be."

Keith was also sorry to lose Paul Morgan, and the creation of Ilmor was a serious blow for Cosworth, particularly as its first product, the Ilmor-Chevrolet 265A, would go head-to-head with one of Cosworth's best income streams, the DFX. The very construction of the Ilmor name – a contraction of the founders' surnames, as with Cosworth – is a nod to Mike and Keith. But many at St James Mill Road felt the parallels went much further – too far in fact – maintaining that the Ilmor product bore an unhealthy resemblance to the DFX.

TALKING AT INDIANAPOLIS; WALKING AT TORRANCE

The Ilmor-Chevrolet 265A was first shown in public at the 1986 Performance Racing Industry show at Indianapolis, where it appeared on the Chevrolet stand.

Cosworth also had a stand, featuring what company insiders irreverently called the 'Mexican version' of the DFX, a polished show engine. Keith was due to attend the show, not least because he wanted a good look at the DFX's new rival, and planned to arrive on the second day.

"All through the first day," recalls Ian Bisco, "this guy kept coming up and standing over the DFX, spouting all his performance theories and becoming a real pain. He kept asking for Keith. He was there again the next day when Keith finally arrived." The visitor promptly buttonholed Keith. Ian's colleague, Ken Jacobs, remembers what happened next.

"He went on about how he'd worked at a prominent Indy engine builder for years, and had developed a rotary-valve engine: he said he could take it to Keith and start it on his desk." Keith listened to the visitor for a few minutes, then replied that he'd looked into rotary valves before and concluded that they weren't appropriate for a performance engine because they didn't permit enough airflow. But the visitor was having none of it.

"Suddenly, Duckworth interrupted the guy, in a loud commanding voice, and said 'You know, we are both assholes, but the difference is that I am on the outside looking in and you are on the inside looking out.' With that, the dumbfounded guy quietly turned and slowly, sheepishly walked away in disbelief.

"Years later I saw the same gentleman at another trade show. He started to go on about how he worked for a prominent engine builder. I said, 'I remember you, you were at the PRI show when Duckworth was there!' He quickly concluded his visit to our booth and went on his way."

In due course Keith got a good look at the Ilmor engine and, when quizzed about it back on the Cosworth stand, responded that he thought it was a "... neat little package."

DKD made a number of visits to Indy, but only one to Cos Inc in California, and that entirely by chance. It happened around 1985, and Ian Bisco remembers it well.

"We were at Early Avenue and I was running our mobile engine dyno that we had built to run the BDPs we sold for midget racing. The dyno was mounted on a frame with three wheels, so we could push it outside to run it in the driveway – it ran to 9000rpm and 300hp, quite noisy! One day I was standing over the controls running at max speed when out of the corner of my eye I saw this guy walking up the road past our driveway, carrying a small travel bag, briefly hesitating to watch what was going on before disappearing towards the front of the facility.

"I thought, shoot, that looked like Keith! So I shut down the engine and wandered up front to the office. Sure enough it was; he had come by to say hi and see what we were at. He stayed about half an hour, then we called him a cab for the airport.

"A couple of days later I learned why he was in the vicinity. Garrett turbo was only a quarter-mile away; we were often in touch. Apparently, Keith had flown over to discuss turbo issues with the GB and, when the meeting concluded, had asked 'I don't suppose you guys can tell me where the Cosworth facility is?' They offered to drive him over but Keith opted to walk, and so turned up completely unannounced."

All designers draw on their previous experience when creating something new, but Mario is adamant that the Ilmor-Chevrolet 265A engine is not a mere DFX copy. "I know we have been accused of taking their stuff but that wasn't the case. I was convinced that I could design a better engine than the DFX, smaller and more compact – I was full of confidence at that young age!"

Mario and Paul left in October 1983, just one month after the DFY's Detroit victory, and in November set up their company in Brixworth, a few miles from Northampton. Two years then passed before the Ilmor-Chevrolet 265A made its track debut, but by 1987 it was winning races, and the writing was on the wall for the DFX.

With Cosworth heavily committed to developing a new F1 engine, the company was in no position to respond to Ilmor's challenge. Malcolm Tyrrell tuned into Keith's concern.

"I think he believed Cosworth didn't have the resources to engage in a performance race with Ilmor, so instead he tackled the problem from another direction. During late 1984, we tested a sonic orifice device, similar to that which was successfully employed in F3. This would have limited the useful rev range and hence limited power output. As there had been some serious crashes and fatalities at the Speedway ... USAC expressed interest in the principle, but despite serious lobbying, we never did succeed in getting the orifice adopted. As Roger Penske had a significant influence with USAC, and he was using the Ilmor engine, I believe the tide was running against us."

Northampton eventually responded in 1989 with the introduction of the DFS, a short-stroke (hence the 'S') update of the DFX. The DFS took advantage of improvements built into the normally-aspirated 3.5-litre DFR, which is discussed later in this chapter. It only won one race, in the hands of Bobby Rahal at Meadowlands in 1989, but continued to be used by a number of teams until it was replaced by the all-new XB in 1992.

With Mario gone, it fell to Geoff Goddard to handle the F1 turbo project. He felt honoured, for of all Keith's admirers at St James Mill Road, none held him in greater esteem than Geoff. Late in 1983, Keith and Geoff got together to decide how best to hit FISA's moving regulatory target, aiming to have a new engine ready for the 1985 season.

Initially it seemed that FISA would choose fuel limitation as the way to restrict power, and that as a result most teams would have some 650bhp at their disposal. BMW had already demonstrated that such an output could be reliably produced with a four-cylinder engine, which had the benefit of lightness and simplicity, and of course Cosworth had a well proven four available in the BD. Moreover, Brian Hart had proved that it could be successfully turbocharged, with his 1981 415T engine for Toleman.

Cosworth's new F1 contender was not a 415T derivative, it was a purely Northampton design. Called the BB, it was an alloy-block BD, ECU-controlled and running at up to five bar boost, courtesy of both a turbocharger and a supercharger, the latter driven from the crankshaft via a continuously variable transmission (CVT) from Ford. The theory was that the combination of the two would not only aid efficiency, but also reduce lag.

The idea of using a CVT soon had to be abandoned, because of problems at Ford's supplier, Van Doorne, but in the event that didn't matter, because a more fundamental problem arose: the engine kept breaking its crankshaft at 11,000 rpm and three bar boost. Channel Four, which had arranged with Ford to follow development of its new F1 venture on its *Equinox* series, found itself filming broken engines in the test cells, with engineers and technicians inspecting the debris to find the cause.[1] The commentary blamed block distortion, but the problem was later traced to the crankshaft bending at the rear.

By this point the 1984 season was well under way, and it was becoming clear that the BB would have to develop closer to 700bhp than 650 to be competitive – a tall order for an engine that was proving fragile. Moreover, there remained the possibility that if combining supercharger and turbocharger proved effective, it would be almost immediately banned.

DKD decided to cut his losses. There is a crucial moment in the film where Keith is walking around the Silverstone pits during the 1984 GP and says to Kranefuss: "We have to start again." Maybe this was staged for the camera, maybe it really was the first Kranefuss knew of DKD's decision and the cameraman just got lucky . Either way, the BB was abandoned and Keith started looking at another idea he'd had: a flat-six.

The attraction of a flat-six was that it offered maximum room between the banks for a turbo and ancillaries. This was important because he was planning an even more ambitious forced-induction arrangement than on the BB, one which would expose the foolishness of the present rules once and for all. For nearly a decade he had watched his company be disadvantaged by rivals crawling one by one through what he regarded as a loophole. Now he wanted to drive a coach and horses through it.

Unlike the BB, the flat-six would have no supercharger, just a turbo. But the turbo would be enormous and its output would be linked to the crankshaft by a compounding arrangement. The design of the latter was never revealed, but its effect would be to power the back wheels from two sources: reciprocating engine and turbine.

Geoff Goddard explains the principles. "The engine would be turbocharged at very high boost, say 10:1: so high that, in practice, all the compression of the mixture would be done before it entered the cylinder. A small amount of expansion work would arise out of the ignition, but much of the mixture would be unburned, so [primarily] the cylinder is acting as a pump to put mixture into the exhaust. There the mixture feeds into a huge multi-stage axial turbo (hence the wide angle, to get the plenums far enough apart), where temperatures are high enough to ignite it without any external assistance. With a turbo compound like that, we could arrive at the circuit with double the power of the rest of the field!"

Keith checked with FISA in Paris and was told everything was legal, at least with the rules as they currently stood. But the inference was that, if the engine really was that powerful, it would probably be banned as soon as it won a race.

Ford, knowing that such an outcome would probably be accompanied by shouts of "Cheat!" from the other teams, thought that would be bad publicity. Keith thought that completely dominating your rivals at the first attempt was the best possible publicity! However, Ford was funding the project, so DKD was obliged to forget compounding and adopt a more conventional approach.

With no monster turbo to accommodate, the best compromise was a 120° V6, – wide enough to keep the centre of gravity low, but narrow enough for each bank to have its own turbo mounted outboard, where it could be easily cooled. As a nod to the GA, Cosworth called it the GB, and its development was approved by Ford in September 1984. In a break with GP tradition, the engine carried Ford's logo, not Cosworth's, and in fact was known outside Northampton as the TEC (Turbocharged Engine, Cosworth). The aim was to have it ready for the 1986 season, by which point atmos would be banned. The GB would be the only Cosworth product on the grid.

The engine that was finally fired up in the test beds in August 1985 was a remarkably neat, compact design which generated 750bhp on pump fuel. Its development was a major commitment for Cosworth and stretched the company's facilities to the limit, employing up to 100 people at its peak.

One of them was Steve Miller, who joined after spending 12 years with turbocharger manufacturer Holset. His name had been mentioned by Brian Hart: shortly afterwards he had an interview with Keith and Martin Walters, and that evening he was offered a job masterminding the turbo installation on the GB. (Steve stayed with Cosworth for 13 years, and is currently managing director of Ilmor.)

"I'd never met him before the interview, but characteristically, Keith made his mind up fairly quickly – he didn't about engineering, but he did about people – and I decided to move.

"When I got there in 1985 there was a missing generation. Some of the older employees were still there, and there were young people they'd just hired, but there wasn't a great body of experienced people in their early 30s to mid-40s. In the early 1980s I'm not sure there was the throughput of interest on the engineering jobs. There was quite a lot of arrogance and total belief in what the company was capable of, so the turbo engine was a bit of a rude awakening."

There were no signs of that rude awakening in the test cells – the problems only began once the engine was in the car. As with the DFV, Ford chose the team to receive the engine for the first year, opting for Beatrice, a team named after its principal sponsor. Beatrice was not Mike Kranefuss' choice, but it was commericially neat for Ford because the company controlled rental company Avis, a major customer for Ford cars. Carl Haas owned the team, Lola built the chassis and the drivers were Alan Jones and Patrick Tambay.

Even before the GB made its first run in the car, personnel changes at Beatrice resulted in the sponsorship drying up. Preparation and morale suffered, as did relations between Ford and the team, reaching a low point in Portugal when Mike Kranefuss discovered that the team had been holding clandestine talks about selling up to Bernie Ecclestone.

DKD was frustrated, but could not be too critical, because the engine wasn't up to scratch either. Cosworth had been away from the podium for several seasons and had lost touch with developments at the top teams, all of which were now using special fuels and enjoying far more power than the GB was producing.

Geoff Goddard recalls "Keith was told by the FIA that they were going to rule out the rocket fuels that had won the championship for BMW, and we must start with pump fuel and the lower compression ratio and power that dictated. Hence at our first GP with the GB we turned up with probably the lowest power on the grid and spent the weekend sniffing the exhaust fumes in the pit lane."

When the GB debuted at the 1986 San Marino GP at Imola in April, Jones qualified a lowly 21st on the grid, way off the pace and slower than his team-mate in a stopgap Hart-engined car. In the race, he climbed to ninth before succumbing to a broken gear linkage and a split radiator. The contrast with the DFV's debut at Zandvoort could not have been more marked. Kranefuss was mightily unimpressed. Keith, who attended the race with Martin Walters, was variously angry, disappointed and embarrassed.

Keith and Martin had arranged to get a lift back to the UK in the Ford jet, and after the race they were running for the connecting helicopter when Keith felt breathless and unwell. Things improved once he settled in the aircraft, but he resolved to get a check-up as soon as he got home.

The day had one more surprise in store, as Steve Miller relates. He was not in the jet, but then he didn't need to be, because the story rapidly passed into Cosworth lore ...

"The jet landed at Stansted and Keith arranged for Cosworth's pilot, Graham, to pick them up there. But Graham had not fuelled the helicopter properly – I'm not sure he was altogether that well organised! – so they came up to the back of the Cosworth site and just managed to slide across the river and over the electricity cables before the thing ran out completely and stopped. He managed to put it down just in time.

"By now Martin Walters was not very happy, but Keith, in his usual way, said 'No problem.' He managed to find an empty five gallon oil drum, nipped up to Westaways, the garage at the end of the road, filled it up with diesel – the helicopter would run okay on diesel for a short while – and there he was, with a five gallon drum and a funnel at 11 o'clock in the evening. One minute they are luxuriating in a Lear jet, the next he is up to the garage. That was one of the beauties of Cosworth, the top man was identifiably an equal at the tea station."

When Keith went for his check-up following the discomfort he'd felt at Imola, it was very bad news. The health issues which had been a concern ever since his heart attack in 1973 had resurfaced with a vengeance, and major heart surgery was now on the agenda, surgery which at one stage had him fighting for his life. From this point on Keith consistently had one eye on retirement, and gave a great deal of thought as to how best to prepare the firm for his departure.

Back at St James Mill road, the priority was to extract more power from the GB and a vigorous development programme was started immediately after the engine's Imola debut. By the end of the 1986 season the engine was in Honda territory, developing 1000bhp in qualifying set-up, thanks to special fuels, different cylinder heads, higher compression (up from 6.5:1 to 8:1 by the end of the season) and a higher rev limit (up from 10,500 to 12,000). Moreover, the extra 250bhp was not achieved at the expense of reliability: mileages of 600 between rebuilds were being achieved and Geoff reckons no engine ever dropped a valve – even when a driver missed a gear – a tribute to the soundness of the basic design.

There was no way the GB was likely to win in a Beatrice car, so in reality Ford's only options for 1987 were to switch teams or pull out altogether. However, Haas had a three year deal, so the latter course would have left him free to sell the team to Bernie, and with it the right to use the GB. Kranefuss wanted to avoid this, so he settled with Haas and nailed Ford's colours to Benneton and its new B187.

The GB was now part of a viable package, and by mid-1987 drivers Thierry Boutsen and Teo Fabi were capable of qualifying not far behind the Williams Hondas and were regularly in the points. There was every reason to believe that 1988 could bring victories.

Those victories never came, not because of any weakness in the engine's design, but because FISA moved the goalposts again. For 1988, FISA was considering reducing turbo engine size to 1-litre, but at a meeting in Paris Keith explained in graphic terms why that would not get to the root of the problem. It was public relations considerations, not technical ones, which had prevented him producing the GB in compounded form and merely reducing capacity to 1-litre would not prevent someone else from trying something similar. To illustrate his point, he put forward a *reductio ad absurdum*, where a combination of BB and GB induction arrangements would be mated to an engine which is simple in the extreme. The gist of it was this:

"You may think 1-litre would knock the power down, but you may be interested in my own proposal for a 1-litre blown engine: a simple twin-cylinder two-stroke. Within the regulations you can have supercharging and turbocharging, and this would have both.

Oh, and I forgot to mention that the turbocharger will be made by Pratt & Whitney, and the engine will probably run a bit rich, so there will be plenty of unburned fuel coming out of the exhaust, which will be feeding into the Pratt & Whitney turbocharger. To save boring you with any more detail, how much power would be required? We can start off at 2000bhp but if you want to move up from that, it is quite okay."

Finally, after a decade, Keith's ideas had gained traction at FISA. The decision was made that, for 1988, boost would be limited to 2.5 bar, and, the following year, turbos would be banned altogether.

Ironically, these changes spelled the end of the GB's career. Ford was reluctant to spend money on an engine with only one season ahead of it, and Keith wasn't keen anyway, because the power lost by lowering the boost could only be regained by raising the rev limit even higher, something the engine was not designed for. The decision was taken to run an atmospheric engine for 1988 in readiness for the all-atmo era starting in 1989.

The end of the GB was a blow to everyone at Northampton, where there was great pride at having caught up with Honda in just two years, despite having a far smaller budget and far fewer engineers.

Richard Bulman took a positive view of the GB. It had not been burdensome financially because Ford had paid for it all, and, in F1 terms, it had brought Cosworth in from the cold – the company had learned a huge amount. Richard consistently supported the racing side of the firm, even though it now generated only a minority of Cosworth's turnover. Motorsport had created the company's cutting-edge reputation, and in his view continued involvement was the best way of protecting it.

The GB was primarily Geoff Goddard's design, though in his own words "... you can never negate Keith's input, he is always in the background."[2] In truth, he no longer wanted to play a foreground role in the design office. Ever since his heart attack in 1973, he had been increasingly inclined to work from home; now, with retirement in the back of his mind, he was seen less and less at Northampton – and sometimes when he did arrive, it was at a time when his employees were least happy to see him.

"Keith's working day tended to consist of him working at home until around three o'clock in the afternoon, when he would drive to Cosworth," says Malcolm Tyrrell. "Typically, when you had planned some social event that evening, Gloria's voice would come over the PA, asking you to ring Keith's extension. You then knew that you were in for a very late night. We used to try to feign deafness on a Friday afternoon, but Gloria's increasing frustration as we failed to respond to her calls led to an even more demanding 'If anyone knows the whereabouts of A N Other, will they *please* get him to ring extension 201!'

"Then the outside world didn't exist any more. Five o'clock would come and go, six o'clock, seven, eight – and at the end you'd be frightened to say anything in case it opened up another three hours of engineering debate and discussion!"

There was certainly plenty to discuss, for in addition to the F1 programme and the need to counter the Ilmor threat in the US, news came through in 1986 that Renault had solved its valve spring problems by developing pneumatic valve return. "Keith was absolutely floored at the simplicity of the concept," recalls Malcolm, and asked Geoff why couldn't they have invented it. All those thousands of hours spent testing, developing and replacing valve springs!

Geoff's reply was that the idea had been invented long before,[3] Renault's achievement had been to make it work in practice. "The problem is finding a seal that will survive,

Continued on p249

Regarded by many as the ultimate sporting Cossie, the 1987 Sierra Cosworth RS500 was fettled at Aston Martin Tickford, and available in right-hand drive only. It used the YBD engine: exactly 500 were built.
(Courtesy Ford Motor Co)

The YB series engine became Cosworth's most famous roadgoing powerplant.
(Courtesy Ford Motor Co)

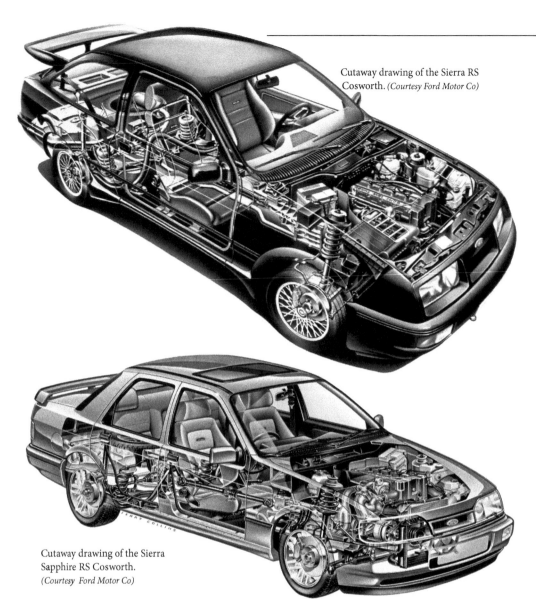

Cutaway drawing of the Sierra RS Cosworth. *(Courtesy Ford Motor Co)*

Cutaway drawing of the Sierra Sapphire RS Cosworth. *(Courtesy Ford Motor Co)*

A night out in the late 1990s for Keith and Gill in their personal Sierra Cosworth, one of the first built. They later replaced it with a Sapphire similar to the one on the opposite page.

In Cosworth form the Sapphire was a real Q-car: only bonnet louvres and a small spoiler gave a clue to its abilities. *(Courtesy Ford Motor Co)*

The Astra GTE, with its Red Top engine featuring Cosworth KBA heads, was the hottest hot hatch around in the late 1980s. *(Courtesy GM)*

The top Sierra before the arrival of the Cosworth was the XR4x4, which used a 4WD transmission mated to the 2.9-litre Köln V6. When Cosworth was later commissioned to develop a 24-valve head for Scorpio, which used the same engine, no one was better placed than Roger Duckworth to create a one-off rally special, a 24V XR4x4. The car was featured on p52 of the November 1994 edition of *Rally Sport* magazine, and its combination of 300bhp and a 66/34 rear/front bias provided Roger with a lot of fun, and some modest successes, in the Mintex National Rally Championship. *(Courtesy Writtle Photographic)*

First Principles

Mike Kranefuss, looking more genial than he felt at the 1986 San Marino GP. *(Courtesy Ford Motor Co)*

Members of the Beatrice team at Ford's Boreham premises in 1986, with Walter Hayes centre left and DKD to his right. *(Courtesy Ford Motor Co)*

Alan Jones debuts the GB in the Beatrice at the 1986 San Marino GP. Its GB engine (below left) eventually brought Cosworth back into F1's front rank, but arrived too late to show its full potential. *(Courtesy Ford Motor Co)*

The BDP's credibility was greatly helped by the success of one of its earliest proponents, Larry Howard Racing. This shot shows an early example of one of the team's BDP-engined Midgets at Ascot Park, with the engine still on downdraught injectors (hence no visible air-cleaners) and its cover still in primer. At the left rear is Ron Weeks, who assembled the car. *(Courtesy Ian Bisco/Cos Inc)*

The Pocono 500 in 1988: a DFS with electronic fuel injection. Pictured are (l-r) Gilbert Lage (ex Renault F1 mechanic), driver and team owner Dick Simon, Ian Bisco, Arie Luyendyk, Malcolm Tyrrell, and (working on car) Andreas Leberle. Note the location of the CART pop-off valve (Gilbert has his hand on it) positioned in a low-pressure area of the plenum to maximize boost. *(Courtesy Racemaker Archive)*

A lighthearted moment in the Cosworth test shop with the DFS and Kraco team members. Pictured are (l-r) Malcolm Tyrrell, driver Bobby Rahal, Cosworth's Steve Miller, team owner Maurice Kraines and team manager Barry Green.
(Courtesy Malcolm Tyrrell/Cos Inc)

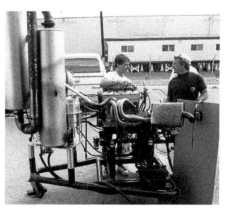

The mobile dyno used to test BDP Midget engines outdoors at Cos Inc. Sleepy Tripp, a very successful racer of these cars, is in the blue shirt.
(Courtesy Ian Bisco / Cos Inc)

1987 Benetton B187, with
the GB: Thierry Boutsen in
the Brazilian GP, in which he
finished fifth.
(Courtesy Ford Motor Co)

By 1990 the DFR was a customer engine. This is the Arrows pit at the Hungarian GP.
(Courtesy Ford Motor Co)

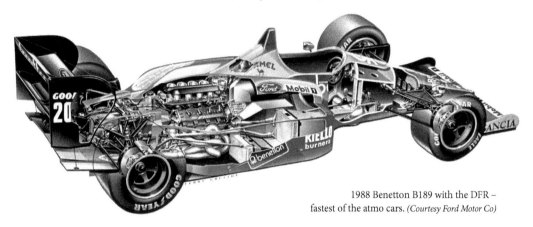

1988 Benetton B189 with the DFR –
fastest of the atmo cars. *(Courtesy Ford Motor Co)*

1988 Benetton B189 with the HB:
Alessandro Nannini at the engine's debut
race, the French GP. *(Courtesy Ford Motor Co)*

(Top) DKD visits the Ford dyno facility at Boreham in 1986 to see an RS200 engine on test. Graham Dale-Jones is on his left, Peter Ashcroft of Ford Competitions on his right. On the far right of the photo is Dick Scammell. *(Courtesy Ford Motor Co)*

(Above) Mark Lovell / Roger Freeman taking their RS200 to second place in the 1986 Scottish Rally. *(Courtesy Ford Motor Co)*

Costin House, as was – the Mahle headquarters in St James Mill Road in 2012. *(Courtesy Norman Burr)* they run at 15-20 bar compression pressure, that gives you a very high temperature, you've also got friction heating from the sleeve, so the seals run at about 470°C. You find yourself exploring PTFE loaded with carbon for the seal."

Renault had been obliged to innovate because the design of its cylinder head rendered it particularly prone to valve spring problems. Cosworth had no immediate need of the technology, but nevertheless Keith promptly started development of the company's own pneumatic valve gear. He knew it was the future, not least because it allowed camshaft designers more freedom. But in Malcolm's words, "... there were lots of pitfalls on the way – the surface finish of the cylinders, roundness, seals for the air, heat treatments – we had an army of engineers pushing that programme forward."

A particular challenge was the level of machining accuracy required. "Ben Rood made our air-valve-spring boring machine," says Geoff. "We put it in a sealed room, floated it on air so no vibration could come through the floor, the spindle was running on air bearings at 8500rpm, for rigidity the toolpost was a hundredweight of granite, with a diamond tool attached to it. We could then bore holes at four-tenths of a thou per rev, that got you to .0018microns of Ra[4] – a perfect mirror that doesn't split light as a machined surface. That's why you had to have Ben on board. We'd say 'We've got to make some of these things, how do we do it properly?' and Ben would go and invent a machine to do it."

Hart's problems were in large measure caused by the banning of Group B in 1986, which had caused Ford to can its purpose-built rally car, the RS200. The cancellation was a big financial blow for Brian Hart Ltd, because although production cars used a Ford-produced 250bhp BDT, the works rally cars were powered by a 540bhp Evolution version, dubbed BDT-E and designed and built by Hart. (Incidentally, thanks to the abandonment of the BB programme, this engine remains the ultimate development of the BD concept: it eventually produced over 600bhp when developed for rallycross.)

In November 1986, with Cosworth stretched to the limit, Keith suggested to Brian Hart that Cosworth take a controlling interest in his company, and in February 1987 the deal was done, cementing a relationship that went right back to the days when Brian was a Cosworth employee. Cosworth would gain much-needed design capacity, Hart would gain much-needed income.

Ford was also more directly involved in the merger. Cosworth was just starting work for Ford on what would become the FBA, a 24-valve conversion for the Ford Köln V6 that would eventually find its way into the top of the range Scorpio, but simultaneously and quite independently Hart was working on a similar conversion of his own. Brian's engine was aimed at a different market – racers and drivers wanting an aftermarket tuning package – but nevertheless there was an embarrassing degree of overlap. Ford, conscious of the bad publicity that could have resulted from two valued associates being at odds with one another, was more than happy with the marriage.

With retirement on the horizon, Keith needed to strengthen the board, so he proposed Dick Scammell for a directorship, and he joined the board in October 1986. Mike Costin insisted to Richard Bulman that Mike Hall should be similarly promoted, thus maintaining the race/road balance at the top of the company and giving the latter's contribution the recognition which in Costin's view was long overdue.

Another significant corporate change was the setting-up in 1987 of Cosworth's own electronics division. Various bought-in systems had been tried up to that point, the current favourite being from Piero Campi at EFI Technology, but Ford was very keen for Cosworth to switch to its EEC IV engine management package, a change that involved a lot of work, as the EEC IV was never intended for racing. The new department was staffed by a combination of Ford and Cosworth engineers under the direction of Dick Scammell, and was to grow steadily as electronics played an ever larger part in race-engine design.

Kees Mense worked in the test cells during the GB's development, and later ran the electronics department (1994-99). "I remember running the GB in Test Cell 3, we'd cut the top of the plenums off, so that we could see if the injectors worked. Dick Scammell was holding some boards over the top of the plenums as a choke and we started the engine; unfortunately the fuel had sprayed back on to the boards that Dick was holding and they caught fire, so Dick had to throw them on the floor.

"While the engine testers were running around extinguishing the engine and Dick's boards, Keith was leaning against the back wall of the test cell, calmly debating what the problem could be. A quick discussion with Piero Campi ensured that we got one of his systems, so that we could begin developing the package, but we ran the Ford system in the car."

The reintroduction of atmos for the 1987 season, a move only announced in October 1986, created a sudden demand for an off-the-shelf engine of the new, larger 3.5-litre capacity. Since Cosworth had already produced 90mm-bore engines in 3.0- (DFVss, DFY), 3.3- (small DFL) and 3.9-litre (large DFL) sizes, the logical starting point was to create a new variant around this bore size and mate it with DFX rods, plus a new crank to get the required 68.6mm stroke. The result was the DFZ, designed by Geoff Goddard and John Hancock and produced in record time, just six months from drawing board to car. That season it powered Tyrrell, AGS, March and Lola cars, atmo honours going to Jonathan Palmer and Tyrrell's DG016, who won the Jim Clark Trophy and the Colin Chapman Cup respectively.

A different version of the DFZ was produced at Hart, where the merger had brought an old name back into the Cosworth orbit: John Lievesley, who had worked with Keith back in Edmonton. John developed a Hart version of the DFZ, using different cams and heads from the Cosworth version and, John reckons, good for an extra 20bhp.

(As an aside, the DFV itself was far from finished. Excluding the DFX, there were some 500 DFVs and derivatives in the field and in 1985 FOCA and FISA agreed to create F3000, a new 'stepping-stone' formula for aspiring F1 drivers where the engines could be put to good use. F3000 replaced F2 and in the interests of safety and reliability limited revs to 9000, coincidentally the DFV's original limit back in 1967. A rash of new DFV variants followed, some from Cosworth, many from others, all trying to make the best of the powerplant within the F3000 regulations.)

The DFZ continued to power a number of F1 cars in 1988 but something better was needed for Benetton, who continued to be Ford's preferred team. A two-year programme was agreed for the move back to normally-aspirated engines, starting in 1988 with a thoroughly re-engineered DFV, dubbed DFR. From 1989 onwards, an all-new engine would be designed, the HB, with the DFR relegated to the role of customer unit and thus replacing the DFZ. As before, Geoff Goddard took the leading design role.

At this time Ford had connections with Yamaha, who had designed performance versions of several Ford road cars, and the Japanese company had designed a five-valve head to fit the DFV, its object being to produce a rival to Honda in Japanese F3000 racing. The jury was out as to whether the Yamaha head was really an improvement over the original, because at the relatively modest 9000rpm permitted for F3000, any gain was unlikely to be evident, nor was it, but great things were promised of the head and Ford persuaded Cosworth to adopt it for the DFR.

The engineers at Northampton had their doubts, and when the heads finally arrived from Japan months later than planned, they were proved right. Output was worse than the four-valve original and there were other problems too. In January 1988 Cosworth abandoned the five-valve head (though Yamaha persevered with it, unsuccessfully, in the Zakspeed team) and all hands were turned to producing what became the definitive DFR, with four-valve head. The new engine looked very like the traditional DFV, but in practice was thoroughly updated, with bigger inlet valves on increased valve centres and many other changes, some 80% of the drawings receiving alterations. Entering service with Benetton during the 1988 season, it was Geoff Goddard's take on the ultimate DFV and generated 600bhp at 10,800rpm – not enough to threaten the turbos, but easily enough to beat the rest of the atmo field.

So as the 1989 season approached, all was set fair for the new 3.5-litre HB and the Benetton B189 it was to power. For the first time in six years, Ford had a chance of getting back on the top step of the F1 podium.

The first decision to be made was the configuration. Benneton wanted a light, compact car, so the V12 was rejected despite being – theoretically – able to breathe better and rev higher. Competition V10 engines were a relatively unknown quantity at the time, so Cosworth fell back on the layout it knew best, the V8, but with a 75° vee angle to keep engine volume to a minimum. The downside of this was that, unlike the DFV, whose block was large enough to be stretched to nearly four litres, the narrower, lower HB had virtually no scope for growth.

Geoff Goddard and John Hancock handled the mechanical design, Martin Walters the electronics and Keith, as normal, was never far away. "Quite a number of the conceptual things were mine, and structurally the V8 HB is really the son of V6 GB turbo," (*Cosworth*, p253). Ford supplied the EEC-V engine management unit, a development of the EEC-IV used on the GB.

When the HB made its debut at the French GP at Paul Ricard in July 1989, few technical details were released because of the level of commercial secrecy by then surrounding F1, but the car was clearly on or near the pace. Alessandro Nannini ran second behind Alain Prost until he retired with a collapsed rear suspension, and a week later at Silverstone he took the HB to third place and its first podium. It was a graphic illustration of how much Cosworth had learned from the GB.

Thanks to a number of other points finishes, including an inherited win in Japan when Ayrton Senna was disqualified following his infamous collision with Alain Prost, Benneton finished the 1989 season fourth in the constructors table.

The HB was steadily developed over the next four seasons, during which it recorded many podiums, including five first places, and eventually acquired pneumatic valves, in 1993 HBE form. But Keith had little to do with this process, for in August 1988 he decided to retire and relinquished the chairmanship. In April 1989 he was presented with a cutaway model of his famous second-compound quill drive as a memento of his chairmanship.

The secrecy which surrounded any new F1 engine in the 1980s illustrates how the world had changed since Cosworth's early days. As Bernard Ferguson remarks, "An interesting thing about Keith and Mike, and why they were a bit alienated by racing in later years, was that they never actually minded people seeing what they were doing. They weren't very guarded on their technical secrets, they said 'Yes, they might see it and they might copy it, but if they don't understand it, it won't work.' But there are people smart enough to deduce how it works. And employees are a lot more mobile now, they take secrets with them."

Keith had a Duckworthism which explains his disinterest in excessive secrecy:

> *CERTAIN PEOPLE DIDN'T SEEM TO UNDERSTAND ANYTHING.*
> *IT WAS NO GOOD DOING ALL THE SUMS, AND THE DRAWINGS, IF*
> *THERE WAS NO UNDERSTANDING. THERE'S A LOT OF DIFFERENCE*
> *BETWEEN REGURGITATING KNOWLEDGE AND ACTUALLY BEING*
> *ABLE TO UNDERSTAND HOW THINGS WORK.*

Not only had the world moved on, but Keith had too, and on his own admission he was now past his best as a designer. Creative people – in any field – often do their finest work in that sweet spot in their lives where the arrogance of youth is balanced by the wisdom of experience. "We did it because we didn't know it was impossible," is a sentiment often voiced by high-achievers.

Keith had hit that sweet spot with the DFV. Now, although his foresight was as astute as ever and he was still peerless at conceptualising, he was uncomfortably aware that he had become slow and uncertain when it came to detailing. He knew too much, could foresee practically every problem – real or imagined – and would get bogged down trying to design them all out.

One of Keith's last acts as chairman was to agree to the creation of a Cosworth museum. John Given persuaded him. "Initially he wasn't at all interested, saying what he was wanted the future, not the past. But finally he begrudgingly did allow some money for the project, and Valerie [John's wife] was taken on as the archivist in 1989 and stayed for eight years. I was allocated some money to collect up engines that we no longer had – for example the SCA – most of which came from America. A lot of people helped."

Coincidentally, Walter Hayes retired around the same time as Keith, so Ford put on a magnificent party for the two at the Savoy in London, with Stuart Turner as speaker. "It was one of the thrills of my life to be paying tribute to both of them, I think I began by congratulating them both on winning their battle against anorexia!"

Mike Costin was the obvious candidate to become the new chairman. As co-founder of the firm, he had given half his name and over half his life to the venture. But no one ever accused Mike of being power-hungry, and he suggested to Bob Graves that he take the job instead. "It was tempting – what a thing for my CV! – but I thought it would be bullshit. I said to Mike, 'You started it, you end it!'"

Just one month into Mike's chairmanship, in September 1988, Jackie Stewart opened the new headquarters of Cosworth's road car division, built at Bob Graves' insistence to accommodate the company's huge growth in this sector. Appropriately enough, it was called Costin House.

An early casualty of Keith's retirement was Cosworth's ownership of Hart. Though the two companies had always co-operated closely, the takeover had proved a step too far for Brian – with Keith gone, the old empathy at St James Mill Road seemed to be missing and he felt his company's skills were being under-used. Within a few months he had agreed with Mike to buy back the shares and eventually he resumed full control.

Despite DKD's departure, the name Duckworth still appeared on the Cosworth payroll, because six months earlier Roger had joined the firm, working in the road car division under John Dickens and ultimately responsible to Mike. Fresh from Brunel University, Roger was just a regular graduate employee, and staff soon came to respect him in his own right, realising that he had no desire to be Keith Duckworth Jr, and was quite happy being himself. Steve Miller sums up the feeling among Roger's colleagues, saying "It's a credit to Keith that Roger never had that spectre of treading in his father's footsteps and failing as a result. He's an independent spirit, much to be admired."

Roger hadn't walked straight into the firm. "I'd spent a year working at Hewland before going to university, like an apprentice. Six months in the build shop, and the other six months making crown wheel and pinions in the machine shop with a Gleason cutting machine. Lapping and deburring, a nice hands-on practical job for a year and living independently with a room in a landlady's house. After a few months I realised that this wasn't the thinking part of engineering.

"Dad didn't force me to go to university, he didn't have a great opinion of academia, but he advised me to do it, saying that at some point I might have to prove myself to somebody and might need the letters after my name. He didn't expect me to come out with a first, and that was a very good attitude from my point of view, because I wasn't the hardest working chap you could imagine. Actually I got a Desmond: a 2:2. I did a thin sandwich course in mechanical engineering, and in my six month spells at Cosworth I did time in the inspection area, on road engines, race engines, dyno test etc.

"I never had to work with Dad, because after the Sierra project he wasn't much involved with the road-engine side."

In fact, at St James Mill Road no one would be working with Keith anymore. But as will become clear, Keith's contributions to British engineering, and British industry, were far from over.

Footnotes

1 The BB saga and the early development of its successor, the GB, can be seen at www.YouTube.com/watch?v=AoFyJw9Dkuo. There are two further programs at www.YouTube.com/watch?v=xbB1qwhKaaE and www.YouTube.com/watch?v=gqfVAGOaGEc. The latter two can be accessed either direct or via www.atomictoasters.com/2012/12/designing-the-1986-cosworth-f1-engine, which has further information.
2 P28, *Cosworth*, Ken Wells (William Kimberley Ltd, 1987).
3 A number of patents had already been filed on the subject of pneumatic valves, notably by Fred C Meyer of Wright Aeronautical Corporation in 1941 (US 2342003 A) and Jim Lyons in 1964 (US patent US 3120221 A). There were also some earlier British patents.
4 Ra is a measure of surface roughness used in machining.

Chapter 18

Flying from the heart

Keith's decision to retire in 1988 was a great relief to Gill. She had always known his health would need monitoring, but it was not easy to persuade him of the seriousness of the situation. He was a strong, active man with a great deal of drive and a lot of stamina, happy to keep going even when his body was actually crying 'enough.'

She did what she could. "He did credit me with helping his health, making him eat better and take exercise. But when I'd take his breakfast up to bed in the morning, the room would be full of smoke."

Gill was in no doubt about the origin of the problem – "When he designed the DFV it really was the ruination of him," – but 30 years of heavy smoking had certainly taken its toll. Colleagues described the atmosphere in his office as 'smog-laden,' and Gill reckons he lit-up between 20 and 30 times a day, though he did make sporadic attempts to stop and cut down, not least because he wanted to get fit enough to regain his pilot's licence. Steve Miller recalls him scoring himself by counting the stubs in the F3 rocker cover that served as a generous-sized desk ashtray.

In 1982 Keith travelled with Gill to London for an angiogram. "They put some dye into his arm and he had a major allergic reaction to it. But they concluded there and then that his arteries were 60 or 70 per cent bunged up and he needed a bypass."

Keith was reluctant. "I feel fine," he said. So nothing was done, even though without it, he knew there was zero chance of getting back in the Brantly's pilot seat.

Four years later, after feeling unwell at Imola, he went to a heart specialist in Northampton. "They put him on an exercise cardiograph," recalls Gill, "and left him there until he was exhausted, it was a wonder it didn't kill him. He was obviously peculiar in that ECGs showed no damage whatsoever, no one knew why. You would think the exercise cardiograph would have highlighted this, but the heart specialist said he just needed a bit of medication.

"Then four days later, on the Friday, he woke up in the night and said 'I think I'm having a heart attack, I don't feel very good.' He looked ashen. But we made a pot of tea and then he decided to get some more sleep." Gill had a desperately worrying night. She'd lost her father only a few weeks before.

"In the morning he rang the heart specialist who said he had to come into hospital. He spent the whole morning in the office trying to tidy up his very disarrayed affairs, then in we went. They transferred him from Northampton to Oxford on Saturday afternoon and on Sunday the specialist said 'You've got to have a heart bypass *now*, I don't know how you're standing up, there are no arteries there, I don't know how your heart is managing to function.' He was not allowed out of bed once we had arrived at Northampton. Yet he had no angina, no pain. That was the trouble, other people would have stopped.

"They operated at 8.30 on Sunday morning and we had a big panic, because at that time the normal technique was to take the body temperature down to operate, and Keith's wouldn't come back up. He came out of surgery at about one or two o'clock, but five hours later he was still not doing very well, despite foil blankets and the like.

"He eventually progressed and came home and he never had any further heart surgery. But he should have done, because I think they could have improved some of those arteries."

Keith never did regain his wings, but after the surgery he stopped smoking, immediately and permanently. For someone so addicted for so long, to stop overnight was a remarkable act of willpower.

Despite not being PIC (pilot in command) since 1973, Keith had never lost his love of the air. In May 1976 Cosworth had bought G-BDOY, the five-seat Hughes 500C, which was kept until 1987, when it was replaced by a Hughes 500D, G-ONTA, a five-blade design with a high T-tail. It had originally been destined for an African head of state, but the order was cancelled following political turmoil and the aircraft went to Northampton instead. Eventually, Cosworth replaced G-ONTA with a second 500D, painted orange and brown.

"Keith liked the Hughes because they are fast and sporty; they're a Ferrari," says Gill. "They're noisy – I could hear that high buzz from three or four miles away when they were coming home – and not that comfortable. If you had five people on board the fifth had to be small and sit between the pilot and the other dual control front seat. But they're wonderful sports machines to fly.

"My most memorable flight in the later one was into a very murky Brands Hatch GP. Everyone was late and slot times were being missed, and there were eight or more choppers circling in 'hold.' Then we had to dash in onto the correct marker and heli out for another journey! Just rows of helicopters, putting down, unloading and taking off again … It's a wonder I ever wanted to learn after that!"

The Hughes was Cosworth property, and although Keith continued flying with Graham for at least five years after the company was sold in 1980, Keith and Gill decided they needed their own machine, something with two seats that Gill could learn to fly and that they could share.

From the mid '70s Keith had been observing the design and production of the Robinson R22. A new concept in personal helicopters, it had taken Frank Robinson – based coincidentally in the same town as Cos Inc, Torrance in California – seven years to get it to certification. Keith liked what he saw, and, in October 1980, bought G-BJBS, one of the first six R22s to come into the UK, imported by a fledgling Sloane Helicopters, working out of a portable office at Cranfield.

It was some time though, before Keith would allow Gill to take the controls. The early R22s suffered blade delamination problems – a potentially catastrophic flaw – and Frank Robinson's first fix was, in Keith's view, "a negative improvement." It took the best part of two years and a total redesign of the blades before Keith thought they were okay.

Finally, on 24 May 1982, with Keith now happy with the aircraft's integrity, Gill sat in the left-hand seat of G-BJBS and less than two months later, on 19 July, she became a fully fledged pilot. "Keith was hugely supportive, especially in the early days when some cross-country flights seemed daunting. He never appeared envious that he was not allowed to fly, he just encouraged me."

By 1990 the R22 was running out of flying life and was traded in against a similar model, G-MDKD, which came with the bonus of an additional fuel tank and the Duckworths' choice of registration. In 1998 this too was replaced, the couple's third R22 being named G-FOLI, after their home. This one was powered by a Lycoming 360 and unlike the others was registered in Gill's name.

Gill still flies, and now, with over 30 years' experience to draw on, she is very much at ease in the air. "In fact, the instructor who I flew for my re-validation this year said how competently I flew! But I am hugely respectful of the privilege it is to fly a helicopter."

The Folly's hangar was built to accommodate three helicopters – "... my Robinson R22 at the far end, Cosworth's Hughes in the middle and his Brantly (actually that was Cosworth property as well) tucked up the other end. The Brantly came here from the Toy Shop when that was turned into factory space – it was sitting on the lawn when my parents had their golden wedding in 1984, because the hangar wasn't finished."

Stuart Turner tells an amusing story about helicopters and Keith. "I reported to the vice president of supply. Someone had convinced him that with all the company planes based at Stansted, a lot of time was being wasted going up and down to Ford HQ at Warley, so it was suggested that we buy a helicopter. 'Let's get one and demonstrate it' we said. So we acquired this helicopter and me and the vice president of supply decided to fly to Northampton to go and see Keith. We had our meeting, got back in the helicopter, gave the pilot the thumbs up – and it wouldn't start.

"Keith disappeared back into the factory for a moment and emerged with a screwdriver, ostensibly to investigate – though he was winding us up really. I can still see the grin on his face! But I said 'Forget this!' We went back on the train – and Ford never did buy a helicopter."

One way or another, helicopters provided Keith with many hours of pleasure in the years leading up to and following his retirement. But his contribution to British aviation would come not from rotorcraft but from microlights. And since by the time of his retirement he had already been flirting with them for the best part of a decade, we need to do some catching up …

Keith loved innovation, and the 1980s were a decade of unprecedented innovation in leisure aviation, thanks largely to the advent of the microlight. It was almost inevitable that he would be drawn to them.

The origins of this decade's turbulence can be traced back to the dawn of aviation. The very earliest heavier-than-air machines were unpowered gliders, simply because engines were so inefficient they could scarcely lift their own weight, let alone pilot and airframe. Once the Wright Brothers overcame that hurdle in 1903, aircraft improved exponentially, but the thrust was towards military and commercial use. Affordable, practical small aircraft were few and far between, and in the decades before and after WWII, the options for the common man who wanted to fly for fun on a small budget were to build your own or go gliding.

Homebuilt small aircraft – typically with wooden structures, fabric covering and modified VW Beetle air-cooled engines – became popular with enthusiasts in the

1950s and '60s, but these were only scratching the surface of the potential market – most would-be aviators had no interest in building, they just wanted to fly.

Meanwhile, gliders had become increasingly slick and sophisticated, with big wingspans and elegant low-drag lines. They were very rewarding in the air, but the downside was that they needed a winch, a tow, or a bungee to help them take off. As a result, gliding became a club activity, working from established sites.

The man who would change that, and change leisure aviation irrevocably in the process, was NASA engineer Francis Rogallo. He had been interested in flexible wings for many years, and in the early '60s proposed using one as a satellite-recovery vehicle. NASA rejected it in favour of parachutes, but exhibition water-skiers picked up the idea. Anxious for something new to excite the public, they strapped the delta-shaped wing of aluminium tube and fabric on their back to lift them off the water at speed.

As understanding of the devices' aerodynamics grew, the delta wing became a popular amusement for 'aviation hippies', launching themselves off the Californian sand dunes, and by the early 1970s it had morphed into the hang glider. It was a revolution: here was something you could strap to a car roof-rack, assemble on site, and fly. All you needed was a slope to run down, a suitable breeze and (in theory at least) the landowner's permission.

By comparison with a traditional glider, performance was poor, but their aluminium-alloy tube and Dacron technology improved by leaps and bounds, and by the late 1970s hang gliders were selling by the thousand worldwide. A small industry evolved, international competition blossomed.

Naturally, people living in flatland areas wanted to join in the fun, and the obvious solution was to create a powered hang glider by attaching a small two-stroke to the keel of the structure. It was soon discovered that there were both practical and aerodynamic difficulties associated with this, problems which have since been solved, but which at the time were serious enough to prompt French enthusiast Roland Magallon to develop an alternative: the trike.

This was a simple three-wheeled tubular structure supporting both pilot and powerplant, which hung from the pivot point of the hang glider, where the pilot's harness would normally attach. At a stroke, the powered hang glider's principal problem – instability due to the thrust line changing every time the pilot altered pitch – was removed. It was simple; it was brilliant. A new breed of aircraft had been born, the flexwing microlight, so-called because its wing was designed to flex in flight.

Meanwhile, in America and Australia, where light aviation had always been more accessible than in crowded Britain, designers were applying the hang glider's tube-and-Dacron technology to aircraft with traditional wings, tail and control surfaces, and traditional stick-and-rudder-pedal control, thus creating fixed-wing microlights.

Keith got his first ever sight of a microlight when a Cosworth employee brought a Weedhopper, an early American fixed-wing microlight, to the works. Weedhoppers fly quite well, albeit within a very modest performance envelope; derivatives are still in production in India,[1] but early examples were poorly constructed and featured an in-house designed single-cylinder two-stroke which was rightly lambasted as the very embodiment of crudity and unreliability. Oliver Achurch remembers Keith describing it as "... looking as though it was made of recycled pots and pans."

Nevertheless, the aircraft sowed a seed in Keith's mind, because at the time microlights needed no pilot licensing or airworthiness certification in the UK. He became convinced that tiny aircraft like this had a big future in bringing aviation to the common man, and began learning all he could about this embryonic industry.

Keith was by no means the only person at Cosworth to be excited by microlights. Dick Scammell bought a Goldwing – the highest-performing fixed-wing of its day – but it never flew because, whereas microlights using hang-glider technology were often supplied in simple kit form, the slippery Goldwing got its shape from glassfibre-covered foam: a job the buyer had to do himself. Dick never did complete this time-consuming process, and the unfinished project is still in a loft at the Folly.

The definition of a microlight varied from country to country (and still does), but typically is based on one or two seats, a maximum weight (initially 150kg empty in the UK), and either a maximum stall speed or a maximum wing loading (initially 10kg/ m^2): the aim being to restrict the aircraft's kinetic energy to a level where it is unlikely to damage anything on the ground, and therefore does not need full airworthiness regulation. The definition says nothing about what sort of wing it should have, what materials should be used, or how it should fly – designers had a completely free hand.

Thus, to be around very light aviation in the early 1980s was as close as the late 20th century man could ever come to the atmosphere of the Edwardian motor industry. New manufacturers were appearing by the month, their enthusiasm matched in many cases only by their lack of business acumen and, in a few sad cases, engineering ability. The buzz was palpable and the pace of development astonishing: everywhere new ideas were appearing and old ideas were being re-examined. There were new engines, new materials, new configurations; even new control systems.

It was one of these new control systems that next drew Keith's eye. Neither flexwing nor fixed-wing, the American Aerolights Eagle was an unconventional but very popular machine. Yaw was controlled by a stick connected to tip rudders on the wingtips, while pitch was controlled by the pilot, whose seat could swing fore and aft to alter the centre of gravity, and was connected to an elevator mounted up front on a canard wing. With a pitch system designed to be self-correcting, and no separate roll control to worry about, the Eagle was designed to be easy and safe to fly.

In 1979 Keith took Trish and Roger to Enstone Aerodrome in Oxfordshire to see one demonstrated by microlight pioneer Gerry Breen. Seven years earlier he'd been one of the first people in Britain ever to fly a hang glider; now Gerry was the UK's Eagle importer. Oliver went, too, and this visit gave birth to their shared passion for microlighting.

Like most early ultralights – as microlights were called in the USA – the Eagle was better suited to the light winds of North America than the much breezier UK. Cruising speed was only 30mph, it was not easy to control in turbulence, and the feeble twin Chrysler Westbend 820 9hp two-strokes were not the most reliable powerplants (as well as being, in Oliver's words, "... a real bugger to start"), but you could put down the craft practically anywhere, and everything happened so slowly that if your landing did degenerate into an 'arrival', there was every chance you'd walk away from it.

Keith bought one. G-MBSN was registered to DKD on 9 June 1982, and the proud owner promptly headed back to Enstone, where instructor Simon Baker stood ready to help him and Roger learn to fly it. Two-seat Eagles did eventually become available, but Simon didn't have one at the time, so his training routine consisted of briefing the pilot as best he could, attaching the Eagle – sans engines initially – to the back of an old London taxi which had its back specially removed for the purpose, and towing the machine along the runway. Once the pilot had the hang of the controls, he could detach the rope and glide off on his own.

So far so good. Tow training completed, Keith duly let himself loose and proceeded to head away from the airfield, only to get into trouble – probably due to turbulence – and come down in a field of standing corn nearby. "All we could see was his head!" chuckles Oliver. Man and machine were unscathed, and soon made their way back to the Folly, where the engines were attached and 'self-training' continued from a nice flat field owned by a friendly farmer nearby. It was all great fun, but not very productive, as Oliver relates. "Keith could get up all right, the aircraft climbed and descended okay, but it always seemed to go in an anti-clockwise direction! After about ten minutes he returned to earth and it turned out that we'd assembled a bolt and wingnut the wrong way, so that the steering would only go one way!"

DKD's interest in the Eagle quickly waned. He was not an adrenalin junkie: his pleasure in flying derived mostly from controlling the aircraft and this one, for all its genuine merits, was not easy to control in typical British conditions. Moreover, the CAA had announced that following a spate of accidents, caused mostly by poor piloting, all microlight pilots would require a licence from 1 September 1982. It would be simpler and easier to get than a lightplane or helicopter qualification, but nevertheless it was not good news for Keith. Less than three months after buying his Eagle, he was back on the ground again. Henceforth, his interest in microlights would centre on their design and manufacture rather than their flying.

A more viable aircraft was the Quicksilver MX (G-MJUI) that Oliver bought around the same time. Designed in the US as a fixed-wing hang glider, and thus originally something of a curiosity, it moved very much into the mainstream once an engine was added. Oliver's used a Cuyuna 430R, a 428cc in-line two-stroke air-cooled twin, which gave a useful 10mph increase in cruise compared to the Eagle, accompanied unfortunately by a tendency to hole its rear piston. Control in turbulence was significantly better than the Eagle, the airframe was simple but robust, the controls held no surprises for the conventionally trained fixed-wing pilot, and the whole package caught the imagination of the public in a way that no aircraft has managed before or since: at the height of the microlight boom in 1982 the maker, Eipper Aircraft, was building them by the thousand. A rash of Quicksilver clones appeared, and at the time of writing the original is still in production, in much updated form.[2]

The MX was a practical aircraft in that you could go places in it, but only slowly. At 40mph airspeed, you were in for a long haul if you hit a 30mph headwind. "Coming back up the A5 one evening, the cyclists were passing me!" laughs Oliver.

Initially, DKD had little involvement with flexwings, probably because the hang glider-style controls were alien to him, operating as they do in the opposite sense to traditional fixed-wings. Nevertheless, European pilots liked them and by the early 1980s the tide of fixed-wing American imports was waning: making flexwing microlights was a natural progression for hang glider manufacturers, who turned their hand to making versatile power-only wings and robust trike units, able to get safely in and out of small, soft, rough fields in conditions which would ground many fixed-wings.

All manufacturers, regardless of the breed of microlight they espoused, had a common problem as regards the power unit. Microlights had only evolved because air-cooled two-strokes had reached a power-to-weight ratio where they could be added to a glider without completely corrupting its ability in the air. None of these engines were designed for aircraft: motorcycles, snowmobiles, chainsaws and – the tabloids' favourite – lawnmowers all donated their power units with varying degrees of success, but none were ideal for aviation, because big, slow props are much more efficient (and much quieter) than small, fast ones.

Even the relatively low-revving units, of which the Fuji-Robin was probably the best in the early 1980s, needed some kind of reduction drive between engine and prop and, with levels of engineering integrity varying markedly throughout this fledgling industry, no engine manufacturer was willing to engineer one for fear of product liability claims arising out of the failure of some unrelated component. Indeed, every Fuji-Robin engine arrived from Japan in a crate marked 'Not for Aviation Use.'

At this point, Roger Kimbell enters our story. He didn't meet Keith until 1989, but from 1982 their orbits were beginning to connect, without either man being aware of it.

Roger ran a construction equipment business in Northamptonshire called Mawsley Machinery. "We were selling Fuji-Robin engines into the construction and garden industries on a local basis and, though we didn't know it, we were the engine's biggest British dealer. So when we'd been going three years, we were offered the import rights and I went for it, largely because of the number being sold into the microlight industry. The volume of aviation sales made the figures stack up very well.

"I had no flying experience at all at that point, though I'd always been interested in aircraft. Later, in 1988, I gained my pilot's licence on a lightplane, and subsequently converted to fixed-wing microlight."

Roger's success with the Robin was partly because a contact of his, Nick Lowe, developed a V-belt reduction drive for it that was more reliable than most. Many 'engine failures' on early microlights were not actually engine-related at all, but failures of the reduction drive, so the availability of a viable reduction system naturally boosted demand for the engine.

Nevertheless, it was clear to the entire industry that a purpose-built microlight engine with an integral reduction drive was badly needed. The void was filled by Austrian engine maker Bombardier-Rotax, who took the bull by the horns in 1983 by introducing its 377 and 503 twin-cylinder in-line two strokes with attached gearbox. No more V-belts, no more 'Not for Aviation Use,' here was a complete powerplant which could be bolted onto the airframe with confidence. Every importer was in direct contact with factory quality-control personnel: problems were investigated, fixes promulgated, service bulletins updated – a proper professional aviation approach.

Rather than take the fight to Rotax, Fuji-Robin got completely cold feet following the Austrians' initiative and, by 1984, had abandoned aviation sales completely, despite having dominated the British market and amassed a healthy share of US and Continental sales. Roger Kimbell and Nick Lowe were not best pleased, but Rotax never looked back. Within five years approximately 80% of microlight production worldwide used Rotax engines, and the situation is little different today, for as microlights have grown and matured, the Rotax range has evolved in parallel. At the time of writing, Rotax's flat-four watercooled four-stroke, the 912, powers some 45% of the UK microlight fleet, and most of the rest is kept aloft by earlier Rotax two-strokes.

Keith already knew the UK Rotax importer, Nigel Beale. "I met Keith in the early '70s when he was a judge on the Shell Marathon. We won it with Conrad [Nigel's son] driving: we used a 50cc Honda four-stroke with stop-start, and got 1309mpg!

"Then Keith got interested in hovercraft and bought three from me around 1980, when we were called Cyclone Hovercraft. His son Roger raced one: when we lived at Caldecotte near Milton Keynes, he came over in the helicopter with him and we went buzzing round the local area." To complement his company's activities, in 1987 Nigel and his friend and hovercraft racing rival Bill Sherlock set up Cyclone Airsports for Bill to run as a Rotax service centre.

The microlight business soon swamped the hovercraft side of the Cyclone Hovercraft, so the company was renamed Skydrive accordingly, retaining the Rotax agency until late 2014, a run of 33 years. There is an old adage in aviation which states that the only way to make a small fortune out of flying is to start with a large one, but being the Rotax importer is perhaps the only exception to this rule. Although Nigel has put a lot back into microlighting over many years and remains a popular figure, it was a standing joke among microlight manufacturers that he was the only man in the entire sport who made any money out of it!

The textbook case of Rotax's commercial bravery and far-sighted investment is worth relating because Rotax did for microlights what the DFV did for F1 and the DFX did for Indycar – it opened up the sport by providing a reliable and affordable powerplant. And the name on the cam cover could have been Cosworth instead of Rotax: Mike and Ben consistently urged Keith to design an aviation engine, not just out of enthusiasm but because Cosworth had both the engineering resources and the production facilities to satisfy a market of that size.

Gill reckons Keith always wanted to design an aviation powerplant but somehow never got round to it, perhaps because of pressure of work elsewhere. Maybe he was worried about product-liability claims. Mike reckons he was put off by the bureaucracy of certification, but microlight engines don't require it … Perhaps he just didn't want anyone's death on his conscience: even the best engines fail sometimes.

He may never have designed an aircraft engine on his own, but Keith did have a hand in several designs by other people. One of the first was the Hewland two-cylinder engine designed around 1984, which, predictably, is a liquid-cooled unit, as neither Mike nor Keith had any time for air-cooling. "Bangs create heat, how do you dissipate that heat?" Keith would ask. "Pour water on it. You certainly don't blow on it, you'll be there forever!" The Hewland twin was never widely used, but it morphed into the triple which found a home in the ARV Super 2, conceived by Richard Noble of World Land Speed Record fame, and designed by pioneer microlighter Bruce Giddings.

One engine Keith decided not to have anything to do with was the Lotus Magnum. He and Mike went to Lotus to look at it in 1982, not long before Colin Chapman died, aware that the Lotus founder had been working on an aircraft project for over a year. Called the Mercury, it was an advanced composite-construction canard design intended to exploit the microlight definition to the limit: noted American canard expert Bert Rutan would design and test-fly the airframe, Eipper in the US would handle marketing, and Lotus had responsibility for the engine.

They were curious about the Magnum 2.25 because its configuration was unusual. A four-stroke air-cooled 480cc flat-twin of modular construction (the intention was to double it up to make a flat-four model in due course), it compensated for its inherently poorer power-to-weight ratio compared to a two-stroke by adopting direct drive, bolting the propeller direct to the engine to save the weight of a reduction drive. Direct-drive engines were nothing new, but had lost favour because it was very difficult to realise the weight saving in practice. To keep prop speed sensible, they needed to be low-revving, and this made them heavy for their output. Chapman's master stroke was to take the drive off the camshaft, thus achieving a built-in 2:1 reduction without any weight penalty. Weight of the twin was projected to be just 19.2kg, output 25hp at a lowly 2500rpm (a prop speed of just 1250rpm).

Far from being a master stroke, this turned out be a complete mis-hit. Not only was the engine far too fragile (Mike describes the insides as "... more like a watch than an engine"), but the camshaft lacked provision for damping the torsional vibrations emanating from the prop. Mike and Keith, who knew from the DFV how damaging these could be, immediately concluded that the design was useless. DKD also declined to invest in the aircraft, though the Mercury did survive the post-Chapman reorganisation, being taken over by a Newbury-based company called Aviation Composites, in which Lotus had a stake. Fitted with a proprietory two-stroke, the prototype test flew in 1983, and in September 1988 was exported to the USA. However, it was never put into production, and the Lotus flat-twin never powered an aircraft.

Of more significance to Keith's story is a motorsport name from Cosworth's earliest days: Campbell-Jones. Mike, the little boy in the back of John Campbell-Jones' car who'd got bored with being dragged around race tracks, had turned into a passionate and innovative aviator. His first venture into microlight design was a prototype tube-and-Dacron fixed-wing called the Ladybird, produced in 1982 in conjunction with a Welsh hang glider maker, Hiway. This company went broke the following year, so Mike, by now trading as Microflight and joined by instructor-entrepreneur John Hollings, moved the operation to Shobdon airfield in Herefordshire.

One day in 1985 Keith and Mike arrived in the Hughes with the Cosworth pilot. "I think they must have been a bit bored that day and wanted to take their helicopter for a ride," says Mike C-J. "The Ladybird had fabric-covered wings but at Shobdon I developed it into the Spectrum with composite wings, unusual because they were a wet lay-up process, all in one go. I think that got Keith excited because later, after I left Microflight, Keith introduced me to Arrows F1 as I was very fired up about the potential of composites and had ideas about using them for car chassis. But they weren't really interested, all they wanted was fibreglass workers."

Mike C-J's contract required him to stay out of powered-aircraft manufacture for a period after leaving the firm, but he would be back in Keith's life before long ...

Microflight continued for several years, but by early 1992 had succumbed to the high-overheads low-volume problem which bedevilled the entire British microlight industry following the CAA's introduction of airworthiness regulations in early 1984.

The CAA's bureaucratic blunderbuss had two barrels. Manufacturers had to have Category A rating, obliging them to satisfy the authority as regards production processes, stock control, quality control, service support etc. Aircraft would have to be type-approved to a new technical standard called *BCAR Section S,* after which identical aircraft could be sold to the public. Both regimes were to be handled by CAA engineers at aircraft-industry rates per hour.[3]

Many manufacturers disappeared immediately, others struggled on for a while, and then died. Some, who had hang gliding roots, returned to them because unpowered aircraft were not affected. Those who survived found themselves constrained from innovating, as even the smallest improvement involved more bureaucracy, and were burdened with huge new overheads which made their product less affordable on the home market, and in many cases completely unsaleable abroad, where indigenous manufacturers – in France, particularly – were under no such constraints.

As this turmoil unfolded and his retirement approached, Keith was watching and waiting. He was never averse to funding ventures that he believed had a good product, and felt sure that sooner or later a suitable project would emerge. He'd said as much to Nigel Beale and Bill Sherlock, but at the time of his exit from St James Mill Road in 1988, neither had need of outside investment. That would change in the years ahead …

Another useful portal to the microlight world proved to be Pete Davies, who set up Sky Rider Aviation at Coventry Airport in 1987. Pete has a habit of popping up wherever there is some interesting flying going on – he worked as a flexwing instructor in Blackpool, then helped with the test flying of the radical and very successful Shadow, a ground-breaking composite-construction fixed-wing introduced in 1983. By March 1988 he was importing the Air Command gyrocopter[4] from America, and it was this which brought Keith to his door shortly afterwards.

Although gyros attracted a lot of interest prewar, the development of their much more versatile rotorcraft brother, the helicopter, subsequently relegated them to the role of aviation curiosity. Unlike a helicopter, a gyrocopter cannot take off vertically because its blades are not powered, but rely on forward airspeed to rotate them. To provide that airspeed, the machine has a normal aviation powerplant, usually rear-mounted like a flexwing microlight. The gyro can land almost vertically, and when flown skilfully is fantastically manoeuvrable in the air, but can be unforgiving if the pilot gets it wrong.

In the past decade and a half, helped by the advent of the Rotax 912 and a lot of serious research and development (particularly by German company AutoGyro), the gyrocopter has been transformed into a practical sport aircraft, but back in 1988 its image remained that of a machine built in tiny numbers by or for aviation eccentrics. Air Command tried to change this to popularise and mass-produce the gyro.

Keith didn't buy a gyro that day, but he did get on very well with Pete, and the pair subsequently spent time together exploring various aviation opportunities. "He just turned up at my office," recalls Pete. "Initially he wanted to talk gyros, but as he learned about my background in the microlight industry, we started talking Shadows – another aircraft that he seemed to respect – and other products that he might want to get involved with. I had a pretty good grasp of what was working in the UK sport aviation field, and of what was bubbling in the background."

At the time of his retirement, Keith had no investment anywhere in the microlight scene – he was still merely an interested observer who had bought an Eagle a few years back. But you always return to your first love, and the teenager who'd been flying model aeroplanes on the golf course long before he first rode a motorcycle or drove a car, would be irresistibly drawn into the industry before long.

Before we find out how though, we need to return to the company he left behind.

Footnotes

1 Current manufacturer is Raj Hamsa Ultralights of Bangalore, India (www.x-air.in).

2 Current manufacturer is Quicksilver Aircraft of Temucula, California (www.quicksilveraircraft.com).

3 During Keith's time the legislative regime was only very slowly lightened, some control being delegated to the BMAA, but at the time of writing the system is under more serious review with single-seaters now exempt from airworthiness legislation and further simplifications likely.

4 Gyrocopters – gyros for short – are sometimes known as gyroplanes or autogyros. Initially, Gyrocopter was the name of a specific model of gyro but modern practice is to use the word as a generic term.

Chapter 19

Cosworth after Keith

Keith's departure from St James Mill Road may have marked the end of his chairmanship and day-to-day involvement, but when a person has given almost his entire working life to a venture, and when many of his closest friends continue to work there, he cannot simply walk away. And Cosworth didn't want him to: in April 1989 the board appointed him Life President of the firm – a purely honorary post, but gratifying nonetheless – and, particularly in the early years of his retirement, it was not unusual to find him chatting to the engineers in the design office.

Over time, his visits became less frequent, as successive changes of management and ownership gradually alienated him from the company. Indeed, it was the imminent announcement of one such change that had prompted his retirement, because during 1988 it became clear that the entire UEI group was likely to be sold to media company Carlton Communications. An engineering company like Cosworth was an irrelevance to Carlton, which wanted UEI for its electronics expertise, and Keith realised Cosworth would soon be sold off, prompting yet more upheaval that he had no desire to be involved with.

The sale to Carlton was finally announced in May 1989, the company paying no less than £492M for the whole of UEI. At St James Mill Road it was no secret that this was unlikely to be the end of the matter, but in the short term at least, life went on as normal. Carlton founder Michael Green realised that in Cosworth he had acquired a success story, and decided to leave well alone: the company's assets remained untouched, and the Cosworth board was still free to operate as it saw fit.

Richard Bulman, sensing that this happy state of affairs might not last long, decided it was time to make some investment decisions. Jack Field remembers Richard saying "We've got £5M in the bank. We can afford to invest £2M." Jack had for some time wanted a new Indy engine "... to blow Ilmor into the weeds," and Richard needed no encouragement, for he believed Cosworth needed an independent presence in the US, not just an engine spun off an F1 unit. So shortly afterwards the board authorised a budget of £1.25M to develop a new Indycar engine, the XB, to wrest back the US market DFX had lost to Ilmor. Steve Miller, latterly chief engineer on the DFX, was in charge of the project, with Stuart Grove handling the design of what became the first major powerplant development of the post-Keith era.

Also agreed were a raft of improvements at Cos Inc's premises on Early Avenue. Jack explains "We needed a new test shop, we were still sending engines round the corner to be tested at $600 a time [at Parnelli Jones' old race shop] and we were pouring waste down the drain. We needed to start treating that properly, and we needed a clean room. I asked Ian Bisco what all that would cost, he said $100k. I told Richard $200k.'

Before any other major investment decisions could be taken, the inevitable happened and Cosworth was sold again. In April 1990, after less than a year in Carlton's ownership, the company became part of Vickers plc, a huge engineering conglomerate with interests in marine engineering, ordnance production and car manufacture – it owned the car division of Rolls-Royce. The price was £163.5M, an astonishing figure compared to the £6.2M the company had realised in 1980.[2]

With the company's independence gone, life at St James Mill Road changed markedly for the worse. Cosworth's cash reserves were absorbed into Vickers' coffers. Suddenly, the firm no longer owned its own buildings, but had to lease them back from the group at unattractive rents. All significant investment had to go through the parent company. These things may have made perfect sense in the Vickers boardroom at Millbank Tower in London, but at the sharp end it felt all wrong. Down at the Red Rover the phrase 'asset stripping' regularly entered the conversation.

The ruse Richard employed to construct the Octagon illustrates the constraints of the new orthodoxy very well. Cosworth wanted to graft a new eight-sided headquarters onto the front of Factory 1 (the shape being dictated by the need to avoid underground fuel tanks), but under Vickers' rules the Cosworth MD could only sign off capital projects up to £10,000. So Richard built it out of cash and told Vickers afterwards – a move that did not go down too well.

Worst of all in the eyes of longstanding employees, the Vickers management seemed to have no feel for racing or race-engine design, and no desire to perpetuate the spirit which had driven the company for so many years. Cosworth's road-engine business now dwarfed the racing side, and in Vickers' eyes was its main attraction.

Richard had been steadily finding his feet at Cosworth. He had made many changes – he introduced graduate training, for example, and completely restructured directors' pay – but they were mostly evolutionary rather than revolutionary. Keith's retirement did not spark a mass exodus of staff, the most significant departure being that of Mike Hall, who retired in March 1990.

By contrast, a number of senior employees left during Vickers' ownership, some because they, too, were approaching retirement, others because they simply saw no future working for the new regime. Three of the earliest departures were the sales director, the chairman, and the managing director, in that order.

Jack Field was Cosworth's great survivor. Jack and Keith hadn't always seen eye-to-eye, and he got off to a rocky start with Richard, too, when at one of their first meetings he called him naïve. Like Keith, Richard had been less than happy having such a rough diamond at the helm of the Cosworth racing sales effort. Like Keith, he'd tried appointing a replacement, and, like Keith, he'd rapidly backtracked when it became clear the newcomer simply wasn't master of his brief.

Happily, within a few months of Richard's appointment a truce had been declared. Richard realised that Jack's wealth of experience and his standing in the eyes of workforce and customers alike made him a great asset, and Jack realised that he needed Richard's support if he was to retire at 60 on good terms, as he'd always promised himself.

STATESIDE HAPPENINGS

Although names came and went at the top of the Cos Inc letterhead, the same two people were in charge at Torrance throughout all the upheavals in Britain – engineer Ian Bisco and administrator Penny Storch, both of whom were made vice-presidents in 1993. This gave the American operation valuable stability, and it is perhaps not entirely coincidental that during this period Cosworth enjoyed more competition success in the US than in Europe.

The investments put in place by Richard Bulman before the Vickers takeover proved timely, for as soon as the XB started winning, the Cos Inc premises became very busy.

"We very nearly won Indy at our first attempt in 1992," says Malcolm Tyrrell. "We led the race with Michael Andretti driving for 95% of the time and towards the end of the race we thought we had it in the bag when the guy out on the pitboard said, 'I smelt rubber when he went past.' The belt driving the fuel pump had failed, but by next season this overworked multi-duty item had been replaced by two separate drive belts and the XB went from strength to strength.

At Cos Inc, Ian Bisco soon found himself under pressure, despite the improvements sanctioned by Richard only a couple of years earlier. "It became obvious that the XB was the engine to have and we needed more space. I looked around several units nearby and chose one on Fujita Street which at the time seemed a little large, at 23,000ft². Of course this had to be approved by the UK and I will never forget taking Peter Nevitt and Victor Smith[1] to see it. Upon walking into the huge empty building Peter started shaking his head and said 'No bloody way!' "A week or so later I got the okay from Victor; apparently approval had been pushed through while Peter was away. By the end of 1993 we'd moved into our current premises and at its peak I had close to 80 working there!"

Although the XB and its derivatives had a long and successful career in American racing, it was briefly and unexpectedly interrupted in 1994 by the arrival of a new Ilmor engine, the 500I, which had been developed in secret.

To give competitors an alternative to pure-bred racing engines, Indy 500 rules permitted pushrod engines based on production units to run at significantly greater turbo boost, and to have larger capacity – 3.43- versus 2.65-litres. For several years extremely fast engines based on the Buick V6 had exploited this provision; during their evolution they acquired revised oil/water and scavenge pumps and the Paul Morgan/Martin Walters fuel-injection system, with all these components being supplied by Cosworth – perhaps not surprisingly as ex-Cosworth man Keith Leighton was working on them!

Nevertheless, the engines always proved too fragile to challenge for top honours. One day DKD found his way into Keith Leighton's garage at Indy and was given a tour. "I gave Keith a complete showing of these engines in various states of build – he couldn't believe how crude they were!"

Mario Illien takes up the story. "The Indycar rules were relaxed year after year to favour pushrod engines, but that had failed every year, so at the end of May 1993 they made everything free. As long as you had a central camshaft, pushrods and two valves per cylinder, that was it. I said 'Now we build a new engine, from the ground up.' That year we had a good 200hp more than anyone else. Then the engine got banned! But I expected that."

An unexpected but very welcome side-effect of the 500I's success was that it brought about a rapprochement between Mario and Keith. "Later in 1994, after we'd won the race and got on pole, blown everybody into the weeds, I saw him at Silverstone and he said 'Forget all about it, I respect what you did.' He was big enough to say it. I think he respected our initiative because it seemed no one else had thought of doing it."

But who would replace him? Jack had consistently championed the cause of Bernard Ferguson, as discussed earlier in this book, and in 1990 Richard offered him the job for the second time. First time around, when Bernard had been working at Wellingborough, he had sensed that Richard was unsure of his suitability. "The very idea of someone with long hair and a northern accent representing the company to the racing world – who he thought were all rogues and vagabonds anyway, so I thought it would have been a perfect fit! – did not appeal at all, and he made me a derisory offer."

This time Richard was more confident, and more generous. The result was that the Cosworth racing sales office acquired a new chief, one who would make a great success of the job and eventually become a director of the company.

The good thing about Jack's imminent departure was that it provided an excuse for a party. Actually, lots of parties, as Steve Miller recalls. "He had this endless series of leaving 'dos, and somehow he managed to persuade Richard to get these supported by the company. I think the final one was a marquee in a field with a pig roast and loads of beer."

One man, already an ex-employee and known to love a beer, had no intention of missing this, and Keith enthusiastically joined in the festivities. So enthusiastically, in fact, that Steve remembers him "... getting passionate about something, swivelling round in a hurry, and spraying the assembled masses with beer."

This was thoroughly in character, as Keith himself had admitted some years earlier during an after-dinner speech to Vandervell GKN. He'd asked Alf Vickers whether a journalist's description of him as an extrovert was fair, and Alf's analysis was that Keith "... was normally fairly shy but two pints of beer made [him] a raging extrovert!"

Bernard arrived in the sales office after Keith's retirement, and had previously served in the road car division under Mike, so his career overlapped very little with DKD. Nevertheless, Bernard came to know him very well: the pair were similar in outlook, background and accent and got on famously, so by degrees he became one of Keith's principal windows into Cosworth. And when there was an official event where the presence of the Life President was needed, it fell to Bernard to organise things.

In July 1991, 15 months after the takeover and on his 61st birthday, Mike Costin closed his office door for the last time. He was motivated not wholly or even largely by sale to Vickers – once Keith went, he'd never intended to stay long – but the changes certainly made the decision easier to take. In retirement, Mike has devoted much of his time to his beloved gliding, and he remains a very active and popular participant in the British soaring scene.

The new chairman was not vice-chairman Mike Hoffman, a man who had been appointed by Peter Michael of UEI, and for whom Richard had considerable respect, but ex-Ford man Dr Peter Nevitt. Walter Hayes had once said "Never employ anyone from Ford," his point being that corporate culture and the needs of a company like Cosworth are simply incompatible, but it was abundantly clear which way the wind was blowing.

Richard had decided almost as soon as the takeover was announced that his future no longer lay at Cosworth – he'd had his fill of corporate politics at Hawker Siddeley and had no desire to return to them – but Hoffman had urged him to stay on for a while to smooth the changeover, and he'd agreed. The appointment of Nevitt did nothing to encourage him to extend his stay and he finally departed in October 1991 to take on a variety of non-executive roles in other companies. For him, the independence of Cosworth had been one of the most attractive aspects of the job; now that freedom was gone.

He looks back with fondness on his time at Cosworth. "I was, I realised later, imposed on Keith after he 'lost' the company to UEI and he was in the most painful of transitions. I hope I always listened to him because his analysis was not just informative but an experience that has influenced my thinking ever since. So many PLCs have been destroyed by city short-termism. Keith once said that the problem with the city crowd was that they did not realise they were dishonest. How prophetic!"

Ben Rood, the fourth pillar of the management establishment to leave under Vickers, said his goodbyes rather later. He counted Keith as his best friend, and St James Mill Road just wasn't the same once DKD retired. Nevertheless, he agreed to stay on to help Mike. When Mike also went, Ben felt inclined to follow suit but, says Jane Rood, "Dr Nevitt who took over got on well with Ben and asked him to stay. He turned down full-time but stayed part-time for several years."

The legacy Ben left behind at Cosworth was of incalculable value. He once remarked that "There are no new ideas, everything has been done before: it is only technology catching up with it that enables it to succeed this time around,"[3] and as far as production technology is concerned, no one did more catching up than Ben.

Everyone at Cosworth had a favourite Ben creation. Mike recalls his 'donkey's dick,' his ingenious extending line-boring machine for camshafts, which bored first two bearings conventionally and then used them to support itself while it drilled the third, and so on. Malcolm Tyrrell admires the equipment he made to productionize the insertion of valve guides and seats into V6 Scorpio heads: a job that had hitherto been done manually by heating the heads in the oven, cooling the guides and seats in liquid nitrogen, and then fitting them one at a time. Geoff Goddard remembers the equipment for making pneumatic valves, as described in chapter 17. And everyone remembers machining heads between centres.

Roger Duckworth sums up the man. "My dad thought that Ben was a lot of the reason for the success of Cosworth. He would help my father design stuff that could be made, and then design the machinery to make it, and advise him on tolerances and finishes and the like. The commercial success of the DFV was a lot to do with keeping the price and running costs down to a sensible level, because you could replace bits, and they fitted and they'd work just as well as the originals. And that manufacturing consistency, in Dad's opinion, was down to Ben."

When Ben finally retired he undertook consultancy work for Ilmor, but Jane Rood recalls that he "... found considerable resistance to his ideas." Nevertheless, he must have made his mark eventually, because, in Mario Illien's words, "We machine heads between centres now."

Often the 'consultancy' was ad hoc, because his middle son Geoffrey worked for Ilmor in the US, and still does. "He would phone every Sunday night and talk engineering for at least an hour with his father," says Jane. "If there was a problem at Ilmor, Ben would go to his drawing board – later his computer – do a drawing and email it to him." The arrangement continued right up till Ben's death in March 2011.

Despite the upheaval, it would be wrong to claim that Vickers' eight-year ownership of Cosworth was unproductive. A full analysis of the company's post-DKD output is not appropriate here, but on the racing side the salient points included a second Queen's Award for Export Achievement (in 1992, to match the one granted in 1986), the successful completion of the XB for Indycar (started 1990, introduced 1992, won the Indycar championship with Nigel Mansell in 1993), steady improvement of the HB series in F1 (1989-93 seasons) and the introduction of the AC. The latter was an F3000 engine introduced in 1993 to replace the DFV, and which went on to dominate the category. To Geoff Goddard's delight, it also won the Design Council's British Design Award the following year. There were low points too, such as the abandonment in 1992 of project VB, the Ford V12 F1 engine, but unexpectedly this led directly to one of the highest points of all. Geoff Goddard was tasked with hastily developing a replacement for the V12 in the form of the V8 EC, which was spun-off the HB, and took Michael Schumacher to his first world drivers' title in 1994.

The German's victory was a great moment, the first time a Northampton product had powered an F1 champion since Keke Rosberg took the title for Williams in 1982. But the days of Cosworth refusing to provide 'special' engines were long gone. F1 engine design now demanded huge budgets and major motor manufacturers were calling the tune. Their favoured team received the latest powerplant, others got 'customer engines'. A derivative of the EC, the ED, was offered as a customer engine for the 1995 F1 season, the same year that work started on a new 3 litre V10 F1 engine, the JD. The later VJ and VJM engines were derivatives of it.

During this period there was also considerable touring car activity. Two projects were started in 1993 – the 2.5-litre V6 KCA for the Opel Calibra (won the 1996 International Touring Car Championship) and the 2-litre FCA for Mazda and Ford (powered Paul Radisich to the World Touring Car Cup in 1993 and '94). Three years later another 2-litre Mazda/Ford touring car project was initiated, the QG.

The best known Cosworth-powered competition car of the era was also a road car: the Escort Cosworth. It was produced in far smaller numbers than its Sierra Cosworth predecessor (some 7000 as against nearly 31,000) but owes its existence to the same person: Stuart Turner.

"If I'd known anything about engineering, the Escort Cosworth probably wouldn't have happened. We were having a planning meeting around 1989 and my product planner was saying, 'Fiesta's too small for rallying, Escort's gone front-wheel drive, the Mondeo will be too, what the hell are we going to do?' And like an idiot I said 'Why don't we take the Sierra Cosworth, take the body off, shorten it and see if the next Escort body will go on?' It was a stupid bloody idea, and I can still hear the engineers' laughter. And eventually someone said, 'Well, let's try it.' I realised no one was going to do this on paper, but we had a skunk works near Wellingborough, John Thompson's Auto Racing Technology outfit, and he actually did one in the metal.

"I took it to head office and all the top brass drove it up and down the A12 and came back saying 'Fantastic, wonderful fun, now go away and think of something more sensible.'

"Then it was realised that Karmann were making the American version of the Sierra, the Merkur XR4Ti, and the cabriolet version of the Escort, so they were playing about with both cars, and the project went on from there. Then I retired! But not before writing to my colleagues 'This will win the Monte Carlo Rally.'"

The Escort Cosworth did indeed win the Monte (in 1994), and nine other World Rally Championship rounds besides. It never took the WRC title, but was nevertheless a formidable contender on the stages and remains a very sought-after car, not only as a competition machine but also as a road vehicle.

One example of the latter is in regular use by Ursula Duckworth, who is very fond of the car because her son Roger was heavily involved with developing its powerplant, a variant of the Sierra Cosworth unit dubbed YBT. Work on the engine started in 1990, and the first Escort Cosworths left the production line two years later.

In parallel with that project, Roger also worked on the FBA, the 24V version of Ford's 2.9-litre V6. Conceived shortly before Keith's retirement, it was designed to power the top model of Ford's executive car, and first appeared in the 1991-94 Granada Scorpio (badged simply Scorpio outside the UK and Ireland). Latterly it was used in that car's 1994-98 replacement, also called Scorpio, but blessed with bug-eyed styling so controversial that at launch *Car* magazine described it as "Ford's new Edsel."

The Scorpio never sold well, but it drove better than it looked and sold well enough to provide good business for Cosworth. "The engine was entirely built at Wellingborough," explains John Dickens, "the blocks and the little jackshaft that drove the oil pump and distributor were Ford, but the rest was ours."

Along with Ford's YB, Mercedes' WA and Opel's KB, the FB series constituted the backbone of the road-engine division, the part of Cosworth that had most attracted Vickers. But nothing is forever: the Sierra Cosworth went out of production in 1992 and the Escort Cosworth four years later, while the W201 series Mercedes was finished by 1993. The KB lasted longer, but eventually production was transferred to Germany. Clearly, major new design-and-produce contracts were needed. Cosworth had been bought on the assumption that these would be forthcoming, but although a big variety of new work was brought in, it was not enough.

Long-term Cosworth staff were not particularly surprised by this: they knew very well that Keith and Mike's business plan had been to have no plan. With no bank or outside shareholders to please, they'd been ideally positioned to grab opportunities as they arose. A more contrasting style to Vickers' management could scarcely be imagined.

Steve Miller summarises Vickers' attitude very well. "It was your archetypical city-run corporation, it had a hundred-odd people in Millbank Tower that all drove round in Rollers with drivers, and a number of companies underneath them, but they weren't very good at corporate governance. They bought Cosworth with the expectation that had come out of the Sierra and the Scorpio and the Opel KA and KB and the Mercedes job, that the company was going to continue to expand like topsy, but of course a lot of that work was opportunistic. You were a bit of a twit if you drew that line forwards.

"We ended up with huge turmoil in senior management because Vickers couldn't accept that there wasn't this growth there. So it got into the usual thing of changing all people all the while." Peter Nevitt was replaced in 1993 by a new chief executive, Chris Woodwark, and three years later ex-Rolls-Royce man Charles Matthews became managing director. Steve calculates that during the 1990s, 24 people came and went on the six-man Cosworth board, one of the casualties being Bob Graves.

"I ended up with a boss that I was never going to see eye to eye with – he wasn't a practical engineer. There were all sorts of stupid things going on, so I got out. When I left in 1997 there were about 450 employees I think, without Torrance." Early in 1998 he joined Ilmor, where he is now managing director.

Geoff Goddard left to join Tom Walkinshaw's TWR Racing company in 1995, having had earlier dealings with the firm on account of its using the Cosworth HBC engine in the Jaguar XJR-14. "Vickers suddenly filled the board with people who were non-engineers," he complains, "yet Cosworth had always been a design-led company." At TWR he designed, among other things, the DB7 engine. He later did consultancy work for Renault and GM, and is now professor in motorsport engineering design at Oxford Brookes University.

John Dickens was 'encouraged to leave' in 1995; a year later Dick Scammell retired.

Under Keith and Mike, jobs had, as far as was practicable, been organised around the talents available, rather than the other way around, and when Cosworth archivist Val Given remarked that "You could be yourself at Cosworth," she echoed the feelings of many. "But Vickers couldn't understand this flexibility," says Geoff.

Richard believes that Keith foresaw this exodus and was saddened by its inevitability. "Keith knew in his heart of hearts that after he left, Cosworth couldn't avoid becoming ordinary."

Bernard Ferguson was no more enamoured with life under corporate ownership than anyone else, but stayed. "In my opinion, Vickers wanted to get rid of the cult of the Duckworth, so during that period a lot of bland people replaced a lot of dynamic people, which made Keith very uncomfortable. The whole control thing had gone already in real terms, now the relationship and familiarity of it was starting to slip away as well.

"I didn't see him often, mainly our association developed over the phone – lunchtime, office time, evenings … He needed sounding boards: as the company repeatedly changed hands he became very perplexed by things he didn't understand ... he always wanted to understand why something was happening ... It was very difficult to explain all the changes rationally, sometimes all you could say was 'That's just how it is.'"

"It was either common knowledge or a common myth that at one point Keith and Mike tried to buy the company back." In fact, as Mike confirmed to the author, it was myth – wishful thinking perhaps, or a throwaway remark in the pub – and it is easy to see why the pair never seriously considered such a move. A buyback would have involved huge borrowings, the kind of stress neither man wanted.

Predictably, given the parent company's priorities, the thrust of investment at Cosworth during Vickers' ownership was in technology applicable to road cars. One of the first initiatives was a technology demonstrator called the MBA, a 2.5-litre 90° V6 designed and produced entirely in-house and fitted experimentally to an Audi 90.

The project was initiated after Keith retired, but John Dickens remembers him discussing it with the engineers involved. "It was designed by John Hancock and team," says John. "We pedalled it round to all the auto manufacturers, towed it behind my Scorpio as an example of what Cosworth could do to create a high-performance engine without a brief. We took it all round Europe, to test tracks, demonstrations and the like. That was the biggest money we ever spent internally on a speculative project."

The MBA was never put into production, but it opened new doors, and ideas from it found their way into other designs. It introduced Cosworth to Daewoo, a company it had never previously worked for, and hence to the design contract for the JEB V6 engine.

A Product Development Centre was opened in Worcester in 1993, complementing the recently completed plant at nearby Warndon which handled heat treatment and general finishing of raw castings. In addition, the Coscast process was licensed to various overseas producers, the first being Ford USA, which set up a mass-production foundry at Windsor, Ontario in 1994 to make some one million castings per annum.

Cosworth then built its own mass-production foundry, capable of producing some 400,000 items a year, near the Worcester North M5 junction. The output of this third casting plant, opened in 1995, included block castings for the Rover KV6 (from 1996), V6 blocks for Audi (from 1996) and cylinder heads for the Jaguar AJ-V8 (from 1997).

Also in 1995, a new £2M Emissions & Driveability Centre was opened in Northampton, and the same year saw Cosworth acquire Intelligent Controls Inc, an engine electronics and diagnostics specialist based in Novi, Detroit. The firm was renamed Cosworth Intelligent Controls Inc.

Despite these investments, and a lot of legwork by John Dickens, the big design-and-produce contracts simply weren't forthcoming. There were some interesting design projects, including the Aston Martin V12 (the SG, started in 1996), and 'in-house' work for Rolls-Royce, such as improvements to the venerable R-R 6.7-litre V8 and development work on the turbocharged 4.4-litre BMW unit scheduled to replace it. However, projects like this were not enough to keep the factories humming, and Cosworth fell back on a myriad of contract machining jobs.

The company also started spreading its net beyond the motor industry, and one Vickers-era initiative which deserved to succeed – and very nearly did – was the idea of building a small aircraft engine. The project that Mike and Ben had always wanted Keith to pursue finally started after his retirement, when a small 'aircraft office' was set up at St James Mill Road to co-ordinate the effort, and John Dickens got in touch with Lycoming and Contintental. Between them, these two US manufacturers had provided the majority of lightplane engines for several decades, but by the end of the 1990s both the powerplants and the aircraft they powered were outdated. Microlights were growing-up fast, and the more sophisticated examples now made traditional lightplanes from Cessna and Piper look embarrassingly cumbersome and expensive.

Continental signed an agreement with Cosworth to develop and subcontract manufacture a new 100hp engine, a direct rival to Rotax's highly successful 912S, and Cosworth took on engineer Mark Wilksch to further the project. Unfortunately, the early 1990s coincided with a dramatic slump in lightplane sales. As a result, Continental got cold feet and cancelled the project when work was well advanced.

In 1998 the Duke of Kent visited Cosworth to celebrate the company's 40th anniversary, but no amount of royal endorsement could conceal the fact that the Vickers was a group faced with many challenges. Cosworth was not the problem – despite the run-down of the major road-engine contracts, it was still a profitable enterprise – but the Rolls-Royce/Bentley side of the business needed major investment which Vickers could not afford. As a result, the R-R business was put up for sale, and Vickers let it be known that it was not averse to selling Cosworth as well.

Ford was aware of the situation and was concerned for the future of its motorsport activities, but did not want to bid for Cosworth as a whole. Mercedes was said to be interested, but in the end it came down to rival bids from the Volkswagen Group and BMW.

Strategically, BMW seemed the obvious choice because it already supplied some engines and other components to Rolls-Royce, and Vickers accepted its bid of £340M, only to change its mind days later when VW trumped it with £430M for R-R plus Cosworth. In June 1998 the deal was done, and the Vickers era was over.[4]

That was far from the end of the matter, however. VW's acquisition of Cosworth had severely compromised Ford's sporting interests, and in the next two months intense negotiations ensued which resulted in Ford buying the racing side of Cosworth (including Cos Inc and the electronics department) from VW in August 1998. The German group then handed the rest to its Audi division, thus splitting the firm into two companies, called Cosworth Racing and Cosworth Technology, respectively. They corresponded roughly to the two divisions set up by Keith and Mike at the beginning of the Sierra Cosworth project.

But there were still complications regarding the foundry operation, which had always served the whole of Cosworth. The Coscast process was Audi's main interest in Cosworth, as its products were superior to anything available in Germany at the

 Continued on p281

Keith refuelling the R22 from jerrycans on the Scottish island of Mull in 1990, on the lawn of the local garage. Rather than bother taking fuel to the island's airstrip, the proprietor told Keith it would be easier to take the aircraft to the fuel!

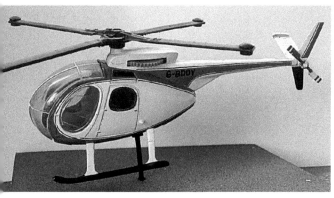

This model of Cosworth's first Hughes 500, G-BDOY, stands proudly on the Duckworth sideboard.

Tony Everard of the Helicopter Club of Great Britain presents Gill with the Whirlybird Trophy in 1996. Keith was always very supportive of his wife's competitive flying, and never griped about no longer having a licence himself.

G-ONTA, Cosworth's second Hughes, outside the hangar at the Folly.

Out and about in the R22: Visiting Middlethorpe Hall in York, June 1995 (above), and flying into Lower Slaughter Manor in February 1996 (left).

Start of the Rotax revolution – the 377 two-stroke with integral gearbox. *(Courtesy BMAA collection)*

A publicity leaflet for the Lotus Magnum microlight and its power unit. Keith and Mike looked at both, and declined to get involved with either. *(Courtesy BMAA collection)*

Keith took no photos of his Eagle, but this is a similar machine from the same era. Owner Alex Shaw (left), is enthusing Jim Hambleton. *(Courtesy Jim Hambleton/BMAA collection)*

If Dick Scammell had ever finished his Goldwing, it would have looked like this. *(Courtesy BMAA collection)*

A Quicksilver MX at Lake Windermere in the early 1980s. Oliver's example had wheels rather than the floats shown here. *(Courtesy BMAA collection)*

Above is an early example of a powered hang-glider – an SK 2SS wing with Soarmaster power unit – in the hands of French pioneer Bernard Danis, who took this machine to 5990ft in 1978. Landing and takeoff are on foot, à la hang-glider, the wheels are merely for backup. Note how the thrust line alters with the pitch of the wing: a fundamental limitation of the layout which led to the evolution of the trike …
(Courtesy BMAA collection)

… the very first of which is shown here. Dating just one year later, the picture shows designer Roland Magallon psyching himself up for the machine's maiden flight at Guyancourt airport near Paris.
(Courtesy UlmMag/BMAA collection)

The significance of the DFV quilldrive can be judged by this model of it, presented to Keith after his retirement, and inscribed: 'Keith. On your acceptance of Honorary Life Presidency. With these quills you wrote a new book in the history of motor racing. The Board, Cosworth Engineering, April 1989.' *(Courtesy Norman Burr)*

The XB took Nigel Mansell to Indycar victory in 1993. Here, he makes a pit stop in Milwaukee.
(Courtesy Ford Motor Co)

Left: The front row at Indianapolis 1993: (l-r) Arie Luyendyk (Ganassi Racing Lola), Mario Andretti (Newman Haas Lola), Raul Boesel (Dick Simon Lola) – all XB powered. *(Courtesy Malcolm Tyrrell collection)*

The XB in the Newman Haas car for its very first test at Elkhart Lake. Note 'Cosworth' on the cam cover; only after this successful test did Ford agree to sponsor it. *(Courtesy Ian Bisco/Cos Inc)*

The British Design Awards ceremony in January 1993, celebrating the XB: (l-r): Malcolm Tyrrell, Dick Scammell, Ian Sturman, Peter Nevitt, Jack Dunkley, Neil Smith, Steve Miller, Roger Broome. *(Courtesy Malcolm Tyrrell collection/Cosworth Enginering)*

The 1994 Spanish Grand Prix, Barcelona. The pit crew check the engine as Michael Schumacher waits to race. *(Courtesy Ford Motor Co)*

Escort Cosworth action in the 1995 Swedish Rally, provided by François Delecour. *(Courtesy Ford Motor Co)*

The 24V Scorpio's FBA 24V engine.
(Courtesy Ford Motor Co)

The MBA engine technology demonstrator.
(Courtesy Cosworth Engineering)

Press launch photo for the 24V Scorpio, showing Dame Kiri te Kanawa outside the Royal Opera House.
(Courtesy Ford Motor Co)

The closed-cycle diesel system test rig at Kettering. The man in braces is Dr Morley, son of Rolls-Royce engineer Fred, while on the left is Harvey Fox; the others are visiting Russian naval personnel, a rear admiral and a captain. The photo is dated 24 September 1997. *(Courtesy Harvey Fox/Cosworth Deep Sea Systems)*

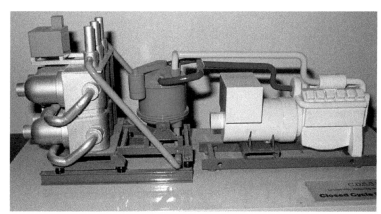

A model of the closed-cycle diesel powerplant, showing the absorber and water management system. *(Courtesy Harvey Fox/Cosworth Deep Sea Systems)*

Cosworth's headquarters, the Octagon, under construction around 1991. Behind it is the original Factory 1. *(Courtesy Ian Bisco/Cos Inc)*

Test flights of the Dair-100 engine were made in this Luscombe – seen here on display at a subsequent PFA rally. *(Courtesy Diesel Air)*

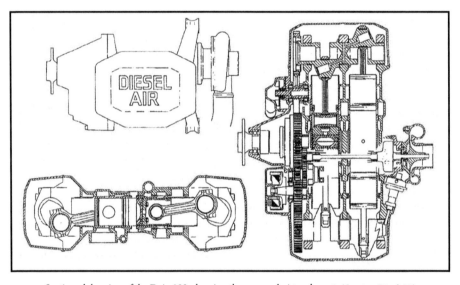

Sectioned drawing of the Dair-100, showing the opposed piston layout. *(Courtesy Diesel Air)*

The engine on show at a PFA rally.

Mike Daniels (left) and David Soul at the Weslake testbed with the Dair-100.

time, but there was no way Ford could allow the innards of its competition engines to be seen by a potential racing rival, so after the split Ford bought licence rights to the process and paid to install it at Grainger & Worrall's foundry at Bridgnorth in Shropshire, the first castings coming out of the moulds in April 2000. At the time of writing this is still the source of Cosworth Racing's castings.

Audi's 1998 purchase bought it three foundries: the original small research foundry at Hylton Road, the larger production unit in Warndon and the big mass-production installation nearby, opened by Vickers in 1995. However, by 2005 Audi had decided that the largest plant was uneconomic and closed it, the relatively slow Coscast process proving incompatible with the very high volumes required. Around the same time, Ford reached the same conclusion regarding its big Coscast foundry in Canada – this too closed. Coscast is still viable for more modest outputs of up to some 20,000 per year, but as alternative techniques have improved, its quality margin has reduced and it has become more of a niche process.

That same year, Audi decided to sell Cosworth Technology. The remaining foundries, the Wellingborough factory, Costin House and its associated buildings on St James Mill Road were all bought by Mahle, a major German automotive components supplier. There are still some familiar Cosworth names on the payroll, not least Mike Costin's eldest son Chris, who still works in what used to be Costin House, but the Cosworth logo has now disappeared from all these premises and its products in favour of Mahle Powertrain. Since 2005, Cosworth has only appeared on the products of the racing side of the company.

In Keith's eyes the latter was always the heart of the firm, hence his quip, after the dust had settled on this corporate maelstrom, that probably the greatest achievement of his career had been to create a company resilient enough to survive being owned by Vickers.

By the end of 1998, his son concluded that his future did not lay at St James Mill Road at all. After the Audi takeover Roger and three of his colleagues decided to leave and set up their own company in Milton Keynes, ending a decade at Northampton which had seen Roger rise from graduate to chief development engineer. He had enjoyed broadening the road-engine department's portfolio beyond Ford work into projects for other manufacturers and saw little prospect of that variety continuing under Audi.

The new venture was called Integral Powertrain, and started early in 1999, Roger being joined by Cosworth colleagues Luke Barker, Darren Cairns and John McLean, each party owning 25% of the shares. Keith was unsure of the wisdom of this arrangement – "A partnership is a bad ship" he opined to his son, showing his scepticism of ventures where there is no overall leader – but the quartet proved him wrong and the company has prospered; at the time of writing there are some 75 employees on the payroll.

The dismemberment of Cosworth was messy, but by 1999 Ford had, for the first time, the genesis of a works F1 operation. Not only could it design and make its own engines rather than simply putting its logo on someone else's, but it was on the verge of having its own team: that January it bought a 51% share in Stewart Grand Prix, a logical step as it had favoured Jackie Stewart's outfit for several years, and in June the company acquired the other 49%. Just three months later it announced that Stewart Racing would run under the colours of Ford's Jaguar division from 2000 onward. The structure was complete.

With Ford in charge, Northampton remained the focus of the motorsport operation, but the integration into the wider Ford organisation, which had started back with the GB, intensified. The company put a great deal of effort into F1 during the 1990s and 2000s, but the history of that effort is outside the scope of this book. Suffice to say that the F1 world was by then so intensely competitive and so well funded that even the resources of Ford were not enough to guarantee an impact.

Inconsistent leadership didn't help, for Cosworth's second era of big-business ownership was characterised by almost as much senior management instability as its first. Initially Neil Ressler was in charge, but as he was based largely in the US, Dick Scammell was persuaded to come out of retirement for a year to run Northampton. In 1999 Trevor Crisp took over, then in 2001 Brendan Connor acquired the CEO's hat and continued to wear it until 2003, after which Tim Routsis took over.

Cosworth's Ford era did generate some successes. In September 1999, just after the Ford takeover, Johnny Herbert took the European Grand Prix at Nürburgring in a Stewart-Ford, and in 2003 Giancarlo Fisichella won the chaotic rain-disrupted 2003 Brazilian GP in a Jordan-Ford, the last F1 victory for any Cosworth engine. Jaguar F1 never won a race, its best points being a brace of third places courtesy of Eddie Irvine – Monaco 2001 and Monza 2002. No constructors' championships went to Ford-powered cars, and after Schumacher in 1994 no Ford-powered driver won the drivers' championship.

WRC rallying was also frustratingly devoid of silverware, the company failing to win a world title at any time during its ownership of Cosworth, despite the latter becoming increasingly involved with engine design and preparation.

Cosworth had more success in North America, where technical director Bruce Wood oversaw the introduction of two new engines, the XF in 2000 and the XG in 2003. The turbocharged 2.65-litre XF was aimed at the Champ Car World Series, and in 2003 was reworked for more longevity, renamed XFE and adopted as the specification engine, while the normally-aspirated XG was intended for Indycar. The XG was initially something of an orphan as Ford was little interested in the series at the time, but was subsequently dusted off and, ironically, successfully developed for Ford's great rival Chevrolet.

However, F1 was the heart of the operation and by 2004 Ford felt it could no longer justify the expense of owning an F1 race team. At the end of the season it sold Jaguar F1 to Red Bull and, with Jaguar F1 gone, the commercial logic for continued ownership of Cosworth disappeared. The company was sold to the present owners, Kevin Kalkhoven and Gerald Forsythe, venture capitalists who are active in US Champ Car and Indycar, and who have since diversified Cosworth into electronics, component manufacture, aerospace and defence work.

After trying unsuccessfully to float the company in 2010 they put the firm up for sale in 2012 – the firm posted a loss that year. Subsequently they decided to retain ownership and announced substantial expansion plans involving a new site further along St James Mill Road. The sad fact remains though, that at the time of writing, there is no Cosworth-powered car on the F1 grid.

Footnotes

1 Victor Smith was finance director under Richard Bulman and stayed on after Vickers took over.

2 Vickers plc had no connection with Vickers Shipbuilding & Engineering (VSEL), where Keith's old university friend Noel Davies was chief executive. The two had earlier been part of the same group but the shipbuilding side was nationalised in 1977 and after denationalisation became part of GEC. Nor did Vickers plc have any connection with Alf Vickers!

3 p45, Cosworth: Creative Power, Ken Wells, (Prancing Tortoise Publications/ Kewkar Racing 1991).

4 BMW and VW/Audi's tussle for the R-R car division continued for some time. The aero-engine side of R-R had been split from the vehicle side at the time of the Vickers takeover, but had retained the rights to the name. Since then, R-R Aero had entered various aviation joint projects with BMW. It agreed to sell the R-R Motors name to its partner, and refused to consider any bid from VW, which thus found itself owning the the physical assets and the R-R radiator and Spirit of Ecstasy mascot, but not the right to use the badge. Matters were eventually resolved by VW retaining the Crewe factory and the Bentley brand, and BMW taking over R-R and starting afresh with a new factory at Goodwood – transitional arrangements being put in place as regards use of BMW engines etc.

Chapter 20

Diesel diversions

Although DKD had little to do with diesel engines during his working life, two projects involving them figured in his retirement – one for submarines, the other for aircraft. As regards the latter, he'd been thinking for some time that if they could be made light enough, diesels were the way forward, not least because their fuel was easier to handle. Now that he had more time, he could give the idea more attention.

The submarine project was already ongoing. In fact, it had been bubbling away gently at Cosworth since about 1982 when Harvey Fox, who was in charge of diversifying Cosworth's client base at the time, spotted an article in *The Sunday Times* about work on a closed-cycle diesel engine capable of running underwater for extended periods by Newcastle University's Marine Engineering Department. Encouraged by Keith, he approached Prof Thompson at the university, and Cosworth agreed to sponsor the research. Later, when Harvey took over as general manager at Wellingborough, a corner of the factory was devoted to what became his pet project.

Existing underwater designs used exhaust gas compression, and were depth-limited as a result. The Newcastle system overcame this but had a limitation of its own, as Harvey explains.

"They used potassium hydroxide to absorb the CO_2 from the diesel combustion; this was effective but the time underwater was limited to the amount of potassium hydroxide the submarine could carry."

Something better was needed, so Keith hired, on a part-time basis, two retired engineers from Rolls-Royce Aero Engines: former Derby senior engineer Fred Morley, and former head of projects at Ansty Albert Jubb. What evolved was an absorber and water management system: seawater was taken on board, the carbon dioxide was dissolved in it, and the water then pumped overboard. The oxygen lost overboard in the CO_2 was replaced from liquid oxygen stored onboard, while the nitrogen was recycled, any small losses being made good with an onboard supply of argon.

"Keith wasn't directly involved, but took a keen and detailed interest in this development," Harvey recalls. "The biggest problem was that the old-school R-R engineers insisted on talking in Imperial units!"

Naturally, overcoming the pressure differential between the inside and outside of the boat absorbed some of the engine's power but the system proved acceptably efficient, and by 1988 Cosworth felt confident enough to set up a separate company in Kettering, a few miles from Northampton, to build a 120kW version of the powerplant, aided by UK and EEC grants. "The total auxiliary power required is about 15kW for something in the region of 120-150kW," said Harvey, writing in Cosworth's own publicity booklet in 1987.[1] With the system capable of operating at depths of up to 500m, Harvey envisaged applications with submarines, torpedoes, pipe laying, trenching, oil-rig inspection etc.

Cosworth Deep Sea Systems Ltd was formed 2 August 1988 – the same month DKD retired – with Keith as chairman and Harvey Fox as MD. Mark Hunt took over Harvey's previous responsibilities at Wellingborough.

When Cosworth came under Carlton's umbrella in 1989, Carlton founder Michael Green took an active interest, and when it was sold to Vickers in 1990 its submarine offshoot was left out of the deal, almost by default as the Kettering facility was geographically separate from the rest of the firm. It was subsequently renamed Carlton Deep Sea Systems Ltd (CDSS).

Thyssen Nordseewerke in Emden and RDM in Rotterdam became enthusiastic supporters of the system, as both companies were building submarines that could make good use of it. "After rigorous testing at Kettering to their standards, I obtained a contract to build a 280kW system for Thyssen for a possible installation in a German 205 class submarine. Within two months, I obtained a second contract for a similar system from RDM," said Harvey.

Things were going well: sea trials of the Thyssen boat began in 1993 in the Baltic Sea, where it was judged to be the quietest submarine to date, while RDM continued with its own modifications to optimise noise emission. The South Korean Navy ordered a third system – successful trials were conducted there in 1997 – and there were constructive discussions with Russia and Beijing, until the Ministry of Defence put a stop to both.

Cosworth's name even came to the attention of the Pentagon, both as regards submarines and because the US military was intrigued by the possibility of putting race engines in its torpedoes, the idea being that although the target would be able to hear the weapon from a mile off, it would not have time to get out of the way! "However, our team was too small to expand into further projects," says Harvey. "Keith followed our activities right through the 1990s, even though he had retired."

Harvey reported annually to Carlton via future Prime Minister David Cameron (then Michael Green's director of corporate affairs) and Carlton MD June de Moller, "... but I was never really sure if Carlton understood our business, and in 1998, as I was about to retire, they sold the company to British Aerospace who moved the test rig to its submarine facility at Barrow-in-Furness."

Keith's involvement stopped completely at that point. Several CDSS employees relocated to Barrow, but with the Cold War over, the pressure to improve submarine technology had lessened and the project gradually lost momentum.

DKD's other Cosworth-connected retirement enterprise was to produce a small diesel aircraft engine.

The roots of DAIR, or Diesel Air Ltd as it is properly known, go back to 1988 and two individuals at Olney in Buckinghamshire: David Soul and Robin Read. The Soul family had been established in the area for generations and owned Olney House, in which Robin rented an office. David's main occupation at the time was running the family coach company, so he had a general interest in engineering, and in aviation and commercial diesel engines in particular, especially two-strokes like the Foden FD6 and Rootes TS3.

David's interest in engineering led him in the early 1990s to commission Robin to find a small engineering business for sale. "Robin suggested I help Weslake promote its 2-litre horizontally opposed aircraft engine in the light-aircraft market. I touted it to various aircraft manufacturers, one of whom was the Europa designer, Ivan Shaw. He was not impressed with it, considering it too heavy, and suggested I talk to Mike Costin, who had built a Europa." This was easily arranged because Robin was an ex-Lotus man and knew Mike already.

Mike, in turn, put David in contact with Mark Wilksch, who had been taken on at Cosworth to further the abortive Continental contract discussed in the previous chapter. "Together we conceived a project to produce an aircraft diesel engine. There was a great deal of talk about the coming demise of leaded gasoline, and we both felt the market was ripe for a new engine type.

"Wilksch Airmotive was formed around 1994, and Mark and I worked together for about 18 months. The Wilksch engine was a two-cylinder two-stroke diesel with exhaust valves and air ports in the cylinder, similar to the Detroit Diesel. Unfortunately, we didn't see eye-to-eye, and parted company in 1996, with Mark buying back my initial investment." Wilksch Airmotive is still active.

"After a few months of engine withdrawal symptoms," continues David, "Robin and I put our heads together and conceived the idea of a baby Jumo 205" – the Junkers opposed-piston diesel of the WWII era.

A contract was signed with Michael Daniels, son-in-law of Harry Weslake, and by then carrier of the Weslake engineering flame, to build three prototypes of the Dair-100, an 1810cc, flat-twin, two-stroke diesel with two opposing pistons in each cylinder. Each bank of pistons drives its own crankshaft which runs in a crankcase without any internal seals. Crankcase volume is thus constant, and a supercharger is used to transfer the air charge through a series of holes in the cylinder walls. The two crankshafts are geared together.

David and Robin then began an investment-raising exercise, helped by John Dickens, who by this time had left Cosworth. "I put together a group headed by industrialist Anthony Poeton and ex-PWC[2] partner Barry Baldwin," says John. "Unbeknown to me, Robin had also been talking to Keith, seeking both engineering input and investment. DKD said no initially, but his interest perked-up when he heard of our little group, thinking he would be able to dabble technically without any management hassle. Similarly, our group was encouraged by Keith's presence."

The result was that by April 1997 Diesel Air Ltd was in business, Keith having overcome his misgivings and agreed to invest. He joined John, David, Anthony and Barry on the board. Despite his financial commitment, DKD had little design input to the Dair-100, most of the work being done by Weslake designer Chris Downton with some backup from Cosworth's John Hancock, who, at Keith's suggestion, helped out on a freelance basis after he left Cosworth.

After many hurdles and a lot of development input from David, in 1998 the engine finally achieved its target of 100hp at 2600rpm, and, in December the following year, it made its first flight, powering the company Luscombe with David at the controls.

At this point Roger Munk enters the story, a friend of Robin, and an airship enthusiast. Back in 1996, as proprietor of Airship Technologies Ltd, he'd asked John Dickens if Cosworth would be interested in designing a cheap, light diesel engine suitable for an airship, but John decided there was little mileage in it for Cosworth, for it was clear that the budget was minimal.

Now, with the Dair-100 having made a successful maiden flight, Roger expressed an interest, buying two for his new small airship and going as far as buying out Robin's shares to give himself a stake in the enterprise.

Many PFA[3] flyers were also interested in the engine, but actually getting units to customers proved problematic, as John explains. "The small matter of CAA certification consumed a lot of time and interest, as did the quality of parts used on prototype engines. Eventually we encouraged Neil Lefley, formerly of Cosworth, to join as part-time general manager to oversee prototype production and a move from Weslake to low-level production at Scott Gibbin in Peterborough.

"Keith found the whole exercise greatly vexing," recalls John, "due to management issues and the less-than-ideal manufacturing conditions through which the early engines came to life. Conversely, he was fascinated by the concept and some of the detail engineering, which was compromised by lack of financial and technical resources."

In the circumstances, buyers were in no hurry to place deposits, and Advanced Technologies Group – which by this time had succeeded Airship Technologies Ltd – was no exception.

"Roger Munk's company was particularly difficult to deal with, both technically and especially commercially," continues John. "He requested a design analysis of an eight-piston 450bhp version for a new range of multi-role airships, and this was completed in 1998, despite very limited funding. So when he offered to buy out the directors and take over the company late in 2001 we agreed quite quickly."

The price Keith received for his shares was, Neil recalls, around half what he had invested, but by this stage DKD no longer trusted Roger Munk and was glad to be out. Twelve engines were laid down and Roger had plans to use them in a military programme for the USA, and in airships for the Chinese navy. Sadly, his company failed a short while later and Roger himself passed away in 2010. David Soul bought back the rights to the engine, and at the time of writing Diesel Air Ltd is still operational and continues to develop the engine.

Footnotes

1 p43, *Cosworth*, Ken Wells (William Kimberley Ltd, 1987).
2 PricewaterhouseCoopers
3 The PFA (Popular Flying Association), has since been renamed Light Aircraft Association, and is the representative body for constructors of homebuilt aircraft in the UK. It administers some microlight-legal aircraft, but should not to be confused with the BMAA (British Microlight Aircraft Association), which adminsters both home-built and factory-built microlights.

Chapter 21

Keith after Cosworth

Keith had always loved travelling on two wheels; it was a passion he never lost. He owned a huge variety of motorcycles over the years – including a Honda CX500 in the mid '70s and a Kawasaki KMX 200 in the early '80s – but his family completely lost track of them all, especially during retirement when all sorts of bikes came and went.

Keith's taste in machinery is best described as quirky: he loved things that were new and different. Now that he could enjoy motorcycling whenever he liked, he found himself frequently rubbing shoulders with like-minded people. And when he discovered that one of them, Roger Kimbell, had also been involved in microlights, the two quickly became good friends.

"I met Keith in 1989 through motorcycling and a mutual friend, David Watts," relates Roger. "The first time we rode together, we went to Silverstone. I remember standing on the pit wall with him; the rotary-engined Norton race team were competing, and I said to Keith 'You wait till they take off, they're going to win.' All the normal-engined bikes shot off the line, leaving the Nortons behind, but I said 'Wait till they come round, they're going to win this.'

'Don't talk rubbish' was the response from Keith (his language was actually rather more colourful!), but by the end of the first lap, one of them was in front and the other in third; they won the race one-two. That's when the ribbing started: 'Why didn't you develop the rotary engine instead of messing about with 16,000 revs, four valves per cylinder and all the rest of it?' At that point he would go off like a Roman candle and put his thoughts forward about how they weren't 600cc but equivalent to 1800cc.

"It became a theme really ... there were times when the words 'rotary engines' were mentioned and Keith would look the other way or go away. He didn't want to be wound up, thought it was bad for his heart!

"He also had a great dislike of the architectural profession, so if you couldn't get him going on the subject of rotary engines, architects was a good bet. He disliked just about everything about them – what they did, how they did it ... Probably it arose from the construction work at Cosworth. No doubt they were trying to do the best by their client within the constraints of local planning regulations, but as far as Keith was concerned, if they couldn't do what was expected of them they were no bloody good – and neither was the man installing his central heating or repairing his swimming pool."

"Obviously few minded," adds Gill, "because most of them still come back to the Folly! They say how much they miss their chats and banter with him."

Once people got to know Keith they would ride over any criticism, knowing full well that it was usually made with a twinkle in the eye. When Oliver Achurch was installing his own central heating, Keith took a good look round the work, then sat down at Oliver's kitchen table and started scoring each aspect of the job out of ten. Oliver was delighted when he got a few nines.

At Roger Kimbell's suggestion, Keith joined the Sreknaw Motorcycle Fellowship, a completely informal unconstituted local motorcycle club whose irreverent ethos is encapsulated by its name (try reading it backwards!). Thus accompanied, he had a huge amount of fun, fell off a few times, consumed a considerable volume of beer by way of compensation, and had many entertaining and passionate debates in the saloon bar.

Roger continues "The joy of being with Keith was that despite his knowledge, his background, his amazing personality, and of course wealth, none of that came into it. He was just one of the boys out on a bike having a bloody good day out. He expected everyone to pay their way, just like him. He loved his beer, the lower the alcohol the better, so that you could drink plenty of it – what he called 'session beers.' He had a great thirst but he became very entertaining when he'd had more than he perhaps should have done.

"His riding skills weren't up to the level of some of the better riders and he did have the odd tumble, some of which had to be kept quiet from Gill, with bikes recovered and quietly dealt with. He hurt his shoulder quite badly once, when he ran off onto some grass." That particular achievement warranted a mention at the Sreknaw annual 'ladies night,' an occasion not to be missed, not least because females were definitely not allowed. "Keith got all sorts of awards for falling off and causing havoc or mayhem," recalls Roger, and this particular year was presented with a photo of a crash helmet underneath a street sign which a Sreknaw member had come across quite by chance. The name? Duckworth Fell.

At this point we must introduce another major influence on Keith's motorcycling career: journalist Paul Blezard.

"I first met Keith on a memorable day in a memorable month – October 1992 – thanks to two things: our mutual connection with former motorcycle racer and Cosworth engineer Peter Williams, and an extraordinary cabin motorcycle, the Swiss-built Peraves Ecomobile.

"That day I took the Ecomobile to the National Motorcycle Museum in Solihull and the Motorcycle Industry Association (MCIA) in Coventry. Before I left the MCIA I phoned Peter and asked if he'd like a ride on this extraordinary 150mph machine and, as he answered in the affirmative, I duly turned up about an hour later just as it was getting dark. After a couple of miles Peter said, 'I think we should show this to Keith Duckworth,' and directed me to the Folly. I took Keith for a ride too, and was pleased to discover that DKD was at least as keen on motorcycles as he was on cars."

Continued on p297

Keith on board his Yamaha GTS 1000. Originally there were other riders in shot but after DKD died his Sreknaw friends wanted a photo to remember him by, and edited it to place him centre stage.

Keith tries Mark Crowson's QuickaQuasar for size at Silverstone in 2000. *(Courtesy Graham Robb)*

When a Sreknaw member saw this sign, he couldn't resist setting up a photo.

The Hossack steering fitted to Keith's Triumph 900 triple in 1993. *(Courtesy Norman Hossack archive)*

Left: Passion in the pub during a 2002 Sreknaw session: Malcolm Clube extols the virtues of rotary engines (top) to an incredulous Keith (centre), who vents his feelings on the subject in no uncertain terms (bottom). The other riders are Howard Robinson (top) and Mike Brogden (centre).

Keith with his scooter collection circa 2000: (l-r) Peugeot Speedake 50, Honda CN250 Helix, Malaguti, BMW C1, Go-Ped, Suzuki Burgman 400. *(Courtesy Paul Blezard)*

At Silverstone, DKD inspects Graham Fryer's homemade FF, with Difazio hub-centre steering and Honda VF500 motor. His own and three other Voyagers are behind him. *(Courtesy Graham Robb)*

DKD says goodbye to his Voyager after loading it onto purchaser Ian Kew's trailer.

Paul Blezard on Yamaha's YP250 Majesty with Givi Screen, and Keith on his Honda Helix in July 1996.
(Courtesy Paul Blezard)

Royce Creasey shows DKD the revised hub for his hub-steering system to avoid pad 'knock-back' on the Voyagers surrounding them at Silverstone.
(Courtesy Graham Robb)

DKD with the group which helped recommission his Lotus Elan.

Along with Mike, Keith contributed to a number of Triumphs, but this was the first to receive his attention: the Daytona Super III. *(Courtesy Roland Brown)*

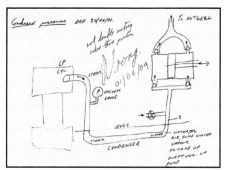

Keith with steamlaunch *Olive* at Lake Vyrnwy in Wales and (above), an example of the many pages of notes he generated while working out how to get the best from it. This sketch dates from 2001, but, in 2004, was rejected as wrong.

Oil in a day's work! Having fun with the Aquascooter in the pool at the Folly.

Enjoying Venice with Gill around 1993.

On the London Eye with Gill in May 2003.

This doctored version of the famous Brunel photo, with Keith's head substituted for that of the Victorian master, was a present from Walter Hayes to Keith, and still hangs in the Folly. The dedication reads 'Keith Duckworth – Life President … but more importantly, Engineer! For all the victories and the enduring pleasure of your company.'

A quiet afternoon in the Tinker in Menorca, around 1993.

Keith received the President's Medal from Sir David Davies of the Royal Academy of Engineering in 1998. DKD upset his audience immediately afterwards by saying they weren't practical engineers …

Goodwood Revival 2000, with everyone dressed in period gear: (l-r) Sue Ferguson, Frances Scammell, Keith, Bernard Ferguson, Gill, Dick Scammell.

Sailing the Tinker in Menorca with Gill.

A large, framed copy of this print hangs on Mike Costin's wall. It shows Keith and Mike driving a pair of Lotus 18s at the Lotus 18 Formula Junior Drive Day at Goodwood, 25 April 2000. They were not going fast when this photo was taken, Keith being much less at ease in the cockpit than Mike, as their expressions show.

With Mike and Ben at Stoneleigh Park in 1995, to receive the Sir Henry Royce Award from the Institution of Engineering & Technology.

Keith and Mike in July 1996. *(Courtesy Paul Blezard)*

A family get-together at the Folly around 2003, before a game of football on the bottom lawn: (l-r) Amber, her husband, Jonathon, their children, Toby and Hebe, DKD, Gill (in front of Gill), Tina and Simon's son, Mattie, and Simon.

A family gathering at Blackburn in the 1990s: (l-r standing) DKD, nephew Tony and brother Brian, holding his grandson, Daniel Anderson. Em is seated in the centre with another great-grandchild on her left.

Roger poses with his mother, Ursula, at his wedding in September 1997.

Gill with Auburn Girl ('Chessie'), after their wins at Atherstone RCQ in 1999.

Above left: Ah! The wheel's fallen off! Keith with his first grandchild, Isabelle, Christmas 2002. Keith had a real soft spot for Izzy, despite feeling generally ill at ease with small children, and doubting the wisdom of bringing them into the modern world at all. At the time of writing, Izzy is 13, and, in the words of her father, "... shows great logic in her thinking." A chip off the old block, perhaps?

Above right: In the stable yard at the Folly, making running repairs to grandson Mattie's pedal car.

Gill in action on Tudor Crown in 1993.

Main image: Having fun with a Honda Pilot. The aftermath of Keith attacking a gateway somewhat narrower than the machine (left), and DKD plays with the Pilots' replacement, the Power Turn (above).

Gill Duckworth with Pitsford headmaster Noel Toone, opening the Duckworth Building, with a Cosworth V8 taking centre stage. *(Courtesy Pitsford School)*

A couple of years later there was an interesting postscript to the Ecomobile adventure when the machine's creator, Arnold Wagner, returned in a newer version of his brainchild, accompanied by a friend driving a second machine fitted with an experimental single-sided steering system.

"I arranged for the Swiss pair to call in chez Duckworth, en route to Donington Park, but it's one of my greatest regrets that, for unavoidable reasons, I wasn't present when they met. Both men are giants of engineering and automotive design but their verdict on each other amused me greatly. Afterwards, each told me, separately, that they thought the other was crazy!

"I came to know Keith quite well and spent many enjoyable hours in his kitchen discussing the pros and cons of different motorcycles and alternative steering systems and layouts, particularly Feet First or recumbent bikes (FFs). And of course we had some *very* long conversations on the phone ...

"I put Keith in touch with Bob Tait who designed the hub steering system used by Malcolm Newell on the most impressive of the Phasars and Quasars that he built single-handed in his Wiltshire workshop." Keith rode over to Bob's Warwickshire home where, Tait recalls, "I got my prototype hub-steered Norton twin out and Keith had a close look at it while I took his Triumph Trident 900 for a spin."

"Coincidentally," says Paul, "the last thing I ever did for *Top Gear* (at the 1992 Bike Show) was to explain, in just 30 seconds, the basic principles of hub-centre steering on the Yamaha GTS 1000, introduced by a youthful Jeremy Clarkson. The GTS was the first large Japanese motorcycle without traditional telescopic forks and Keith purchased one just a few months later. We both liked it, especially the way it could be braked deep into corners without unsettling the steering.

"This brings me to the saga of the 'Hossacked' Triumph Trident 900. Norman Hossack had designed a double-wishbone motorcycle steering system many years earlier, based on his experience both as a bike racer and as an engineer at McLaren, and I enthused to Keith about his ideas. The Hossack looked superficially more conventional than the single-sided mounting of the GTS system but still separated the front suspension of the bike from its steering and maintained a constant wheelbase.

"In 1987 I'd enjoyed several hundred miles on a Hossack-converted BMW K100RS road bike, so I was delighted when DKD decided to have his own Triumph 'Hossacked.' I rode Keith's stock, 100bhp Trident to Norman's place near Harefield and a few weeks later rode the converted machine back. It was transformed: it steered much more quickly without being unstable and was better on the brakes. I wrote Keith a very positive private report to that effect, but he was less impressed than me, believing the bike needed more suspension travel, plus a longer wishbone to increase the trail and hence stability. So just before Christmas 1993 I rode the Triumph back to Harefield for a new wishbone.

"Keith found the newly modified machine better than before, but it was still not quite as he'd hoped, though his fellow enthusiast David Watts tried it and liked it."

One reason Paul and Norman were so pleased to see Keith modify his Triumph was that DKD undertook consultancy work for Triumph throughout his retirement. Norman had earlier tried and failed to interest the recently reborn concern in his ideas, but Keith's influence ensured that Triumph's test riders made a proper assessment of his modified bike. Keith always wanted Triumph to be more technologically innovative, though this was easy to say from his standpoint: unlike proprietor John Bloor, he didn't have to factor in the associated costs and risks.

"Unfortunately," says Paul, "the test riders liked it less than DKD and decreed that the design was not stable enough for a production bike. I was really disappointed because, unlike DKD, I actually preferred the Hossack to Keith's hub-steered GTS."

This disappointing episode proved a major turning point in Norman's life, and he moved to California, where he still lives, to design high-tech medical equipment. But he remains grateful for Keith's support, both with Triumph and for writing a letter of recommendation to help him get a US work permit.

"I had many hard arguments with Keith but I found them all most stimulating," Norman told Paul Blezard recently. "I also spent time arguing with him about my 'square piston' two-stroke engine design. It's sad that he passed away before I got videos of it working up on YouTube – he would have loved to see the way it ran."

Norman finally got significant recognition – but no money – over a decade later when, in 2004, BMW launched its K1200S sports-tourer with a 160bhp across-the-frame engine and a Hossack-copy steering system which it called Duolever. In its 2015 range, BMW has five models using Duolever steering.

"In May 2014," Paul continues, "he received further recognition when the reborn Spanish company Bultaco launched two completely new electric motorcycles in a spectacular ceremony at the refurbished St Pancras Renaissance hotel in London, both fitted with a Hossack-copy 'Dual Link' steering system – and they flew Norman from California to see it. Keith would have been really pleased for him."

The next FF bike to appear at the Folly was a project close to Paul's heart: the all-British Voyager 850. "I'd followed its development from its earliest days as a Ducati 450-powered bike created in the back room of Royce Creasey's terraced house in Bristol in the early 1980s. I was the first journalist to ride the Reliant-powered, Moto Guzzi-gearboxed, Volvo-seated prototype when it made its debut with Royce on *Top Gear* in the ten minute FF segment I wrote and presented in April 1988. Unfortunately, the project stalled for want of investment and the manufacturer, SCL, put all five prototypes up for sale, two of them appearing at Bonham's auction at the Stafford Classic Bike Show in April 1994.

"During 1993 I'd sent Keith a lot of FF articles – he'd become intrigued enough to call Royce Creasey – so I was delighted when he bought Voyager 03 at the auction. I hoped that Keith would use his skills and contacts to hone his Voyager into something closer to what it was originally supposed to be in terms of weight and performance, perhaps making use of his microlight connections. It struck me as ironic that a Pegasus microlight weighed only 210kg, and even with a 580cc two-stroke Rotax engine in 'quiet' mode still made 50bhp, whereas the true weight of the Voyager was 280kg and its 850cc four-cylinder Reliant engine developed under 40bhp."

But it didn't happen: his verdict on the Voyager amounted to "If I wanted to build an FF, I wouldn't start from here, with a Reliant engine and a Moto Guzzi gearbox!"

Nor did he want to start afresh: by this point Keith had his hands full with microlights.

"However, he was interested enough to join the Best Foot Forward club and to come to a talk I gave at Southampton University in May 1996. It was entitled *Why bikes should be more like cars,* and was primarily aimed at a group of graduate mechanical engineering students who were working on an FF project, but it was open to all, and quite a few FF enthusiasts turned up. Keith tied it in with a Sreknaw run and everyone was surprised and delighted when he arrived on the hub-centre steered GTS 1000. Later the same month Keith lent me his Voyager to take to the BMF Rally at Peterborough.

"Keith rode the Voyager himself to Silverstone three times for the annual October Voyager gathering at the 750 Club's Birkett six-hour endurance event. One year he followed me to the BMF Rally on the GTS 1000 while I rode his Voyager. I remember him complementing me on how quickly I was able to hustle the rather overweight, underpowered beast along, but another Voyager owner, Colin Russell, says that Keith was no slouch in the Voyager himself."

Colin recalls: "Keith was a very useful rider – I once followed him in his Voyager out of Silverstone after the Birkett and he was flat out as soon as he got out of the main exit. I struggled to stay with him on my own Voyager and most of the journey was 90-100mph stuff – great to see him enjoy himself. He looked very safe and confident on the road.

"I think if the Voyager had been 90kg (200lb) lighter and had 50bhp more, it might have 'floated his boat' more. It did suit his outgoing personality though, because he liked to be the centre of attention. He particularly liked the Birkett: a ripple would go out that Duckworth was in the pits and he would do his 'royal' walk, stopping at various open-mouthed F750 racers and then enthusiastically chewing the cud, much to our amusement. I think the racers thought we FFers were his minders! He did not hold motorcycle manufacturers in high esteem … they were all producing fairly mediocre bikes with antiquated chassis. Not at all the Keith Duckworth way."

Blezard again: "Keith told me about a big 'moment' he had in the Voyager when the front pads got knocked back in their calipers and he arrived at a corner too fast; he left the road, but managed to stay upright. Royce maintains the knock-back occurred as a result of leaving the road, rather than being the cause of it, but I've spoken to another Voyager rider who experienced pad knock-back more than once with the original hub design. In any case, whatever the sequence of cause and effect, Royce redesigned the hub to combat the problem."

Paul remembers a discussion with Keith about the pros and cons of racing an FF. "I said it was good to keep both wheels on the deck under maximum acceleration and spread the load between both tyres when braking, while Keith said that having the rear tyre deal with all the acceleration and the front tyre deal with all the braking gave the tyres a better chance to cool down between the two conditions …

"I always had a big smile on my face when I argued with Keith, as did he, although it was a bit intimidating when he got out a pencil and paper and started drawing diagrams annotated with equations."

"In 1997," recalls Paul, 'he acquired both a Honda VTR 1000 sports bike and a Honda NTV650 middleweight, although the latter was actually bought with a view to

FF-ing it. He also bought a a big four-cylinder BMW K1200, mainly because he was intrigued by the Telelever steering system, which was BMW's favoured alternative to telescopics until the Hossack patents ran out. However, he swapped the bulky BMW for a friend's much cheaper Yamaha FZ600 Fazer simply because he enjoyed riding the little Yam so much more – it was a jewel of a bike."

At the other end of the motorcycling scale, Keith and Paul shared an appreciation for scooters, particularly Honda's long and low feet-first CN250 Helix. They each had one – "... the difference was that his had been bought new and was immaculate whereas mine was a battered 'stolen recovery'. When mine broke down he lent me his for a while and also made a generous contribution towards my repair bill."

The Helix was one of Keith's favourite bikes – he told Paul he'd never sell it because it was so useful for local journeys – and was the first of a series of scooters. "In 1995 he bought one of the first Peugeot Speedake 50s in the UK and was intrigued enough by the Peugeot's CVT to do a whole series of data-logging tests with it, experimenting with different gearing and states of tune. Then when Suzuki launched its 90mph Burgman 400 Keith bought one of those, using it for a meeting in London despite the 150 mile round trip distance. He liked its comfort and underseat luggage space, but eventually swapped the 'Burger' for one of Yamaha's ton-up Tmax 500 twins.

"In 1996 Yamaha brought out their YP250 Majesty, which took Europe by storm, out-selling everything else with an engine and two wheels over 50cc and kick-starting the superscooter revolution. That July I rode Yamaha UK's press Majesty 250 to the Folly and Keith and I spent a really enjoyable summer's day comparing and photographing the two scooters. I also compared the Majesty to Keith's Voyager and wrote up the story for *Motorcycle Sport & Leisure* magazine.

"In the summer of 2000 I became features editor of *Twist & Go* scooter magazine, and I interviewed Keith for the publication. He told me his first bike was a 'bloody terrible' BSA 250 sidevalve and that he passed his test at seventeen on a 1932 Scott two-stroke, which was a rare bike even in 1950. 'If the Scott backfired it could start running backwards and that could be very embarrassing!' His first experience of riding a scooter was in 1957, when he borrowed John Campbell-Jones Lambretta to ride to work at Lotus: 'It was wet and a dog jumped out in front of me. I tried to avoid it but I hit it and went flying. All the passers-by went to look at the whimpering dog and ignored me, but the scooter was okay and I remounted and continued to work.'

"Keith also bought an ABS-equipped example of BMW's ground-breaking C1 125cc 'safer-scooter'. He was impressed by its weather protection as much as anything else and once rode it the 130 miles to Swindon and back. I remember having quite a heated (but good natured) argument with Keith about low and high centres of gravity, a debate provoked by the top-heavy feel which the roof gave the C1, making it very intimidating for beginners. He tried to convince me that the higher C of G actually made it easier to balance, using the example of balancing a hammer with the head at the top. I said that was bollocks because it was a completely false analogy. He, of course, said that I too was talking bollocks ..."

Keith was a fan of the C1 but he was in a minority – Roger Kimbell, for one, was unimpressed. "I didn't like it, but he did. He'd turn up on it when we went steamboating."

Steamboating may sound an unlikely interest for a man always inclined to look ahead, but every rule has its exception, as Roger explains.

"In discussion one day he started to tell me about his university days, and how his engineering degree had required him to understand steam tables and the workings of various steam-propelled devices. He knew a lot about it, and I said I'd always been interested in acquiring a steam launch.

"So we teamed up with Paul Holdsworth, who ran my Robin engine company – he was an ex-naval chap – and David Watts; between the four of us we spent the grand sum of £1500 and bought a 13ft boat called *Bluebell*.

"It had been built recently but with very old technology. The engine was a twin cylinder but without any condensing apparatus, so you constantly had to top it up with water from the canal or river. It was coal-fired, and it gave us a great deal of pleasure to trundle it down to the pub. We kept taking pals for days out and eventually we sold it and bought a much bigger, 21ft boat, a Frolic called *Olive*, which had been worked commercially on the Broads. Oil-fired, it had a lovely surrey canopy over it and a twin-cylinder compound engine, so that the exhaust gas from the high-pressure cylinder operated the low-pressure cylinder – much more efficient – and a hotwell that recovered the water from the low-pressure cylinder. That was the theory, but it relied upon creating a vacuum, and that kept Keith busy for hours trying to work out what was wrong. I've got a book full of drawings and notes about what we should be doing.

"This was completely the reverse of his interest in the new. But steam has a fascination for engineers: you've got maximum torque at zero revs like an electric motor, you've got almost total silence – something you could never accuse Keith's engines of! – and there is a charm about them. This later one took 50 minutes to get up pressure, and it was a requirement that all the crew turn up armed with at least a pork pie and a bottle of red wine (or a crate of beer). By the time we'd got steam up, all the pork pie had gone and most of the booze as well. We never did run it in the most efficient fashion; the arguments were legion.

"Initially, we had it on the Grand Union Canal. Latterly, we kept it at Oundle on the Nene; we used to trundle up to the Kings Head at Wadenhoe, or go the other way. Often, Keith would burst into song, he knew the words to every rude rugby song you can imagine, and he was also amazing in that he could sing hymns beautifully and word-perfectly. Often, he was happy just to keep the engine running and let the rest of us consume the wine, but if he did join in he'd get very voluble – I'm sure he could be heard several fields away."

The steamboat was hardly used after Keith died – "... it didn't seem the same without him," says Roger – and it sat in the stable yard at the Folly until it found a new home.

Returning to motorcycles, Keith's choice of a Triumph for his suspension experiments was logical, because, from January 1990, he and Mike had a consultancy arrangement with the company, one result of which was that Triumph loaned him a number of bikes. It was a happy, relaxed arrangement – just half a day a fortnight, occasionally more if there was a particular problem to be solved – which continued for the rest of his life.

The timing was serendipitous, because Triumph opened a new factory at Hinckley in Leicestershire around the time Keith retired, a factory which was effectively home to a new company. John Bloor, the enthusiast behind the rebirth, is a self-made man who founded a thriving housebuilding business and subsequently bought the Triumph name from the receiver when the company went bankrupt in 1983. To keep the name alive while he planned the marque's rebirth, he licensed continued production of the famous Bonneville to Les Harris for several years, but by 1987 the first new-generation engine – a 1200cc four-cylinder – was bench testing, and, in 1988, Bloor funded the construction of a brand new factory on a 4ha (10 acre) site at Hinckley.

Bloor's mission to recreate a major international motorcycle manufacturer from scratch was a huge personal commitment, and one for which DKD had enormous respect, so he was delighted to be asked to join the team. There was certainly plenty to do, for just eight months after he started at Triumph the company burst back onto the motorcycling scene with a range of six models at the Cologne show: the Trident 750 and 900 triples, the touring Trophy 900 triple and 1200 four, and the more sporting Daytona 750 triple and 1000 four.

Keith found the whole Triumph enterprise fascinating. He was well paid for the work, but Gill says he'd have done it for nothing, "he was so interested in what was going on." The investment level was huge: it is estimated that £70M-100M went into the company before it turned a profit in 2000. "Keith said the value of the CNC machines installed in the new factory around 2004 was unbelievable," recalls Gill.

The new company had to build its design team from scratch. Triumph had employed a number of very bright young engineers, but they lacked background and production experience; Keith and Mike's job was to imbue them with the same design ethos and sense of direction which they'd so successfully forged at Cosworth.

One Triumph engineer who was heavily influenced by this process is Paul Carey, now the company's chief powertrain engineer. He joined in 1995 as a design engineer after working for an aerospace instrumentation company, and has petrol in his blood. He started riding trials at Islwyn Motor Cycle Club in 1978 and clearly remembers the good/bad old days of the British motorcycle industry, so Keith's stories struck a chord.

"I started working with Keith immediately after I joined. The Daytona Super III was in progress, so that was practically my inauguration. It had very high compression so we had some issues with it, I remember discussing them with Keith."

Paul Carey continues: "Keith's role was very much advisory, more than consultancy. I don't think he'd want to put his name to any particular bike or project, he helped out in lots of ways – a piston scuffing problem here, a valve spring issue there, perhaps a lubrication problem, etc."

DKD did have his limitations, though, and was old enough to recognise them. When Triumph was taken to court over a fatal accident resulting from an engine throwing a conrod and thus jamming the gearbox, he declined to join the defence team and persuaded Geoff Goddard to go instead. He knew he wouldn't be able to stop himself making counterproductive remarks. "If I go," Keith told him, "I'll sit there and try and prove the judge is an idiot!" Triumph won the case.

"Meetings were very educational!" recounts Paul. "We always looked forward to them. Keith and Mike were very down to earth and didn't expect any special treatment, we used to feed them on packet sandwiches and Maxpax instant coffee and they didn't bat an eyelid. Being two old characters, they used to bounce off each other very well. Keith would never hold back, and on the odd occasion when he and Mike disagreed over something, you could almost sit back for five minutes and let them work it out between themselves – very entertaining. You felt very relaxed around them.

"You knew where you stood with Keith, as long as you were very open and honest and didn't put on a front and accepted when you were wrong. I never felt intimidated by him, I felt very open and friendly towards him.

"Sometimes I'd sit in as we subjected junior engineers to Keith, to talk through various problems. It was quite a rapid learning curve for some – they'd be trying to explain their difficulties and I could hear them digging themselves deeper and deeper into holes, and I'd just let them carry on. After they'd finished he'd just sit there and contemplate and then say 'Well, I think what you've actually said there is complete and utter rubbish,' – or something rather stronger!"

Keith got it wrong himself sometimes. "I've been in meetings when he'd be going down a path, and later – either in the meeting or by fax in the evening – come back to me and admit: 'No, I was talking absolute bollocks, ignore it.' He was very honest."

As Paul's career at Triumph progressed, he tried to instil in his colleagues the philosophies he'd picked up from Keith. After the Daytona Super III he went on to design derivatives of engines for different chassis teams, and then designed the 806 engine, the four-cylinder 600cc unit which powered Triumph to its IoM Junior TT win of 2003. "Keith helped us with that in phases. He and Mike didn't lay out the engine, but they were very good at bouncing ideas around and talking through problems. Triumph also had some development help from Steve Miller, by then working at Ilmor.

"Keith believed in going back to basics and thinking things through from first principles, and I'm of the same mindset. Although initially he came across to the design engineers as very blunt and to the point, he made them think about what they were saying and what they were designing before they cut any metal. He once said to me that the only way he made a business out of making racing engines was to make 90% of his errors on paper. The same goes for us. Could we have got those philosophies from elsewhere? Possibly, but for us Keith was very much part of that learning process."

"Towards the end of his consultancy Keith said he felt that he was learning something from us! Mike used to talk about attending the University of Duckworth: I'm privileged to have spent a small amount of time at that university."

After Keith died, Triumph was very keen for Mike to continue coming in, and for a short while he did, accompanied by Martin Walters, but with Keith gone Mike felt it wasn't working so well and didn't represent value for money for Triumph.

Paul remembers Keith using a variety of transport, both two- and four-wheeled. "He used to turn up at Triumph in many wacky vehicles. Most of the time he drove an old Sierra

Sapphire Cosworth; he also had a Subaru Impreza." But whatever car he had, adds Oliver Achurch "... it never seemed to have any screenwash and the clock was never right!"

In fact he had two Subarus, as Roger Kimbell explains. "He bought the first one secondhand after the grey Sierra Sapphire was stolen from his garage one night. The Subaru's first owner had taken his four Cairn Terriers everywhere with him – the smell was appalling and Keith spent a fortune trying to get rid of it. So he bought a new one, the bug-eyed model, to replace it. He thought the Subaru were wonderful."

The purchase of the Subarus surprised Roger, because Keith always reckoned the inline four was the perfect configuration. "He would go on and on about what was wrong with a straight six, which I love, but for him only a four would do. And of course the DFV was effectively two inline fours on a common crank, like a Ferrari. He had strong views on F5000 engines, and commented in the pre-turbo era that if they were tuned to give the output required for F1 they would never hold together.

"I did persuade him to sell me the second of the Elans he got from Lotus, a fixed-head Series 3. It had stayed idle in his shed for donkeys' years, which seemed to me a criminal shame, but he wouldn't be persuaded as far as his white Sierra Cosworth was concerned. When I got the Elan running I went over to show him and offered him a drive, and I've never been so scared in my life. I suppose it was actually quite safe, but the pace ..." Sadly, Roger didn't have the Elan for long: on its way back from an MoT it caught fire and was destroyed. The Sierra fared better: after a lay-up of some 20 years, it was restored to full health in 2013 with the help of Malcolm Tyrrell.

Interesting though all these projects were, Keith had not retired simply to carry on engineering. Now he had time to travel for pleasure, to support Gill's riding activities, to relax with her in Menorca and spend time with his son Roger, daughter Trish and stepdaughters Amber and Tina – activities that Gill, always conscious of his health issues, was more than happy to encourage.

Keith knew his heart and arteries could give trouble at any time and, much though he loved playing with boys' toys and having a pint with the lads, he found it greatly reassuring to know that Gill was not far away. When she went on a three-week safari trip with her daughter Tina in 1995, Keith felt decidedly uneasy, so much so that, subsequently, Gill never left his side for more than a night or two.

As with any family, there were ups and downs. 1997 certainly counts as an up, for in September that year Roger married his girlfriend Julie and just a couple of months later came home 11th overall and first amateur in the 1997 Network Q Rally of Great Britain, the British round of the World Rally Championship. He followed it up in 1998 with a win in the Mintex National Rally Championship. These were proud moments for Keith, who had always encouraged his son's rallying exploits. Roger and Julie now live in the village of Whittlebury with their children Isabelle (13) and Jamie (11). He still competes in five or six events per year, family and business commitments permitting, one of his more recent successes being first place in the 2012 Sunseeker Rally.

The following year, 1998, brought a double blow for the Duckworth family, starting in June with the death of Keith's mother. The redoubtable Em lived independently until the last few days of her life and finally passed away in June at the age of 95. She was extremely proud of both her sons and never lost her fascination with technology.

In March that same year Trish bought a farm near Battle in Sussex with her partner Tony, but tragedy struck just a few months later, in December, when Tony died. "Dad came over the day after, which was very sweet of him. I'm a busy person when I'm upset, so I said 'I want to ride', and asked him to open the gate for me. Could you believe it? – he left it open and all my horses went charging off down the road!

"I handed him the horse that I was going to ride and said 'You'll have to hold this one', and rushed off to round them up. When I got back," she laughs, "he was just standing there with this horse whizzing round and round him and he was looking completely bemused. He made me swear not to ever tell Gill – 'She'll never let me hear the last of it!'"

Trish still lives at the farm with her current partner Andrew and several horses, which are effectively her full-time occupation. Her time at Brighton Poly was followed by a career in London, where she found herself running wine bars, but eventually she realised that her heart was no longer in it and, aided by the money put in trust for her by Keith, opted for a country life instead.

Gill's daughters inherited their mother's love of animals. While still living at the Folly, Tina competed in eventing with great success, from Junior through to Senior classes, and her achievements gave Keith a lot of pleasure. She became a physiotherapist and married Simon – they have two children, Mattie (11) and Sophie (9). Amber became a vet and married Jonathan – their children are Hebe (21, at Oxford reading biology), and Toby (19, at Portsmouth University).

There was never any shortage of social events for Keith to attend outside the family, among the more notable being the unveiling of the statue to Colin Chapman at Mallory Park circuit, in July 1998. There Keith met a man whom he probably didn't remember very well, if at all, but who remembered him vividly from over 40 years before.

In 1998 Victor Thomas was running the Historic Lotus Register, but in 1958 he'd been the proud owner of an Austin 7 Special and a regular at 750 Motor Club meetings, held in a pub between Wembley and Hangar Lane on the North Circular Road. Victor often noticed Chapman, Costin and Duckworth there together – "I think I once touched Chapman's sleeve!" he grins – and reckons part of the attraction for the Lotus trio was the chance to sniff around rival Eric Broadley's latest creations. "The car park was the thing, you'd spend hours there, people would give a demonstration of how fast they could go on the dual-carriageway past the pub!"

While reminiscing with Victor, Keith found himself looking back over his career. "I was very pleased in hindsight with what we did with the DFV, we raised the rev limit by a quantum leap and all our rivals had to follow suit, but my biggest regret was that I never even thought of pneumatic valves."

Another trip down memory lane occurred in 2002, when Bo celebrated its centenary and its former minders – Keith and his university friend Noel among them – were invited by Imperial College to celebrate at the Gaydon Heritage Motor Centre, where it was being kept. It was a good day out, but both men were disappointed to learn that the James & Browne was now being maintained commercially, which to their minds defeated the object of it being in the custody of a university motor club.

Sometimes there would be a phone call from Bernard at Cosworth, inviting the company's life president to a formal occasion. "I'd look after Keith and Mike and make sure they were where they needed to be, which of course gave me plenty of chance to talk to them." The Goodwood Festival of Speed was one such event and, as the 2003 festival was scheduled just four weeks before Keith's 70th birthday, Bernard organised a surprise. "We wheeled in Murray Walker and without any warning he did a speech for Keith, which was very nice."

The impromptu celebration was one of the highlights of 2003 and gave a welcome lift to a year which had earlier brought the very sad news that Keith's elder brother Brian had died at the age of 72. The news was unexpected because, of the two siblings, Brian had generally enjoyed the better health.

One way of getting over a very unpleasant shock was to spend time thinking about mechanical things, and back at the Folly there was no shortage of toys just waiting to be played with. A whole succession of devices provided stimulation and amusement during Keith's retirement, starting in the late 1980s when Keith's favourite was the Honda Pilot. He bought one, raced it, then bought a more powerful version.

Oliver Achurch remembers these machines well. "They were quite a popular sport for a while, but they were really a sand buggy for having fun in the dunes, not for racing across rutted countryside and forests and through gates that weren't really wide enough. Keith failed to negotiate a gateway during one exploit and was recovered with only three wheels on his Pilot!

"I was in the agricultural supply industry at that time, so I got involved when he required a trailer to transport both Pilots. I should have known that it was never going to be straightforward. To get the spring rates on the trailer correct, we ballasted it to the equivalent weight of the two Pilots, but that required me to be on the trailer with a G-meter to record the shock loads when he was driving on a country road. This was pretty exciting, trying to note down the figures while Keith was simultaneously trying to view me in the rear view mirror and drive, especially as he was not beyond forgetting that the trailer was wider than the car."

Gill continues "We decided they were too quick and hairy on our hills for guests to play with, and as Trisha loved playing on them, Keith gave her one for her 40th birthday. When he realised they did his back no good, he gave the other complete one to her and her partner Andrew. We were still finding bits long after Keith had died." Andrew and Trisha still enjoy them at their farm.

Kinder to the posterior was the Power Turn, a rear-engined device with two totally separate Briggs & Stratton power units, each controlled by a separate hand throttle and connected to one wheel. Two small jockey wheels prevent the vehicle turning over backwards when the driver gets it wrong, which can happen very easily as there is no steering wheel, and the front wheels merely castor, forward propulsion and steering both being controlled by judicious use of the throttles. Injudicious use can result in extremely tight turns, utter confusion and general hilarity, but Keith found it very tame after the Pilots and it only ever came out for children and guests to play on.

When tiny motorised stand-up scooters started appearing in the paddocks at race circuits, one of these naturally had to be added to the toybox. In fact Keith bought two: a lightweight tuned-up Go-Ped and a bigger, Ferrari-red Malaguti which looked a bit like a miniature jet-ski with wheels. Complementing these was an Aquascooter, a two-stroke device for powered snorkelling. Keith and Oliver decided to try it out at the Folly.

Roger Kimbell once remarked that "Gill was always slightly suspicious of anything Keith got up to with his mates," and what happened next suggests she had good reason.

"Gill and Shirley had gone out for the day and Keith and I thought we'd run it in the pool." continues Oliver. "What we didn't realise until we'd finished was that there was an oil film on the top of the pool."

The farce that followed was analogous to two schoolboys who have kicked a football through the kitchen window and hope that if they clear up the shards no one will notice the broken pane, as Keith and Oliver began a frantic attempt to clean up the pool before their wives returned. "We managed it, almost, but we kept very shtum about how bad it had been before! We used the Aquascooter extensively in Menorca but never again in the pool!"

None of these toys made a significant dent in Keith's bank balance and he had no interest in acquiring expensive objects simply for the sake of it. He gained far more satisfaction from using his money to help others. Both he and Gill felt that the Salvation Army did a lot of vital but thankless work; the YMCA too has cause to be grateful to him, as has a water project in Africa. He made several donations to his old school, Giggleswick, but by far his biggest philanthropic gesture was to buy Pitsford Hall so that it could continue to be a day school that served the locality.

Pitsford School, located four miles north of Northampton, opened in 1989 and has since acquired a new science block and a new junior school, Keith contributing to both projects. The latter, an ultra-modern high-efficiency building, was named Duckworth Junior School in recognition of Keith's generosity and was opened by Gill in 2012.

After Keith's death, Gill established a scholarship in his memory for a sixth-form student to study science at Pitsford. There was talk at one point of broadening its scope to include other disciplines, but she robustly resisted the suggestion, knowing precisely what her husband's priorities would have been.

The memory of the bank's antics in the early years of Cosworth never left Keith and he was always sympathetic towards fledgling businesses. "Keith did loads of business expansion schemes," says Gill, "there was a tax advantage, but most times he lost the money anyway!" This neither surprised nor particularly bothered him: although he looked carefully at anything he was asked to invest in and steered well clear of no-hopers, he knew perfectly well that the success rate of young businesses is not high. If the idea seemed viable and he judged that the people involved had the right commitment, he was inclined to give them a chance. A Robin Hood museum in Nottingham and a Cornish company making yachting components are just two of the start-ups which would not have happened without his support.

There were many others, but one business support scheme dwarfed them all: his commitment to the British microlight industry.

Chapter 22

The microlight legacy

Aviation in one form or another took up more of Keith's retirement than any other activity. He put far more time and money into microlights than any other sector of aviation, but his interest in flying was varied. To explore other avenues, he set himself up as a small business called Duckworth Aviation not long after his retirement.

Duckworth Aviation's activities centred on two projects with Mike's brother, Frank Costin. The first involved Frank modifying a Fisher Horizon, a wooden American lightplane. Keith and Frank then set about getting its permit to fly through the PFA, only to find that the engineers there were unhappy with some aspects of the machine. Frank fastidiously improved the aircraft, working at a mushroom farm near Sywell until they lost the lease, at which point the Horizon was moved to the Folly. Six months later, in 1995 when it was nearly ready for its Rotax 618 engine to be installed, Frank died.

After that the project stalled, and the other aircraft also remained unfinished. It was Frank's own design for a high-performance glider, which had a high tail to facilitate its planned development into a motorglider, a ducted-fan arrangement being mooted for the powerplant. But his creation did at least fly as a pure glider, Oliver towing it aloft at Bruntingthorpe for its maiden flight. In due course this aircraft, too, found its way to the Folly – indeed, the fuselage plug is still there.

From the early 1990s until 2004 (particularly from late 1997 till 1999), Duckworth Aviation used the services of hovercraft enthusiast David Kemp, a former employee of Bill Sherlock and friend of Nigel Beale's son, Conrad. David found himself helping out at the Folly in dozens of ways, including running thrust tests on various paramotors, for which a small dyno was installed. But on quiet days he might equally be found changing the oil in the helicopter, or even helping Keith investigate a drainage problem in the field.

His biggest single project was not related to aviation at all. Assisted by Neil Lefley, by this time retired and occasionally helping out at the Folly, Keith and David fitted one of DKD's racing karts with a much simplified, cable-operated version of Cosworth project VA, the driver-controlled rear axle developed for F1 by Cecil Schmacher in 1978. They tested it at Whilton Mill kart track near Daventry; it functioned perfectly and definitely helped lap times, though the drivers who tried it weren't talented enough to use it properly! After the test Keith picked up the phone to Patrick Head at Williams and David heard words to the effect of "Hello Patrick … you remember that axle idea that FISA banned? Well, it works!"

Undertaking engineering projects at the Folly was all very well, but Keith still wanted to fly for himself, and he wondered if a person in his state of health could acquire a microlight or gyrocopter licence, as the requirements seemed less demanding than for a lightplane. His thoughts turned to gyros and to Pete Davies' Sky Rider company, which had the import rights for the American Air Command machine.

For his part, Pete had taken a shine to Keith's beloved Brantly helicopter, which was still sitting in the hangar, mothballed. They agreed a swap, and in March 1989 Keith became the proud owner of G-BPSB, an Air Command Elite single-seat gyro with Rotax 532 engine. The Elite was later joined by a second example, a two-seater which was otherwise identical to the solo machine.

Pete and a friend spent many happy hours at the Folly recommissioning the venerable rotorcraft. "Because the Brantly hadn't flown for a long, long time we had to strip it down and check the engine for corrosion etc, though we didn't expect to find any. In fact it was in excellent condition. The Brantly is a great old machine with some interesting technology, I thoroughly enjoyed working on it."

The swimming pool at the Folly is next to the hangar, and Gill encouraged Keith to swim regularly, to keep himself in shape. "She certainly tried to keep him in order!" laughs Pete. And often, "… he would pop in [to the hangar] to see what we were doing."

The conversation wasn't always about aviation. "Sometimes Keith would throw questions at us about use of toluene fuels in F1 cars, or boundary effects on aerofoils, or interactive suspension. We weren't motorsport people and he wanted to know what we thought and how we viewed it from a layman's perspective. It was a fascinating mix of questions – he was always one to bounce ideas off people. But he did get wound up by things quite quickly and never ever suffered fools gladly."

"I thought of him as a bit of genius, one of the very few designers I've met who cannot only design to a virtually perfect standard but also tell you how it was going to be machined and manufactured, and the tolerances. Most designers will come up with a design and regard manufacturing as someone else's problem. He was also one of the few guys who could pick something up and straight away understand how it worked. Sometimes he liked something purely and simply because of the way it was engineered."

"Keith was very pleased," recalls Gill, "he enjoyed watching and giving advice while they were rebuilding; they did the work over the winter and flew it away in spring."

"I kept it for several years," continues Pete, "I used to fly it out of my back garden, but eventually decided I couldn't afford to run it any more and sold it. It's still on the British register, owned by the Eaglescott Brantly group."

Keith's desire to get back in the air was not his only motive for getting involved with gyros. "He was looking at them with a view to asking himself, 'Can I improve it, can I build one to my own design, is there a market for it?' explains Pete. Unfortunately, the Air Command Elite in its original form was a flawed design and after several fatal accidents it was grounded. The problems were eventually resolved and the grounding lifted, but by then Keith had moved on to other projects. After his death the gyro was sold to local enthusiast Glyn Mowll.

There was one way in which Keith could get back into powered flying without licence issues: by piloting a foot-launched aircraft – either a powered hang glider or the powered version of a paraglider (known as a paramotor). These machines had been in legal limbo ever since their invention because, as powered aircraft, the CAA regarded them as subject to pilot licensing and airworthiness approval, yet it could find no practical way of enforcing either – try doing drop tests on the undercarriage! In 1996 the CAA finally admitted defeat and exempted them from both requirements, confirming the freedoms which existing owners had been clandestinely enjoying for years.

As a distant cousin of the parachute, the paraglider derives its shape from the air inflating it, so unlike a hang glider it has no rigid parts and can be packed into a rucksack. Allied to its ability to land and take-off at walking speed, this unique portability ensured that from the late 1980s the paraglider's popularity mushroomed. It has since become the most popular breed of aircraft ever devised.

In the late 1990s paragliding was booming, but paramotoring, as an officially recognised branch of aviation, was still in its infancy, as were the techniques needed to train new pilots. Around 1997 Oliver Achurch, who was between jobs at the time and wondering what to do, thought paramotoring instruction might be an interesting livelihood. "I'd been to Sweden to be taught the basis of wind handling and launching at Paramotor Performance, so Keith and I thought we'd have a go."

At first, they decided to try launching by towing. "All the books say that towing a paraglider with a vehicle is a big no-no," says Oliver, "because you're immediately airborne, so it's absolutely critical to control the speed; you can do that with a winch, but you can't do it accurately enough with a vehicle.

"Nevertheless, we thought we'd reinvent the wheel. Keith at that time had a Kawasaki Mule, a very small 4x4 pick-up. And although we were only half bright, we did at least realise that should have a means of releasing the *piloti* if he got into trouble, so we got Bill Brooks[1] to send up a quick-release link, which we fitted to the roll bar on the back of the mule."

"So with me as *piloti* and Keith as driver, all went well until I developed a lock-out – that's when the wing veers off to one direction and dives into the ground. There is no way back from it. Keith was so busy watching what was happening to his mate struggling with this lock-out that he didn't think to operate the release. Fortunately the weak link broke and the line whipped back – I still have a chip off one of my teeth to remind me of that day. With me having landed in a heap on the ground and with blood coming from my mouth, but still in one piece, we decided there and then never to try it again."

Instead the pair turned their attention to winch launching. "I bought a winch from Michel Carnet,[2] which used a Piaggio motorscooter with a variable-speed drive. They were quite popular for this purpose: you took off the back wheel, mounted the scooter on a frame and that was the basis of your winch. I took it a stage further, whereby the line from my winch went 500m upfield to an anchor point, a pulley mounted on my

Jeep, and then all the way back to my student, who was thus just a short distance away and able to communicate easily by intercom. With the wing laid out and the student ready and comfortable, we'd take up the strain and gently get him no more than a metre off the ground before letting him settle down again. Then we'd ask whether he'd enjoyed the experience. This was all without an engine backpack attached. Then we'd do it with an engine fitted but not running, then finally with an engine running – just a short hop at first, to get the feel of the loads.

"We wanted to find out about the loads on the line, so we took the winch to one of the paddocks at the Folly and 'borrowed' Gill's bicycle with a basket on the front. We fitted strain gauges to the winch and coupled it to the front of the bike – the hook for the front lamp looked a good attachment point. Then at the appropriate time I signalled 'take up the slack,' and told Keith to set the winch going, having first pointed out that I really didn't want to disappear into the mechanism at the other end if I failed to detach.

'The field was far from flat, having been well poached by horses. Keith applied the power and, next thing I knew, the bicycle had disappeared from between my legs and was being dragged across the field, while I was busy picking myself up off the floor. A discussion ensued. I said 'I really think you should try and restrict the amount of power that is required at any given moment.'

"So for the second attempt we set off at a reasonable acceleration, but he didn't seem to slow it down at any time. The winch was on max power, I was leaping around, my legs were going crazy on the bike and the handlebars were all over the place, and I was getting hellishly close to the winch before he cut the power. Keith thought it was hilarious, he was having far too much fun to worry about my health. I wish we had filmed that day. *Last of the Summer Wine* couldn't hold a candle to our antics. We did get data off the strain gauges though!

"I then took it a stage further and started to teach people to fly. I built a winch on the front of an ex-British Telecom van, fitted it out with shelves and equipment inside, plus poles up front for a windsock on one side and an anemometer on the other. I could arrive at the field in my Jeep and park 500m away, put on the pulley and then tow students up. Unofficially – and that's exactly what it was – I taught 16 people to fly. I even did the odd corporate day, just handling wings. By the time guys from London, who'd never done anything but push a pen or sit in a seat, had experienced a day doing ground handling, they were absolutely knackered and ready for a beer."

Keith never flew a paramotor: he got as far as doing some ground handling with Oliver before the pair decided that his hand-eye coordination was not really up to flying it safely. However, he took a continuing interest in paramotor development and owned several, conducting experiments with David Kemp to measure thrust output.

Oliver's paramotoring tuition petered out after a couple of years, because by 2000 he was fully occupied as a director of Pegasus. But his departure from the foot-launched flying scene was not the end of Keith's involvement with paramotors, because Mike Campbell-Jones had re-entered the story. Indeed, the wing which Keith had been attempting to fly had been designed by him.

After leaving Microflight, Mike C-J had been contractually obliged not to work with powered aircraft for four years and had turned to gliding instead, working with John Lee between 1984-88 to create a composite glider called the Lightwing. It was an interesting project "... the first attempt at making an aircraft all in one go using wet lay-up and a male-female mould," he explains, but it was more of a hobby than a living.

"So I went to France to some friends who used to have a hang gliding school and they showed me their first paraglider. I returned with the idea of starting up a paragliding school, which we called Welsh Borders Paragliding School. This was around 1988, when everyone wanted to learn."

It was highly successful, and for a while Mike C-J's operation was Britain's only full-time paragliding school. When the recession hit in the early 1990s Mike started doing winter training in Spain under the name Paramania, and became interested in paramotoring, which he realised would benefit from purpose-built wings, designed to work efficiently at the higher speeds power made possible. The challenge was to achieve this while retaining good control at low speeds, and the answer was to incorporate a pitch-positive section which the pilot could trim in flight. By 1997 Mike was on the Welsh hills, trying the first wing to incorporate this idea, dubbed Reflex on account of its pitch-positive wing profile, and a year later he set up his own company, Reflex Wings, to make it.

Keith, always ready to fund an interesting aviation initiative, had some exploratory discussions about investing. However, they came to nothing as Keith wanted more control than Mike was willing to concede, so DKD remained on the sidelines as an interested observer.

Two things soon became evident: first, that adding a reflex section was a genuine technological advance, and second, manufacturing what was, after all, a textile product, with all that implied in terms of labour-intensive production, was not cost-effective in the UK. So a deal was struck with Polish manufacturer Dudek, which was already making paragliders under its own name, to make the Reflex under subcontract.

Business prospered until Mike C-J became ill with cancer in 2001. "At that point everything changed. Keith called me in hospital and said 'What can I do to help?' He gave me a choice of just accepting some money to sort myself out, or letting him help me keep Reflex Wings alive. In the end we decided to pay off Dudek, who were our main creditor, and in return to transfer all the stock of wings to Keith. He kept them at the Folly and whenever I wanted a wing to sell I had to go his place and collect it, which was fun.

"While I was in hospital I told Peter Dudek my ideas for the next generation of wings – use of diagonals, more aspect ratio and so on – and once I recovered a bit I went to a Hungarian competition where I found a new Dudek wing incorporating all my latest ideas! I went to the factory in Poland and hit the roof."

A deal was eventually struck, where Mike would finish development of Dudek's new wing and Dudek would then make it for Mike to sell as the Paramania Action. But trust had been damaged, and Mike later parted company with Dudek altogether. Many paraglider makers now use reflex sections on their power wings.

Making the best of the Reflex meant finding more thrust, so Mike also turned his attention to power units. Starting in 1998, he had already done some development work to improve the M3, a backpack produced by Paramotor Performance in Sweden, and Keith had helped with fatigue calculations to ensure the starter motor they had planned for its 210cc German Solo engine would not fall into the prop, as had happened with a rival French machine. This development was in the hands of Gordon Heeks, father of Dan, one of Mike's erstwhile instructors, and was ongoing when Mike fell ill.

However, it went off in what he regarded as an unauthorised direction while he was too ill to control matters, and on his recovery he refused to pay Gordon's bill. Keith, who knew both the Heeks and Campbell-Jones families, and had no desire to fall out with either, found himself witnessing an escalating and increasingly unpleasant legal contest which, in view of the relatively small sums involved, had every likelihood of ending Lawyers 1, Litigants 0. Sensing that he was uniquely placed to inject some common sense into the situation, he gathered the parties round the table and subjected them to some characteristically blunt talking, by the end of which they had been persuaded to accept a compromise, which at least made the most of the available resources.

In hospital Mike had continued think about his own power unit, which he called the Vortex, and once he was fit he turned it into a reality with a little help from Keith. Along the way DKD was finally reacquainted with Mike's father, John Campbell-Jones, Cosworth's first landlord. "I was so pleased to meet him again," smiles John.

"Keith loved anything that flew," continues Mike, "we used to have long conversations about engines and many other subjects. You could call him up at any time to discuss them, and he would dash them on the rocks for you!

"It was really weird, Keith was always there. He sent Oliver with me to Florida to assess whether there was a US market for Reflex wings and the Vortex paramotor. If I ever needed advice or help, he was always there for me. But he'd tell you exactly what was what, with his very dry sense of humour, particularly if you said you were interested in Wankel engines!"

Mike C-J was not the only British paramotorist influenced by Keith. Paul Bailey, whose well-crafted paramotors have attracted many compliments, and who, in recent years, has successfully diversified into the manufacture of small paramotor and microlight engines, is another admirer. "Originally, my business was converting Cosworth engines for saloon-car racing, and Keith was always my hero, my idol. It wasn't until I got into microlighting that I actually met him and had real conversations and discussions about things, including the first generation of my four-stroke engine. I wish he was still around because there are a couple of questions I'd love to ask him …"

Entertaining and interesting though the footlaunched scene undoubtedly was, its impact on Keith's retirement was dwarfed by that of microlights, to which he would commit huge amounts of time and money during the 1990s and beyond. To explain how and why, some background is needed.

By 1985 the hang glider and the flexwing microlight had diverged, with virtually all flexwings using purpose-built wings which, though they still looked like hang gliders, could not be flown without power. As airworthiness approval could only be given on complete aircraft, makers of wings and makers of trike units either amalgamated or cooperated, so that by 1984 the plethora of UK flexwing companies at the start of microlighting was down to just six. The three major players[3] were Pegasus, Mainair and Southdown, all making complete two-seat aircraft, while two smaller companies (Hornet and Medway) made two-seat trike units fitted with Southdown wings. The sixth firm was Aerial Arts, which produced complete single-seaters – a niche market.

Keith watched this process of attrition and amalgamation with great interest. He was convinced that further consolidation was both desirable and inevitable if the industry was to survive in the UK, which he very much wanted.

The first sign of this came early in 1987 when Southdown closed its doors. The rights to Southdown's well-liked Raven wing were sold to Medway, which thus became a maker of complete flexwing aircraft. By 1989 Hornet had developed its own wing, the ZA, only to succumb to management issues just one year later. Medway is still very much in business, though proprietor Chris Draper has always been a robustly independent figure and his sales volumes have never been huge. Thus by 1990 the two-seat market had become dominated by two suppliers, Mainair and Pegasus, based at opposite ends of the country and very different in character.

Mainair was a family firm at heart, founded in Rochdale just a few miles from Keith's native Blackburn by John Hudson and his wife Eileen and with a reputation for solid engineering and customer service that was second to none. Mainair pilots were fiercely, almost tribally, loyal, so much so that when John tragically died while test flying a new model in spring 1989, they rallied round and encouraged Eileen to head up the company on her own, despite her suffering badly with rheumatoid arthritis. Even for someone in the best of health, it would have been a brave decision – very few sport aviation companies survive the death of their founder in a flying accident – but for Eileen it was nothing short of heroic. That she succeeded is due in large measure to her appointment in 1990 of Jim Cunliffe as factory manager and ex-Hornet man Roger Pattrick as chief designer, who together gave the company stability and direction.

Pegasus' great strength was its design flair, thanks particularly to the services of the multi-talented Dr Bill Brooks. Cranfield-educated Bill is one of the world's most versatile aircraft designers with a CV that includes chief designer at Farnborough Aircraft company, chief technical officer of the British Microlight Aircraft Association (BMAA), chairman of the Royal Aeronautical Society's human-powered aircraft group, successful participant in Channel 4's *Scrapheap Challenge* (his aircraft always won) and – crucially for our story – chief designer at Pegasus. Anything emanating from the Pegasus factory at Marlborough in Wiltshire could be guaranteed to look slick and fly beautifully. With good reason, Pegasus, too, had many devoted fans.

A particularly fine example of his work is the Quasar, introduced in 1990 as Pegasus' top of the range model. Its futuristic trike unit was composite clad with a square-section alloy tube structure underneath, while up top was the company's recently introduced Q-wing, a combination good enough to win that year's Reserve Grand Champion award at the world's largest sport aviation jamboree in Oshkosh, Wisconsin.

Keith enjoyed airshows and went to Oshkosh himself the following year with Oliver. They hired a Winnebago and went travelling, and when they spotted Road America at Elkhart Lake they stopped on the off-chance and asked to look around. It was a quiet day at the circuit; someone asked casually where they were from.

"Northampton," was the reply.

"Do you know a company called Cosworth, or Keith Duckworth?"

"You're standing right next to him."

"It's amazing the effect that had," says Oliver. "People came out of the woodwork from all over and Keith found himself sat under a tree telling the story of Cosworth to a rapt audience." The scene was almost biblical, Keith looking for all the world like a prophet preaching to the faithful. "It was one of the most memorable experiences of my life," recalls Oliver.

Keith liked the Quasar but had far less time for the way its manufacturer operated. Formed in 1984 by the amalgamation of hang glider manufacturer Solar Wings and trike maker Ultra Sports, Pegasus was much broader-based than Mainair and harder to control; not only did it still make hang gliders but it also encouraged flying schools to operate under its banner. In Keith's ideal world, Pegasus and Mainair would merge to create one company with the design skills of Pegasus and the management of Mainair, but no one in Rochdale could be tempted in this direction, so he concentrated his attentions on the Wiltshire company, sensing that it would need his help before long.

By the time it did, he had already made his first investment in the microlight industry. Late in 1990 he lent Bill Sherlock £40,000 to fund the UK type approval of the AX-3, a greatly improved Weedhopper being produced by Mark Mathot of Ultralair in France. Cheap and cheerful fixed-wing microlighting had been slow to catch on in the UK, but the Australian Thruster had opened up the market in 1987 and Bill felt there was room for a competitor.

Earlier in 1990 Bill's Cyclone Airsports company, originally merely a Rotax service agency, had evolved into a flexwing manufacturer almost by accident, when Nigel Beale of Skydrive had acquired the rights to Aerial Arts' Chaser flexwing in lieu of unpaid engine bills when its maker went broke. The Chaser was (and is) a fine aircraft and notched up dozens of victories in international competitions over many years, some of them in Nigel's hands. It deserved to survive, but Nigel felt a conflict of interest would arise if the Rotax importer were also an aircraft manufacturer, so he encouraged Bill to take over production instead. Thus by October 1992, Bill had both a flexwing and a fixed-wing to offer. Combined with his engine service facility, this ensured that in due course Keith was repaid in full.

Things were much less rosy at Pegasus, and by the start of 1991 the financial situation was dire. In the short term, matters were resolved by director Tom Beese raising money and forming a new company, Holdcontrol plc, to buy out Pegasus' trading arm, Solar Wings Ltd. Keith was chairman of the new company and a major investor, but it soon became clear that far more funds were needed to stabilise the operation, so he increased his stake, the basis of the deal being "Pay me back or give me shares in lieu." Before long, he found himself in control of the company.

This was not part of the plan! Management had never been Keith's chosen activity, and he certainly didn't want to spend his retirement doing it. But he was committed, financially and mentally, and determined to make a success of the enterprise even though he found the process desperately frustrating. It is one thing to build a company from the ground up, the way you want it, but quite another to try to make sense of someone else's.

Gill worried constantly about the potential effects on his health, and remembers seeing him from the garden through his study window, talking on the phone to Marlborough, gesticulating furiously and getting more and more irate and red in the face.

Keith was hands-on at Marlborough for three productive but stressful years, Gill often flying him there in the helicopter. There was plenty for him to do. A new mainstream flexwing, the Quantum, was introduced to general acclaim in spring 1993 and that summer the company moved a to a new factory at nearby Manton, a change made all the more timely by the fact that the Marlborough premises had been damaged by fire the previous autumn.

For Bill Brooks, designing the Quantum meant getting to know Keith and his ways of working, and it was the beginning of a fruitful relationship.

"Keith would arrive, either in a Robinson R22 with Gill or on one of his collection of unusual motorcycles. I would immediately be bombarded with advice, like the use of bronze welding to avoid temper change in 4130 steel tube. He was a great mentor to me, almost like a second father. My own father was an engineer of a similar nature, it was a bit much to have two of them criticising and cajoling me into better things!

"At the time I was doing composite structures research for BAe at Cranfield for half the week and would often ride up to the Folly on my 350cc Matchless and stay the night. I enjoyed those evenings very much, though I had to tune up my feeble intelligence first, to get near to his level. We would delve deeply into the philosophy of engineering design, as his greatest pleasure was to think down to the fundamental level and work out principles from scratch. We would explore resonance and transmissibility of rubber mountings, different explanations for the way an aerofoil produces lift and why the thread pitch of connecting rod bolts should be intentionally mismatched to the caps, to improve stress distribution.

"Keith could be bombastic and overbearing, but time and again I found his judgments and predictions turned out to be right, so I learned to pay attention. However, he was full of fun and could take a joke. One sure way of winding him up was to tell him how good the Wankel rotary engine was. He would go a puce colour, his eyes would bulge – 'Combustion chamber's all the wrong shape! Think of the surface area to volume ratio! How is the flame front supposed to know how to travel to the edges? What about the tip seals and cooling? An explosion is a sphere, how the hell are you going to contain a sphere in a square?' – the tirade would go on for several minutes until he began to realise he had been set up. I still miss him."

By 1994 the pressure of his responsibilities at Pegasus was getting Keith down, and the more relaxed lifestyle long advocated by Gill was appearing increasingly attractive. He started looking for someone to take over the helm, but Jim Cunliffe at Mainair could not be tempted, and Oliver was not interested.

Finally he turned to Bill Sherlock, who had already proved a trustworthy partner. If Keith lent Cyclone Airsports the money, would he be prepared to buy out Keith's stake in Pegasus and take over the firm? The deal was done, and in August 1994 the merged operation took shape, based at Manton but with Bill in charge and John Fack handling marketing. Flexwings would be marketed as Pegasus, fixed-wings would sell under the

Cyclone banner, and hang gliders would retain their traditional Solar Wings badge.

With Bill having a controlling stake and Keith, Nigel Beale and Conrad Beale as minority shareholders, DKD could now step back from day-to-day management.

With his desire for a merger with Mainair frustrated, in the late 1990s and the early years of the new millennium, Keith concentrated on helping the Manton team broaden and update its range. Two major projects followed in succession: a sophisticated fixed-wing to complement the simple AX-3, and a new flexwing called the Quik, featuring a high-performance wing – effectively a top-of-the-range replacement for the Quasar but aimed at a much wider market.

As resources did not run to designing a high-tech fixed-wing from scratch, it was decided to seek an import deal for an established foreign design. Bill and John rated the Flight Design CT, not least because it was already selling well on the Continent, and as soon as Keith met its German designer, Matthias Betsch, he knew they were right. The two struck up an immediate rapport, aided by Mattias' appreciation of English beer. Here's how he remembers their meeting and the friendship that followed:

"As I'd been a Formula 1 fan from childhood and my idol was Jim Clark, of course I read about Cosworth and Keith Duckworth and Mike Costin. I always wondered how a company could lead for so long in an area where things change every weekend!

"I'd been told that Keith was a very straightforward personality, so I was expecting a very serious person who was not much fun. What a surprise at our first meeting! Yes, Keith was very straightforward, but with the biggest amount of 'British humour' I had ever experienced. And, he said to me, 'I didn't know until today that Germans had a sense of humour!' Keith was very interested in being with bright people with energy and vision, and he understood that such people are not simple, so if a person was bright he would tolerate a lot of peculiarities. He was a real character, it was very good to be with him. I met Gill a few times and found her very energetic, pleasant and bright. I think that their tolerance made them a happy couple.

"Through Keith I came to know other key Cosworth people, like Mike Costin, Ben Rood and Martin Walters, and it became clear to me why Cosworth had been so successful. Everyone had a particular area of expertise and they appreciated and respected each other – they were interested in people, something I'd never before seen so intensively among bright people. I'm sure that was a major factor in their success.

"When I asked Keith about our idea of developing a hybrid aircraft engine, he first said 'Did you talk with Mike already, and what did he say?' Or when there was a starting problem with the Rotax 912S engine, he engaged Martin and, based on the analysis from him, Rotax changed the starter and trigger speed.[4] Or Keith's work on our fuel system, of which he built up a simulation in his workshop at the Folly."

Effectively, the CT was a high-performance lightplane scaled down just enough to be microlight legal; very different from anything Pegasus had sold before. Initially, Keith suggested setting up a separate company to import and market it, perhaps headed by Oliver, as his paramotor training was waning and he was game for a new challenge, but instead the board decided that airworthiness approval would be more easily achieved through Pegasus and opted to employ Oliver on a contract basis.

The CT was advertised early in 2000 but UK deliveries did not start until autumn 2001, as the British interpretation of the microlight weight limit was stricter than Germany's, and much work was needed to make it light enough to comply. Once it did, it was an immediate sales success, making it necessary to regularise Oliver's position.

Like so many of Keith's most productive agreements, the deal was done in the pub. "We talked about it at the Fox & Hounds at Great Brington," says Oliver. "After the first pint I agreed to handle the CT's marketing. After the second pint I agreed to become a Pegasus director, on the grounds that, in Keith's words, I should have some responsibility." So the CT became Oliver's personal baby, until he retired in 2014.

The Quik had an even greater impact and was the belle of the ball when it was unveiled at the 2002 Flying Show at the Birmingham NEC. Here for the first time was a flexwing which offered a genuine 100mph cruise, while retaining docile handling and a manageable landing speed. Hugely influential worldwide, it raised the bar for flexwing design and elements of Bill Brooks' creation can now be found in many rival designs.

Despite being heavily involved in both projects, Bill Sherlock was not around to witness the first deliveries of either. By 2001 the word from Rochdale was that Eileen might retire soon, opening the door to the merger that Keith still believed was vital, and Keith wanted to prepare the ground. Unfortunately Bill was not keen, as Mainair's product line was ageing and could not compare with the new offerings from Pegasus.

His opposition placed Keith in a difficult position. A merger could never work without the senior management's support, but he and Bill had enjoyed a very productive relationship which he did not want to sour. More in hope than anticipation, he arranged for Roger Kimbell, who was not involved with Pegasus but knew the industry well, to visit Manton and assess the situation. However, he only reported back what, in truth, Keith already knew – namely that a merged company would need a new face at the top.

Fortunately Keith had someone in mind – Keith Negal, a great competition flying enthusiast and at that time also BMAA chairman. The introduction came through Nigel Beale as both were heavily involved in the British microlight team. With a practical background (in bomb disposal), allied to huge reserves of energy, remarkable farsightedness and a great sense of fun, he was a man after his namesake's heart. In May 2001 Pegasus acquired a new chairman and not long afterwards, Bill left.

Bill Sherlock has mixed feelings about the way things turned out, but is not resentful, commenting recently that "Keith was a very principled man, I think everything he did was aimed at the long-term good of the wider microlight industry."

The merger finally happened the following year. "We were looking at the numbers game in the pub one night," says Oliver, "and he concluded that the market was not big enough for two. 'I think I should try again to persuade Eileen to sell,' he said. He didn't discuss it with Gill at the time! Over the course of the next few weeks Keith acquired Eileen's shares and then over another pint he said 'I'll have to tell Gill what I've done.' She was not a happy girl."

Keith Negal took over as chairman of both companies in November 2002 and stayed for some three years to oversee the process of integration which created the present company, P&M Aviation. Sadly, he died from cancer at the age of 62 in February 2011, his obituary describing him as "...only slightly quieter than a Rotax 912 and even more influential,"[5] a reference not only to his work with DKD but also to his enormous international contribution to sport flying.

Eileen Hudson too, is no longer with us, finally succumbing to her debilitating illness in December 2008.

Happily, the company they and DKD left behind continues to be a credit to them. Jim Cunliffe rose to become chief executive at P&M and stayed until retirement in 2009, when Roger Pattrick took over, while Bill Brooks continues to lead the design team, his latest creation being the semi-enclosed PulsR, the most sophisticated flexwing yet. P&M still operates at both sites but is certainly a leaner and more effective organisation than the one Keith encountered at Marlborough back in 1991. Broadly speaking, DKD got what he wanted and his vision has been proved right by events. Thousands of pilots worldwide have cause to be grateful for his willingness to commit huge sums of his own money, totalling some £1.6M, to ensure the continued quantity production of microlight aircraft in the UK.

In 2003 Keith bought Bill Sherlock's shares and, with the Duckworth family now in full control of the merged company, Gill was finally able to convince Keith to divest himself of his microlight responsibilities, which from her viewpoint had brought nothing but stress, worry and expense to their retirement. It was agreed that his niece Julia Anderson, an accountant by profession, would become a director – a position she still holds.

Keith never lost his restless curiosity, but by his standards the remaining years of his life were relaxed and peaceful. After he died, his P&M shares were divided between Gill, his children, Gill's daughters, and Keith's nieces and nephew in Blackburn. The day-to-day running of the company was entrusted to the directors with the shareholders having oversight. Gill gave her shares to her step-granddaughter, Izzy.

Footnotes

1 Bill Brooks was chief designer at Pegasus, a microlight company discussed in this chapter.

2 Michel Carnet is a highly successful competition paramotorist and winner of numerous national and international competitions.

3 The term 'major player' is very much relative: these were all very small operations, with the largest employing perhaps 20 people and making around 100 machines a year. Despite this tiny commercial base, very high technical and production standards were required of them by law and, unlike motorsport, there was no possibility of external support from the wider industry. Leisure aviation is in effect an adventure sport and the last thing commercial civil aviation wants to be associated with is adventure. So even the best-run microlight company will never be a blue-chip investment.

4 The definitive fix did not come until later, when Conrad Beale developed the Soft Start module for the Rotax 912S, which was subsequently abopted by the factory.

5 p22 Microlight Flying, February 2011, published by the BMAA.

Chapter 23

Vale

Keith was frustrated. The hangar doors at the Folly had been giving trouble for some time, not folding properly when the switch was pressed, and eventually he had called the supplier. The result? The technicians had been on site three days and now the doors were not working at all.

Surely it couldn't be beyond the wit of man to fix a hangar door? He phoned Oliver Achurch and Martin Walters, and on Tuesday 6 December 2005 the three friends set to work. After another three days' effort they got the doors to function, but not to Keith's satisfaction.

It had been bitterly cold work. Not only is the Folly's hangar exposed, on top of a hill, but with its doors wide open there was no way of heating it. Nevertheless, on the Saturday afternoon he decided to brave the cold again and complete the job, leaving Gill in the house with her granddaughter Sophie, who she was looking after for the day.

It was characteristic of Keith to get wrapped up in what he was doing and forget to wrap up in suitable clothing. At 3.45pm, when Gill came out with Sophie in the buggy to see where he was, darkness had fallen and Keith was still up on the ladder, lightly clad and working on the runners. "Don't open the doors," he said. He'd spent the whole afternoon greasing the chain that operated the door, bracing himself by resting his knees against the rungs of the ladder. "The ladder was a horrible thing," recalls Oliver, "a bit loose on the rung; Gill had told us to scrap it but we'd never got round to it." Nevertheless, Keith was pleased, he was making progress.

Gill was not pleased at all, she was annoyed at his foolishness. "When he came in he was desperately cold and he sat at the kitchen table shivering. 'Get in a hot bath,' I told him, but Keith insisted he was alright. 'Just give me some tea,' he said. He did eventually warm up, though he was restless that night. He did get colds and flu badly many winters and spent time in bed. This often happened at Christmas or New Year – I don't think he liked all the fuss attached to them – and this was ten days before Christmas. I thought 'Oh no, here we go again.'"

Next morning he had a temperature of 39°C (102°F) and was complaining of stiffness around the chest. Gill was worried that another heart attack might be imminent, but Keith reckoned it was just the result of his exertions the previous afternoon, so she gave him paracetamol to calm his temperature.

Continued on p329

A pair of Cyclone AX-3s over the English countryside. This French import was the first microlight to benefit from Keith's investment.

Old and new in the hangar: behind the tail of the Hughes G-ONTA is a sorry-looking Brantly awaiting Pete Davies' TLC.

Right: Keith (in red flying suit) with Ian Lee (dark blue flying suit) at Long Marston in 1990 with Ian's Air Command gyro. Shortly after this photo was taken, Ian was involved in a fatal crash and the type was grounded. As a result, Keith's own Air Command gyro (above) stayed in his hangar: this was as far as construction progressed.

Inside DKD's hangar, a Piaggio Skipper scooter converted to a mobile paraglider launcher. The rear wheel is retained but its tyre is replaced by a pulley. Note the drawing board in the background, and Honda Pilot alongside. *(Courtesy Paul Blezard)*

A Reflex wing in flight around 1998. The reflex shape which gives the wing its name can be clearly seen on the wing's upper surface. Inset: Keith's test rig for measuring the thrust developed by various paramotors. The instrumentation can be seen on the shelf and the remote control at the bottom. *(Courtesy BMAA collection)*

Keith trying out an Adventure paramotor backpack in 1999. *(Courtesy BMAA collection)*

Mike Campbell-Jones' Spectrum as it looked at the 1983 Weston Park fly-in. *(Courtesy Norman Burr/ BMAA collection)*

State-of-the-art flexwing design in 1990: the Pegasus Quasar.

DKD and Oliver – a rare shot showing wine on the table rather than beer.

Pegasus sales manager John Fack (right) shows a potential customer around the Quantum at the BMAA's annual show in Telford in 1993.
(Courtesy BMAA collection)

Mainair staff in 1998: Roger Pattrick in front of Jim Cunliffe in the aircraft, and Eileen Hudson in the black dress.
(Courtesy BMAA collection)

A Quik with (l-r) test pilot Robin Kraike, DKD, Bill Brooks and Roger Pattrick. This shot was taken at the 2003 Popham show shortly after the merger with Mainair. DKD was often seen at fly-ins, but because he never sought the limelight, few pilots realized the depth of his commitment.

Bill Brooks about to give an excited passenger her first microlight flight, in P&M's latest, the PulsR.

Gill riding Pie, with Tina in front and Sophie behind, on a sponsored ride at Kirtlington in 2014.

Gill riding her grey mare Red Bog Lady (Lily) to a win at Aston-le-Walls in 2013.

The very successful Flight Design CT, type-approved through Pegasus. *(Courtesy BMAA collection)*

Standing in the doorway of the home he loved.

The Quik in flight.

Enjoying the 1991 Oshkosh show.

The last photo taken of Keith, playing on a scooter in the stable yard on 21 October 2005.

Sir Jackie and Lady Helen Stewart arrive for the service. Sir Jackie gave the penultimate address from the pulpit, followed by Stuart Turner (above right).

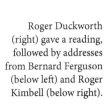

Roger Duckworth (right) gave a reading, followed by addresses from Bernard Ferguson (below left) and Roger Kimbell (below right).

Gill Duckworth with her daughter, Tina, and Tina's husband Simon.

The display of DKD-related machinery in front of the church, with more in a covered awning nearby, was a fitting tribute and attracted great interest. This is the Lotus 91 with which Elio de Angelis notched up the DFV's 150th win in the Austrian GP.

Trish Duckworth and her partner, Andrew (left), and Patrick Head (right), who was one of dozens of motorsport figures to attend.

Start of the service, with the BRDC's memorial wreath (inset) just visible on the centre of the steps.

DKD's engineering life in summary: a 1960 Lola MkII FJ car powered by one of his first 105E-derived engines (right); the Lotus 49 and its DFV powerplant (below); and examples of projects nurtured during his retirement years: the P&M Quik microlight and the Triumph Rocket III Classic, with a modern Daytona 675 Triple for company (bottom).

"We were due to go out with some friends for drinks that Sunday and he decided he'd come," continues Gill. "So he got up, got dressed, and we went along, it was a fabulous day for the time of year. I didn't see much of him for an hour or so, and when I did he looked ashen. 'I don't feel very good,' he told me."

So they came home early, Keith complaining in the car that his knee was hurting terribly. He went straight to bed, the knee by now looking very red and very angry. It had been suspect ever since his schooldays, when he'd hurt it playing rugby. During National Service it had put him in hospital for a cartilage operation and subsequently, of course, it had not been improved by the occasional unplanned separation from a motorcycle.

"It did play up occasionally," recalls Gill. "We went to Tenerife one year and he would go and ride a big waterbike the second day we were there – it was one you sat astride, he hadn't seen that type before and wanted to try it. He wrecked his knee and spent the whole of the rest of the holiday on the bench!"

Keith had a fitful night. The next day Gill was due to go with her sister-in-law for a spa day. "It was all booked and we were both looking forward to it. Keith said he'd be okay, so he stayed in bed and I made him some sandwiches and took everything upstairs. He didn't look great, he just didn't want to move because the knee hurt. Although this problem wasn't exactly new, and I thought it was probably just another episode, I thought it prudent not to leave him alone too long, so I asked Oliver if he would drop in around lunchtime."

When Oliver arrived he became very worried indeed; Keith looked extremely poorly. He couldn't get hold of Gill initially, so he took it upon himself to call the doctor, who examined Keith and concluded that he had a bacteriological infection of the knee. Infections of that type can take hold very quickly and the doctor was in no doubt: Keith should be in hospital. He called an ambulance, which arrived around 4.30pm.

By this time it was clear to everyone that Keith was deteriorating quickly. He could no longer walk, so the ambulance crew tried to manoeuvre him down the stairs in a walking wheelchair. "But he was a big man," explains Oliver, "and they said he was too heavy for the two women in the ambulance to cope with; they'd have to call for assistance. I said 'There's no way we're going to do that, we're going to get him downstairs and into your ambulance.'

"He was in so much discomfort that he couldn't move his leg into a position where it could be supported by the chair. I asked him how much he could move it, and Keith sketched out a design for a rest that I could make to support it in that position. I went into the workshop, cut a piece of plywood, found a couple of G-clamps and made it. I then supported the rest while the medics took the wheelchair down the stairs, one at a time. That's how we got him off to hospital." Sadly, this simple construction would turn out to be Keith's very last piece of engineering design. True to form, it had worked first time.

The accident and emergency department of Northampton General Hospital that Monday night was not a good advertisement for the NHS. Staff were heavily overstretched and it was 11pm before Keith was transferred to a bed. "Nobody would pay any attention, I was going nuts!" says Gill. "Eventually a very stressed young doctor came down, knew who Keith was – he was a motor racing fan – and got him into a ward. When I took a taxi home at 1am, I felt a bit better about things, and by the time I arrived next morning they'd already operated and flushed the knee out."

It had been imperative to operate as soon as possible. Tests had revealed that the infection was massive and there was a risk of permanent damage to the knee joint. Gill spent the next day with him but he looked poorly and his knee was very painful. The doctors asked him how he felt.

"Not too bad," was the reply.

"I don't think he'd analysed what was going wrong," says Gill. "He always played down his big health issues."

It was a very uncomfortable evening. The ward was noisy – "... there was unlimited visiting so there were people making a racket opposite until 11 o'clock – and it was stiflingly hot."

When Gill rang the hospital on Wednesday morning she was told he was to have a second operation that day to flush out the knee. She rushed off to see him, before he went into theatre but ended up spending all day with him waiting, as he was at the end of the theatre list. He was not allowed to drink, and as the day wore on he became very thirsty and unhappy. Gill tried to keep him comfortable with ice blocks and sips of water, and when they rushed in about 4.30pm to take him to theatre, they said he was dehydrated and needed a drip!

The second operation involved a general anaesthetic – a much more risky procedure – but Keith came through it. Gill rang about 7pm to find out how he was.

"They said 'Come in, he's being very difficult, he won't keep the oxygen mask on, he won't keep any clothes on the bed.'" She drove into Northampton and cajoled her husband.

Keith had a quiet, if confused, Thursday, and that day Gill had a chance to have a proper chat with a doctor. "He said the knee was really serious stuff; he wouldn't have proper mobility in it. I thought, if he can't ride his motorbikes ... all sorts of stupid things go through your head at times like that. The physios got him out of bed but he looked in terrible agony and the doctor came along and said 'Don't let him move that leg.'"

On Friday Keith looked much better, and Gill made enquiries about moving him to a private hospital which she hoped would be more restful. However, the doctors advised against it: Keith was not out of the woods yet and he might still need Northampton General's specialist facilities and equipment.

On Saturday they took off the dressings, but the doctors were not yet confident that the knee infection was beaten, so there was the possibility of another trip to theatre. As a result Keith got very little to eat and felt very weak. At this time a sickness and diarrhoea bug was going round the ward, though, fortunately, Keith didn't catch it. Unfortunately, Gill did. "Come Saturday I had this projectile vomiting. I went to see him Saturday night but felt terrible and thought I'd better go home. In fact, I took one of their cardboard bowls with me and as I drove past Althorp I vomited as I drove, I didn't have time to stop!"

On Sunday morning she returned and asked the nurse on duty if Keith was due for another operation, as there was a 'nil by mouth' notice over his bed. The nurse said he wasn't, but added that, as Gill was clearly unwell, would she please leave in the interests of infection control? Gill was having none of it – at least, not until she had washed Keith and given him his breakfast.

Back at the Folly, her family had rallied round. Her daughter, Tina, went to see Keith later that day, as did Oliver, and her other daughter, Amber, took charge of the house and promptly ordered her mother to bed. She woke up around 6pm, phoned the hospital and was put through to Keith. They didn't speak long, but she noticed his breathing was much quicker than usual: a bad sign as he breathed much faster than Gill at the best of times. She promised to come and see him next morning.

Sadly, it was not to be, and that phone call would turn out to be their last communication. Just three hours later she was called into the hospital urgently. Amber drove her, and when they arrived they learned that Keith had suffered a ruptured aortic aneurysm. Doctors were fighting to save his life and Gill, protesting, was shepherded away. By the time she was allowed at his bedside it was all over, the fight had been in vain. It was the evening of Sunday 18 December.

Trish, Roger and Tina had seen him before he died, Tina visiting on Sunday afternoon followed by Roger with four year-old Izzy, but Gill had not had that chance.

She returned to the hospital on Monday morning to collect his belongings. "I felt a bit cheated that I hadn't seen him at the end," she says, "but when I walked out of the hospital that was that. I decided not to complain, I felt it would be bad for me and would not bring him back."

Over the coming weeks and months she mused over what had happened and tried to make sense of it all. Whatever the hospital's failings as regards the treatment of his knee, Keith had died from a completely unrelated problem which, given the dire state of his arteries, could have happened at any time. In all probability, the trauma of the infection and two operations had made it more likely, but there was no direct link.

"I should have been more proactive," she reproached herself. "His heart was done privately in Oxford in 1986 and the NHS didn't have access to his history. I should have pushed that they looked harder at his heart and arteries. If they had scanned him they could have seen the state of his aorta. They had ECGs on him which weren't flagging up anything out of the ordinary, but I knew they didn't work on his skin. The trouble was, in the hospital you never saw the same person twice.

"Thinking back, he'd said to me on the Friday before he died that his stomach felt really uncomfortable. Normally when you feel bloated it goes when you lie down, but this didn't. However, he never mentioned that to anybody else.

"His health had been going downhill for a while. We would sometimes take the dog for a walk, down to the bottom of the field, and one day about six months before he died, he got back and said 'I can't do this,' and he never went down there again. Some days I'd walk past the study window and he'd be asleep. I should have pushed harder and told him to go and see a heart specialist, but he was happy enough."

In the years since her loss, Gill has become a little more philosophical about his passing. "Looking now at the daily grind so many partners have, of caring for someone with illnesses like dementia or lingering cancer, someone who day by day is becoming less and less like the person you knew – maybe we were lucky to be spared that. Naturally we slowed down a bit as we got older, but we did enjoy a pretty active life right to the end."

When they married in 1986, Keith told Gill he reckoned they had a good seven years left together, but in the event they were married for 19. Seventy-two is no great age by modern standards but is more than he expected, given that he smoked heavily for many years and led an intense, stressful lifestyle; and that his father died at 43 and his grandfather at 39. Coincidentally, his brother, Brian, was also 72 when he passed away in 2003.

Throughout their time as a couple, Keith and Gill knew that it might suddenly be cut short. For Gill, fears for his health manifested themselves in everyday concerns. If he was late coming in from outside, she'd worry that he might have collapsed at the bottom of the field. If he was quiet in the night, she'd reach across to reassure herself he was still breathing. And she was constantly watchful of his diet, exercise regime, and general stress levels.

For Keith, from the moment of his first heart attack in 1973, his fragile health had informed every major career decision. It was the reason he never designed another complete engine after the DFV, the reason he appointed Alf Vickers, the reason he sold Cosworth, the reason he retired at 55. However, even in retirement, he'd continued full-on with microlights, motorcycle design projects – his own and other people's – and charitable work. Nothing was going to stop him doing what he wanted to do.

But as anyone who has lost a loved one knows, knowing in advance that it is likely doesn't make it any easier to deal with when it happens. It was particularly hard for Gill because she'd lost her brother to a brain tumour that April and had herself had an operation that October to remove spurs on her collarbone which had sawn through the tendons, causing her blinding pain. 2005 was Gill's annus horribilis, its only bright spot being the arrival of her sixth grandchild, Sophie, on 1 July.

The years following Keith's death were tough in a different way, as she set about tidying up his myriad business affairs and dealing with a hangar, workshops, sheds and storerooms full of tools, engineering equipment, mechanical toys and vehicles of all descriptions. Wherever possible, she tried to find an appropriate home for things rather than just selling or scrapping them – the Pilots went to Trish, Oliver got the BMW C1, and so on.

The first of DKD's domains to be tackled was his study. "I had to find everything needed to start sorting out his estate, which turned out to be far from straightforward," says Gill. "Keith did not like to throw anything out, so his office at home had become an 'Augean Stables!' I tried to get him to sort it out on many occasions, and he would fill a few sacks with papers and burn them, but he never made much impression on the piles!"

However, the engineering-related material needed to be sorted by someone with technical knowledge. At the time of writing Malcolm Tyrrell is still helping her go through boxes of papers of potentially fascinating engineering topics, nine years after Keith's passing.

Progressively, Gill's focus became her horses. Throughout the 1990s, as the children spent less and less time at home, she had been training and competing with her horses more and more. Now they filled her life, along with flying the R22. She rode the lovely chestnut mare Auburn Girl to success in eventing for the last seven years that Keith was alive, and for four more years after he died, until arthritis stopped 'Chessie' from competing.

Gill then had a back operation, and eventually found and bought Red Bog Lady (Lily) a young grey mare that she trained and with whom she still competes, the highlight being their win in the BE 80 National Championship in 2012. Last year she took on a re-homed 'gypsy' pony, Pie, from World Horse Welfare, as a companion for Lily. Pie has now trained on with Gill to win dressage and Family Pony classes, and has been on sponsored rides with Tina and Sophie.

News of Keith's death stunned Cosworth and the wider motorsport world alike. Viewed rationally, for a man with known coronary issues to die at the age of 72 was not such a surprise, but viewed through the lens of personal contact, it seemed almost inconceivable that it could happen to this man; that almost overnight such a powerful personality and towering intellect could simply disappear.

Messages of sympathy poured into the Folly and to Cosworth, and obituaries were written by the dozen. One of the best, from Mike Lawrence at Pitpass.com, is reproduced opposite. A website was set up for people to post their tributes and attracted no fewer than 547 contributions, but, unfortunately, www.keithduckworth.com was taken down

OBITUARY

Keith was once shown around the engine department of one of the Detroit Big Three. As the world's most successful designer of racing engines, everyone hung on his every word. Someone asked him what he thought of their engines, and Keith said they were crap. Consternation all round. Keith said, "Imagine you are the gas inside a cylinder. You've got a bloody great piston coming up your chuff and you want the quickest way out. Have you provided the quickest way out?"

That was typical Duckworth. He was blunt and didn't waste words. He also had the ability to take something as complicated as thermodynamics and reduce it to a simple image which a child could understand. It was that clarity of thought which made him such a formidable designer. Provided you did not pretend to know more than you actually did, he would take infinite pains to explain things.

Keith Duckworth was the most delightful company provided you accepted that, at any moment, he was likely to go off at a tangent into politics, philosophy and religion. I always found that invigorating. If you went to interview him on a motor racing subject, it was one hour of racing and three hours of something else.

Although he came across as this blunt, confident, no-nonsense Lancastrian, he was actually very modest about his achievements, and he was always prepared to give credit to others where it was due. Though it is nearly 20 years since he had a role to play at Cosworth, the company still likes to boast that it is guided by his inspiration.

It can be argued that Keith Duckworth was the greatest engine designer there has ever been. Even if you disagree, you have to take him into consideration. I am only sorry that never again will I hear him putting the world to rights.

– Mike Lawrence (Pitpass.com)

---

before it had been properly archived, so only a small proportion of the tributes survive.[1] A selection of them is included on the following pages, along with comments from others who knew him. Some of the words are from names familiar to readers of this book; others are from ordinary enthusiasts around the world, but all of them are heartfelt.

Keith gave dozens of interviews to the motoring press during his career, but one of the most revealing – it was certainly a favourite of John Dickens, who liked it enough to circulate it round the Cosworth managment – was printed in the December 1987 edition of *Car* magazine. Talking to Phil Llewellin, DKD started, naturally enough, with motorsport:

"If you're going to get involved in anything as daft as motor racing, there are two options. You either learn to laugh at adversity, or eventually they cart you off to the funny farm. Faced with those alternatives, the wise man cultivates the humour of despair. That's the most important thing in life, and the ability to laugh has always remained with me."

Asked his favourite racing driver, he did not hesitate. "You can't beat pure, natural talent, so it would have to be Jim Clark. There's nowt like natural ability. This learning is really for the bloody birds."

Soon he moved on to broader issues, such as his disdain for social sciences. He seemed to regard the very phrase as self-contradictory, commenting "They should not, in my opinion, be university subjects. They are flannel, trash, bullshit, and not worthy of a degree. Unfortunately these bullshit subjects have taken away semi-bright people

– who might have done something useful – and made them useless. A lot of people are gaining great height by standing on piles of bullshit."

Talk of being useful quickly brought him round to politics. "If you're going to do anything useful, you're going to come up against politics, and politics always makes it impossible for good sense to prevail."

He summed himself up like this: "I'm just an interested and enthusiastic engineer who gets upset when he doesn't understand things. I would be perfectly happy to have 'He tried to understand things' carved on my gravestone."

The actual words on his gravestone were written by Gill and are rather more informative; they can be seen in the churchyard at Long Buckby, not far from his home:

Keith Duckworth OBE, 1933-2005. Founder of Cosworth,
Designer of the DFV engine which won 150 Grand Prix races from 1967-1981.
An exceptional man and engineer of the 20th century.

His funeral on 4 January 2006 was a small, private affair, but several weeks later, on 23 February, a service of remembrance was held at All Saints' Church, Northampton, with donations invited to BEN (the automotive industry charity) or the Salvation Army. It was a celebration of his life, and was appropriately upbeat and full of humour – as is to be expected when Bernard Ferguson, Roger Kimbell, Sir Jackie Stewart and Stuart Turner are addressing the congregation.

Outside the church a selection of Cosworth-powered cars was proudly displayed, along with a P&M Quik microlight. Inside, the church was packed, with dignitaries from Northampton, friends, colleagues and dozens of famous names from the world of motorsport. And, just in case anyone had forgotten why they were all there, the service ended with the roar of the DFV filling the church. As far as possible given the circumstances, it was a joyous occasion befitting a man for whom humour was as essential a part of life as an understanding of the second law of thermodynamics.

We end with a quote of which DKD would surely have approved, even though it comes not from him but from Henry Ford, founder of the company with which he enjoyed such a long and fruitful relationship. By sheer chance, on 11 October 2012, the day Steve Miller was interviewed in connection with this book, this was the 'thought for the day' on the tear-off calendar on Steve's desk:

"Thinking is the hardest work there is, which is probably the reason
why so few engage in it."

Footnotes

1 See www.prezencesa.co.uk/keithduckworth/comments.php.

TRIBUTES AND OBSERVATIONS

I met Keith in the summer of 1958 at Brands Hatch. My first impression was of a man with a great ability to think and to cut through to the essentials of the subject, together with a wonderful gift for a visual description of any mechanism. We began working together almost immediately and this continued throughout the rest of his life. He was the man who most influenced my life from the very beginning. We had a great friendship and together with Mike Costin would put the world to rights whenever we met together. It was not an easy ride, mind in neutral was not allowed, but humour would always prevail. It was altogether a most rewarding association. The world felt noticeably more stable each time we met.

A great man, much undersung for his part in the development of motor racing. Without his influence, engine development would have staggered along much more slowly, and F1 as we now have it may not have been possible.

I am very proud and grateful to have known him. I shall miss him greatly.

– Ben Rood

I'm just a fan and I just want to say goodbye to a legend. RIP Keith. My sincere condolences to the Duckworth family.

– Lorenzo Francesconi, Italy

He was fascinated by almost anything technical, one of the great masters. But you were either in his camp or not, it was a quite abrupt divide!

– Mario Illien

One of my most precious memories of DKD came when I was first arranging to write my book *Cosworth, the Search for Power*. Naturally I had to be interviewed by Keith before I got approval. Looking at me fiercely from across his desk, he thought about it, grinned amiably, then retorted: "Over the years, a lot of people have written a load of bollocks about me. Oh well – if anyone is going to make a complete mess of writing Cosworth's history, it might as well be you!"

After which he gave me endless hours of hilarious reminiscence. The man was a genius, a treasure, a tyrant, an iconoclast – and a man who never believed anything until he had worked it all out again for himself. Did you ever see a more perfect example of a one-off? Keith was it.

– Graham Robson

A true legend who will be sadly missed. Thank you for all the motorsport knowledge. Cosworth forever! With love, Cosworth fans from Romania.

– Tomi Pop, Romania

There were a number of times when my career came quite close to Cosworth. I became chairman of Ricardo for the last eight years of my working life, and Ricardo was Cosworth's main competitor. I'd just become chairman when Keith died, I'd expected him to pull my leg about that …

– Sir Noel Davies

In the Imola paddock for an F2 race I saw Mr Duckworth walk over to a low-end team that was having trouble starting their BDA. I went to watch and learn. He got it started for them and they started in with their rev-rev-rev method of warming the engine. Asking if he could help, he grabbed the throttle linkage and cranked the revs way up, where he held them, explaining that the easiest way to warm a race engine was to raise the revs to the point where the engine made the most internal noise and to hold the revs there until the noise quieted down – at which point it was warm and ready to run. Pragmatic, effective, and to the point. Just like the man.

– Steve Matchett

I didn't know him, I know nothing about engines, but as far as I am concerned, the DFV was the reason for the best period of Formula 1 racing, from the late '60s to the early '80s. Thank you, and may you rest in peace. A fan from Canada.

– Bob Fennelly, Canada

I asked him over a pint one night what would he would wish to be remembered for. After his usual lengthy pause he said, "That with the knowledge available at the time, I could not have done it better."

– Oliver Achurch

Father of shallow included valve angles. A fundamental design element that changed performance engines forever.

– Kirk Stratford

I believe Keith was the nearest thing to a modern Brunel. He unlocked, spectacularly, how you made the four-valve head work. When he laid out the DFV, computers were in their infancy, so every nut and bolt in it was stressed manually. And he finished it in about nine months, and it worked!

– Bob Graves

So very sorry to hear this sad news. As an ex-employee of Cosworth I met him on a daily basis. A fine man, a deep thinker who will be sorely missed. I have but fond memories. Thank you Keith.

– Roy Jones

Keith was interesting, and it didn't matter what he was talking about. He loved an argument and sometimes you sensed that whatever you said, he'd immediately disagree even though actually you were probably both on the same side. Sometimes we'd say to him "You are a rude bugger," and he'd reply, "I might be rude, but I'm right."

– Roger Kimbell

"When facts are scarce, bullshit is rife!" Keith would say.

– Malcolm Tyrrell

He had a great sense of fun and a great sense of humour and despite the fact that he was a very strong personality and wasn't always the easiest guy to work for, you couldn't help but like the fella. He was a very honest man.

– Steve Miller

Keith was multi-talented, super-confident, deep-thinking, forthright, stubborn, dismissive of fools, gregarious in company, dangerous in argument … a one-off in every respect.

– Mike Costin

Appendix

Engines and other major projects at Cosworth

Listed on the following pages are all major design and/or manufacturing projects undertaken at Cosworth under Keith Duckworth's chairmanship. The list is chronological by year, and alphabetical within each year. It is believed to be complete as regards the company's output under its own name, but is not exhaustive as regards consultancy or subcontract machining work. Neither does it include any freelance work undertaken by Keith.

Keith reduced his involvement with Cosworth gradually and still visited the works occasionally after his retirement in 1988, so it is impossible to state a hard and fast cut-off point for his input. Hence, the list includes a number of 1990 projects, on the grounds that many will have been in progress at the time of his departure, and ends with the XB engine, the first major product of the post-DKD era. Most dates refer to the year a project reached fruition, rather than the start of design work.

The list is based on an earlier publication[1], but with many corrections and additions. In particular, it now includes non-engine projects (shown in italics) and many later projects omitted from the original list. Footnotes discuss the most significant corrections.

All projects involving design work are shown with project codes. This alphabetical drawing office system was introduced around 1967 for all projects, not just engines. It was applied retrospectively to existing engines: drawings for the earliest designs – Mk1 to MkXVII – were given the code Mk, the BD series drawings carried BA, the DFVs DA, the FVAs FA, the MAEs MA, the SCAs SA, and the twin-cams TA. Subsequent projects (beginning with the CA and continuing alphabetically, but omitting letters already used) were simply known by their two-letter code. Where appropriate, a third letter was added to indicate the variant.

Year introduced	Name	Project code	Size (cc)	Power (bhp)	Max speed (rpm)	Description
1959	MkI	Mk	997	n/a	n/a	The first modified four-cylinder pushrod 105E Anglia engine. An experimental engine not made for sale.
1960	MkII	Mk	997	75	7500	The first production racing engine. A development of the MkI and used in Formula Junior. Used A2-profiled camshaft.
	MkIII	Mk	997	85/90	7500	An improved version of the MkII using A3-profile cam with a strengthened bottom end and optional dry-sump lubrication.
1961	MkIV	Mk	1098	90/95	7750	A bored-out version of the MkIII fitted with bigger valves inter alia.
1962	MkV	Mk	1340	80	5000	An inexpensive modified four-cylinder pushrod Ford 105E Classic engine made for Lotus for installation in the Lotus 7. It had few modifications since it was intended only for road use.
	MkVI	Mk	1340	105	7000	A racing version of the MkV. Very few were made.
	MkVII	Mk	1475	120	7000	A bored out version of the MkVI. Very few made.
	MkVIII[2]	Mk	1498	90	6000	An inexpensive modified four-cylinder Ford 116E Cortina engine produced for the road-going Lotus Super 7, which replaced the MkV. Fitted with an A2-profiled camshaft, five main-bearing crankshaft and twin 40 DCOE carburettors. A large number were produced.
	MkIX[3]	Mk	1498	125	7000	A racing version of the MkVIII.
	MkX[4]	TA	1498	n/a	n/a	A one-off experimental engine, this was the forerunner of the production Lotus Twin Cam engine as fitted to the Elan. The production engines, however, had a capacity of 1558cc, utilizing twin overhead camshafts (chain driven) with a crossflow cylinder head.
1963	MkXI	Mk	1098	110	8000	An updated version of the MkIV Formula Junior engine but with a very much improved specification. A very successful engine and a major development in Cosworth's history.
	MkXII	TA	1594	140	6500	A bored-out racing version of the Lotus Twin Cam engine with dry-sump lubrication, though using standard connecting rods and a cast-iron crankshaft.
	MkXIII	TA	1594	140	6500	A development of the MkXII with improved dry-sump lubrication and latterly using steel connecting rods and crankshaft.

	MkXIV	Mk	1498	100	6000	Another modified Ford 116E engine made for the Lotus Super 7 but with more power than the MkVIII.
	MkXV	TA	1594	140	6500	A wet-sump racing Lotus Twin-Cam engine fitted to the Lotus Cortina for (then) Group 2 saloon car racing.
	MkXVI	TA	1498	140	6500	An 81mm-bore version of the MkXIII. It was very popular with the (then) current formula in New Zealand and Australia, to where almost all these engines were exported.
1964	MkXVII	Mk	1098	120	8500	A downdraught version of the MkXI engine with an improved crank design. Few were made, partly due to the brazing problems involved in modifying the cylinder head to a downdraught configuration. More a development than a production project.
	SCA	SA	997	115	8750	SCA = Single Camshaft type A. The first extensively Cosworth designed engine, based on the Ford 116E Cortina cylinder block, which was the only 'standard' component. Gear-driven single overhead camshaft, five main-bearing crankshaft and a bowl-in-piston combustion chamber. A very successful engine which won the Formula Two Championship in 1964 and 1965. Uprated to 130bhp @ 10,000rpm for 1965.
	SCB	SA	1498	175	8000	A 1500cc type B version of the SCA made for experimental purposes only. Successfuly raced by Mike Costin in his Brabham BT10.
1965	SCC	SA	1098	135	9500	Same as the SCA but with a larger bore. It was destined for a North American sports car formula but only a few were made. Many SCA engines, however, were later sold to the USA and converted to SCC specification.
	MAE	MA	997	100	9500	MAE = Modified Anglia series E, the Ford 105E. A very successful Formula Three engine made in large quantities. A modified cylinder head introduced in 1966 improved the performance slightly but after 1965 few complete engines were made. Many kits and parts, however, were sold to other engine specialists throughout the duration of the 1000cc Formula Three regulations.
1967	DFV	DA	2993	408	9000	DFV = Double Four Valve. Cosworth's first F1 engine and the most successful engine ever used in Grand Prix racing. First fitted to Jim Clark's Lotus 49 at the 1967 Dutch GP, which it won. In total DFV and derivatives won 155 GPs and 12 World Championships. Also twice an outright winner of the Le Mans 24 Hours. A lightweight V8 with four valves per cylinder and the first Cosworth-designed cylinder block. Uprated to 430bhp @ 9500rpm

Year	Engine	Type	cc	bhp	rpm	Description
						for 1970, 450bhp @ 10,250rpm (1971), 465bhp @ 10,750rpm (1975), 495bhp @ 10,750rpm (1977).
	FVA	FA	1598	218	9000	FVA = Four Valve type A. An unbeaten F2 engine, winning all F2 Championships from 1967 to 1971 – the duration of the 1600cc regulations. Based on Ford 116E Cortina block, used four valves per cylinder with gear-driven DOHC. Uprated to 235bhp @ 9750rpm for 1969.
	FVB	FA	1500	200	9000	An experimental 1500cc version of the FVA made to examine the power output possibilities for the DFV. Successfully raced by Mike Costin in his Brabham BT10.
1968	BDA	BA	1601	120	6500	BDA = Belt Driven type A. A road-going engine designed for Ford for installation into the Escort RS1600. Using the 1600cc crossflow Ford block, its design is based on the FVA but with toothed-belt drive to the twin overhead camshafts. Four valves per cylinder.
	DFW	DA	2491	358	9750	A successful 54.0mm short-stroke version of the DFV made for the Tasman Series.
1969	CA	CA	-	-	-	*Four-wheel drive F1 car with magnesium DFV engine. Never raced; now in museum with standard DFV engine.*
	FVC	FA	1790	235	8750	A long stroke version of the FVA made mainly for the European Two Litre Sportscar Championship, which it won twice.
1970	BDB	BA	1700	200	8250	A development engine made for Ford for rallying application. Modified BDA with enlarged bore. Only one made by Cosworth but many sold in kit form.
	BDC	BA	1700	230	9000	A fuel-injected racing version of the BDB with larger ports and valves, developed mainly for Group Two saloon car racing. Only one engine made by Cosworth but many sold in kit form.
1971	BDD	BA	1598	210	8750	Formula Atlantic version of the BDA with 45 DCOE Webers. Only one engine made for development but many sold as kits. Later engines on 48 DCOE Webers managed 215bhp @ 9000rpm.
1972	BDE	BA	1790	245	9000	A Formula Two version of the BDC bored to 85.8mm and with siamesed block; fuel-injected. Uprated to 255bhp @ 9250 for 1973.
	BDF	BA	1927	270	9250	The BDF improved on the BDE by becoming closer to the 2000cc F2 engine limit, although its 88.9cc bore was achieved only through brazing liners into the siamesed block. It won more F2 races than any other engine in 1972.
	EAA	EA	1995	275	9000	Based on the Chevrolet Vega block: Cosworth's

first non-Ford-based stock-block engine. An aluminium four-cylinder similar to the BDA in layout and also using belt drive. Destined for sportscar and F2 racing but never used in the latter.

Year						
1973	BDG	BA	1975	275	9250	An improved version of the BDF but with greater reliability due to better head-gasket arrangements. The 1973 F2 engine. Uprated to 285bhp @ 9250rpm for 1976.
	BDH	BA	1300	190	10,000	A small-capacity version of the BDA based on the Ford 1300cc crossflow block. Used in Group Two saloons and sportscars.
	FVD	FA	1975	275	9000	A modified version of the FVA made for experimental purposes only. Not produced because BDG gave similiar output and was cheaper.
	GAA	GA	3412	415	8500	Based on a Ford Essex V6 block, designed for use in Group 2 saloon-car racing. Also successful in F5000: gave 445bhp @ 8750rpm in this spec, from 1975.
	HA	HA	(2000)	-	-	2 litre V6 engine intended for F2; never built.
	PA	*PA*	*-*	*-*	*-*	*Customer piston drawings (pistons for Cosworth engines carried appropriate engine prefix).*
	ZA	ZA	n/a	n/a	n/a	Pushrod Clubman engine based on four-cylinder Ford crossflow block, instigated at Cosworth Components.
	(various)	ZA	-	-	-	In addition to the above, ZA codes also used for miscellaneous items, including those drawn up at Cosworth Components by Frank Webb.
1974	BDJ	BA	1098	145	9500	Designed for American SCCA Formula C. Used modified BDH head with smaller valves and fuel injection. Uprated to 150bhp @ 10,000rpm for 1975.
	BDL	BA	1425	296	9000	Experimental turbocharged BD engine. Not pursued because of head-gasket problems.
	JAA	JA	750	65	7000	A production motorcycle engine designed and built for Norton Villiers.
	LA	LA	-	-	-	Infinitely variable transmission based on Hobbs concept and intended for F1 use. Abandoned at prototype stage.
1975	BDM	BA	1599	225	9250	Large-valve fuel-injected version of the BDD.
	BDS[5]	BA	1975	235	8250	Brazed-block version of BDB rally engine kits, but used BDE heads and either carbs or injection depending on the event. Up to 285bhp possible on fuel-injection. BDS designation used over several years for all manner of special rally-spec engines, which were sold as kits for outside assembly.
	DFX	DA	2645	840	9500	57.3mm-stroke turbocharged version of the DFV designed for Indianapolis-type racing in

341

	Code	Type	cc	bhp	rpm	Description
						the USA. 80 inch Hg-boost version. In this and its latter form, the DFX would win more than 150 IndyCar races including 10 consecutive Indianapolis 500s.
	JAB	JA	750	95	9750	Racing version of the JAA.
1976	BDX	BA	1975	285	9250	1976-spec BDG supplied as kits for SRE to assemble. BDX was also used for certain one-off BD-based projects.
1977	BDN	BA	1599	210	8750	Modified BDD for Canadian Formula Atlantic series. Used 45 DCOE Webers.
1978	KAA	KA	2400	240	7000	Rally version of the Opel Ascona 400.
	VA	VA	-	-	-	*Rear axle allowing each wheel to be driven independently; intended for F1. Abandoned at prototype stage.*
	(various)	MISC	-	-	-	*Used from the outset of the project code system for miscellaneous drawings, including the Cosworth powerboats of 1978-80.*
	-	-	-	-	-	Machining and assembly of 400 cylinder heads for Vauxhall Chevette HS.
1979	BDP	BA	1845	235	8500	Fuel-injected alloy-block version of the BD-race engine, drawn by Alastair Lyle in 1977 and run in October 1979, Used 87.0mm bore, ran on methanol at 14.5:1 compression. Not marketed at this capacity, but larger version sold later by CosInc for use in Midget racing (see 1984).
	OAA	OA	1600	170	7800	A VW Golf-based Formula SuperVee engine.
	PM	PM	-	-	-	Pontiac parts. Some doubt about the meaning of this designation, but it is believed to refer to work done in connection with the Pontiac Fiero powerplant.
1981	BDT	BA	1778	200	n/a	Turbocharged version of alloy-block BDA designed by Ford for Escort RS1700T and assembled by JQF Engineering in Towcester; little Cosworth involvement except to build 200 kits. Enlarged version (1803cc, 250bhp) used in RS200.
	BDU	BA	1975	235	8250	Gasoline version of BDP for off-road racing.
	DFL	DA	3995	540	9250	90.0mm-bore by 77.7mm-stroke version of the DFV, designed for Group C sports car racing. Manufactured under licence for Ford.
	DFL	DA	3995	n/a	n/a	Turbocharged version of 3.9 litre DFL..
	DFL	DA	3298	490	n/a	3.3 litre version of DFL with 64.8mm stroke, raced successfuly, notably in Group C2.
	WAA[6]	WA	2297	270	n/a	Twincam conversion on Mercedes-Benz M102 four-cylinder, intended for competion. Only a few built due to cancellation of rally programme, but roadgoing version later made in large numbers – see 1984.

Year	Code		cc	bhp	rpm	Description
1982	DFVss	DA	2993	520	11,000	90.0mm-bore by 58.8mm-stroke version of the DFV used in F1.
	DFY	DA	2993	530	11,000	Similar to the DFVss but with its camshaft carrier integral with the cylinder head. Only five examples were made, for Tyrrell Racing, winning the 1983 Detroit GP.
	-	-	-	-	-	Subcontract machining and design work for TWR racing, on Group A version of Jaguar V12.
1983	AB	AB	-	-	-	Auxiliary pumps pack for Chevrolet V8 sprint racing engine, based on production small-block. SOHC conversion for same engine also designed, but only reached prototype stage.
	BDR	BA	1601	120	6250	Based on the BDA. Sold as a conversion kit, 150bhp and 170bhp 1700cc versions fitted in top-of-the-range Caterham Super 7 sports cars.
1984	*AF*	*AF*	-	-	-	*Cosworth Filtron filter.*
	BB	BB	n/a	n/a	n/a	Experimental turbocharged F1 four-cylinder: alloy BD block with F1-spec cylinder head, compounded with CVT gearbox; featured in Channel 4's Equinox documentary series. Drawings later redesignated BA.
	BDP	BA	1975	245	8500	Production version of BDP (see 1979 for original).
	BF	*BF*	-	-	-	*Cosworth Filtron filter.*
	CBA	CB	1993	n/a	n/a	See 1984 YAC below.
	CF	*CF*	-	-	-	*Cosworth Filtron filter.*
	F3000 DFVss inj	DA	2993	n/a	n/a	Modified DFVss with mechanical injection.
	HF	*HF*	-	-	-	*Cosworth Filtron filter.*
	PF	*PF*	-	-	-	*Cosworth Filtron filter.*
	WAA[7]	WA	2297	187	n/a	Twincam conversion on Mercedes-Benz M102 four-cylinder, originally for competition (see 1981), then for road use in 190E 2.3-16.
	YAA	YA	1993	n/a	n/a	Prototype naturally aspirated engine based on Ford T88 block (Ford Europe's equivalent of Pinto).
	YAB	YA	1993	n/a	n/a	Prototype turbocharged version of YAA.
	YAC	YA	1993	n/a	n/a	Prototype dump-port version of YAA, later redesignated CBA to avoid confusion with 1990 YAC. Not pursued.
	YBA	YB	1993	n/a	n/a	Prototype modified YAB.
	YBB	YB	1993	204	6000	Turbocharged four-valve-per-cylinder twin-camshaft engine based on the Ford T88 block and developed from the YAB. Designed specifically for the series production Ford Sierra RS Cosworth.
1985	-	-	-	-	-	Production and assembly of cylinder heads for Metro 6R4 engine, which used a number of

					DFV components. No final engine assembly and no formal input to design, but some informal consultancy from Mike Hall.
	BDT-E	BA	2137	540	n/a	Evolution version of BDT developed by Brian Hart for RS200E.
	DFX	DA	2645	700	12,000	48 inch Hg boost version of 1975 DFX, for revised regulations.
	DFXss	DA	2645	n/a	n/a	Modified DFX
1986	EB	EB	3400	n/a	n/a	V6 for Buick-Oldsmobile-Cadillac, prototyped but never put into production due to internal GM competition from Chevrolet-Pontiac.
	F3000	DA	2993	420	8750	F3000 specification DFV, limited to 9000rpm.
	F3000ss	DA	2993	n/a	n/a	Modified DFVss
	F3000inj	DA	2993	n/a	n/a	Modified DFV, long-stroke, electronic injection.
	GBA	GB	1497	750	n/a	First version of F1 turbocharged Grand Prix engine developed for Ford.
	YBC	YB	1993	280	6000	Group A rally engine based on the YBB.
	DBA	DB	3000	370	n/a	DOHC version of the Pontiac Iron Duke engine for use in the USA. Sold in kit form.
	DFV3000	DA	2993	n/a	n/a	Modified DFV for F3000; long-stroke, mechanical injection.
	DFVss	DA	2993	n/a	n/a	Modified DFVss for F3000, short-stroke, electronic injection.
	DFZ	DA	3495	560	10,250	3.5 litre normally aspirated Ford F1 engine to compete for the Colin Chapman Cup in GP races.
	DFZ Hart	DA	3495	580	n/a	Modified DFV, 3.5 litre, for Brian Hart
1987	DFZ Lowered	DA	3495	n/a	n/a	Modified DFV, lowered sump.
	GBA	GB	1497	1000+	12,000	Final version of turbocharged GP engine ready to race in 1988 before the rules changed.
	KBA	KB	1998	156	n/a	Sixteen-valve twin-camshaft version of GM Vauxhall/Opel 2 litre engine.
	Sport V8 3.3	DA	3298	n/a	n/a	Modified DFV, mechanical injection, for International Motor Sports Association.
	YBD	YB	1993	225	n/a	Uprated 'Evolution' version of the YBB for installation in the limited edition Sierra RS500. Modifications include eight fuel injectors (instead of four) and a larger turbocharger.
	YBE	YB	1993	n/a	n/a	Special version of YBB, only for Ford-approved special installations.
	YBE1A	YB	1993	n/a	n/a	Version of YBB for Ford Industrial Power Products, for use in Panther Solo.
	YBF	YB	1993	400+	n/a	Racing version of the YBD, for kits and re-development.

1988	DFR	DA	3495	600	10,800	F1 engine for 1988 Benetton.
	DFS	DA	2645	710	12,000	Revised turbocharged engine for CART/Indy racing.
	DFS DFXss	DA	2645	n/a	n/a	Modified DFXss.
	FMS	DA	2645	n/a	n/a	Modified DFX with fuel-management system.
	JBA	JB	(2900)	n/a	n/a	Ford V6 SOHC engine with 12 valves, Köln 2.9 based.
	WAB	WA	2498	195	n/a	Increased capacity version of WAA.

1989	DFR4	DA	3495	n/a	n/a	Modified DFV to 4v.
	DFS89	DA	2645	n/a	n/a	Modified DFX
	HBA	HB	3498	600+	12,000	Benetton Ford F1 engine. Won the Japanese GP.
	WAC	WA	2490	330	n/a	Short-stroke version of WAB for saloon car racing.
	YBE2A	YB	1993	n/a	n/a	Version of YBG for Ford Industrial Power Products, for use in Panther Solo.
	YBG	YB	1993	220	6000	Uprated YBB compliant with 83US emissions and unleaded fuel.
	YBG (Air)	YB	1993	n/a	n/a	Modified air-conditioning version of YBG.
	YBJ	YB	1993	220	6250	As per YBG but to European 15.04 emissions rules, not 83US.
	YBJ (Air)	YB	1993	n/a	n/a	Modified air-conditioning version of YBJ.
	YBM	YB	1993	n/a	n/a	Race version of YBG/J for kits and re-development.
	-	-	-	-	-	Subcontract machining for TWR twin-turbocharged V6.

1990	3.5 Sports	DA	3495	n/a	n/a	DFR with old DFV deep (ie not lowered) sump.
	DFS90	DA	2645	n/a	n/a	Modified DFX, small bearings, short stroke.
	DFR5	DA	3495	n/a	n/a	Modified DFV to 5v.
	DFR90	DA	3495	n/a	n/a	Modified DFR89.
	DFR90B	DA	3495	n/a	n/a	Modified DFR, small bearings.
	F300090	DA	2993	n/a	n/a	Modified DFV, short stroke.
	F3000SB	DA	2993	n/a	n/a	Modified DFV, small bearings.
	FBA	FB	2933	192	5750	Naturally aspirated 24-valve double-overhead-camshaft engine based on a development of the Ford 2.9 litre V6 pushrod cylinder block. Designed and developed specifically for the series production Ford Granada Scorpio.
	FBB	FB	2933	n/a	n/a	4x4 version of FBA.
	FBC 2.9L	FB	2933	207	6000	Modified version of FBA based on 2.9 litre block.
	FBC 3.4L	FB	(3400)	n/a	n/a	Modified version of FBA based on 4 litre block
	FBD	FB	(4000)	n/a	n/a	4 litre version of FBA
	HBA	HB	3495	630+	13,000	1990 spec version of HBA, for Benetton Ford F1. Won in Japan and Australia.
	HBB	HB	3498	n/a	n/a	Previous season's HBA modified for Jordan Racing and Fondmetal.

HBC	HB	3498	650	11,500	Previous season's HBA modified for TWR in Jaguar sports car racing and then for Minardi.
JBB	JB	(4000)	n/a	n/a	4 litre SOHC engine derived from JBA.
LB	LB	n/a	n/a	n/a	Race research engines.
MBA	MB	(2500)	n/a	n/a	2.5 litre V6 Cosworth concept engine.
NB	NB	n/a	n/a	n/a	Terrier development.
YAC	YA	1993	n/a	n/a	Naturally aspirated verison of YBG for kit car with carburettors. Unrelated to 1984 YAC.
YBP	YB	1993	n/a	n/a	Ford Cosworth CE14 Escort engine with EEIV injection, MY93.
YBR	YB	1993	n/a	n/a	Ford 4x4 rally engine.
YBS	YB	1993	n/a	n/a	Ford 4x4 Group A rally kit.
YBT	YB	1993	n/a	n/a	Ford Cosworth CE14 Escort engine, MY92 rally verison of YBG.
YBT (Air)	YB	1993	n/a	n/a	Modified air-conditioning version of YBT.
XBA	XB	2645	n/a	n/a	CART/USA turbo engine for Indycar racing. The first Cosworth racing engine to be designed without Keith Duckworth's input.

Footnotes

1 Source: pp46-48 of Cosworth: Creative Power, Ken Wells (1991, Prancing Tortoise Publications/Kewkar Racing).

2 See 4.

3 See 4.

4 Shown as 1963 in Cosworth: Creative Power, altered because an engine of this description was used to great effect by Jim Clark at Nurburgring in 1962, and because the Lotus Elan with the production version of the engine was available towards the end of 1962. To retain chronological consistency, engine types MkVIII and MkIX have also been brought forward from 1963, as it seems unlikely that Cosworth would jump two marks and then backfill later.

5 BDS designation shown as 1982 in Cosworth: Creative Power but, as text explains, actually in use well before then.

6 See 7.

7 WAA was omitted from source list, presumably in error as later versions of the WA series were listed.

Also from Veloce Publishing –

The Official Biography
of **John Chatham**

Team Healey

'Mr Big Healey'

Norman Burr : Foreword by Simon Taylor

The authorised biography of one of the best-liked bad boys in British
motorsport, John Chatham – driver, racer, repairer, rebuilder, tuner, trader and
lover of Austin-Healeys. With 150 photographs, many previously unpublished,
this is an important and entertaining account of one of motorsport's biggest
characters.

ISBN: 978-1-845842-57-4
Hardback • 25x20.7cm • 160 pages
• 200 pictures

For more prices and other information, visit our website at www.veloce.co.uk
• email: info@veloce.co.uk • Tel: +44(0)1305 260068
* prices subject to change, p&p extra

Also from Veloce Publishing –

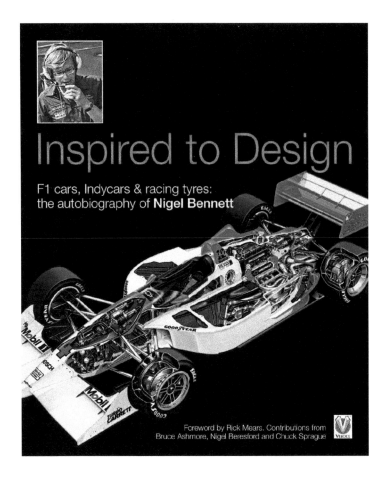

In this unique autobiography, Nigel Bennett describes his life and career, from growing-up influenced by car design, to his education, and the building of his '750 specials.' He describes his work as Firestone Development Manager, recounting many tales of the outstanding designers and drivers of the period. Detailing his work in Formula 1, as a Team Lotus engineer, and then as Team Ensign designer, he also covers his Indycar designs at Theodore, Lola Cars, and Penske Cars. Life after his retirement, his involvement in boat design and with modern F1 teams, is also recounted.

ISBN: 978-1-845845-36-0
Hardback • 25x20.7cm • 176 pages
• 194 colour and b&w pictures

For more prices and other information, visit our website at www.veloce.co.uk
• email: info@veloce.co.uk • Tel: +44(0)1305 260068
* prices subject to change, p&p extra

Index